Memory and Intelligence

JEAN PIAGET

and

BÄRBEL INHELDER

in collaboration with

HERMINE SINCLAIR-DE ZWART

Translated from the French by

ARNOLD J. POMERANS

BASIC BOOKS, INC., PUBLISHERS

NEW YORK

Library of Congress Catalog Card
Number: 72-89197
SBN: 465-0445-X
Printed in the United States of America

Translated from the French
Memoire et Intelligence
Presses Universitaires de France
© 1968

73   74   75   76   10   9   8   7   6   5   4   3   2   1

75—5304

Contents

v

CONTENTS

PART III
THE REMEMBRANCE OF CAUSAL STRUCTURES

vii

CONTENTS

Preface

Our interest in the subject matter of this book calls for a word of explanation. Having assumed that mental operations concern the transformation of states, we decided to look more closely into the latter and hence to examine the problem of mental imagery.[1] In so doing we came to appreciate (Chapter 7) that action may, in certain cases, be more conducive to the formation and conservation of images than is mere perception, and this raised the problem of the memory.

We accordingly devised a number of preliminary tests to determine what our subjects remembered, after an interval of an hour and again after a whole week, of situations or states resulting from such operational processes as a series of decantations (which involves a grasp of logical transitivity) or the construction of a serial configuration. This led us to the (fairly obvious) conclusion that the memory of children is bound up more closely with the way in which they interpret a model at various stages of their operational development, than it is with their perceptions. But while this result was what anyone taking the operational, as opposed to the associationist, view would only have expected, a chance encounter with one of our subjects persuaded us to look further into the matter. When this subject, who had been questioned about the memory test six months earlier, turned up for quite a different investigation, and was asked what he remembered of the first one, his reply showed that he did, in fact, recall it, but that he had schematized it further. This raised a special problem. The long-term memory is generally believed to deteriorate or at best to remain unchanged, while the operational schemata are known to persist or to progress in the course of the child's development. Does that mean that memories pursue their own course regardless of the intelligence, or, on the contrary, that, depending on the situation (simple or conflicting) and the level of development (near to, or far from, the solution of the implicit problem), they rest on operational schemata, and hence introduce either

[1] J. Piaget and B. Inhelder: *Mental Imagery in the Child*, Routledge & Kegan Paul, 1971.

systematic distortions resulting from the mechanism of the schemata or else mnemonic improvements due to progress in intelligence? The reader will see that all our investigations tend to show that the memory does indeed interact with the intelligence: sometimes there is spectacular progress in recall after a lapse of several months (as in the case of serial configurations—Chapters 1 and 2); at other times there are distorting schematizations designed to resolve a conflict (e.g. numerical correspondence *v.* spatial magnitude—Chapter 4), etc.

And once the problem of the memory had been raised in this way, we went on to speculate about the relationship between its figurative aspects (from perceptive recognition to the memory-image) and its operational aspects (the schemata of the intelligence, which are conserved much better than what is commonly called the 'memory in the strict sense'): the structuring needed for mnemonic retention seems, in fact, to be highly systematic and even to be endowed with a biological sense, at least if, as is usually supposed, the memory is based on the integrity of the RNA, which has a structure of its own. Beyond that, we have been led to stress the fundamental importance of the 'reconstructive memory'. It fits between the elementary mnemonic level of simple recognition and the higher mnemonic level of recall.

In short, the reader will be presented not only with a number of experimental facts but also with several theoretical notions, the validity of which the future alone can decide. For the rest, there is one aspect of these studies that has greatly encouraged us in our work: the surprising discovery, in a sphere apparently remote from that of cognitive operations, of a precise succession of operational stages, whose existence we ourselves might have begun to doubt had we listened to all those who do not, or rather do not yet, believe in the validity of the operational approach.[1]

J.P. and B.I.

[1] Our sincerest thanks are due to Messrs Vinh-Bang and Beuchat, who have been kind enough to provide the illustrations in this book.

Collaborators in this Work

PIERRE MOUNOUD, Superintendent, Centre of Genetic Epistemology; Assistant at the Institut J.-J. Rousseau (Chs 3, 6, 11, 14)
JOAN BLISS, Assistant at the Institut J.-J. Rousseau (Chs 4, 5, 8, 15, 16)

and

Christiane Challande, Assistant at the Institut J.-J. Rousseau (Ch. 10)
Jean and Marie-José Delcourt, former Assistants at the Institut J.-J. Rousseau (Ch. 20)
Muriel Depotex, former Assistant at the Institut J.-J. Rousseau (Ch. 2)
Catherine Fot, former Assistant at the Institut J.-J. Rousseau (Ch. 12)
Monique Levret-Chollet, Assistant at the Institut J.-J. Rousseau (Chs 1, 2, 18)
Laszlo Luka, Physician at the Medico-Pedagogic Office, Geneva (Ch. 19, §3)
Robert Maier, Assistant at the Institut J.-J. Rousseau (Ch. 13)
Olga Maratos, former Assistant at the Institut J.-J. Rousseau (Ch. 5)
Sylvia Opper, former Assistant at the Institut J.-J. Rousseau; Assistant at Cornell University (Ch. 17)
Andrula Papert-Christophides, Assistant at the Institut J.-J. Rousseau (Ch. 19, §2)
Paul Petrogalli, former Assistant at the Institut J.-J. Rousseau (Ch. 19)
Elsa Schmid-Kitzikis, Assistant at the Institut J.-J. Rousseau (Ch. 9)
Tuât Vinh-Bang, Assistant at the Institut J.-J. Rousseau (Ch. 7)
Gilbert Voyat, former Assistant at the Institut J.-J. Rousseau, Research Assistant at M.I.T. (Cambridge, Mass.) (Chs 14, 20)
Christiane Widmer, former Assistant at the Institut J.-J. Rousseau (Ch. 10)
André Bauer, Demonstrator at the Institut J.-J. Rousseau (Ch. 19)

MEMORY AND INTELLIGENCE

The Problem of the Memory and
its Place among the Cognitive Functions

In contrast to perception, which is the appropriation of immediately present data, the memory might be considered a fairly direct apprehension of past associations or experiences. In that case, the most elementary form of memory, recognition, can be split into two elements only: perception and recall, which would reduce the rôle of the memory to the simple conservation of some component of the antecedent perception.

But this approach raises a host of problems. To begin with, reactions to immediately present data are purely perceptive, and perception itself (which is an organization of sense data) involves several structuring planes. Far from being a mere imprinting mechanism, perception also involves identification or assimilation, and hence contains a schematism: when a subject recognizes an object he has previously perceived, it is difficult to decide whether his recognition is based on the remembrance or conservation of perceptive schemata, and in what form, or whether it reflects the organization of the sense data by these schemata, and again in what form. Moreover, perception is invariably extended by interpretations based on assimilation to the sensori-motor, conceptual, pre-operational or operational schemata, and it is obvious that remembrance must impinge on these interpretations or significations, no less than on the antecedent perceptions themselves.

The analysis of even the simplest cases thus leads us to treat the memory as a form of actualization, involving the conservation of the entire past, or at least of everything in a subject's past that serves to inform his present action or understanding. But in doing so, we greatly complicate the problem of mnemonic processes—if they can only be explained in terms of the conservation of the entire past, how do we explain that conservation itself, and how can we isolate those factors which belong to the special province of the 'memory', and as such, lend themselves to observation and experimentation?

1

§1. *Remembrance and the conservation of the past*

An individual's past is first ('first' in chronological order) his entire heredity, and treating heredity as a form of phyletic memory, as a storehouse of 'genetic' information, is a far cry from analysing particular acts of recognition, let alone recall by means of a memory-image. And yet the conservation of the genetic past affects our every action, all our acquired knowledge,[1] our every recognition or recall.

Our first problem, then, is to distinguish between the acquired memory (or the memory proper) and the phyletic memory or conservation and utilization of hereditary information. Now that distinction is much more difficult than it seems. Let us suppose, as ethologists do, that an animal responding to 'releasers' by means of the so-called 'innate releasing mechanism' (IRM; for instance the shape or size of twigs used in nest-building) will come to recognize them even better after training. The improved memory will nevertheless remain a (partial) function of its hereditary mechanism. In human beings, too, it seems most likely that the remembrance of simple geometrical forms is supported, not by an IRM, but by certain functional mechanisms of space perception based partly on innate influences. This applies even to cases in which the memory or acquired knowledge cannot be sharply distinguished from the hereditary factors.

There is an even greater, and for us a much graver, problem; over and above the hereditary schematism, we humans possess a large number of acquired (perceptive, habitual, sensori-motor, pre-operational, operational, etc.) schemata, the conservation of which is a presupposition of all our actions, without being necessarily related to what we commonly call the memory. What, then, is the precise relationship between the two?

The problem is not a purely semantic one, but it does raise a semantic question. In particular, biologists and psychologists use the term 'memory' in three distinct senses:

I. Biologists apply the term 'memory' to the conservation of acquired reactions, at every level of life. Thus, when a bacterium produces an antibody in response to an antigen, two explanations are possible: either the response is due to genetic preformation and selection after the event, in which case we cannot speak of a memory, or else the production of antibodies is a reaction to the structure of the antigen, in which case immunity is considered as an act of 'memory'. *A fortiori*, the term 'memory' applies to the conservation

[1] Modern biologists treat all phenotypic acquisitions as interactions between the environmental factor and the synthetic activities of the genom, i.e. the total chromosome content of the nucleus of a gamete.

2

of the results of organic training or habituation. It is to this extremely broad meaning (acquired semantic responses as well as acquired behavioural schemata) that we refer when we speak of the 'memory' in the biologist's sense.

II. In respect of behaviour only, people often give the term 'memory' an even wider meaning, covering the conservation of habits or the results of training, together with the recall of memory-images and acts of simple recognition. This raises three main problems.

In the first place, it seems clear that all habits presuppose the recognition of certain signs: when the limpet returns to its place on a rock after high tide, it obviously relies on certain proprioceptive or exteroceptive signs: its habits clearly involve acts of recognition. Depending on the vocabulary we choose, we can then say that habit is a particular case of memory, or else that it merely concerns that part of the memory we call recognition. It follows that we must distinguish between two separate elements: (1) the conservation of the sensori-motor schemata constituting the habit; and (2) the recognition of perceptual signs whose significance is determined by these very schemata. In fact, no matter whether we apply the term 'memory' to the whole process, or merely to recognition, the reproduction of an organized set of movements (sensori-motor schemata) is something quite other than the recognition of perceptive signs.

In the second place, if we include in the memory the conservation of (and the possibility of repeating or actualizing) all habitual schemata, there is no reason for excluding from it the conservation or actualization of all other schemata (action, knowledge, and operations). Thus, when the child learns to place objects into series or classes, the schemata are conserved and can be actualized whenever they prove useful to him. This means that their conservation is of a kind with that of the habitual schemata. No wonder, then, that one of the chief problems we shall be examining is the relationship between what is commonly called the memory (recognition and recall) and the conservation of the underlying, acquired (as distinct from inherited) schemata.

In the third place, we must carefully distinguish not only between the repetition of schematized actions (from habits to operations) and recognition or recall, but also between two distinct ways of conserving the past. That conservation can bear (1) on repeatable processes, as happens precisely with habits and operations, and (2) on singular events or objects, as when we recognize one particular face among hundreds and recall it by means of a strictly individual-ized memory-image. This distinction between the repeatable and the

3

singular coincides in part with that between the conservation of schemata and mnemonic recognition and recall, but this correspondence needs further definition. Thus, when we learn a particular poem by heart after a series of repetitions, are we conserving a schema or are we engaging in acts of recognition and recall? Our answer is: we are doing both, which maintains the distinction but raises relationship problems. On the one hand, poetry, once learned, is open to recall, but that recall, being complex, involves an element of learning, which comes back to the construction and conservation of a schema. On the other hand, apart from more or less general schemata, there may also be individualized ones, just as a system of logical classification can contain singular classes.[1]

We must accordingly pay close attention to the precise way in which we formulate our problem. In particular, we shall not apply the term 'memory' indiscriminately to all types of conservation of previous forms of behaviour, but we shall use the terms 'schematism' or 'conservation of schemata' to refer to the ability to reproduce whatever can be generalized in a system of actions or operations (habitual, sensori-motor, conceptual, operational and other schemata); and the term 'memory in the wider sense' to refer to the type of memory which, *inter alia*, involves this 'conservation of schemata'. It might be argued that the existence or construction of a schema (for example a seriation or classification) is something quite other than its conservation, since the latter presupposes the existence of a specialized memory. But the special characteristic of a schema (as distinct from a single action) is precisely that it links up similar situations, and hence gives rise to reproductions or generalizations, so that the conservation of a schema is identical with its own existence. True, the idea of a construction involving its own conservation raises a further problem, and moreover an essential one in respect of what we shall call the 'memory in the strict sense'; namely, determining whether the source of the repetitions lies in simple 'associations' (which are also conserved by virtue of their very construction), i.e. in repetitions of external events or in regular sequences imposed by experience, or whether the existence of a schema involves an assimilation factor, that is active generalizations and reproductions reflecting attempts to interpret external sequences—regular or irregular, apparent or factual. But this problem transcends that of the memory, for it concerns the intelligence itself, and the cognitive functions as a whole.

III. By 'memory in the strict sense', we shall refer to reactions associated with recognition (in the presence of the object) and recall

[1] However, individualized schemata are invariably part of a general system, and hence exceptional in appearance only.

4

(in the absence of the object). Its distinctive characteristic is that it refers explicitly to the past: the subject 'recognizes' an object or a sequence of events if he has the impression of having perceived them before (rightly or wrongly, for there are also false recognitions); and the memory-image involved in mnemonic recall differs from the representative (reproductive or anticipatory) memory-image in that it goes hand in hand with (general or detailed, correct or mistaken) localizations in the past, i.e. with the impression that the object or event has been experienced or perceived at a given (possibly non-localizable) moment in time. Another, perhaps even more characteristic distinction, though inseparable from the first, is that the 'memory in the strict sense' and the memory-image only bear on such situations, processes or objects as are singular and recognized or recalled as such (whereas schemata are general), and on such representative images as, while being individual, symbolize a general schema (the image of a square as the symbol of all squares). Thus, if we employ, say, the concept of 'stigmergy', a recent notion introduced into animal psychology by Grassé, we are simply conserving and applying a schema, albeit one we have acquired by external transmission. However, if we recall finding that concept in one of Grassé's treatises on zoology, we are falling back on a memory, inasmuch as we are referring to a particular situation we ourselves have encountered and which we can localize in time more or less accurately.

This example also suggests the possible existence of intermediate stages between remembrance and the conservation of a schema. Thus, a student having no interest in, or use for, stigmergy can nevertheless remember that concept step by step during an examination, (via 'signifiers', termites, the works of Grassé, etc.). But these intermediate stages, which may be compared to the stages involved in learning a poem by heart, do not invalidate the structural and functional duality linking the conservation of a schema used in practice to a memory that is both particularized and also (roughly) localizable in time.

The first difference between the memory thus defined[1] and the

---

[1] In addition to recognition and recall, we can also distinguish a third type of memory based on the acceleration of acquired knowledge that comes with re-learning. Thus, when the results of learning are apparently forgotten, it often happens that the repetition of the original learning process gives the same (or better) results, but in less time and with a smaller number of repetitions. This has suggested the existence of 'memory traces', and hence of a special type of memory distinct from mnemonic recognition or recall.

But it is essential to distinguish between what a subject can 'do' and the acts of recognition or recall that may accompany his actions. In the case of the mere reproduction of actions, we remain in the realm of sensori-motor schemata (habits, etc.) and the greater capacity that comes with re-learning simply goes to conservation of schemata is therefore that the schemata are actualized in the present situation without explicit reference to the past, unless this re-utilization is accompanied by remembrance, which may sometimes be helpful but is never essential: a habit, for instance, can appear without the subject's remembering its formation; seriations can be applied without recall of the past, etc. From the developmental point of view, it should be noted that a complete sensori-motor schema arises during the first twelve to eighteen months of existence, that is well before the formation of mnemonic recall (which is related to the semiotic function). However, the application of that schema presupposes a measure of recognition (similarity of situations, etc.), much as an elementary habit implies the recognition of signs. In general, the process of assimilation engendering a schema must be reproductive, generalizable and recognitory all at once, for it involves repetitive, extensive and discriminatory factors, thus providing a primitive link between the schematism and the recognitory memory (the appearance of which represents a considerable advance over mnemonic recall). The better to grasp the nature of this link, we must first of all distinguish between two extreme types of recognition.

The first of these is purely mnemonic and appears during the re-perception of a given object, for instance when the infant first distinguishes his mother from a stranger. The second type has a somewhat pre-notional, and in any case clearly schematic, character: it involves the assimilation of a given situation to a schema, as when the baby, seeing a new object, but one that is suspended in the same way as other objects it has previously seen, recognizes it as a swinging toy. It is in this second sense that assimilation is always recognitory as well as reproductive and generalizing. This leaves us with the problem of establishing whether mnemonic recognition derives from recognitory assimilation, or vice versa, or whether the two are always conjoined. But even in the last case, mnemonic recognition would only be a particular aspect of the over-all schematism, and hence fail to provide

---

show that the initial schema, constructed during the original experience, is not completely destroyed. If, on the other hand, the retraining process is accompanied by recognition (of the experimental set-up or of the actions themselves) and *a fortiori* by recall (memory-images of earlier experiences) then, of course, we have 'memory in the strict sense', over and above the conservation of the schemata, and this, once again, precisely because an explicit reference to the past is involved.

In other words, if all we have is easier reproduction based on earlier actions, the reference to the past is not in the mind of the subject, but only in that of the experimenter, in which case we can only speak of a schematism or the conservation of schemata. If, however, the reference to the past is made by the subject himself, then, and only then, shall we employ the term 'memory in the strict sense'. (An analysis of re-learning by one of our subjects will be found in Chapter 3, §3.)

an explanation of the conservation of schemata by the memory in the strict sense.

Moreover, if one of the fundamental differences between the schematism and the memory in the strict sense is, that the first, as we saw, invariably comprises the general or repeatable, while the second, like perception itself, generally involves singular objects and events and hence fails to give rise to schemata, operations or ideas, except by means of concrete figurations (or, as we shall see by part-deductive reconstructions more or less closely linked to language), then we are left with the following central problem: we must establish to what extent the memory involves a reconstruction, which is what P. Janet meant when he said that the memory was bound up with 'narrative conduct', and to what extent it lingers on, between the imprinting of the data and their recall, thanks to the conservation of unconscious pictures (such as Penfield was able to resurrect by electrical stimulation of the temporal lobes). Now, it is quite possible: (1) that these memories based on 'unconscious' traces (if they exist at all, and even if they are not integrated to the extent Freud and Bergson claim they are) may essentially be of an imaginal and concrete nature; (2) that they may be, in one way or another, linked to action schemata (possibly giving rise to affective schemata);[1] and (3) that the memory may only be able to embrace the most abstract processes (causal sequences, concepts and operations) to the extent that it relies, *inter alia*, on deductive or verbal reconstructions, thus placing itself even more closely in the system of schemata. But all this is no more than a hypothesis at this stage, and we hope that the facts we shall be presenting will throw fresh light on the matter.

In general, the differences between schema and memory seem to result mainly from the fact that, whereas the former reflect the internal organization and dynamics of behaviour, i.e. an organization the conservation of which is the expression of its own activity, the second is either a figurative interpretation or a reconstruction of the results of that activity, without (or prior to having) a direct bearing on the latter. But in order to clarify these, our guiding, hypotheses, we must enter a qualification, without which they may seem quite trivial or even meaningless.

Advocates of the theory of learning usually contend that all forms of mental development, including the evolution of schemata, are the result of learning, and that the memory is nothing other than the conservation of these results (including the schemata): in that case our main hypothesis would reduce to distinguishing, within the memory, between the figurative or symbolic elements and the motor

[1] See J. Piaget: *Play, Dreams and Imitation in Childhood*, Routledge & Kegan Paul, 1951.

elements. However, in the light of earlier[1] and current[2] studies of learning processes, we have found that these processes cannot possibly account for mental development, since mental activity is based not only on what a subject 'learns' continually from the environment, but also on such factors as self-regulation and equilibration, in short on organization. Now, these factors, far from being the results of learning, preside over it. Similarly, all organisms adapt themselves to their environment by virtue of a process of internal organization based on interactions which, admittedly, cannot be split up but nevertheless run counter to the hypothesis of purely external acquisitions. Seen in that light, the schemata, although continuously modified by learning (i.e. by accommodation but coupled to constant assimilation), are part of the general process of development and not the result of learning alone, and this is why the problem of the conservation of the schemata is a problem quite distinct from that of the memory in the strict sense.

In short, our starting hypothesis is meaningful only in the framework of a general theory of development, distinct from special theories of learning. Hence, it may prove useful to determine the rôle of the memory in the general system of cognitive functions.

§2. *The place of the memory in the system of cognitive functions*

An organism is a machine engaged in transformations, or more precisely in two types of transformation: (1) it assimilates the environment even while it is subject to its constraints, i.e. it constructs and conserves such forms of organization as are capable of perpetuating exchanges with the outside world; and (2) it changes the environment by its reactions and especially by behaving in such a way as to extend and particularize these two types of interrelated transformation in accordance with the following scheme:

I. The inputs of the system are perceptions, though perceptions are by no means the sole sources of knowledge: in order to 'know' an object, the subject may act upon it, thus giving rise to the feedback FR which carries the results of the action X, i.e. of the transformations TR, back to the input I.

The internal system does not reduce to a set of associative paths between the inputs I and the outputs X, but consists of an organization O which

---

[1] See Volumes VII–X of *Études d'épistémologie génétique: Apprentissage et connaissance* (VII); *Logique, apprentissage et probabilité* (VIII); *L'Apprentissage des structures logiques* (IX); *La Logique des apprentissages* (X), Presses Universitaires de France, 1959.
[2] Studies by B. Inhelder, M. Bovet, H. Sinclair *et al.*

8

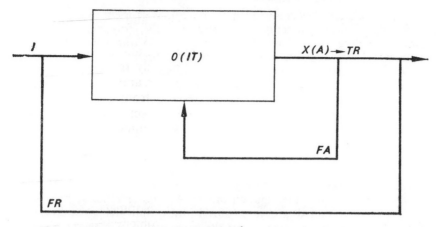

FIGURE 1

I = input (entry);
O = organization (system of internal transformations);
$X(A)$ = output or actions leading to TR = transformations of reality;
FR = feedbacks based on the results of TR;
FA = feedbacks based on $X(A)$.

adds various elements to what is put in at I. Hence, the cognitive organization is made up of the assimilation plus the transformation of the data I. However, the internal transformations IT constituting the schematism at all its levels— from the most elementary habits to the most highly evolved operations—spring only in part from the subject's innate resources (spontaneous movements, reflexes, hereditary cerebral function, etc.) and are, moreover, constructed piecemeal under the growing influence of the actions $X(A)$ culminating in the transformations of reality TR. This accounts for the feedback FA leading from these actions $X(A)$ to the internal organization O as constituent elements of the schemata.

As for the outputs X, we have referred to them as transformations of reality TR and not of objects alone, to mark the fact that they can also involve the subject's body, for instance by leading it to imitate, or accommodate to, the properties of the object.

Schematized in this way, the cognitive functions give rise to two great distinctions that prove useful in defining the place of the memory. The first opposes *figurative* to *operational* functions. The latter, which range from elementary to higher operations, are characterized by their ability to transform objects. This, as we have kept stressing in other works, does not mean that logico-mathematical structures are derived from objects as such —they are abstracted by reflection and construction from actions performed on objects and not from the properties of the latter: that is precisely why the feedback FA links the actions in X to the internal organization O (which explains the relative independence of the system of schemata). The figurative functions, by contrast, have no tendency to

9

transform objects, but tend to supply imitations of them in the broadest sense of the term. The figurative instruments, therefore, bear mainly on static configurations, which are relatively easy to translate into images; even when they concern movements or transformations, they do so in order to produce the appropriate configurations, not the changes of state. This is what happens during perception (in I) which, though governed by the assimilatory schemata (whence the partial isomorphism of perception and the intelligence), is essentially a form of object accommodation, so much so that the perceptive activities imitate the form of the object (for example when the eye follows its contours). This is also what happens during imitation (in $X \to TR$), which, from the sensori-motor level onwards, provides an image based on the corporal actions of others and often of objects, and whose role in subsequent representations of one's own body is well known. Imitation, though immediate and external at first, later assumes 'differentiated' and internalized forms, thus giving rise to a new and basic figurative instrument for the construction of mnemonic recall, namely the mental image, which, as we have tried to show elsewhere,[1] is based on internalized imitation. Similarly, symbolic play, graphic images, etc. all constitute or utilize figurative instruments born of imitation.

The formation of the figurative functions is thus closely linked to the feedback FR leading from the results of the imitative actions in X to the perceptions in I. The operational functions, on the other hand, correspond to the transformative actions of the object in $X \to TR$, as well as to the internal operations in $O(IT)$, joined by the feedback FA. This does not mean that no figurative element is found in the internal organization $O(IT)$; since imitation is one of its many products (in X) and since perception presides over the inputs in I, we may take it that all operational schemata in $O(IT)$ have at least one figurative aspect, not in the form of a constituent or motor element (the image would only be an element of thought if the internal system, instead of being a transformative organization $O = IT$, were a simple collection of associative transmissions) but in the form of signs or symbols which ensure recognition (from recognitory assimilation to perceptive recognition) and recall.

II. This brings us to the second great distinction we must introduce if we are to cover the entire field of cognitive functions: that of *signifiers* and *significates*.[2] Understanding and intervention in X are manipulations of objects, which they endow with meaning based on prior assimilation to the organization in O. Now, these meanings or significations include both significates, i.e. the schemata constituting the schematism $O(IT)$ and also signifiers. Among the latter we can distinguish three types, two provided by the instruments of the figur-

---

[1] J. Piaget and B. Inhelder: *Mental Imagery in the Child*, Routledge & Kegan Paul, 1971.
[2] By 'significate' we refer to the meanings themselves, i.e. to the schemata or concepts (involved in the understanding) and not simply to the objects (in extension) to which these meanings apply.

ative function, and a third which is collective and poses a special problem.

The most elementary signifiers (and hence the first to appear) are the perceptive *signs*, since, as Piéron,[1] following the great Ampère,[2] has so shrewdly remarked, sensation is a symbol (in the sense of general signifier), not a faithful copy of the object (whence we speak of it as imitation in the wider sense). A sign is only part of an object (a branch protruding over a wall is a sign of the presence of a tree) or one of its aspects (a shimmering may be a sign of a hidden sheet of water) or it may be a causal effect (the track of an animal, a spot, etc.). In short, a sign can serve as a signifier of all sensori-motor schemata, and when we say that all perception is 'significative', we mean that all signifiers consist of perceptive signs, while significates consist of schemata transcending the mere sense data (identifications, correlations, etc. inherent in sensori-motor and action schemata no less than in conceptual schemata).

The next highest order of signifiers is constructed during the second year of life and marks their differentiation from the significates: these differentiated signifiers are no longer simple parts or aspects of the perceived object but intervene during more or less similar or deliberate acts of recall in the absence of the object; in other words, they are *symbols* first and foremost (in the strict sense in which linguists oppose 'symbols' to 'signs'). They are simply the figurative elements (excluding perception) to which we have referred earlier, namely, images, symbolic games, etc. Now, as we have tried to show elsewhere,[3] it is imitation which, by developing beyond the initial sensori-motor level to become deferred and internalized, is the source of these differentiated—figurative and symbolic—signifiers. The use of such figurative symbols goes hand in hand with the beginning of representation, and we refer by 'semiotic function' to the use of such symbols, no less than of the signs we have mentioned. It should be stressed that, as regards the organization of the operational schemata $O(IT)$, there are no grounds for holding that the sensori-motor schemata, as significates, contain their signifiers as perceptive signs—representative or operational schemata do not demand the use of adequate signifiers—they are constructed from the sign systems[4] we shall be discussing below. But language is collective and does not meet all individual needs: while it is adequate to the designation of the general schemata common to all individuals, it cannot signify every detail in the experiences or actions of the individual, quite especially in what concerns the memory, the subject matter of this book. Hence, it is only natural that symbolic images as signifiers relating to differentiated and individualized schemata should interpose themselves between perceptive signs and common language.

[1] H. Piéron: *The Sensations*, Yale University Press, 1952, pp. 412 ff.
[2] See Barthélemy-Saint-Hilaire: *La Philosophie des deux Ampères*, Didier, 1866, p. 34.
[3] J. Piaget: *Play, Dreams and Imitation in Childhood*, Routledge & Kegan Paul, 1951.
[4] Natural (languages) or artificial systems (algebra, etc.).

The third level of signifiers is therefore constituted by language, or by the system of differentiated and collective 'signs', and as such either 'arbitrary' or conventional. In order not to complicate our model even further, we have not distinguished between the individual and the socialized components in the actions $X \rightarrow TR$, which become inseparable at a very early stage. Now, every social group has a language and, by virtue of it, acts on the internal, cognitive organization of its individual members: we must therefore complete our scheme with two further feedback systems, $F'A$ and $F'R$, which represent the continual pressure, on the organization $O(IT)$ and on the inputs I of the collective actions $X \rightarrow TR$, of each subject, though, needless to say, there is no point in trying to distinguish them from FA and FR. The only thing to remember is the presence, by the side of imaginal signifiers, of linguistic signifiers, which serve to signify the schemata of the organization $O(IT)$, because they play an unmistakable rôle in the work of the memory.

Before returning to the latter, which is quite obviously related to the figurative aspects of knowledge and to the various signifier systems, let us briefly sum up what we know about the relationships between the figurative instruments of knowledge and the semiotic function (symbols and signs). These can be represented by two intersecting ellipses (Figure 2). There are first of all those figurative elements that do not participate in the semiotic function, among them

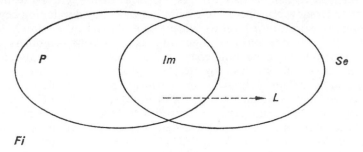

FIGURE 2

Fi = figurative instruments; Se = semiotic function; P = perception; Im = mental image, etc., L = language.

perception, which, though representing a system of signifiers, does so by means of signs that are not differentiated from the perceptive data. Next, there are the figurative cum semiotic mechanisms, for instance mental images, symbolic games, deferred imitation, gestural language, etc. Lastly, there are the semiotic instruments which are not figurative in themselves, namely, the system of signs. Natural languages belong to this category. However, a subject's use of this system is not necessarily devoid of all figurative aspects. In particular, children often use language as a set of symbols instead of a system of signs. Even adult use of language often resembles figurative speech; apart from onomatopoeia, we employ a whole range of metaphors and expressions characteristic of what C. Bally has called the 'affective language'. But even in these, predominantly semantic, cases, the sign structures *qua* signifiers are subject to the normal rules of linguistic usage, so that the laws governing them cannot be reduced to those governing the behaviour of the mental image or such of its symbols as lend themselves to individual constructions. Language, on the other hand, differs slightly in this respect, as we have just seen; while being closer to the figurative factor (and especially to imitation) in its initial stages, from the age of two years it moves gradually in the direction of the arrow in Figure 2.

III. Having briefly outlined the system of cognitive functions other than the memory (in the strict sense, as defined in §1., III) we shall now try to define the place of the latter in our scheme. But here we encounter several unresolved problems, and it is, in fact, because of these that we originally decided to make this study. It would, however, be idle to expect us to resolve them in this Introduction (if solved indeed they can be).

The central problem of the memory hinges on the pronounced heterogeneity, from the investigator's (no less than the subject's) viewpoint, of the experimental data and the events in the 'black box' (Figure 1), with generous contributions from the transformative organization $O(IT)$. The observable facts are situated at the input I and the exit $X \rightarrow TR$: they relate to what the subject recognizes (as having been perceived previously) and to what he manages to recall. As for the hidden mechanisms in $O(IT)$, which ensure the conservation or reconstruction of the memory, we know very little about them, at least in the case of mnemonic recall.

In respect of the observables, on which we shall concentrate for the moment, it seems clear that the memory is very closely bound up with the figurative and semiotic functions, and this for two complementary reasons.

The first of these is that mnemonic recognition and recall are based on figurative or semiotic mechanisms. Recognition, a primitive process found even in lower vertebrates, occurs in the presence of the object and consists of perceiving the latter as something known, as something perceived in the past. In other words, it is a double utilization of that figurative mechanism which we designate as perception. As for mnemonic recall, it involves the use of a memory-image, i.e. an image or a 'narrative' which in turn involves language, that is a figurative cum semiotic mechanism (image) or a purely semiotic

13

mechanism (it should, however, be remembered that, while the spoken word itself is not figurative, the memory, or acoustic image of the word, is just that).

The second reason is that all semiotic mechanisms, be they figurative (images, symbolic games, etc.) or not (language), are themselves based on the memory. A mental image, even if its only function is the representation of a state, is always a memory-image: it is only constructed or only reappears in the absence of the object of its perception. The sole valid distinction between reproductive images and memory-images is that the first bear explicitly on a particular object or event located by the subject in his past, while the second remain implicitly bound up with perception, also in the past, which they try to imitate or copy, and hence they, too, are based on mnemonic recall.[1] Similarly, language, too, involves the memory of words etc., and there are many cases of aphasia whose behaviour suggests that, while the loss of this type of memory impedes the use of language, it does not affect the operational schemata. In other cases, speech impediments go hand in hand with figurative defects (poor spatial representations), again without operational disturbances, and this in situations where reasoning about transformations does not involve the representation of non-perceived states.

§3. *Problems for investigation*

The close link between the memory and the figurative or semiotic mechanisms brings us to the central problem of the conservation of memories, and hence of the memory 'traces' involved in recognition or recall, i.e. of the non-observable mnemonic processes situated in the black box $O(IT)$ of Figure 1. This problem calls for a closer examination of the different types of conservation mentioned in §1.

I. Fundamental in this connection is the difference (and we must still establish whether it is one of kind or of degree) between the conservation of an operational schema (actions or operations) and the conservation of memories which, as we saw, is bound up with the conservation of the figurative or semiotic elements.

The conservation or recall of a word is something quite other than the word itself, for there is nothing to compel a word to enter the memory (this becomes clear whenever we learn a foreign language): a word lacks a self-regulatory mechanism (except on the collective level of linguistic constraints[2]) demanding its conservation in the individual's memory. Similarly, the memory of an image is something

---

[1] There remain the anticipatory images, but these are based on analogies with prior experience.
[2] This presents us with another vast problem for investigation.

quite other than the image itself, for there is nothing in its own functioning to demand its self-conservation. True, an image is already a memory-image inasmuch as it refers to prior perceptions, but this memory can be lost.

A schema, by contrast, conserves itself by virtue of its own functioning, and does so in the psychological sense of the conservation of the past. This is because its own mode of composition involves logical conservation, i.e. the invariance of the over-all system under all transformations. The characteristic feature of an operational schema, for instance, is that it involves a reversible structure, i.e. one that is not time-bound (even though reversible operations are the culmination of semi-reversible regulations which are unidirectional in time). This ensures the conservation of the system by its inner logic. As a result, the memory of an operational schema, such as a classification, a seriation or one-to-one correspondence (we say memory of a schema in contrast to the memory of the concrete objects that might have been seriated or classified, etc.) coincides with the schema itself, which, having once been constructed, is conserved throughout the life of the individual, except for pathological reasons. In other words, the memory of a schema is something quite other than the memory in the strict sense. A *Gestaltist* once told us that what we have said of the memory of a schema is true of the memory of most things; the memory of a *Gestalt*, for instance, is simply the *Gestalt* itself. To this we can assent, provided only that we grant that a *Gestalt* represents a schema (which can be generalized by virtue of its symmetry, regularity, etc.). However, we cannot say the same of a perception as such; moreover, a 'bad' form or irregular *Gestalt* is not automatically preserved in the memory, so that its recall is not identical with its perceptive imprint.

At the other end of the schematic spectrum, it is worth recalling that living organisms, too, conserve themselves by virtue of their own functioning, and that they continue to live, at least in such of their immortal parts as the genoms, without a special conserving function or memory of their own organization. It may be said that this conserving function does, in fact, exist, and that it is called heredity, but since the genom is a regulative system (and not as was formerly believed an atomistic collection of independent genes) we must clearly distinguish between heredity, i.e. the transmission of particular characters by division and multiplication, and the organization as such, which is not transmitted in the proper sense of the word, but simply continues and conserves itself as the necessary condition of all such transmissions.[1]

[1] See J. Piaget: *Biology and Knowledge*, University of Chicago Press, 1971, Chapter VII.

Returning now to the psychological sphere and to the schematism acquired or 'constructed' in the course of an individual's development, we find that the contrast between the memory in the strict sense and the conservation of the operational schemata grows less marked as we descend to the lower levels of development, for instance to the sensori-motor schemata and, quite particularly, to the habitual schemata. In fact, a habit can be lost, and its conservation is bound up with the way in which it functions. We must therefore look more closely into these lower schemata, and quite particularly into the possible existence or absence of a series of intermediate stages between the conservation of memories and the conservation of schemata.

Let us note first of all that, thanks to their self-conservation by functional regulations, sensori-motor schemata behave very much like operational schemata. Schemata such as the persistence of objects when they are no longer perceived, or the organization of displacements into a 'group', are conserved throughout life precisely because they are elaborated into operational structures. Similarly, though such particular schemata as pulling an object towards oneself with the help of supports, strings, sticks, etc. or as swinging a suspended object, cannot be generalized indefinitely, their general co-ordination (colligation of schemata, order of succession, correspondence, etc.) bears witness to the existence of a permanent schematism, so permanent in fact that we can consider it as the elementary source of all logical operations. We must therefore envisage the possible existence of various degrees of conservation in increasing order of generality and, in any case, we may postulate the self-conservation of certain schemata essential to the functioning of the intelligence (all of them the result of gradual constructions).

As regards the schemata proper to the most primitive habits, some are normally lost (e.g. thumb-sucking) while others are conserved throughout life (e.g. those concerned with visual or tactilo-kinaesthetic exploration). This raises the question of the nature of the mechanism responsible for their conservation or extinction, and we see at once that the conservation results from the feedback which help to maintain the schema as a function of its utilization and results. Is this not equally true of the memory in the strict sense, which becomes consolidated when it is put to frequent and agreeable use, but becomes extinct in the wake of disuse or repression? Perhaps so, but with two essential reservations which force us to treat this process as a problem and not as a starting point for further studies.

In the first place, a habit (and *a fortiori* every schematism higher than a habit) is an over-all system that functions as one whole, and it is precisely this over-all functioning which ensures its conservation as a system, however elementary; the system is, moreover, self-contained and thus constitutes a schema (the more so if this schema is a sub-system of a wider one, as in Hull's 'hierarchical families'). A memory, on the other hand, can either be isolated (the sudden re-appearance of a melody or of the face of a fellow air-passenger) or else be part of a system (which may also be the case with isolated memories), but there is nothing to prove that this system is of a purely mnemonic nature (in the strict sense): on the contrary there is every indication that it involves a great deal of action, and hence a more or less extensive schematism. In that case, we must ask ourselves whether the conservation of the memory in the strict sense is independent of the conservation of schemata, or whether it depends more or less closely on the latter and in what manner. Now, we know of the existence of purely mnemonic schemata (as investigated by F. Bartlett), some of which are spontaneous mnemotechnical procedures. Their relationship with the cognitive schemata has still to be determined by a study on the genetic plane or the plane of mental development in general. Moreover, it is useful to recall and maintain the distinction between the 'scheme' proper to images, and the 'schema' proper to actions, the first simplifying, and the second assimilating, by way of analogies.

Secondly, there is a wide range of mnemonic processes whose elementary varieties are manifestly bound up with the conservation of action schemata: we are referring to recognitions which, in their initial form, are bound up with sensori-motor schemata. In fact every habit is based on the recognition of signs, and the successive phases of an act of practical intelligence, too, are determined by a succession of signs whose recognition is a *sine qua non* of the performance of an action. Hence, we have reason to suppose that mnemonic conservation is subordinate to the conservation of schemata, which comes back to saying that mnemonic recognition is based on recognitory assimilation. With higher stages of recognition, on the other hand, it is possible to recognize an object that has been perceived on just one past occasion, and apparently without the aid of schematisms. But we must then establish whether such singular events do not constitute a special class, i.e. whether this type of recognition is not part of a complex and unconscious system of analogies and contrasts, which would explain why the isolated object attracted sufficient attention in the first instance to be recognized during the second.

In the case of mnemonic recall, finally, the problem of memory conservation is much less straightforward. Between the views of Freud and Bergson, who believe that the entire past is recorded and conserved in the subconscious (but without specifying in what way, as if the mere fact of subsequent recall is enough to explain the alleged conservation of memories during the interval between their original fixation and their eventual reappearance), and the views of P. Janet *et al.*, who assume that all acts of recall are direct reconstructions of the material facts, there is room for every conceivable hypothesis.

This is one of the many problems we shall be investigating, the more so as far too little attention has been paid by other students to the relationship between the possible conservation of the memory and the undeniable conservation of the operational schemata, or, for that matter, to the relationship between mnemonic reconstruction in Janet's sense ('narrative conduct') and deductive or operational reconstructions. Another somewhat neglected approach in the study of mnemonic processes is the comparative and functional analysis of cognitive mechanism, and first of all of the intelligence in its many manifestations; and it is in this light that we shall be viewing certain aspects of the development of the memory.

II. Classical studies of the memory have been surprisingly positivistic, i.e. confined to the analysis of the inputs I and exits X of the black box (Figure 1) by highly ingenious variations of the stimuli, and without any attempt to go beyond the observable facts so as to reconstruct the inside of the box. Ebbinghaus has tried to use psychophysical methods to analyse the laws governing the behaviour of the memory and, ever since, an impressive collection of quantitative data has been accumulated in this particular field.

If, however, we are interested in the contents of the box, which has been kept tightly sealed (by the investigators themselves and not by force of circumstance), we must not only lower our sights but also try to justify our objectives. To lower the sights is easy; we are simply aiming at a qualitative analysis, and far from trying to discover new laws, we are merely trying to discover the mechanisms of the memory and their relationship to those at work in imagery and the intelligence. As for the justification of our project, it is based on two factors. The first is that the inner processes at work in the intelligence are nowhere more accessible than they are in the memory ('thought is a subconscious activity of the mind', said Binet). Moreover, the analysis of intellectual behaviour, i.e. of reactions by subjects at grips with problems, enables us to make certain reconstructions whose validity can be checked more or less acurately by an examination of their implications. Why then should we not attempt to use a similar approach in investigating the behaviour of the memory?

The second factor is that the difficulties surrounding the problem of mnemonic recall are unlikely to prove insurmountable, except in the case of adults whose mental functions have become too complex and crystallized to allow an analysis of the underlying processes. But if we once again apply the genetic method, there is good reason to hope that, in response to questions concerning the memory, we may obtain something other than successes expressed as percentages or as fractions of the general task: we may look forward to the discovery of distinct qualitative stages that can throw fresh light on the very organization of the memory.

But, in order to attain this objective, we must naturally choose and vary our factors, not so much in quantitative terms (number of presentations, intervals between successive presentations, etc.) as in terms of our central problem: the comparison of the memory in the strict sense with the conservation of the pre-operational or operational schemata. That is precisely why we have decided to begin this book on the memory[1] with a study of the remembrance of an operational situation, an hour after the presentation of the experimental set-up, or after one or two weeks, and in several cases after four to eight months. The experimental set-up involved purely static models based on operational transformations (of which the child was unaware), for instance ten rods arranged in order of size, or collections of classifiable objects, or two lines of equal length, one straight and the other broken. In yet another series of tests, the child was shown a series of transformations, such as decantations, as practical examples of transitivity or associativity. The child's operational level being known beforehand, we wondered whether his memory of the experimental set-up would be in the nature of a more or less passive and receptive record of what he had perceived (in terms of perception as such and not of interpretation) or whether he would merely remember what he had understood. Now, apart from some very young children, we found that the memory of our subjects was very closely bound up with their level of understanding. This apparently trivial conclusion is nevertheless worthy of closer analysis, because we were forcibly struck, not only by the correspondence between the quality of recall after a lapse of one or two weeks and the level of operational and pre-operational development, but also, and more strongly still, by the extent to which the memory was bound up with what the child could 'do' or construct at various stages of its life. But the greatest surprise was that in certain cases the memory was found to have improved over several months, and this without further presentations of the experimental set-up. It goes without saying that such facts, which recall Ballard's 'reminiscences', are highly instructive in a study of mnemonic conservation or reconstruction.

[1] The problem of the memory was first raised in our study of mental imagery: in a chapter dealing with the qualities of the image after the simple perception or material reconstruction of the model.

But such improvements are not general and are quite naturally linked to the nature of the particular schema on which the recall is brought to bear or to which the memory is attached. In Chapter 4 we shall see that, if the memory is not bound up with a dominant schema (such as seriation) but with two schemata which remain unco-ordinated for a relatively long time (e.g. numerical correspondence which is grasped at the age of seven years, and the conservation of lengths which is only grasped at nine years) the resulting conflict tends to weaken the memory, which, for lack of adequate operational support, takes refuge in illusory solutions. Hence, it seemed desirable to present the experimental material in increasing order of opera-tionality. Some arrangements were chosen because they either lent themselves to an operational interpretation or else made a mainly figurative impression: e.g. a rotating triangle with different figures in each of its apices; drawings of an inclined or recumbent bottle partly filled with a coloured liquid; a snail placed on different parts of a figure eight lying on its side, or two transparent U-tubes with liquids at equal levels in one, and unequal levels in the other (which had a stopper). Other arrangements included various geometrical figures supporting rods in more or less arbitrary positions, so that the memory could only rely on a minimum number of operational schemata.

In short, since we had set out to discover the possible relationship between the memory and the operational or pre-operational schemata we had to use experimental arrangements that were relatively simple to schematize. But we should like to stress from the start that, though schemata reflect the general aspects of actions or opera-tions, while memory-images bear primarily on concrete or singular objects and configurations, the distinction is not at all clear-cut. By the side of very general schemata corresponding to the logical operations most constantly employed, we must also allow for the existence of increasingly particularized schemata, and this in more than one sense. At the operational level, we may expect to find greater schematic specialization as we pass from a system to a sub-system (rotations as sub-groups of displacements, etc.) and quite particularly as one and the same schema is applied in distinct ways (seriation of lengths or surfaces, weights, etc.). At the pre-operational level the schemata become increasingly particular as we pass from articulated intuitions to simpler intuitions bound up with a particular action, and above all as we pass from habitual schemata to action schemata susceptible of momentary, though not to continual, repetitions.

The simplest explanation of the relationship between the memory in the strict sense and the schemata is therefore that the first is merely a translation or figurative aspect of the second. Recognition makes its entry hand in hand with the perceptive signs proper to the sensori-motor schemata, and we may take it that, at all levels, recognition is similarly bound up with increasingly particularized assimilatory schemata. Recall may be considered a product of the combination of a certain, more or less, inferential, reconstruction, with the use of 'memory traces' subject to subconscious conservation. Now, reconstruction most certainly involves the utilization of what schemata are at the subject's disposal during recall, if only to re-capture the temporal order, which is obviously not part of the con-servation as such. As for the latter, the 'memory traces' or evidential elements it utilizes or helps to maintain may be conceived as consisting of, or being bound up with, the concrete and imaginal representation of particularized schemata, which they serve as more or less exact individual symbols, much as language designates the more general schemata. In that case, the (more or less fragmentary) conservation of a memory, must be based on that of the schemata (of habit and intelligence) and must normally be completed by a reconstruction involving the schemata currently employed.

III. Having outlined the general hypothesis on which we have based this book, and which has informed all our experiments,[1] it might perhaps be useful if we developed it at once, so as to clarify our interpretation of some of the facts we are about to examine.

The meeting ground between the conservation of the operational schemata proper to action or intelligence and the figurative elements of perception (recognition) or of the memory-image (recall) proper to the memory in the strict sense must be sought in the links between the assimilatory schemata and the various possible ways of accom-modating these schemata to the assimilated objects, no matter whether the objects be present, as in cognitive adaptation, or whether they belong to the past, as in the memory.

Every schema is the result of an assimilatory activity whose special characteristic it is to incorporate new or known data, or to repro-duce and sooner or later to generalize what has been discovered. Assimilation therefore fashions the schemata, and the latter are nothing but the structural result of the former—a circular process comparable to that relating judgments to concepts.

However, every assimilatory schema must perforce accommodate itself to the objects it bears upon, or else the assimilation becomes distorted (either centred on the affective behaviour of the subject as

[1] In fact, when we set out, we intended merely to study the remembrance of operational situations. But as this Introduction may have shown, a host of new problems cropped up as we proceeded.

happens in symbolic games, or else modifying reality according to momentary whims or desires). In other words, there can be no assimilation without accommodation, nor, conversely, can there be accommodation without assimilation, which helps to explain the inseparable links between recognition and memory-images, on the one hand, and assimilatory schemata on the other.

In fact, accommodation is the starting point of the figurative aspects of knowledge. On the perceptive plane, perceptive schemata are assimilatory inasmuch as they represent a general tendency to identify and compare, but they are also accommodative inasmuch as they serve to explore the perceived configuration, to follow its contours and articulations, etc. On the general plane of action (as on the perceptive plane) accommodation balances assimilation in all adaptations to new situations and in all attempts at intelligent understanding, but it can also go further and tend towards imitation (much as assimilation tends towards play). Imitation, already at work in the perceptive exploration of the contours of an object, gives rise to a sensori-motor or sensori-tonic function whose development leads, well in advance of the construction of the semiotic function, to a kind of representation by means of material actions, increasingly moulded by the external models. Now, it is this type of imitation which, once deferred and interiorized, constitutes the source not only of the mental image, but also of the semiotic function *qua* distinction between signifier and significate.

Since, moreover, the memory in the strict sense relies on figurative instruments—perceptive in recognition and imaginal in recall (and also on strictly imitative instruments in the case of 'reconstructions', which must be situated between recognition and recall), it quite obviously depends on a differentiated and individualized accommodation to the models, and hence on assimilation to the schemata, in which accommodation plays an essential part.

This raises a further problem which, moreover, is not specific to the memory and already crops up in imitation (i.e. in a particular form of mnemonic 'reconstruction'); given the indefinite diversification of the accommodations underlying memory-images or recognitions, does the memory rely on assimilatory schemata as much as it does on individualized accommodation? Now, there are no such things as accommodation schemata (only 'schemata'), for every schema is the result of assimilations. Moreover, the latter, no less than the schemata representing their results, tend towards generality, whereas all forms of accommodation, and particularly the memory-images that may result from them, tend towards singularity: indeed, it is only inasmuch as accommodation is particularized that it becomes the source of the figurative instruments. But the special

22

property of schemata—precisely because of their characteristic generality—is that they involve hierarchical colligations, the most general schemata comprising sub-schemata, and so on, down to single-term schemata, whose particular mode of assimilation is identification. Accommodation, on the other hand, can be more or less elaborate and exact, or remain global, but, in any case, does not involve such colligations. Hence, there is no contradiction when we treat the memory in the strict sense as a result of differentiated or individualized accommodations, or when we consider the conservation of memories as necessarily bound up with that of the assimilatory schemata. This hypothesis is not a simple tautology amounting to the unqualified identification of conservation with assimilation, which would explain nothing at all, but is based on the assumption that the conservation of an element (or individualized sub-schema) is a function of the conservation of the increasingly generalized schema of which it is a part, and often of the conservation of the system as a whole. Now, this is precisely what we are trying to establish: that memories are linked, in various forms, to action and operational schemata which can be seen to exert a constant influence on the memory in accordance with the subject's operational level.

IV. The fundamental problem of the memory thus tends to shift from the memory in the strict sense to the memory in the wider sense, i.e. it tends to hinge on the conservation of schemata—from the most individualized to the most general. This is because, in our hypothesis, it is the conservation of the latter which must eventually bear the entire weight of the mnemonic apparatus. Now, this central problem is one we have to pass over in silence, and we must do so for two reasons.

The first is that, from the psychological point of view, the conservation of schemata is automatic (see (I)): it is a characteristic of all forms of assimilatory generalization that they constantly renew and conserve themselves by their own reproductive or generalizing activity. The second reason is that if we ask how this continuity, and hence this conservation in its most elementary and formative aspect, is ensured, we are forced to leave the sphere of behaviour, and hence of psychology, for neurophysiology, general biology and even biochemistry.

In the psychological sphere, the assimilatory schemata may be of three types, based on their mode of conservation: (1) pre-operational schemata of the habitual type (in the wider sense and beginning with perceptive schemata); (2) representative and pre-operational schemata tending towards reversible operations; and (3) fully operational schemata. The first are conserved by their own activity

23

(reproductive and generalizing assimilation) but deteriorate when they do not function. The second involve the same but a less stable type of conservation, inasmuch as they tend towards final equilibrium (even if they are later integrated into other schemata) and inasmuch as the phases of this process of equilibration are themselves transitory —which comes back to saying that the phases are not conserved indefinitely, but that each tends towards the next, so that their conservation resembles that of a developing organism or organ. This is precisely what happens when the memory of a seriation improves over the months.

As for the operational schemata in the strict sense, it is characteristic of them that they are in equilibrium as a result of their characteristic reversibility. Now, whenever we say equilibrium we are also saying conservation, and that is precisely why seriation, numeration (series of natural numbers) and similar schemata, once constructed, are conserved throughout life. The clearest proof of the conservation of operational schemata, in the process of construction or newly formed, was provided by one of our collaborators who questioned children of different ages on the conservation of lengths, quantities, etc. over a period of four to five years. During this entire period, he encountered no case of regression from one stage or substage to the preceding one.

Passing now from these simple psychological findings to biological phenomena capable of accounting for the conservation of schemata, we must distinguish between two types of data, each of equal importance to our study. The first results from procedures designed to suppress or weaken the effects of learning: electric shocks or drugs (especially those retarding the formation of RNA). The chief lesson to be learned bears on the spontaneous consolidation of memories, and also on the possible recovery of apparently lost memory traces.

The consolidation of memories is demonstrated by the fact that the results of such shocks and drugs are the less marked the greater the lapse of time between their administration and the original formation of the memory. It would appear that a 'short-term memory' phase, during which the traces are registered or organized, is followed by a 'long-term memory' phase, during which the traces become stabilized. Moreover, the fact that apparently lost traces are subsequently recovered, suggests that this process can be speeded up or delayed by physical means and, quite particularly, by those encouraging or inhibiting the formation of RNA.

The second type of biological data concerns the effects of RNA itself. Babich, Jacobson and Bubash have reported that injecting the central nervous system of untrained rats with the RNA produced in the brains of rats that had been taught to perform a particular task helped the untrained rats to learn the same task, but more quickly. These results, which Gross and Carey were unable to confirm, have since been verified by Fjerdingstad, Nissen and Petersen. Moreover, Baron and Cohen in 1966 made effective use of actinomycin C or D (which inhibits the action of messenger RNA) or puromycin (which acts directly on the proteins synthesized by DNA with the help of RNA) to inhibit the short-term memory (immediately after learning) no less than the long-term memory (which is bound up with the entire process of protein synthesis, while the short-term memory is associated with modifications of protein configurations by RNA).

What concerns us most in these findings is the fact that the imprinting of the 'memory traces' during the initial phase (short-term memory), no less than their conservation during the second phase (long-term memory), seems to be dependent on highly structured substances. In fact, messenger RNA obtains its information from DNA, i.e. it is the carrier of the hereditary schemata which impress their own structure on the proteins. Since it is as part of this type of highly structured organization, and not by means of such 'neutral' substances (comparable to blanks) as, for instance, the cytoplasm of the nerve cells, that the imprinting and consolidation of 'memory traces' is effected, it follows that, from the biochemical level onwards, the memory is subordinate to a structuring process, and hence to a schematism. In other words, the new connections introduced by learning do not constitute independent elements or mere appendages to the hereditary schemata, but serve from the very start as new links in the chain forged by the activity of these hereditary schemata. To put it in yet another way, the essential involvement of RNA, as an emanation of DNA, tends to show that the integration of memory traces demands a ready-made organization (which, in the present case, is directly dependent on the genes but can, at other levels, come to depend on them less and less directly). Here, then, we have a phenomenon which, in our view, occurs at all levels of behaviour; and this is precisely what we mean when we say that the conservation of memories is subordinate to that of the more general schemata or structures. Admittedly, the intervention of the RNA can be interpreted in other ways as well. Before concluding that it is to the acquired memory what the DNA is to the hereditary memory, i.e. a carrier or transmitter, we must first determine (and this is the view of McConnel whose work with Planaria has aroused so much attention) whether the RNA is not responsible for a general sensitization of the organism to the stimuli involved in the conditioning process. The fact that RNA plays an essential role in protein synthesis suggests that it is also involved in the storing of memories, but in what form? All we can say is that the latest investigations are departing more and more from the idea of isolated 'engrams'; in the current view, mnemonic imprints are increasingly treated as being dependent upon structures of higher organization and synthetic power.

V. The main hypotheses we shall be putting to the test in this book may be summed up as follows. The memory is a store of information that has been encoded by way of a process of perceptive and conceptual assimilation. The information itself, however, depends in part on the code, which determines, for example, whether or not it is put to good use. Now, memory changes in the course of a subject's development do not simply reflect the level of his encoding and decoding powers: *the code itself is susceptible to change* during the construction of operational schemata. This explains why the level of memory organization differs with age, reflecting not only the coding level of the subject, but also the transformation of the code in the course of retaining the memory of, say, an experimental arrangement that has not been resurrected in the subject's presence. Hence, also, the need to distinguish between two distinct problems in the conservation of the memory: (1) mnemonic retention leading to decoding and retrieval (recognition, reconstruction or recall) as a function of a code of known level—this is the problem of the memory in the strict sense; and (2) the conservation of the code itself throughout its possible transformations—this is the more general problem of the conservation of schemata in the course of individual maturation.

PART I

Remembering Additive Logical Structures

In Part I (Chapters 1 to 6) we shall be looking at the remembrance of configurations or processes involving the most elementary logical structures: seriations, correspondences, and transitive and associative relations. These structures can be called additive, or, alternatively, linear, because they involve a single dimension. In Chapters 3 and 4 we shall be examining the correlation of two or three series with the help of a single criterion; the use of two criterea in multiplicative correlations (matrices) will be discussed in Chapters 7 and 8.

CHAPTER ONE

Remembering a Simple Serial Configuration[1]

In this chapter we shall examine the remembrance, after a lapse of (a) one week and (b) eight months, of a series of ten rods arranged without the child's assistance in (regularly) increasing order of size. This simple case will provide us with an excellent starting point, because we know a very great deal about most aspects of this structure, both as an operational schema and also as a 'good form'.

§1. *The problem*

In fact

(A) We know that such a series constitutes a 'good', simple and regular *Gestalt*, easily grasped both visually and intellectually;

(B) We have been familiar with the operation involved in seriation for some time, and there are many papers on the subject. Let us briefly recall the observable stages in the process (in the present experiment, the seriation of ten rods measuring from 9 to 16·2 cm presented to the child in a jumble):

Stage I: No real attempt at o·dination.
Stage II: Failure to construct the over-all series, but success in combining rods in terms of absolute qualities (bigness, smallness) or by pre-relations.
    IIA: Unco-ordinated pairs (pairs of large and small elements);
    IIB: Unco-ordinated triplets (one large, one medium-sized and one small element) etc.;
    IIC: Seriation based on the correct alignment of the tops of the rods but without a horizontal base;
    IID: 'Roof'-shaped seriation: top profile rising and then descending (or vice versa);
    IIE: Correct seriation (by trial and error) of from three to six rods, but failure to go further.
Stage III: Complete success (by trial and error), but if new (intermediate) elements are added, the subject does not fit them into place and generally prefers to reconstruct the entire series.[2]

---

[1] In collaboration with H. Sinclair and M. Levret-Chollet.
[2] Subjects at Stage III cannot perform the screen-seriation test, while those at

Stage IV: Operational seriation, which has the following distinct characteristics:

1. The subject proceeds systematically from the longest of all the rods to the longest among the remainder, etc. This involves double co-ordination: any element E is both such that $E < F, G$, and also such that $E > D, C \ldots$;
2. The inserted elements are immediately treated as terms of the series;
3. The subject has grasped the meaning of transitivity: $A < C$ if $A < B$ and $B < C$.

(C) Third, we know (and shall re-examine with the help of several subjects) that graphic reproductions of the series are in full accord with Luquet's findings about the drawing of seven- to eight-year-old subjects, far more like internal representations (Luquet's 'intellectual realism') than perceptions ('visual realism'). Now, it is clearly relevant to our problems that these reproductions, far from being random internal representations or reductions to a single or even to two types, should fit into levels that mirror the operational stages in the child's life, with correct drawings from about five years[1] onwards (telescoping Stages III and IV, the latter having no sense in the case of drawings). There is the equivalent of Stage I in which all the rods are drawn as strokes of equal length. Then there are all the types associated with Stage II, slightly stylized or rather representing what the subject thinks he should be doing and not the objective lengths. Thus Stage IIA is represented by the alternation of large and small elements (pairs) but in such a way that all the large elements are equal and all the small ones as well, or else by a clear dichotomy between pairs or triplets of large and small rods of equal length; at Stages IIA, IIB and IIC there is a similar disregard of the fact that every rod is greater or smaller than any other (connexity).

Drawings of type IID, by contrast, introduce this property, as do those corresponding to Stages III–IV.

(D) Fourth, we are familiar with the anticipatory model of the seriation, thanks to the following experiment.[2] Our subjects were presented with ten graduated sticks, each of a different colour, and asked to arrange them in order of increasing size, after first drawing what they thought the final arrangement would look like. The drawing was to be in black and white (general anticipation) or in the correct colours (analytical anticipation). Analytical anticipation is, of course, as difficult as the operational seriation itself, or even slightly harder (success at seven to eight years). Over-all

---

Stage IV can. This test is performed as follows: ten rods are jumbled up and presented to the child with the request that he hand them back to the experimenter one by one and in the correct order. The experimenter then arranges the rods behind a screen, in the order in which they were handed to him. The screen is raised, and if there are any mistakes, the child is asked to try again.

[1] Often from 4;0 onwards, and in 75 per cent of all cases at 5;0.

[2] J. Piaget and B. Inhelder: *The Early Growth of Logic in the Child*, Routledge & Kegan Paul, 1964, pp. 247 ff.

30

75-5 304

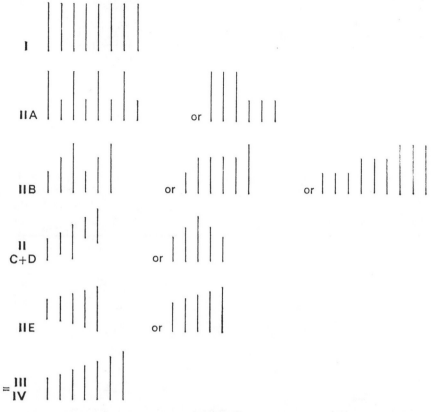

FIGURE 3

anticipation, on the contrary, was found to be correct (horizontal base line, increasing lengths and connexity) in 55 per cent of our five-year-old subjects and in 73 per cent of our six-year-olds. This anticipatory model is therefore simpler than the operation (seven years)—drawing the correct series involves a one-way action, not reversibility ($E > D, C, B, A$; and $E < F, G, H \ldots$). The resulting model has a good perceptive form. It should also be noted that this model appears very soon after the first graphic reproductions, precisely because drawings are aids to perception.

(E) Lastly, thanks to the studies of one of our associates[1] we have precise knowledge about the linguistic expression of the act of seriation. These studies have, in fact, shown that verbal descriptions of the seriation itself (that is, of the final configuration prepared in advance of the experiment and not of the reconstruction demanded for diagnostic purposes after the experiment) can be divided into four categories:

(1) *Dichotomies:* the only terms used are 'big' and 'small', whether the

[1] H. Sinclair-de Zwart: *Acquisition du langage et développement de la pensée,* Dunod, 1967.

31

description involves such categories as a small one, a small one, a small one, a big one, a big one, etc., or whether it involves (purely mechanical) divisions into pairs (a small one, a big one; a small one, a big one, etc.).

(2) *Trichotomies:* and more detailed identifications: 'small, small, small; medium, medium, medium; big, big, big, etc.' or 'small, medium, big; small, medium, big, etc.'; or even 'very small, smallish, medium small, medium big', etc.

(3) *One-way comparative descriptions:* 'smallest, bigger, still bigger . . . biggest'. When asked to describe the series the other way round, the child is baffled because the penultimate term ('still bigger') becomes 'smaller', and this calls for a grasp of relativity.

(4) *Two-way comparative descriptions.*

What is remarkable about these four categories is that they are in such close correspondence with the stages of operational development mentioned earlier. This is borne out by the following percentages obtained from tests with twenty-three subjects at Stage I (4;5–5;11), thirty-eight subjects at Stage II (4;5–5;8), fifty-four subjects at Stage III (4;4–6;5) and fifteen subjects at Stage IV (6;1–9;3):

	Linguistic category			
Operational stage	(1)	(2)	(3)	(4)
I	91	9	0	0
II	26	63	11	0
III	2	59	24	15
IV	0	7	13	80

There is thus a clear correlation between language and operational level.

We can now go on to examine the remembrance of a serial configuration (a series of rods arranged in increasing order of size) and, in particular, to investigate whether the memory of that configuration, after a week or after several months, is based chiefly on the perceptive aspect of the series ('good form'); or on its operational aspect (pre-operational or operational schemata used in the construction of the series itself); or perhaps on various combinations of the two.

In fact, both aspects are more or less clearly involved in all recollections of the series, other than those based on pure perception (A) or pure operation (B). Graphic reproductions (C) quite obviously involve operational ability since, even though the model has been actually perceived, the drawings reflect the same stages as appear in the operational construction (B). Nevertheless, it is clear that perception plays an important part as well, because progress from stage to stage is accelerated and the correct picture is drawn at about the age of five years instead of at six or even seven to eight years, as it otherwise would have been. In the case of the anticipatory image (D), we find precisely the same development, though at a different pace. On the one hand, before the emergence of correct anticipations, we find the same stages as occur in object-drawing (and hence as in operational constructions): there is an accelerated development, though slightly less so than in the case of object-drawing, which means that operational schemata must be at work. On the other hand, correct over-all anticipation is attained without trial and error at the age of five-and-a-half to six years, and not at seven to eight, as happens in the operational construction of the series. It follows that the perceptive model based on the child's earlier and spontaneous experiences, or the 'good' *Gestalt* of the serial configuration, must have some influence on the child's reactions, for the mental image would not otherwise have been able to anticipate the configuration so precociously. Finally, in the case of language (E), the operational factor has become dominant.

With respect to the memory, therefore, the problem is to establish whether the perceptive influences which play so important a part in (C) and (D) also facilitate and accelerate the recall of a serial configuration at all ages or rather from a precocious age (five to six years) onwards, or whether the memory-image (five to six years) involved in recall follows the stages of the pre-operational and operational schemata. Unfortunately, we cannot draw up hypotheses based on the preceding data alone, and we apologize for our inability to offer a detailed hypothetical frame that can be directly confirmed, invalidated, or shown to be meaningless by experiments ... In fact, the child may have two distinct types of perception of the serial configuration he has been asked to memorize. On the one hand, he can look upon it as just another figure to be drawn from memory, as he would a circle, a square or a flight of stairs; on the other hand, the very fact that the ten rods are presented in order of increasing or decreasing length (according as the child first looks at the left or the right extremity) may cause him to see them as objects of possible manipulation or operation, particularly if he is told to describe them verbally (as in one of our techniques). In that case, the memory, as expressed in the drawing, will not bear on the purely figurative aspect of the model, but on what the child would have remembered had he constructed, or tried to construct, the series himself.

In fact, as we shall see, two hypotheses are verifiable—one, partly, when all prior analyses are omitted; the other, more fully, when the child is asked for a verbal description during the presentation of the series, and is therefore forced to have recourse to operational schemata.

§2. *Methods*

We have relied on two main methods (I and II), each with a sub-division (IA and IIA). In all of them, the subject is asked to look at a series, previously constructed, not for the purpose of getting him to repeat the construction but rather to determine how much of it he will remember after a week or several months.

We might, of course, have used other methods, based, for instance, on differences in recollection after direct perception of the experimental set-up, or after its construction or reconstruction (see *Mental Imagery in the Child*, Chapter 9). But then we should simply have rediscovered what we know in any case; namely that action encourages the formation and retention of memory-images, and, what is far more important, that whenever the subject himself constructs a series, there is quite naturally a close correspondence between his memory and his action schemata. Now our main problem is, of course, to discover whether this correspondence also exists in the case of the direct perception of configurations, and not in actions. This explains our choice of technique. In all cases, the equipment consisted of ten wooden rods, 0.5 cm^2 in cross section, and increasing regularly in length from 9 to 16.2 cm.

I. In Method I the child is shown the complete series during the first session. He is not asked to describe it, but is told to take a good look at it and remember what he has seen. During the second session, about a week later, he is asked to: (1) trace out, by running his fingers across the table, what he saw, (2) draw a picture of it. Next (3) the investigator assesses the child's operational level by asking him to construct the series. In order to distinguish between Stages III and IV, we introduce such controls as the insertion of intermediate rods or the construction of the series behind a screen.[1] Then (4), if the drawing of the series is incorrect, the child is shown the series once again, as in the first session, and told to draw it, as a test of his powers of direct reproduction. (5) With ten rods still on the table, or placed back on it, the subject is asked for a verbal description by such questions as: (a) 'What is this?'; (b) 'Are they all the same?'; (c) 'How do they differ?' Finally (6) he is asked to alter the sense of his description: 'Describe them starting from *here*.'

During a third session, about eight months later, the subject is asked to draw the original series from memory, i.e. without being shown it again (he last saw the series during the second session).

Method IA is identical in every way, except that, instead of the drawing

[1] When this test was done, we made no provision to re-examine the subjects after six to ten months—otherwise we would have postponed the operational test until then. However, in §5 the reader will find an analysis of seventeen new cases in which this examination was omitted after six months, and the same is true of the seriations in *M* treated in Chapter 2. The elimination of this factor showed that it did not affect the qualitative nature of the results.

in (4) the child is asked for a verbal description after his practical construction (3). This omission may have minor repercussions during the third session.

II. Method II differs from Method I in that the verbal description, (5) and (6), is demanded during the first session, i.e. when the series is first presented to the child. For the rest, the two procedures are identical.

In Method IIA (as in Method IA) the drawing (4) is omitted; for the rest, it is identical with Method II.

Having described the methods, we can now proceed to the analysis of the results.

We shall start with remembrances during the second session (Method I), i.e. with memories based exclusively on perception and not on verbal descriptions. As we shall see, whereas the memory-drawings by children at operational Stages I to IIC are inferior or equal to the operational performance, at Stages IID to III, by contrast, they are sometimes (seven out of sixty cases) slightly better than those obtained with Method II, thus bearing witness to a slight advance of the memory-drawings over the operational level, much as happens in the case of the anticipatory image.

Next we shall go on to analyse the results of the second session using Method II (verbal description during first session), to discover a remarkable convergence between the 'gestural memory' and memory-drawings on the one hand and the child's operational level on the other. Finally, we shall examine the results of a third session, using Methods I and II (including Methods IA and IIA) combined after eight months, and discuss the remarkable and paradoxical finding that there has been a fairly regular and very gradual improvement in the level of memory-images since the second session.

§3. *Results of Method I* (*second session*)

Method I was applied to sixty-two subjects between the ages of 3;6 and 6;6. The results (see Table I) may be summarized as follows:

(a) Up to about the age of 5;6 years, the recollection (after a week) of the serial configuration, expressed by gestures or drawings, corresponds fairly closely to the subject's operational level (Stages I to IIE);

(b) The same is true of Stage III and, *a fortiori*, of Stage IV, since, once the child is capable of constructing the series, even if only by trial and error, he is, in general, equally capable of reconstructing it by means of drawings.[1]

---

[1] So much so that we cannot distinguish the correct drawings of subjects at operational levels III and IV, to which we shall subsequently refer as III–IV.

(c) On the other hand, it sometimes does happen that subjects below Stage III produce correct drawings of the series they saw a week earlier, which raises the question of whether theirs is straightforward figurative memory (remembrance of the figure as seen), or whether they are drawing the series they themselves would try (ineffectively) to construct by manipulation of the rods (our previous studies have shown the existence of correct anticipatory images in 55 per cent of five-year-olds and in 73 per cent of six-year-olds, although only 46 per cent of the five-year-olds and only 58 per cent of the six-year-olds had reached Stages III and IV).

I. Several children at operational Stage I (no ordination, even by couples or triplets) from 3;5 to 5;6 (mostly from 4;1 to 4;10), produced drawings of type I in the form of groups of lines of equal length, or even of irregular hatches, and one drawing of type II.

At Stage IIA (unco-ordinated pairs), a number of drawings were of type II as well, consisting either of more or less matched pairs (one long, one short, one long, one short, etc.), or of an over-all dichotomy (a group of long lines of equal size followed by a group of short lines of equal size). However, there was also some progress. Thus one subject (5;11) drew a triplet (one short line, several lines of equal length, one long line), while his operational seriation still proceeded by pairs, and another subject (5;9) produced a drawing with the correct topline but no base line (IIC) while his effective seriation remained at Stage IIA. Operational Sub-stage IIB (blocks of three equal lines or unco-ordinated triplets) was found to correspond to memory-drawings of various types (it should be remembered that the operational stage was determined *after* the drawing from memory). Some were of type IIB; some of type IIC (only the top line correct), some of type IID (roof shape); and a few were of type IIE (correct seriation, but only of four to five elements). Two subjects of 4;6 and 5;7, however, produced the correct drawings (III), again raising the question we posed earlier. Subjects at Sub-stages IIC–E produced similar drawings (types II and III).

The drawings corresponding to operational Stage III are worth examining, too, if only because of their lack of uniformity. For, while most of the subjects at this stage produced the correct drawings (III–IV), some who succeeded in constructing the actual series by trial and error nevertheless drew pictures from memory of type IIE (incomplete series), or even of type IIC (only the top line correct) or of type IID (roof). These cases of drawings from memory lagging behind the operational level are exceptions and hence easily explained as such: the lower limit of Stage III is, in fact, somewhat fluid: chance always intervenes in trial-and-error constructions of a series. At all events, the only types of memory-drawing not found at Stage III were of types I (equal lines); IIA (dichotomies); and IIB (trichotomies).

In general, there was a fairly marked correspondence between the subject's operational level and the organization of his memory after a lapse of one week. The only notable exception (not apparently

36

found among subjects tested by Method I) was that a number of subjects at Stage II, though unable to construct the correct series even by trial and error, nevertheless made the correct drawings (III–IV). However, the importance of this exception should not be exaggerated; among sixty subjects from three to 5;11 (eight three-year-olds, twenty-five 4-year-olds and twenty-seven 5-year-olds), they accounted for only seven cases: one 3;9-year-old (taught at a private school where particular attention was paid to drawing); two 4-year-olds (taught at the same place), and four 5-year-olds.

II. Nevertheless, these cases are important in that they might point to the existence of a purely figurative memory, independent of all operational schemata, while all the other data seem to indicate that the remembrance of the series after a week depends far more upon the assimilation of the model to these schemata (according to operational level) than upon simple perception. Three facts suggest that the precocious drawings do not invalidate the second interpretation. First, such drawings are, as we have said, exceptional. Second, not even all children at Stage III were able to draw the series correctly. Third, we saw that anticipatory models help to project the results of a series before the child is able to construct it in practice—it is easier to arrange pencil lines that can be lengthened at will than to arrange material objects which must be compared two at a time before being placed in position. The precocious, correct and exceptional drawings, far from contradicting, would thus imply, the rôle of action in the construction of the memory-image (reproduction or anticipation).

III. However, another and more serious objection could be made. We saw (§1(C)) that copy drawings of the series are not fully successful until about the age of five years. This raises the question of whether the errors in the pencil and finger drawings produced one week after the presentation of the series, and hence their correlation with the operational level, do not simply reflect the child's inability to *depict* the series. Now, while this explanation may apply to children at operational Stage I, producing object- *and* memory-drawings of type I (which is rare above the age of three years), we find that, from four years onwards, many subjects start producing memory-drawings of type I and correct copy drawings of types III–IV. More generally, two arguments can be used to refute the last objection. First, copy drawing is almost invariably more advanced (and increasingly so with age) than memory-drawings, which suggests that the inferior quality of the latter must be due to the memory and not to poor drawing ability. Second, copy drawing evolves through the same stages as memory-drawing and operational constructions, which points to a general isomorphism between the modes of construction, but such that the stages of memory-drawing are synchronous with the stages of operational development and not, as we saw, with those of copy drawing. In other words, it is the synchronism between operational stages and memory levels that constitutes the second argument in support of our interpretation, and so helps to refute exaggerated claims about the influence of drawing skills.

§4. *Results of Method II (second session)*

Sixty-three subjects, from 3;0 to 8;8 were tested by Method II a week after the presentation of the series. One of the youngest refused to produce any kind of memory-drawing. Table I compares the distribution by operational stages of the sixty-two remaining subjects with that of an equal number of subjects tested by Method I.

TABLE 1 *Percentage distribution of memory types elicited with Methods I and II (number of subjects N in brackets)*

	Method I				Method II			
Memory type	I	II	III	N	I	II	III	N
Stages:								
I	83 (5)	17 (1)	0	(6)	86 (6)	14 (1)	0	(7)
II	0	65 (13)	35 (7)	(20)	20 (4)	70 (14)	10 (2)	(20)
III	0	27 (8)	73 (22)	(30)	0	93 (26)	7 (2)	(28)
IV	0	0	100 (6)	(6)	0	0	100 (7)	(7)

Eight of the subjects (from 3;0 to 5;0) were found to be at Stage I (no ordination). After a week, seven of the remaining subjects produced one refusal and six memory-drawings of type I (lines of equal length) and one memory-drawing consisting of twelve lines: four equal lines, six equal but slightly shorter lines, one line equal to the first four, and one very much shorter (one-third the length of the first four). This, then, was a drawing half-way between types I and IIA: the child had simply remembered that the last rod was very short. The verbal descriptions of six of the eight subjects were consistently of type IIA (dichotomy). It should be remembered that the subjects were asked for a verbal description while they were actually looking at the rods, which would have counteracted any tendency to consider them as being equal in length. Now H. Sinclair believes that type IIA dichotomies are more primitive than type IIB dichotomies (large and small lines divided into two distinct groups), since the latter 'involve a basic opposition, essential for the development of language'.

Of the twenty subjects at Stage II, including two intermediate cases who eventually succeeded in completing the series by trial and error (Stage III), four still produced memory-drawings of type I (equalization), two were of type III–IV (correct) and fourteen of type II. These included one of type IIE (correct seriation but of five elements only); a few dichotomies, and a preponderance of drawings consisting of one long stroke at the beginning, followed by a group of medium-size strokes of equal length, and a short stroke at the end. Verbal repetitions of the description given during the first session ranged between dichotomies (five cases) and more detailed identifications ('rather small', 'very small', etc.), all of them in remarkable correspondence with drawings produced during the second session (preponderance of triplets).

The majority (sixteen) of the twenty-eight subjects at Stage III (correct seriation by trial and error) produced drawings of type IIE (correct seriation of four to five elements); six arranged a larger number in order of size but fan-wise (ascending top line and descending base line, or vice versa); only two drawings were correct in every way. The fact that most of the memory-drawings were almost but not quite correct is the more remarkable in that it corresponds to operational seriation based on trial and error, and not yet on reversibility, and in that it goes hand in hand with a similar correlation on the verbal level: eighteen of the twenty-eight subjects used three-part descriptions (or detailed identifications, with a tendency in some to progress towards one-way comparisons); eight subjects used one-way comparative terms; one was still at the dichotomous stage, and one produced two-way comparisons.

These results are the more significant in that all seven subjects at Stage IV were able to draw the complete series correctly. On the verbal level, however, three made two-way comparisons, two produced one-way comparisons, and two gave detailed identifications.

All in all, therefore, unlike the responses of our five- to seven-year-old subjects, who had not been asked to give verbal descriptions during the first session (Method I), the responses of subjects tested by Method II bore witness to a very close correspondence between operational level and memory-drawings, which later did not, moreover, involve systematic anticipations of the practical constructions demanded at the end of the second session. This suggests that the verbal description gave rise to operational analysis which then dominated the memory-image. It might, of course, be argued that the child remembers more of what he has said than of what he has seen, and that we are dealing with verbal rather than perceptual images. However, it is clear that, in this particular area, the memory does not bear on speech or words as such, as it does in the memorization of a quotation or poem, but on significations and concepts. For, as H. Sinclair has shown, the linguistic level depends on the operational level and not vice versa—the exceptional cases in which verbal learning leads to operational progress (as happens precisely with seriation)[1] are due to the fact that verbal learning forces the child

[1] See H. Sinclair-de Zwart: *Acquisition du langage et développement de la pensée*, Dunod, 1967.

to introduce operational correlations. It is as if the verbal description asked for by Method II introduced a structuring (of the child's operational level) into the figurative model, thus generalizing what we can already observe in young children tested by Method I (no verbal description). This result is all the more striking in that the series presented is a good perceptual form, giving rise to correct anticipatory images before operations, and in that five-and-a-half- to six-year-old subjects find it easy with Method I to produce correct memory-drawings of it. Very strong forces indeed are therefore needed to reverse this general trend, and these result from the fact, that as soon as the operational schema has been activated, it replaces the memory-image with another, more in keeping with the operational one.

However, this interpretation poses a new and serious problem: namely that different schemata are conserved in distinct ways: while some are already complete, others are still developing. What we have just been saying raises no special difficulties in the case of completed operational schemata (Stage IV), which are maintained by virtue of their own equilibration. The pre-operational schemata, by contrast, which gave the way for the operational schemata are short-lived, and their preservation, though due to the same functional mechanism, leads to modifications in which what is conserved has only, so to speak, an organizing capacity and no definite form. In that case, what happens if a memory becomes fixed as a function of a stage N schema and is recalled, not a few days later, when the subject is still at Stage N, but a few months later, by which time he may have advanced to operational Stage $N + 1$?

§5. Recall after seven to eight months

Some eight months after the interrogation of our last subjects, we were able to trace thirty of them aged 4;0 to 7;1 years, including eleven who had been tested by Method I, and nineteen who had been tested by Method II (mine by Method IIA). This re-examination was not part of our original plan, since we did not imagine that so simple a series would leave a durable impression on children most of whom (twenty-four out of thirty) were only four to five years old. Fortunately, one of the children, during an encounter with one of us, mentioned the experiment and showed that he still remembered what he had been asked to do. Only then did we decide to re-examine the old subjects systematically.

Naturally, we were most careful not to repeat the explanations we gave eight months earlier, and, in particular, not to mention that the series resembled a staircase. We merely asked, in the most neutral terms, if the subject would once again draw what he had been shown. However, once he had finished his second drawing from memory (the first was done some eight months earlier, one week after the actual presentation of the series), he was shown the series once again, and asked to give a verbal description (as in the second session) so that possible progress in this respect could be assessed as well.

Of the thirty subjects re-examined, six had to be rejected: four because they had taken a language test which included material on seriation; and two because, eight months later, they simply reproduced their own copy drawings (second session), and these turned out to be distinct from their memory-drawings.

Of the remaining twenty-four subjects, only two had made no progress at all, while twenty-two produced memory-drawings representing a marked advance upon the old, thus giving striking proof that their memory had evolved in the course of these eight months. Nor was this evolution haphazard; it did not take the form of a sudden leap from incorrect to correct drawings, but was in the nature of a very gradual progress from one stage or sub-stage to the next, as if the memory were linked to the development of the pre-operational schema.

We shall now look at the results in greater detail, bearing in mind that the subjects had previously been tested by different methods (copy drawings or not during the second session, etc.):

Two subjects progressed from Stage I to Stage IIA. PHI (4;0) had produced a memory-drawing of type I (all the elements of equal size) and a copy drawing of the same type during the second session. His verbal account at the time was 'There were some big ones, then some more big ones, then some little ones,' and there was no attempt at operational seriation (ordination). During the third session, eight months later, his second memory-drawing consisted of six lines, the first three very long, and the last three half the size of the first. TOM (5;5) who had also produced a type I memory-drawing during the second session (he was tested by Method II, and not asked to make a copy drawing), now produced two pairs, followed by two triplets (the first equal, the second consisting of one long, one medium and one short stroke). His drawing was therefore intermediate to type IIA and IIB.

One subject, TIA (4;1) who had produced a drawing intermediate to types I and IIA (seven lines: six equal, and one, somewhere near the middle, shorter than the rest), and a copy drawing of type IIB (long, medium and short lines), now offered a type IIE drawing (fan-shaped with ascending upper and descending base line).

STO (4;5) had made a type IIB memory-drawing during the second session (sixteen strokes: the first eight long; the next four medium-sized; and the last four short) and a type I copy drawing. During the third session he produced the correct series but consisting of only three lines (IIE?).

41

Similarly CHRI (5;7) drew a correct three-element series during the third session, instead of the dichotomy (four long and seven short lines, respectively of equal length) he had produced during the second session.

CLA (4;0) produced an incipient dichotomy (twelve equal and one shorter stroke: type I–IIA) and a copy drawing of equal but descending strokes. During the third session, he started with a dichotomy (fifteen short followed by four long strokes—IIA), but immediately corrected himself and produced a drawing of type IID (five strokes of increasing length) followed by fifteen strokes of decreasing length.

STEP (4;2) was one of the children to produce a completely correct drawing during the third session (a series of ten elements decreasing in size). However, though her memory-drawing during the second session (seven short strokes and three long ones), was of type IIA, her progress over the next eight months should rather be assessed in terms of her original copy drawing, which was intermediate between a trichotomy and a graded series.

These examples will give the reader some idea of what we mean when we say that of the twenty-four 4- to 5-year-old subjects, twenty-two had made clear progress since the second session, in respect of their memory-drawing or copy drawing, whichever was the better of the two. Let us now try to establish what factors were responsible for this advance, and look at the possible interpretations.

The most obvious interpretation is that progress with Methods I and II, as distinct from Methods IA and IIA, was due to improved copy drawing ability, which constitutes a form of reproductive activity, and not simply a record of perceptions. In fact, two memory-drawings out of thirty made during the third session were faithful reproductions of the second-session copy drawings (type IIA) and quite unrelated to the second-session memory-drawings (type I). These two cases were therefore eliminated, and even if they had not been, they would only have increased the number of stationary cases to four, as against twenty-two cases of clear progress. As for the subjects we retained, the following remarks will show that the influence of copy drawing was relatively small: (1) In ten cases, the copy drawings were distorted to an equal extent as, or to an even greater extent than, the drawings from memory; (2) in the two stationary cases (types I and IIB), the copy drawings were correct and could therefore not have exerted any influence. Two other subjects who progressed from dichotomy to trichotomy or from three to five graduated elements, and at the same time produced correct copy drawings, were the only cases of whom we could possibly (though by no means certainly) say that the copy may have had an accelerating influence; (3) a further three cases had clearly advanced beyond their copy drawings (see STEP, above); (4) the ten

42

subjects who had not been asked for copy drawings made as much progress as the rest.

In the second place, the advances could have resulted from the verbal descriptions demanded at the end of the second session, which might well have improved the initial visual memory: in the case of Phi, for example, the third-session drawing was closer to the verbal description than to the original memory-drawing. But this is by no means the rule, and for two reasons. First, as we saw in §4, verbal descriptions generally correspond quite closely to memory-drawings, and though they help the child to conceptualize the series he has seen, comparisons of the results of Methods I and II show that such conceptualization tends, if anything, to retard the figurative development of the drawing or of the memory-image from about the age of five or five-and-a-half onwards. Second, third-session drawings were quite generally more advanced than verbal descriptions during the first or second sessions: for example, dichotomous or trichotomous descriptions made way for symmetrical (IID), abridged (IIE) or even correct (III–IV) seriations. In these cases the verbal descriptions asked for at the end of the third session were more advanced than those given during the earlier sessions: clear progress from one stage or sub-stage to the next was recorded in seventeen cases.

In the third place, the reader will recall that, in both methods, the child is asked at the end of his second session (after a week) to produce an actual construction of the series, so that his operational ability can be assessed. Could it not be that this exercise in practical seriation helps to improve the powers of recall between the second and third sessions? Here, we can give a clear-cut answer. Of the twenty-two cases who showed signs of such progress during the third session, thirteen produced drawings whose level was higher than the operational standard assessed during the second session. Of the remaining nine subjects, one was at Stage IV (his drawing had advanced from IIB to IIE); and eight were at Stage III (correct construction of the series by trial and error, and progress of drawings from types IID and IIE to III–IV). Thus, if the actual operation (construction of the series) does indeed influence the development of memory- and copy drawing, it does so only in subjects who are, in any case, on the threshold of success.

The fact that none of these explanations is satisfactory suggests that the progress noted after an interval of eight months must be real and not merely apparent, i.e. it does not consist in an improved ability to reproduce what the child has somehow absorbed during the first week, but involves a novel element. It only remains for us to see how and why.

But first, we must point out that, since nearly all our subjects

43

were between four and five years old during the first session, we decided to test a further seventeen subjects between the ages of three and four, in order to ascertain whether a similar phenomenon occurred in children who had only just learned to draw. These subjects were tested by Method IA (no description or copy drawing), and were not given the operational test during the second session. Only when there was some doubt about their intention were they asked to explain the drawings. (Examples of their replies were: 'They are all little' or 'a big one, a little one, a big one, a little one', etc.) The distribution of types (during the second session) was: two of type I, seven of type IIA, two of type IIB, three of type IIE, and three advanced cases of type III. Six months later, there were one of type I, three of type IIA, three of type IIB, two of type IIE, and seven of type III. Of these seventeen subjects: one had regressed (from IIA to I) (this never happened with children over the age of four years); seven had remained stationary (41 per cent),[1] and nine (53½ per cent) had made progress from type I to IIA, from type IIA to IIB (doublets to triplets), from type IIB to IIE (triplets to shortened series), or from types IIA or IIE to III. All this goes to show that progress after a lapse of several months occurs even among three-year-olds, although less frequently than in the older subjects. If we combine these seventeen 3- to 4-year-old subjects with the twenty-two 4- 5-year-olds, we find clear progress in twenty-nine out of a total of thirty-nine cases, i.e. in 74 per cent of our subjects.

It is easier to explain why this occurs than how. The over-all results show that even the youngest of our three- to seven-year-olds do not perceive the series in the neutral way in which, for instance, they see a cross or a circle—two patterns that raise no problems in their minds. In our tests, they are forced to examine the series as a source of questions—questions involving the memory, since they are asked to recall a series constituting a complex figure, and also questions about structures, since they interpret the series conceptually, as the result of possible actions. Thus his first memory-drawing (after a week) strikes the child as the solution to a problem, and precisely because there is a problem, he may think that the solution he offers is approximate and not entirely satisfactory. Professor F. Restle of Indiana University has told us that, after asking adults to do a quick multiplication, he found that the majority, regardless of the result, were left with the impression of having gone wrong. Similarly, we may take it that after drawing a series from memory in sets of pairs, triplets, etc., the child, too, will be left with the impression that his drawing, though more or less correct, is capable of improvement. He is then left with a kind of gap, comparable to the Zeigarnik effect,

[1] Including the three cases of type III who could not progress further.

and hence spurred on to look for a better solution. Now, as we all know, this impetus gives rise to a spontaneous organization or reorganization of ideas, so that, on returning to the problem, we find ourselves in possession of slightly improved working hypotheses.

But if these remarks do, indeed, explain why the child should continue to work on the problem after he has provided an answer, they do not tell us anything about the details of his evident progress. It is one thing to reflect on the solution of a logical problem in the light of new ideas or hypotheses, and quite another to keep a memory unchanged. In the case of mnemonic progress as such, we must apparently distinguish between two types of remembrance tending towards equilibrium: (1) the effective memory, reflected in the child's first memory-drawing, and (2) a sort of latent memory preserved in the unconscious and serving as a model for the first. Now, the existence of such a latent memory raises two serious problems: (A) How to explain its formation by a sort of 'subception' or subconscious perception. If the latter did, in fact, exist, as is sometimes asserted, it would consist primarily of such affective impressions as the subject overtly rejects (repression), or else it would bear on a peripheral zone of a group of complex or mixed objects, perceived but not really taken in (Pötzl). This could not be the case with such good forms as a regular series observed at leisure. (B) At all levels, the series is assimilated into the subject's operational schema. How, then, can we suppose that, over and above the series he assimilates, the subject also retains the image of a series beyond his powers of assimilation? And even if this were possible, why should he only make use of this image after a lapse of eight months, and not after a week?

A simpler hypothesis emerges along the lines suggested in the Introduction. If the memory-image is the figurative symbol of an otherwise independent schema—the very schema, as we saw, to which the subject assimilates the series presented to him for memorization—there are only two possible explanations: either the schema is operational—that is, adequate to the assimilation of the series—so that the memory will be conserved for eight months, just as it is for a week; or else the schema is pre-operational, in which case it is bound to develop, and, after eight months, it will quite naturally have been changed in the sense of greater operationality. In that case, the memory attached to the schema as a representative symbol will be modified as well: it is, after all, a signifier and as such forced to adapt itself to its significate (the conceptual meaning). Hence, there is nothing mysterious about the memory progress during an interval of several months, and no need at all to introduce the subconscious conservation of a model series acquired by 'subception': we need

merely take the view that the memory of the series is not the perceptive and imaginal reproduction of the series as such, conceived as an
object completely independent of the subject (and thus unlikely to be
transformed in the course of eight months), but that the memory of
the series is the manifestation of a schema and that it is the latter
which has evolved!

Now, the reason why this schema evolves is because it is associated
with all sorts of spontaneous and common actions, either isolated
(co-ordination of objects) or else performed in the context of other
forms of conduct (causality, etc.). And it is precisely because the
schema develops in conjunction with the general activity of the child
and because it has not yet been equilibrated at the pre-operational
levels that the child, in the very act of producing the best possible
memory-drawing he can, may nevertheless have the impression that
his solution is not a perfect copy of the model he perceived. In that
case, however, it may be objected that he must have conserved a
'trace' of the model in his 'latent' memory, whose existence we have
just denied. However, it should be remembered that what we have
rejected is the idea of a pure memory, independent of the schema,
and preserved as an internal model to which the schema adapts
itself by means of a copying mechanism. What we do not deny is the
existence of a certain duality between the child's actual or developing
schema and the equilibrium form towards which it tends.

Now, this duality becomes most obvious when we confront recollection, which is bound up with the current schema, with recognition, in which the perceptive presence of external objects allows for
momentary equilibration of the schema by adaptation to these
objects. To that end we decided to compare the recollection of the
series after a lapse of eight months with its direct recognition, but
since this idea occurred to us rather late in the day, we were only able
to put it to the test with the last fifteen of our subjects. All were
presented with drawings of: (a) the most common errors (dichotomies, etc.); (b) a symmetrical figure of type IID (see Figure 3); and
(c) the correct seriation.

Of these fifteen subjects (between 4;0 and 5;9), eight recognized
the correct series, three chose either the symmetrical figure or an
isolated triplet ('last year there were three rods' one child said, and
this was, in fact, how he had drawn it from memory), and four were
unable to decide between the correct model and the 'roof'-shaped
series ('No, it was like both of them'). This tends to show that although
recognition is clearly, and quite naturally, well in advance of recollection, it, too, is far from perfect, and in no way points to the presence
of a 'pure' memory presiding over recall as well as over recognition.
We may therefore take it that recognition is ensured by assimilation

to a schema, in temporary equilibrium during the presence of the object, and striking a new balance with each further presentation— the so-called 'latent memory' being nothing but the schema itself. At the sensori-motor levels, where memory extends to recognition but not yet to recollection, it is schemata built up by habit or practical intelligence which enable the subject, by successive assimilations, to recognize the salient signs. At the levels of representation, where the schemata are associated with figurative symbols (internalized imitation) or verbal signs, recall is based on the latter, but in association with the schema itself, or rather with its particular state of development. However, when the subject is once again confronted with the object assimilated to this schema, a new assimilation is likely to occur, thus ensuring the recognition of the object. Now, this recognition leads to the mnemonic equilibration of assimilation and accommodation. Although not identical with the internal equilibration of the schemata, which is a form of gradual organization tending towards reversibility, the momentary equilibration characteristic of recognition nevertheless participates in it, since organization necessarily involves actions on objects. It is for this very reason that recognition may be ahead of recollection, although the mechanism of both is based on the same schemata. And this is undoubtedly why the subject, as he looks at his first memory-drawing, can feel satisfied and dissatisfied at one and the same time: he has succeeded in recalling the object of his memory, and yet fails to recognize it fully.

This raises a major problem. We tend to contrast recognition with recall, not only because the first is genetically the older of the two, but also because we tend to overlook the schemata underlying recall. Our own interpretation of the conservation and potential improvements of memories, on the other hand, is based on the assumption that there is a measure of continuity between recognition and recall, not in the sense that the one can be reduced to the other, but because of the probable existence of a series of intermediate genetic stages which ensure the transitions between the two (see Chapter 5).

§6. *Improved remembrance of a series and the Ballard and Ward–Hovland phenomena*

Short-term and long-term memory

Memory progress has been the subject of a number of studies. In 1903–4, Henderson, Biner and Lousien drew attention to quantitative improvements in the course of successive attempts at recollection, thus apparently contradicting the findings of Ebbinghaus. In 1913 Ballard performed a conclusive experiment on the remembrance of poems or fragments of prose that were presented to the subjects for too short a time to allow of complete memorization. The subjects were asked to recall the lines: (1) immediately after the presentation; and (2) two to seven days later. The results showed an over-all improvement in memory after two or three days, followed by a gradual deterioration. Huguenin, in 1914, Nicolaï, in 1922, and Williams, in 1926, arrived at similar conclusions.

To explain these facts, some authors have invoked a process of mental revision, but when Magdsick showed in 1936 that rats have similar 'reminiscences'—lasting from an hour to a week—this hypothesis had to be dropped. C. Florès, who has described these developments,[1] greatly prefers Brown's hypothesis that the memory is consolidated by successive acts of recollection, and Ammons and Irion, in 1954, were in fact able to demonstrate by experiments with five groups of subjects that those who were asked to recite some lines they had been shown, either immediately afterwards or else two and seven days later, showed a gradual loss of memory (9·23, 6·81 and 6·13 lines on average were recalled on each of the three dates respectively), while those asked to repeat the lines immediately afterwards (9·73 and 9·00) and *once more* a few days later showed improvements when the second session was held after a lapse of two days (10·05), but regression if it was held seven days later (7·96). The role of intermediate (immediate) recall is thus obvious.

The Ward-Hovland phenomenon, by contrast, does not involve prior recall, since it occurs within $\frac{1}{2}$–2 minutes of the presentation. The problems it raises are thus similar to those involved in the organization of the memory during concentrated or prolonged studies and hence impinge upon questions that do not concern us directly.

As for Ballard's 'reminiscences', they bear some resemblance to the improvements in memory we have been analysing, except that progress in 'reminiscence' is, by its very nature, of a chiefly quantitative type, while, in the case of our seriations, the schema itself progresses during two successive sessions. Nevertheless, in the case of Ballard's poems and prose passages, we may take it that the first recall was based less on consolidation than on reorganization; sensing that his recollection does not fully agree with the model, the subject feels an impulse to improve it, just as happens with seriation. For all that, Ballard's twelve-year-old subjects did grasp the structure of the model, and their 'reminiscences' merely served to provide a better copy. In the case of seriation, on the other hand, the first recall proved to be an imperfect assimilation of the model, so that subsequent improvements in the memory must have been due to

[1] C. Florès: 'Memory' in P. Fraisse and J. Piaget (eds): *Experimental Psychology*, vol. 4, *Learning and Memory*, Routledge & Kegan Paul, 1970.

progress of the schema itself as the condition of that assimilation. In other words, after a lapse of a few months, the memory has become attached to a more highly elaborated schema and it is this schema which provides a better reproduction of the model, not some independent process. If improvement in the memory of serial configurations is to be treated as an extended Ballard effect, it is the latter which must be considered a special case of the former, since 'reminiscence' here bears witness to a reconstruction in the full sense of the term and not simply to a 'completion'. In other words, what is involved is more than pure reminiscence as a subconscious form of memory, because the memory itself has become transformed.

Our findings also have a bearing on current discussions about the relationship between the short-term and the long-term memory. There are two schools of thought, one contending that the two types of memory are continuous and that they share certain mechanisms (e.g. Melton): and the other maintaining that they are based on distinct mechanisms (e.g. Broadbent). Some authors (e.g. Tonkonogi and Tsuckerman of Leningrad) believe, more simply, that certain combinations are conserved in simplified form by the long-term memory, while the short-term memory serves to pick them out. If enough importance is attached to the preliminary activities of which the memory is a function and to the variable structure of the resulting 'codes', the problem undoubtedly assumes different forms according to the field on which the memory is brought to bear. In the case of our serial structures there can be no question but that the long-term memory introduces certain new aspects, since the recollection itself has improved. But it is also clear that this improvement is due to progress of the schemata, whose initial forms are already at work in the short-term memory, and hence that the two types of memory cannot be heterogeneous in this case. Other tests, involving particularly the rotation of triangles (see Chapter 15) and causal sequences (see Chapter 12), have shown that the long-term memory is highly schematized, which leads to a weakening of the figurative elements in recall. However, even in these cases, we are faced not so much with a basic difference as with the accentuation of tendencies manifestly present in the short-term memory.

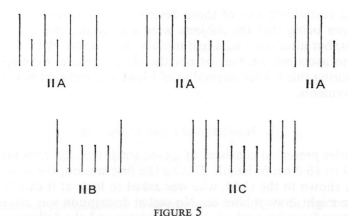

FIGURE 5

superior to that of IIIA. Luckily (and this should be emphasized) we were never forced to make that decision, since all the six subjects who proved to be of type IIIA after ten weeks had earlier produced either a simple seriation or some form other than IIB and IIC.

Type III introduced a new element: seriation involving at least three (and up to sixteen) elements, and no longer by simple pairs. There were four distinct sub-types: simple seriation (IIIA), two successive seriations (IIIB), seriation followed by one large element (IIIC), and seriation followed by two or three ascending elements, these being noticeably fewer in number than the descending ones (IIID).

Generally speaking, all the drawings of type III reflected the difficulty our subjects experienced in reversing the direction of the series when passing from the downstroke to the upstroke of the *M*. A girl of 6;3, for instance, started with a type IIIB drawing, but one consisting of four descending elements, and then declared with obvious dissatisfaction: 'But there was a tiny little one right in the middle: it came to a point in the middle.' She began again but produced the identical result. Nine weeks

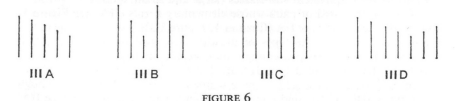

FIGURE 6

ater, she started the same way, but added a large element at the end (type IIIC), explaining that it was 'as big as the first one'. Next, she produced a descending series of four elements followed by four more elements equal in length to the last element of the descending series, but with a rising base line. Finally, she added a large element identical to the first and standing on the same base line. This was one of the many examples illustrating the operational difficulty experienced in reversing the direction of the series, and also the mnemonic difficulty involved in representing the result of this operation by means of a clear memory-image. We use the term 'mnemonic' rather than 'graphic', since our subject (and she was only one of many) was unable to decide between the correct model and an X-shaped figure. Other type III subjects also selected type III drawings during the recognition test.

As for sub-type IIIA or simple seriation, which, as we have said, is difficult to classify with respect to types IIB and IIC, there were good reasons for lumping it together with IIIB, IIIC and IIID. In fact, the subjects who produced drawings of type IIIA (a total of four during the second session, and a total of six during the third session) fell into two groups. The first produced simple series both during the two memory tests and also during the recognition test, thus reducing the complete *M*-shaped model to its first half. The second, and these were the more interesting cases, progressed from IIIA to IIIC or IIID, coupled to better recognition (IVA or V), or from IIIA to IVB or V. Type IIIB subjects behaved in much the same way (see §3).

Type IV (a mere five cases during the second and six during the third session) raised a different problem. All of these subjects endowed the model, or rather their memory of it, with what to us were quite unexpected meanings: a butterfly (IVA), a roof (IVB and C) or an *M* (IVD). We might, therefore, have been tempted to treat these drawings as a special category

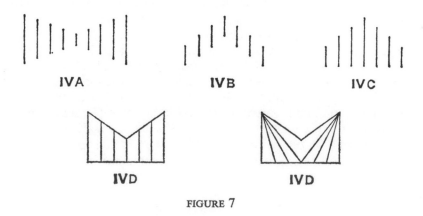

FIGURE 7

quite distinct from all the preceding ones. But, first, all spatial forms can be endowed with such attributes without altering the operative schemata of their construction: thus our simple series was commonly described as a 'staircase'. Second, the 'butterfly' (IVA) presented during the recognition test was sometimes chosen even by subjects who had not previously recalled it, and who at no time attached any particular significance to it. Third, and above all, though these figures do not constitute a necessary transition between types II and V, they were often used as intermediate steps and hence represent schematizations interesting in themselves: sub-type IVA is simply a copy of the actual model, with a missing horizontal base-line; the roof-shapes (IVB and IVC) are inversions of the model (again without the horizontal base); and sub-type D (left) is a correct representation except for the lines joining the tops and bottoms. Sub-type IVD proved of particular interest: the subject, finding it difficult to reverse the direction of the descending series, solved the problem by slanting the elements so that they converged on the two peaks of the M.

Type V finally corresponded to the model. In addition to the completely faithful reproductions, we have also included in it all drawings with two instead of only one central element; and all drawings with a central gap, or even with an exaggerated number of symmetrical or near-symmetrical elements.

§2. *General results*

Before presenting a detailed analysis of the advances and regressions between the first and tenth weeks, which is the main object of this chapter, we must first examine how the five types of recall we have just distinguished correspond to the respective operational levels of our subjects.

These subjects were made up of four children aged 3 years, and fifty-seven ranging more or less evenly from 4 to 6 years. Assessments of their operational level—which, for our purpose, are more important than classification by age—based on the simple seriation test (see Chapter 1, §1) showed that ten subjects were at Stage I, eight at Stage II, twenty-eight at Stage III and nine at Stage IV. The remaining six subjects (two aged 4 years, three aged 5 years and one aged 6 years), could not be classified in this way because their memory of the M-configuration had become confused with that of the simple seriation in the final (operational) test. Since that test was administered during the twelfth week, it was too late to make up the full complement with further cases at Stages II and IV. The accompanying Tables are therefore expressed in percentages, which may facilitate comparisons despite the small number of subjects at Stages II and IV (absolute numbers shown in brackets).

One preliminary remark is called for: only two of the nine subjects at operational Stage IV produced correct drawings (V) after the first week, and six did so after the second week, when all subjects at Stage IV produced correct drawings of the simple series. This shows how much more difficult the M-seriation is, and hence proves the importance of establishing whether the memory of that configuration, too, depends on operational schemata and whether it, too, makes progress during an interval of several weeks.

To these two questions, Table 2 would seem to provide unequivocal answers. Although the operational levels were determined by means

TABLE 2   Comparison of recollections after a week and after ten weeks

Types of memory	N	First week					Tenth week				
		I	II	III	IV	V	I	II	III	IV	V
Stages:											
I	(10)	80 (8)	20 (2)	0	0	0	30 (3)	70 (7)	0	0	0
II	(8)	25 (2)	62·5 (5)	12·5 (1)	0	0	0	50 (4)	37·5 (3)	12·5 (1)	0
III	(28)	11 (3)	11 (3)	53 (15)	11 (3)	14 (4)	3·5 (1)	11 (3)	36 (10)	11 (3)	38·5 (11)
IV	(9)	0	0	78 (7)	0	22 (2)	0	0	22 (2)	11 (1)	67 (6)
Unclass.	(6)	0	(2)	0	(1)	(3)	0	(2)	0	(1)	(3)
Total		(13)	(12)	(23)	(4)	(9)	(4)	(16)	(15)	(6)	(20)

55

of the simple seriation and not by means of the M-shaped configuration (in which the stages are evidently the same but with a shift in average age), there is a clear correlation of memory type with operational level, both after one week and after ten, and this despite the fact that the subjects were at no time asked to construct the M-shaped series, did no more than look at it for a few moments, were not asked for a description of the model, and had no questions put to them.

The most striking result (which we shall discuss in detail in §3) was a considerable progress in recall between the first and eleventh weeks. For the moment we shall confine ourselves to two general comments. In the first place, this progress is reflected in the totals at the bottom of Table 2: if we compare the number of reactions of each type after one week and ten weeks respectively, we find that types I to V have increased or decreased by -9, $+4$, -8, $+2$ and $+11$. The changes clearly proceed in the direction of the higher types: while types I and II together account for twenty-five cases after one week and for twenty cases after ten weeks, types IV and V have increased from thirteen to twenty-six cases. Thus, even if the details of our grading system may be criticized, the system can hardly be faulted as such, the less so since, as we saw, the uncertain types IIA and B do not affect the general picture.

Table 2 shows further how closely memory progress is bound up with operational progress. At Stage I, the memory-drawings are all of types I and II after the first week, and though this is true after ten weeks as well, the proportions have changed: there are now three of type I and seven of type II (as against eight of type I and two of type II). At Stage II, the types range from I to III after one week and from II to IV after ten weeks. At Stage III (partly due to the greater number of subjects) the spread is wider still, though the proportions have changed once again. As for the nine subjects at Stage IV, they progressed from two to six correct drawings, thus showing that they made relatively greater progress than subjects at all previous stages.

§3. Detailed analysis of changes between the first and tenth weeks and recognition

Of the sixty-one subjects listed in Table 2, thirty-four (56 per cent) not only failed to progress from one type to the next but even kept to the same sub-type when they were re-examined ten weeks after the first session—in other words these subjects had made no progress at all. Moreover, four (6 per cent) had regressed. As for the remaining twenty-three (38 per cent), they all made progress in recalling the model.

This remarkable result seems therefore to agree with our findings in respect of the simple series. Indeed, the reason why as many as twenty-nine subjects out of thirty-nine (74 per cent) showed progress in recalling the latter after seven or eight months was, on the one hand, that they had been faced with a much simpler operational structure, and, on the other hand, that the interval between the two sessions was about three times as long. Now, this long interval, which might be expected to blur the memory, on the contrary helps the development of the underlying operational schema and hence improves mnemonic recall. Thus, it is only natural that the shorter the interval and the more complex the model the smaller the progress —the only surprising thing is that the proportion of subjects making progress with the *M*-shaped series should have been reduced from 74 to 38 per cent and not less.

The second remarkable finding, which once again agreed with the results of the simple seriation test, is that progress was gradual rather than sudden. This suggests that the subjects correct their earlier impressions in the light of what schemata are available to them and not because unconscious images belatedly rise up into their consciousness.

In fact, the cases of progress fell into the following groups:

I to IIA (6 cases); I to IIC (1 case); I to IIIA (1 case); I to IIIB (1 case);
IIA to IIC (1 case);
IIIA to IIIC to D (1 case); IIIA to IIID (1 case) IIIA to IVB (1 case); IIIA to V (1 case);
IIIB to IIIC (and almost to V) (1 case); IIIB to V (2 cases);
IIID to IVA (1 case); IIID to V (4 cases);
IVA to V (1 case).

The only sudden leaps from one type of memory to the next but one were from I to IIIA or IIIB, i.e. from representation by equal elements to simple seriation; from IIIA or B to V, i.e. from the first half of the model to full symmetry, and especially from IIID to V (four cases), i.e. from a model with an incomplete right section to the complete model.

Table 3 lists progress and regression by operational stages:[1]

TABLE 3   *Memory changes in ten weeks (in absolute numbers)*

Stages (numbers)	I (10)	II (8)	III (28)	IV (9)	Unclass. (6)	Total (61)
Progress	5	3	8	5	2	23
Stationary	4	4	19	3	4	34
Regress	1	1	1	1	0	4

[1] As determined by simple seriation, during the twelfth week.

All cases of progress at Stage I were advances from type I to type IIA, that is from a series of equal elements to one of simple pairs of long and short elements, but without the inflexion of the top line associated with IIB and C.

Advances at Stage II, by contrast, were from type I to IIC or IIIA (simple seriation) or from IIIA to IIID, leading in all three cases to a differentiation of the elements, and in two cases to an incomplete inflexion of the top line. These two features were also present in advances from Stage III, though here the chief transition was from type IIID to type V, i.e. to the correct figure.

At operational Stage IV, progress invariably involved advances from type III to types IVB and V.

All in all, these results point to a very gradual form of progress, that is to an evolutionary process rather than to an all-or-nothing mechanism or additive composition of data. But can this process, which must be attributed to a gradual equilibration of the schemata, really have any bearing on the memory? Would it not be much simpler and more satisfying to assume that the progress of the schemata is reflected in better drawings rather than in better recollections? And since the young child draws what he knows or conceives of the model rather than what he actually sees, may we not take it that his memory of the M-shaped series in the form of a visual image must be much better than it appears to be, but that it cannot be expressed by means of drawings until such time as his general development is adequate to this task? In brief, while there is, indeed, progress based on the equilibration of schemata, may it not express itself, in the observed reactions, by improvements in draftsmanship and not in mnemonic recall?

It was in order to decide this issue (and for other reasons as well) that we gave our subjects a recognition test during the twelfth week, i.e. one week after the third session, based on a choice between ten life-size drawings (types I, IIA, B and C, IIIA, B, C and D, IVA and V). The test could not be administered to the ten youngest subjects (aged from three to four years and at Stage 1) but proved all the more informative in the case of subjects at Stages II to IV. Table 4 again includes the six subjects we had termed unclassifiable during the operational test because they had either constructed an M-shaped series (five cases) or else simply reproduced their earlier type IIA drawings. We may therefore take it that these six cases were at Stages II (one case) and IV (five cases).

The results of the recognition tests can be summed up as follows ($R > E$ means that recognition at eleven weeks was better than recall at ten weeks. See Table 4: the left section expresses the number of subjects in percentages; absolute numbers in brackets).

TABLE 4 *Recognition after 11 weeks*

Type of figure chosen	N	I	II	III	IV	V	R > E	R = E	R < E
Stages:									
II	(8)	0	12 (1)	50 (4)	12 (1)	25 (2)	4	2	2
III	(28)	4 (1)	4 (1)	18 (5)	14 (4)	60 (17)	10	16	2
IV	(9)	0	0	11 (1)	11 (1)	77 (7)	2	6	1
Unclass.	(6)	0	16 (1)	0	0	83 (5)	1	5	0
Total	(51)	(1)	(3)	(10)	(6)	(31)	17	29	5

Table 4 shows that, despite progress between the first and tenth weeks, only three-fifths of our subjects recognized the correct model (V). Yet it is a well-known fact that recognition is more primitive and simpler than recall. This means that it is more readily accomplished and retained than the memory-image, and not just that it is simpler than drawing as such. Hence Table 4 would seem to rule out the hypothesis that all, or nearly all, our subjects had conserved an accurate memory-image of the model, and that the observed gaps no less than the advances were all due to the graphic factor.

The left-hand section of Table 4 is particularly instructive, since it shows that recognition, like recall, evolves in conjunction with operationality: drawings of type III were selected by half the subjects at Stage II; this proportion then decreased and the correct model was chosen more frequently as we went up the operational ladder (and would undoubtedly have been chosen less often at Stage I than at Stage II, could the matter have been put fully to the test).

Now, it is highly significant that recognition should have been better than recall in a mere seventeen cases out of fifty-one. Moreover, on comparing Table 4 with Table 2, we find that the correct model was recognized by only thirty-one subjects as against twenty correct recollections a week earlier: only eleven subjects had thus made progress in this respect.

All in all, the new data discussed in this chapter thus seem to confirm the interpretations we offered in Chapter 1, both in respect of progress in remembering serial configurations and also of the unlikelihood that such progress may be due to some unconscious image presiding over mnemonic capacity no less than over drawing ability. Instead, the close link between the mnemonic level and that of the operational schemata demonstrates that it is the spontaneous equilibration of the latter, combined with further practice and the demand for inner coherence, which governs the organization of the memory, and which, in the particular case of seriations, explains the exceptional advances we encountered.

Appendix

Another method of verifying the results of our simple seriation tests has been developed by G. Voyat, who applied it to forty-eight 4- to 8-year-old subjects in Boston (Mass.). In this method, the experiment described in Chapter 1 is repeated, but the ten little rods are all of different colours. The children are asked to reconstruct the series straight away, a week later, and again after one month, by means of colour drawings (they are presented with some twenty crayons of different colour) and subsequently by pencil drawings.

The results of this test, which G. Voyat will be publishing in greater detail, show: (1) that colours are badly remembered (one or two correct colours per subject and only two subjects with five colours in the right position) and that colour recall does not improve with age; and (2) that the use of colours tends to depress the operational level slightly. Thus, while pencil drawings of level IV were produced by 0 per cent of the four-year-old subjects, 35 per cent of the five-year-olds, 85 per cent of the six-year-olds and 85 per cent of the seven-year-olds, colour drawings of type V (regardless of colour correspondence) were produced by 0 per cent of the four-year-olds, 26 per cent of the five-year-olds, 67 per cent of the six-year-olds, and 77 per cent of the seven-year-olds. In no single case was the colour drawing superior to the pencil one. Seventy-one per cent of the drawings were of equal quality (in respect of correct seriation only), and 29 per cent of the pencil drawings were superior to the coloured drawings. As for the reactions after one month, the following percentages were established (P = progress, E = equality and R = regression):

	N	Seriation by size			Remembrance of colours		
		P	E	R	P	E	R
4-year-olds	(9)	55	45	0	0	55	45
5-year-olds	(15)	25	75	0	26	54	20
6-year-olds	(9)	23	77	0	0	30	70
7-year-olds	(15)	30	70	0	13	40	45
Average		33	67	0	9	44	65

In other words, roughly one-third of the total number of the subjects examined had made progress in seriation after only one month. It is also interesting to note that most of those who did make progress in this field were precisely the ones whose pencil drawings were superior to the colour drawings. This suggests that the elimination of the colour factor helps the child to structure the seriation schema.

CHAPTER THREE

Remembering Equivalent Numerical Sets Arranged in Different Rows[1]

The central idea of this book is that the memory is not simply a mechanical function of successful or unsuccessful coding and decoding processes, but that it is basically dependent on the nature of the code which, far from being static, changes in accordance with the pre-operational or operational structures, and hence with the schemata proper to the intelligence. Depending upon the characteristics of these schemata, the models presented for coding may give rise to memories that improve as the schemata themselves develop (for instance, in the case of seriations; see Chapters 1 to 2); to systematic distortions (as with corresponding lengths; see Chapter 4); or to mistaken or correct recollections depending on the subject's grasp, not of a given structure, but of a problem raised by virtue of the available schemata (as in the case of unequal levels; see Chapter 14). Using this approach we were quite naturally forced to ask ourselves whether or not distinct stages in the organization of the memory corresponded to the successive stages in the solution of a problem involving operational conservation.

Unfortunately, it is rather difficult to express a conservation problem in terms of memory-images, for its solution hinges on the understanding of the transformations as such (expressed in words, etc.) and not of the configurations. It follows that one must either confine one's investigations to the remembrance of ideas or of verbal expressions, or else concentrate on the configurations, which might be instructive at the pre-operational levels (no conservation), but is of no value at the higher (and more interesting) levels of understanding.

Now, in the case of the child's conception of number, my earlier studies (with A. Szeminska) concerned the conservation of equivalence in the case of rows of elements presented in optical correspondence (the corresponding terms being placed on top of each other), and later rearranged (by spacing out the elements). The same

[1] In collaboration with P. Mounoud.

model can also serve as a memory of such correspondences (without posing the problems of conservation as such), but in such a way that the results can be shown to depend on the subject's level of non-conservation or conservation (which is precisely what we are trying to verify).

§1. *Method and nature of the problem*

The subject is shown a model (Figure 8) consisting of three different but (numerically) equal rows of blue counters: *A*, *B* and *C*. The subject's attention is drawn to the possible relationship between the red control counters (*R*) and the reference row *B* by the request that he cover each blue counter in row *B* with a red counter *R*. He is then asked (= anticipation I) if all the blue counters in row *A* can be covered with the same red counters, and after he has forecast the result, he is asked to try for himself. The same question is asked (= anticipation II) about row *C*. Finally, the child is questioned about the numerical equality or inequality ('Are there as many counters or not?') of the three rows *A*, *B* and *C*. A few minutes later, again a week later, and finally several months later, he is asked to: (1) recall the model by word of mouth and by a drawing; and (2) to reconstruct it with the help of the counters. To assess his operational level he is given the egg and egg-cup test (at the end of the second session): eight or ten eggs are first placed in front of as many egg-cups and then spaced out into a longer row, and the subject is asked if there are still as many, more, or less eggs as are needed to fill the cups.

This correspondence test showed that, from an average of $6\frac{1}{2}$ years, 75 per cent of our subjects had a grasp of the operational conservation of equivalence. The following characteristic stages were observed: (I) Evaluation of the relative quantity by the length of the rows alone, and without reference to the one-to-one correspondence; (II) estimates based on optical correspondence alone, in which case the child believes that the number of individuals in the set (the quotity) changes when the row is extended by the spacing out of its terms; (III) the quotity, unlike the quantity, is thought to be unaffected by extensions of the row ('There are eight and eight, but it comes to more here'); (IV) conservation of both quotity and quantity (in which case, unlike at Stage III, the whole is understood to be equal to the sum of its parts). Needless to say, there are also intermediate stages between one level and the next.

The existence of these stages shows that questions bearing on the superposition of the counters (anticipations I and II) do not suffice to determine the child's operational level. Thus, Nan (4;11) predicted, after having

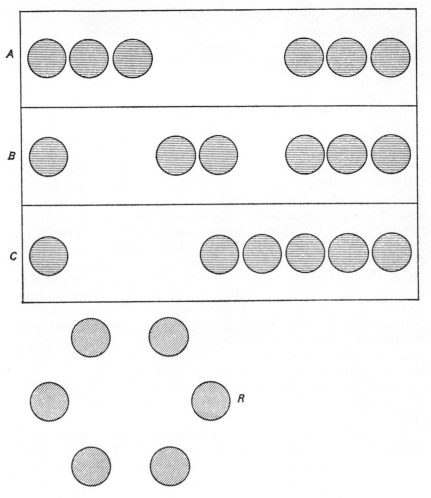

FIGURE 8

covered the blue with the red counters, that she would be able to cover the As because there are enough (Rs), as well as the Cs 'because there are a lot of them'. On the other hand, she believed that A ('not many'), B ('few') and C ('a lot') were unequal, and the egg and cup test showed that she was at Stage II. Bus (5;2) thought it was possible to cover the As with the Rs 'because there are as many', and the Cs with the Rs 'because I know how many there are', from which he concluded that A = B = C. Nevertheless, he did not accept that there were as many eggs as egg-cups after one or the other had been spaced out (Stage III).

Our questions about correspondence and numerical equality were chiefly intended to fix in the child's mind the data we wanted him to remember, and were not meant to be a form of operational 'training': each subject was, in fact, allowed to assimilate the data to the schemata characteristic of his level. In that case, the memory may be assumed to depend much more closely on the operational level than on the 'inputs', i.e. on the child's perception of the rows, and on his subsequent confrontation of his anticipations with the control experiment he himself performs by placing the six red counters on the six blue ones in rows A, B and C. It is, of course, possible to take the opposite view, and argue that it is the 'input', i.e. the information the subject absorbs, thanks to his perception and particularly thanks to his successive manipulations of the counters, that determines which of his reserves he draws upon at the moment of recall. However, we must not lose sight of the code, the central point of our problem: it is either invariant, in which case the inputs must be qualitatively identical for all age groups, and what differences there are must derive from the number of recorded data that can be decoded at the moment of recall (how they are retained during the interval remains an open question), or else the code itself is modified in the course of development, in which case it depends on the subject's schemata (or logic). Our hypothesis is based on the second view, and the superposition test tends to support it: thus Bus concluded from the equalities $R = A$, $R = B$ and $R = C$ as to the general equality $A = B = C$, while Nan failed to arrive at this conclusion from the same data, which suggests that she must have used a different code.

If, knowing the operational level of each of our subjects, we go on to determine the mnemonic form or level of their recall or reconstruction, we shall be able to establish whether and to what extent the latter depends on the former, or whether it simply reflects the data imprinted on the memory at the time of perception or superposition.

§2. *Mnemonic forms and levels*

While it is fairly easy to distinguish different forms of memory by type of organization and frequency distribution, nothing is more difficult than to place them in an hierarchical order. The most obvious method would be to determine their accuracy or efficiency, but, in fact, this determination depends closely on the nature of the supposed 'code'. For example, some of our subjects recalled or reproduced the three sets A, B and C, by dividing them into distinct sub-sets, but ignored the fact that the sets themselves were numerically equal ($6 = 6 = 6$). Did they have a more or less accurate memory than those who drew the three rows with the correct number of elements, but in vertical alignment (no sub-sets)? The problem cannot be solved without reference to the code and to its possible evolution.

Another solution might be sought in development with age, the very criterion that allows us to grade levels in the operational field, where the conservation of quantity seems to be superior to the conservation of quotity simply because it emerges during a later stage of development. But if it is true to say that, until adolescence at least, the operational structures progress rather than regress with age, there is no evidence that this is also true of the memory. We can, of course, suppose that it is, but if we do, we must realize that we are choosing one of three possible hypotheses. One could equally well postulate the existence of an *optimum* age: the memory might be better at the age of three to five years, than, say, at ten or fifteen years. Or, again, we could take the view that the memory of young subjects is richer, but less well-defined or organized (and hence more capricious), than that of older subjects, which may be poorer but is more highly structured. Mere recourse to age cannot therefore provide us with a sufficient criterion for assessing the hierarchical status of a particular level.

Let us, however, suppose that age goes hand in hand with distinct types of memory organization. Let us further suppose that these types are somehow related to the subject's operational level, as quite obviously happens with seriation. In that case, we are entitled to speak of memory levels, not necessarily in the sense of general levels, since each can be specific to a given operational domain, nor yet in the sense of greater mnemonic accuracy, since schematic constructions can have a distorting effect (see Chapter 4), but in the sense of a development capable of affecting the transformations of the code itself. Now, in the case of the numerical correspondence involved in our test, it seems difficult to deny the existence of a relation between the known operational stages and the different types of memory-drawing or practical reconstruction produced by our subjects (twenty-nine children ranging in age from 4 to 6½ years).

Type I. This type was represented by several of our four-year-old subjects and by one drawing by a five-year-old (who moved to type III in his reconstruction). It has the following characteristics: no numerical equality as between at least two of the three rows, and no coincidence of the end terms. These two characteristics seem to point to a mainly figurative form of mnemonic retention and to neglect of the numerical aspect even in the case of simple optical correspondence.[1] The number of elements used by the subjects varied a great deal, in the reconstructions no less than in the drawings: 12, 8 and 9; or 4, 13 and 15; elements etc. Moreover, the

[1] By optical correspondence we refer to one-to-on ⟨figurative correspondence without conservation of equivalence after spatial rearrangements of the elements.

densities of the rows (spaces between the counters in the sub-sets) were arbitrary as well—another indication of the lack of concern with correspondence. On the other hand, each of these subjects remembered that the counters (in at least two of the three rows) were arranged in sub-sets or discontinuous segments, but failed to reproduce them correctly, except for two cases who did so for the single element in C (but increased the remaining five elements), and for one case who reproduced a three-element sub-set.

All in all, therefore, the mnemonic organization of the data seems indeed to correspond to the level of understanding of these subjects, who had not yet grasped the idea of the conservation of equivalence. In fact, all of them were at pre-operational level II, that is, they failed to grasp the conservation of quantity or of quotity (numbers).[1] As a result, none of these subjects believed that the rows A, B and C were equal, not even those anticipating that they could all be covered by the counters R: their anticipation was thus of a general type and devoid of numerical precision: 'because there are enough', 'because there are a lot of both', etc.

Type II. With the second type of memory (eight subjects from 4;6 to 5;6), there was a clear attempt to express the numerical equality of the rows. But this equality was expressed figuratively by placing the rows in over-all optical correspondence, with coincidence of the end terms and homogeneous densities, but without sub-sets or real (as opposed to chance) equality: in the case of all these subjects the rows were either long and closely packed (for instance with 15, 13 and 13, or even with 21, 26 and 23 elements respectively) or else short and superposed (for example with 7, 5 and 6 elements). Though figuratively less accurate in respect of the sub-sets than type I, subjects of type II thus focus their attention on the over-all correspondence, which could perhaps be described as progress towards numerical equality.

Here, too, the level of mnemonic achievement seemed to be closely linked to the level of understanding: apart from one case at pre-operational level II, all the subjects were at level III, characterized by the conservation of quotity, though not yet of quantity. Most of them anticipated that the red counters R would cover rows A and C; and four out of eight concluded as to equality between A, B and C; two out of these four were unable to predict whether or not $A = B$ and $C = R$.

Type III. This type (eight subjects of 4;8 to 5;10) represents progress in remembering numerical equalities in the sense that two of the three rows A, B and C are represented by, or reconstructed with, the same number of elements (4, 4 and 8 or 5, 5 and 8, etc.). As in type I, there is an appreciation of correspondence (coincidence of the ends of the rows and division of the rows into separate sectors or sub-sets) coupled with progress towards the conservation of the over-all numerical equality. However, the subjects still have great difficulty in co-ordinating these two factors, with the result that the sub-sets of the two rows are generally thought to consist of an equal number of elements (for example, one and four elements each for

[1] In Geneva, we found no subjects at level I (evaluation of quantity by length of rows) above the age of four years.

rows of five; one and three elements each for rows of four; etc.). One five-year-old subject, however, produced sub-sets of $2 + 4$ and $3 + 3$ elements for the two equal rows.

From the operational point of view, two of the eight subjects were still at Stage III, but the remaining six had reached Stage IV in the egg and cup test. But while success in that test, which introduces the relationship between container and content, comes slightly before success in the conservation of equivalence, the time-lag is less than six months, and hence insufficient to explain the slight advance of the operational over the mnemonic level. On the other hand, it does account for the fact that one out of the eight subjects with type III recall concluded that $A = B = C$, after having established that each of those three rows was equal to R.

Type IV. Subjects with this type of recall grasp the numerical equality of the three rows, A, B and C (eight subjects of 4;9 to 6;5). For all that, only one subject (6;5) reproduced the rows with complete accuracy. The other seven produced such associations as $3 + 3$, $2 + 4$ and $1 + 5$; or $3 + 3$, $1 + 4 + 1$, and $1 + 5$, etc., which proves their comprehension of the conservation, and often, even, of the associativity of the additive group, and also that their memory has been brought to bear on the schematic significance of the model rather than on its figurative aspect.

Now, every one of the eight subjects, including the one aged 4;9, was found to be at Stage IV by the operational test, and hence had understood both the conservation of quantity and also that of quotity, i.e. the law of additive composition which states that the whole is equal to the sum of its parts.

§3. *Memory and operational schemata*

The preceding analysis suggests that there is a fairly close relationship between type of memory and operational level, but with the memory lagging slightly behind the operational schemata. The data are listed in Tables 5 and 6. Table 5 correlates memory type[1] with the success or failure to anticipate that $R = A$, $R = C$, once $R = B$ has been established, and hence to conclude that $A = B = C$.

Let a be the anticipations $R \neq A$ and $R \neq C$, b the anticipations $R = A$ and $R \neq C$ or vice versa, c the correct anticipations $R = A$ and $R = C$, d the conclusion $A \neq B \neq C$ (or that there are partial inequalities), and e the conclusion $A = B = C$.
Then:

abd = false anticipations and conclusion (despite the verification).
cd = correct anticipations and false conclusion (incoherence).
abe = partly false anticipations and correct conclusion (after verification).
ce = correct anticipations and conclusion.

[1] We have chosen the highest memory type reached by each subject, which is not necessarily the same during immediate recall as it is a week later or during subsequent evocations and reconstructions. We shall be returning to this point.

On this basis, we found:

TABLE 5   *Distribution of memory types (in absolute numbers)*

Combinations	abd	cd	abe	ce
Types of memory:				
I	2	3	0	0
II	2	2	1	3
III	1	0	2	5
IV	0	0	1	7

The Table in itself is enough to demonstrate a close connection between type of memory and operational level: the anticipations provide adequate tests of correlation ability. Moreover, the conclusion $A = B = C$ constitutes another correspondence test inasmuch as it involves the correlation of three differently divided rows by means of R. The Table shows that all subjects of type I were at levels *abd* and *cd*, while all but one subject of type IV had progressed to *ce*, with types II and III occupying positions between these two extremes. In short, there is a clear correlation between types of memory and operational stages.

Let us now examine the relationship between types of memory and operational stages (conservation) as determined by the eggs and cup test (Table 6):

TABLE 6   *Types of memory and operational stages*

Operational stages	II	III	IV
Types of memory:			
I	5	0	0
II	1	7	0
III	0	2	6
IV	0	0	8

Again, the correlation is quite clear, though, interestingly enough, the memory level of the six subjects of type III lagged behind their operational level. (By contrast, the memory level of one type II subject was in advance of the operational level. This was the only case to support the widespread belief that the memory can serve as a substitute for intelligence!)

69

The number of subjects was too small to justify a detailed comparison of recall by means of drawings with recall by reconstructions. As it was, one-third of all the cases produced better reconstructions than drawings, especially during transitions from types I to II, and, quite particularly, during transitions from types II to III (in the remaining two-thirds, the level of the reconstructions was identical with that of the drawings).

As for the relationship between immediate recall and recall during subsequent sessions, we observed only one regression in seven cases, but also one advance (better schematizations, etc., notably at level III). One subject (5;4) in particular produced three rows each with two sub-sets of 9, 18 and 15 elements on immediate recall, and three rows of 6, 7 and 6 elements in two or three sub-sets a week later (type III).

The conclusion is that the memory of correspondences and their conservation under various spatial arrangements, such as recall of seriations, depends on the development of the operational schemata. However, there are two differences between the present case and seriation: whereas the memory level seems to correspond fairly closely to the operational level in the latter, it lags slightly behind it in the former; and while the retention of memories is accompanied by spectacular and spontaneous advances in the case of seriation, the progress is much less marked in the case of correspondences. The explanation is doubtless that while serial operations produce particularly 'pregnant' configurations ('good perceptive and imaginal forms' ensuring economic coding methods, at least in the case of advanced codes), the figurative arrangements of the three rows of counters remain arbitrary despite the conservation of equivalence, in such a way that the operational schema of this type of conservation can only be recalled with the help of figurative accommodation, which introduces an additional difficulty.

For all that, in none of the four types of memory observed was recall or reconstruction limited to the reproduction of the figurative *inputs;* rather were these inputs subordinated, at all levels, to the operational schemata governing their assimilation. We must therefore distinguish between perceptive and verificational *inputs*, including the verification of the equivalences $R = B$, $R = A$ and $R = C$, and the actual encoding of the information. However, the encoding process depends on the code itself and the latter varies with the organization of the schemata. From the moment of encoding, the code is thus an instrument of organization or transformation and not simply a transmitting or translating agent. Moreover, this organization only comes into being with the encoding process, and can be preserved during retention and even up to the moment of recall, inasmuch as the latter is an active process involving a degree of reconstruction. And though this continuous organization may lead to memory progress no less than to distortions, it undoubtedly constitutes a necessary form of mnemonic structuring and one that is dependent on the activity of the schemata proper to the intelligence.

§4. *Recall after several months*

Of the twenty-nine subjects originally tested, twenty-two could be brought back to the laboratory, though most of them only after a year. Owing to this long interval, but more probably because of the special numerical and spatial nature of the model, most of the subjects tended to dissociate its two components: they either remembered the numerical equality and forgot the spatial configuration (twelve reconstructions by subjects of memory type III out of twenty-two), or else they had no precise recollection of the (arbitrary) spatial arrangement of the elements, with the consequent disappearance of type IV and the emergence of two new memory types that were not represented during earlier sessions.

Let us first examine the new types, for their interpretation has a direct bearing on the character of the apparent regressions or advances during this long interval. Both types remembered the existence of unequal sub-sets, but, having forgotten their arrangement, they generally schematized the inequalities. In doing so, they displayed a remarkable preference for regularity; in other words, they tended to introduce structures that were completely or largely absent from the model.

The first of these structures, which is admittedly adumbrated in row *B* of the model (1, 2 and 3 counters), is a *seriation*, but extended to the entire model. Thus Ser, who was found to be of type IV during the second session (after one week), drew six superposed rows of 6, 5, 4, 3, 2 and 1 elements (whereas, during the reconstruction, he first produced three rows, of 8, 7 and 6 elements, and then rearranged them into three rows of 8 elements each (type III memory)). Similarly, other subjects produced seriations consisting of 7, 6 and 5, or of 7, 8 and 9, or even of 4, 6 and 9 elements, etc.

While the first of these new structures was of a notional and numerical type, the second was both numerical and figural: it reflected a marked preference for symmetry, perhaps suggested by row *A* of the model, but once again extended to the entire set. Thus Eri, who like Ser has been found to be of type IV during the second session, drew three rows of 3, 1, 3; 2, 2, 2; 4, 2, 4; elements, and then went on to reconstruct rows of 4, 1, 4; 2, 1, 2; 3, 1, 3; elements. His sub-sets were thus reminiscent of those found in the model, but much more regular in form. Other subjects produced less symmetrical combinations (for example, 3, 3; 2, 1; or even 2, 2, 2; 2, 1, 2; 3, 1, 6; with duplications of the last sub-set), but with a clear tendency to proceed to schematizations.

All in all, there were four seriations and five symmetrical figures in a total of twenty-two drawings, and three seriations and six symmetrical figures in the same number of reconstructions. Do these results represent memory regressions or advances? In fact, they do both: there is progress in the direction of regular schematizations, but regress inasmuch as the numerical equalities and the precise configurations of the sub-sets have been forgotten. In short, there is a failure to synthesize the spatial and numerical components of the model.

By contrast, the remaining thirteen subjects attempted, in their drawings no less than in their reconstructions, to equalize the rows (3 rows in 10 cases; 2 rows in 2 cases; and 4 rows in 1 case). There were rough equalizations of type II in five of the drawings (none in the reconstructions), and complete equalizations of type III in seven drawings and in twelve reconstructions. Type I had disappeared, save for one doubtful drawing resembling a truncated series. Of these thirteen cases, only one drawing and two reconstructions were clear cases of regression (from type IV to type III). The stationary cases were represented by seven drawings (types II and, particularly, III) and by two reconstructions (type III), and progress by five drawings and nine reconstructions[1] (from type I to types II or III or from type II to type III). In short, the Table would point to clear progress in that there is a growing appreciation that the rows consist of an equal number of elements, were it not for the nine cases in whom this appreciation was hampered by the clash between the numerical equality and the arbitrary spatial arrangement, and the tendency to offset it with regular constructions (seriations or symmetries). The general conclusion to be derived from the forty-four drawings and reconstructions produced one year after the first session is, therefore, that they reflect a marked tendency towards regular schematizations, be it by way of numerical equalization, seriation or symmetry.

The conflict between numerical equality and spatial arrangement was, however, relatively mild in our experiment, since the rows were not only constructed with the same number of elements but also had the same spatial boundaries. In the next chapter we shall be looking at a similar, but considerably sharper, conflict, involving the opposition of numbers and spatial boundaries.

[1] This represents progress in the drawings of 23 per cent, and in the reconstructions of 40 per cent of the twenty-two subjects.

Before leaving the subject of numerical correspondence, we must stress that the double polarization of memories in the course of several months, whether tending towards seriation or symmetry (which is a form of figural classification), is highly reminiscent of the construction of number, whose main constituents are seriation and classification. It would seem that whenever the long-term memory fails to retain the model as a whole, it tends to dissociate it in accordance with the underlying operational schemata.

CHAPTER FOUR

The Remembrance of Conflicting Numerical and Spatial Correspondences[1]

Our next experiment was of the same type as those described in Chapters 1 and 2: presentation of static figures without explicit mention of their construction or transformation, but such that the subject may, if he is so inclined, treat them as the results of prior actions or operations, and perhaps modify his remembrance of them in accordance with his operational schemata. Several models were used, involving two lines or two pairs of lines represented by four matches or four strokes drawn on paper. The lines themselves were objectively equal but of different shapes—an arrangement that sets up a conflict between the numerical (4 and 4) and the spatial correspondence, and gives rise to protracted memory distortions instead of the advances we have described in Chapters 1 and 2.

One of the operational schemata which the child may employ without special prompting by the experimenter is the non-conservation, followed at about the age of eight to nine years by the conservation, of a line whose shape has been altered.[2] Thus, if the young child is presented with two parallel superposed lines each constructed with four matches, the equality of lengths is evident and obvious immediately and he will say so directly, but if one of the straight lines is transformed into a zigzag, he will no longer consider it equal in length to the other: in general he will treat the zigzag as the shorter of the two, simply because its end point does not coincide with that of the straight line (ordinal evaluation by terminal points). On occasion, however, he will judge the zigzag the longer of the two, on the grounds that it twists and turns, etc., and it is not until the age of eight to nine years that he will grasp the conservation of lengths, and begin to evaluate lengths notionally by the interval between their end points, irrespective of the path.

[1] In collaboration with J. Bliss.
[2] The conservation of lengths appears, on average, at nine years. At the age of eight years, many subjects recognize that A and A' are each composed of four matches, but nevertheless still believe that the over-all lengths are unequal.

74

Knowing these facts, we can present the child with the two series of four matches illustrated in Figure 9, without drawing attention to the term-to-term correspondence and without asking any questions about the lengths or, *a fortiori*, about the transformations from which these arrangements might have resulted. Once these series have been perceived and/or described by the subject, he is asked—as with the seriations discussed in the last chapter—to recall them, so that his remembrance of them after an hour, etc. can be tested. The general problem is once again to establish whether the memory corresponds exclusively to the perceptible data, or whether it bears witness to various schematizations based on assimilation to pre-operational or operational schemata. Now, the fact that the second alternative proves to be the more common of the two, faces us with a problem: in contrast to the seriations, the two new figures have distinct and possibly conflicting spatial characteristics (schemata of ordinal evaluation and non-conservation, followed by quasi-metric evaluation based on the horizontal distance between the end points, and

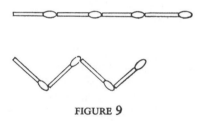

FIGURE 9

finally by conservation in opposition to the numerical approach, i.e. by schemata of optical correspondence or conservation of number). There are several ways of explaining this development.

It is possible, for instance, that, as a result of his spontaneous discovery of numerical correspondence, the subject will remember that the two elements consist of an equal number of components, but that his schemata (ordinal evaluation and lack of spatial conservation) are such that he is forced to base the numerical equality on the coincidence of the extremities of the two lines: in that case, his memory is distorted by inferential transformations leading to the prolongation of that part of the figure which is apparently too short. Conversely, he may take the numerical inequality for granted, in which case his memory will emphasize this fact by decreasing the line that appears too short. As for the general figural accuracy of the memory, it seems likely that an over-all operational grasp of the model (assimilation to conservational schemata and estimates based on the interval or distance) will lead to precise recall, though it is also possible that the child may get there by purely figurative means.

75

In that case, however, we must also allow for the possible existence of diverse spatial schematizations (relations between the empty space underneath the straight line A and the space occupied by A' etc.), and these are certain to be bound up with the operational schemata.

In short, if we are concerned with the modes of mnemonic conservation discussed in the last three chapters, and not merely with the quantitative aspects of mnemonic retention, our experiments may well provide useful pointers to a general interpretation. Now, the chief difference between the new situation and the seriations discussed in Chapters 1 and 2 is that the latter do not give rise to conflicts: in them, the memory was organized in accordance with simple schemata and their continuous progress. The present situation, by contrast, may introduce a conflict between the spatial and the numerical schemata. The main problem, therefore, is to establish whether or not the memory is dominated by this conflict and in what way. It follows that we shall no longer be concerned with the possible improvement or deterioration of memory-images after six months but with the way in which the model may be distorted by conflicting operational schemata and rectified by the gradual resolution of the conflict.

The basic test (Figure 9) was given to seventy-eight 5- to 8-year-old subjects after a series of preliminary experiments involving various methods applied to more than 100 other subjects (divided into groups of different sizes). These variations proved highly instructive, but there is no need to describe them in precise chronological order, the less so since, if we defer their analysis until after we have discussed the main data, they will serve as verifications of our general hypotheses. The reader would nevertheless do well to bear in mind that we did not arrive at our main experiment until after a series of detours, which we have no wish to hide from him, but which it would be tediously pedantic to describe in detail.

§1. *The basic experiment*

Two methods were used, each with some forty children. The only difference between them was that, in the first, the subjects were asked to produce a drawing one hour after the presentation, whereas this additional test was omitted in the second. In both methods, the material having been presented, the subjects were asked for a brief description[1] (no reference was made to the numerical or spatial correspondences involved) and to look at the model carefully so that they might later draw it from memory. Having produced a drawing one hour after the presentation (first method) or not (second

[1] The matches were glued end to end on to a piece of cardboard.

method), all the subjects were re-examined a week later and asked for (1) a memory-drawing; (2) a reconstruction (each subject was provided with more than eight matches); (3) an estimate of the number of matches involved (equal or unequal number of matches in A and A'); and (4) an evaluation of the lengths (the examiner asking whether the paths were as long as each other, and not whether they overlapped).

The results pointed to a clear evolution of memory form with age, i.e. with operational level.

Subjects with the most rudimentary types of memory (type I), which were made up of only a few of the five-year-olds tested, arranged the matches in a single row, either vertically | | | | . . . or horizontally – – – – . . . (corresponding to element A of the model (Figure 9)), or again obliquely and in zigzags (corresponding to element A'). These subjects had clearly forgotten the existence of one of the two elements A and A', which suggests that they either failed to grasp the conflict between the two, or else eliminated it by suppressing one of the terms. But two of the four subjects who reacted in this way, produced superior reconstructions a week later. One of them, in particular, placed three vertical matches in a row, each surmounted by a horizontal match, thus introducing a term-to-term correspondence that helped to resolve the conflict.

Subjects with memories of type II, on the other hand, seemed to be dominated either by the conflict between the equality of number and the inequality of lengths (non-coincidence of the end points) or simply by the figural conflict resulting from this non-coincidence. These two factors cannot easily be dissociated by the present technique, but, as we shall see later (§3, III), if the matches are replaced by continuous lines, the inequality of the elements A and A' is easily recalled, since the memory is no longer forced to come to grips with an equalization problem. It would therefore seem that the discontinuous character and numerical equality of the matches play a special rôle in memories of type II.

It is further characteristic of subjects of type II that they no longer consider the element A' to consist of four matches arranged in the shape of a flattened W, but that they think it is made up of a large number of zigzags. At the same time, they extend the element A so that its extremities are brought into coincidence with those of A'. The conflict is thus resolved by a mainly ordinal evaluation of the lengths. In this regard, we can distinguish three types of reaction. In sub-type IIA the drawings are extended indefinitely (often to the edge of the paper); in sub-type IIB the drawings are shorter but nevertheless exaggerated; in sub-type IIC (found almost exclusively in subjects tested by the second method) the drawings are similar to those of sub-type IIB but shorter, and the segments of A are brought into contact with the peaks of A' to form a closed figure.

Subjects with memories of type III are plainly dominated by the conflict between the numerical equality and the non-coincidence of the spatial boundaries: the element A' is constructed of four (or eight) segments, but stretched out in such a way that the outer summits of the W correspond to

77

II A   II B

FIGURE 10

the extremities of the element A. As for the latter, the number of matches is variable in sub-type IIIA, but precisely four in sub-type IIIB.

In type IV, the element A projects slightly (and correctly) beyond A', but the segments consist of an arbitrary number of elements. This points to a tendency to extend both A and A' so as to bring them into coincidence, but to leave this construction uncompleted because the non-coincidence of the end points has been remembered.

Type V, finally, produces the correct reconstruction of the model (four elements each in A and A') and overlap. In a few rare cases (one in eight), however, the number of elements is incorrect (five), though the figure is still a faithful copy of the model. Hence, there is little need to distinguish between types VA and VB based on this difference.

For greater clarity, and also in order to show that, by and large, these five types of memory depend on age, we shall first of all set out their absolute frequencies (combining the results of both methods, i.e. the drawings after an hour by some, and the drawings and reconstructions by all subjects after a week), in Table 7.

TABLE 7   *Frequency distribution (in absolute number of responses N) of types I–V with age*

	N	I	II	III	IV	V
5 years	(54)	8	29	2	9	6
6 years	(52)	0	25	11	8	8
7 years	(50)	0	15	9	8	18
8 years	(37)	0	6	3	2	26
9 years	(37)	0	4	4	2	25 (27)[1]

[1] The number in brackets (27) includes two subjects who vacillated between types III and V.

Clearly, type I, in which there is no apparent conflict, is confined to the youngest subjects; type II (predominantly figurative solution of the conflict) declines in frequency with age; type III (semi-numeri-

78

TABLE 8　*Analysis of the preceding results (in absolute numbers of subjects)*

	Method a					Method b				
	I	II	III	IV	V	I	II	III	IV	V
5 years										
H	1	4	1	3	1					
W	2	4	0	3	1	2	8	0	1	1
R	2	4	0	2	2	1	9	1	0	1
6 years										
H	0	2	2	3	3					
W	0	6	3	1	0	0	5	2	1	2
R	0	4	4	2	0	0	4	2	1	3
7 years										
H	0	1	1	3	5					
W	0	2	3	1	4	0	5	1	2	2
R	0	3	2	0	5	0	4	2	2	2
8 years										
H	0	2	0	0	5					
W	0	1	0	1	5	0	2	0	1	5
R	0	0	2	0	5	0	1	1	0	6
9 years										
H	0	0	1	0	5					
W	0	1	0	0	5	0	2	2	1	3 (5)[1]
R	0	0	0	0	5	0	1	1	1	7

[1] The number in brackets (5) refers to the two subjects (mentioned earlier) who vacillated between types III and V.

cal and semi-figural solution) is most common at the age of six to seven years; and the correct reproductions (V) do not predominate until about the age of eight years. A more detailed analysis will be found in Table 8. On it, the results of the two methods are shown separately, and so are recall by drawings after an hour (H) or after a week (W), and reconstructions with the help of matches after a week (R).

The first thing to note is that there is little difference between the drawings (W) and the material reconstructions (R) produced one week after the presentation. In fact, the results are identical in sixty-five cases; in a further eleven cases the reconstructions are superior to the drawings, and in two cases only are they slightly inferior. Now, in most of our other experiments, reconstruction was clearly in advance of recall, and this because it fits between recall and recognition. The very similarity between R and W seems to confirm the assumption that, in the present case, the memory is less centred on pure retention than on a form of retention that accords with the subject's schemata and hence tends to suppress the conflict between the numerical correspondence and the spatial boundaries: the few cases of progress from W to R are essentially transitions from type IV to type V, and hence represent numerical advances on the part of subjects who are already aware that A projects beyond A', or else transitions from II to III, i.e. numerical improvements as well, but by subjects who do not recognize or remember the overlap.

Another remarkable fact is that, whereas subjects tested by the first method produced better drawings (W) and reconstructions (R) after a week than those tested by the second method (no drawing after an hour), their recall W after a week was much poorer than their first recall H. Thus, if we compare the results of the two methods, we find that subjects tested by the first produced the following reactions (W and R combined) after a week: four of type I, twenty-four of type II, fourteen of type III, ten of type IV and twenty-two of type V, giving a total of seventy-four reactions; whereas subjects tested by the second method produced three reactions of type I, forty-two of type II, seven of type III, eight of type IV, and twenty-two of type V (eighty-two reactions in all). The second group, therefore, produced a larger number of inferior reactions (I–III), and a smaller number of superior reactions (IV–V) (with A projecting beyond A') than the first. Now, despite the superior reactions of the subjects tested by the first method, whose second recall (W) and reconstructions (R) ought to have been facilitated by their first recall H, the number of inferior reactions increased as between H to W (from one to two of type I; from nine to thirteen of type II; and from four to six of type III), while the superior reactions decreased (from nine to six of type IV and from fourteen to ten of type V). This is further proof that memory retention is dominated by a tendency to eliminate the conflict between numerical conservation and the coincidence of the spatial boundaries rather than by the tendency to copy the model.

It is particularly worth stressing that, while six-year-olds seem to be well ahead of five-year-olds in respect of H, their W reactions (obtained with the first method) are clearly inferior, which suggests that their better recall in H must have accentuated the conflict and produced a stronger tendency towards equalization in W (with the second method on the other hand, six-year-olds are slightly ahead of five-year-olds).

All in all, therefore, the mnemonic reactions to the present experiment (Figure 9) were both very similar to those we encountered in the case of seriation, and very different in respect of their results. In both cases, the child was shown a static model, but one that might be treated as the result of a prior operation: seriation in the first and one-to-one correspondence in the second. In either case, what the child remembered was not the figure he had perceived as such, but a modification in accordance with his operational schemata. In the case of seriation, the most elementary reaction was the suppression of the differences in length, and hence the recall of a series of equal rods placed in a row. In the present case, the simplest reaction (type I) was equally the suppression of the correspondence and the recall of a series of matches placed in a row. In both cases, the memory-images were quite generally bound up with the subject's operational capacities, which proves once again that mnemonic retention and recall are subordinate to the schemata of the intelligence and not simply to the perceptive and figurative aspects of the model.

However, the main difference between the two situations is that, whereas the serial configurations described in Chapters I and 2 do not give rise to a conflict, the obvious numerical correspondence involved in Figure 9 is at odds with the non-coincidence of the terminal points, which strikes children at intermediate stages (before the age of eight to nine years) as being incompatible with the equality of lengths. It follows that, even though they assimilate the model to their operational schemata, or precisely because they make this assimilation but to two schemata at once (one numerical and the other spatial), these children find themselves in a systematic quandary. Thus, while, in the case of seriations, the development of the schemata leads to spectacular mnemonic improvements in the course of six months, in the case of double (numerical and spatial) correspondence, by contrast, the progress of the schemata serves first to acerbate the conflict before it eventually resolves the latter (at about the age of eight to nine years): instead of producing a faithful copy of the model, the child tends to seek an illusory solution of the problem through the equalization of the terminal boundaries. The preponderance of memory-types II–III at the age of five to six years, and the fact that these types still account for twenty-four cases as against twenty-six cases of types IV to V at the age of seven years, bear witness to this situation, which quite naturally impedes mnemonic progress with time, and leads to systematic distortions. It follows that though the memory of seriations and remembrance of spatio-numerical correspondences are based on the same general principle of assimilation to the operational schemata, their results can be diametrically opposite.

§2. Remembrance after six months

Before discussing the various control experiments, we shall first examine the memory of the present model (Figure 9) after six months.

81

We were able to retrace thirty-two subjects tested by the first method, and forty-one subjects tested by the second method, and we shall first describe what became of our five categories:

I. Subjects of type I (suppression of the conflict between the elements A and A' through the elimination of one or the other), who, during the second session (one week after presentation) were only represented by a few five-year-olds, keep increasing in number until about the age of eight years, and can be divided into two distinct categories. Thus, while subjects of type IA produce long zigzags (often accompanied by gestures) or several lines representing a path, a rod, etc., or closed geometrical figures (squares, etc.) or empirical constructions (e.g. a 'factory' with a wavy roof, a mountain hut, etc.), subjects of sub-type IB (not present during the first sessions) try to distinguish between the elements A and A' but combine them into a single continuous (__/_/__) or discontinuous figure (a capital T or V).

II. Subjects of type II (equalization of the boundaries and no recall of the original number of matches or strokes) are found in all age groups, though feebly represented, and quite generally in a form resembling IIC, as defined in §1 (though the figure is often drawn or reproduced upside down and sometimes closed up).

III. Type III, which is characterized, *inter alia*, by a grasp of the one-to-one correspondence combined with the equalization of the two lengths, though represented at all ages during the first two sessions, was only found among subjects from seven years onwards during the third session. It should, however, be added that the figures were sometimes drawn in peculiar ways, so much so that they could have been considered as belonging to a separate set. In the most primitive cases (transitions from the preceding types) the model was represented by four successive horizontal strokes on top of four vertical strokes. Next came irregular figures, all formed of four pairs of parallel strokes, ranging from the near-vertical to the horizontal. In this type, we have also included the very exceptional case of a W, built up of two Vs consisting of four strokes each. This construction involves numerical correspondence and equality of lengths as between the two V's, but no superposition.

IV. Type IV was represented, at the third session, by two subjects aged seven years and nine years respectively. It resembled our description of this type in §1, except that one of the subjects made the overlap too long instead of too short.

V. This type was represented by subjects between the ages of seven years (one case) and eight to nine years.

Table 9 lists the distribution of types by age, as determined either from drawings or reconstructions (the results were identical except for four subjects to whom we shall be returning: in their case we have listed the better response of the two). The figure 0 refers to the absence of any memories.

Table 9 shows, first of all, that remembrance is better in subjects tested by Method *a* (one hour and one week after presentation) than in those tested with Method *b* (one week after presentation only), which throws an interesting light on the subject of memory fixation. The four subjects whose reconstructions and drawing were of different types included two 8-year-olds who had reverted from type V to type IV (a fairly unimportant regression), and two 8- and 9-year-olds who produced drawings of type III and reconstructions of type IV and V.

However, the most interesting difference between this result and the results of the first two sessions (Tables 7 and 8) is that types III to V, characterized by a grasp of numerical correspondence and

TABLE 9   *Types of memory after six months (in absolute numbers)*

	Method *a* (N = 32)							Method *b* (N = 41)						
	0	*IA*	*IB*	*II*	*III*	*IV*	*V*	*0*	*IA*	*IB*	*II*	*III*	*IV*	*V*
5 years	1	2	1	1	0	0	0	0	11	0	0	0	0	0
6 years	2	4	3	0	0	0	0	0	6	2	1	0	0	0
7 years	0	2	0	0	4	1	1	0	2	0	2	3	0	0
8 years	0	1	0	0	0	0	4	0	3	1	1	1	0	1
9 years	0	0	0	1	0	0	4	0	0	0	2	2	1	2
Total	3	9	4	2	4	1	9	0	22	3	6	6	1	3

the gradual resolution of the conflict between number and length, do not appear until the age of seven years, i.e. until the emergence of operationality. This tends to show that the memory after six months is subordinate to the elaboration of operations that endow it with meaning. In this respect, it is interesting to note that one 7-year-old progressed from type II (after one week) to type IV, but in his case, the drawing was a copy of the drawing he had produced after an hour and not of the model itself. The great majority of five- to nine-year-old subjects, however, remained stationary (especially the successful eight- to nine-year-olds of type V tested by Method *a* or else regressed, as witness, *inter alia*, the considerable increase of types IA and IB.

§3. *Improvements in the memory when the element A'*
is compressed

The time has now come to show how the various hypotheses we put forward in §1 were tested by means of experimental variations (which, as we have said, served us as so many preliminary tests).

83

The element A' of Figure 9 consists of four straight but slanting segments (matches) which are readily (and, after a certain age, inescapably) brought into correspondence with the four matches or horizontal segments of the element A. But if the four elements of A' are slightly compressed, the four matches become increasingly dissociated from the element A, and recall more familiar forms: the letter W for children who have learned to read,[1] or roofs, mountains, etc. (which are often drawn in the shape of an M, i.e. upside down). In all these cases, the figures come to look less and less like the segments of the element A, and this fact is of great importance to our investigation.

It should, moreover, be noted that such changes do not so much diminish or eliminate the rôle of the schemata, as cause the dominant schemata to rest on new spatial and topological distributions: recognizing a letter W, a house or a mountain, is tantamount to assimilating the model to a schema and perhaps basing one's memory on the latter. However, there is this great difference from the responses to Figure 9: the conflict between the elements A and A' has disappeared, and this because the elements look completely different. If our hypotheses are correct, the memory will not, in these circumstances, proceed to an equalization of the terminal boundaries, unless, of course, the subject is induced to put them into correspondence by special procedures.

The following four models were used:

(1) Four matches arranged in a line (A) and another four matches combined into a W (A') (Figure 11, I); (2) the same elements as in (1) but with the W (A') placed centrally beneath A, so that the starting points no longer coincide (Figure 11, II); (3) same arrangement as (1) but the couple $A + A'$ is completed by a couple $B + B'$ made up of $4 + 4$ matches in obvious optical correspondence (the experimenter draws the child's attention to the correspondence of B and B', but makes no reference to either the lengths or the operational transformations by which the couple BB' can be changed into the couple AA') (Figure 11, III); (4) the same arrangement as in (1) but the matches of both elements are drawn in corresponding colours (the colour correspondence is not pointed out to the subject); (5) the same arrangement as (2) but, again, with a corresponding colour scheme; (6) for purposes of comparison, Figure 9 was also presented, but, again, in corresponding colours.

I. The results with (1) and (2) (no colours) were quite unequivocal: because the element A' (the W) constitutes a figure quite distinct

[1] In Geneva this happens at the age of six years, though the letters themselves are often recognized at the age of five years.

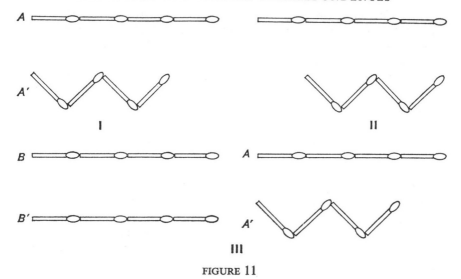

FIGURE 11

from the line *A*, and because there is nothing to draw the child's attention to the numerical cum spatial correspondence, there was no longer the least conflict nor the slightest tendency to equalize the boundaries, except in a few exceptional cases, no doubt influenced by figural considerations.

Of the eleven 5-year-olds to whom we presented the model depicted by Figure 11, I, two were found to have type I recall: after a week they produced an arrangement of matches which showed that they were oblivious of any distinction between the elements *A* and *A'*. (However, after an hour, they both produced differentiated *A*s, though altered beyond recognition.) By contrast, during the reconstruction (after a week), one of these subjects produced a correct *A'* and an *A* consisting of five segments, and the other an *A'* in the shape of a trapezium without a base (four matches), and an *A* consisting of five segments.

One subject proved to have type II (or rather type IIA) recall: he produced a large number of segments in *A'* which joined up with the boundaries of an equally long *A*. His reconstruction was of type IIC: an almost correct *A'* closed by means of an *A* consisting of two segments. This subject must have had some grasp of the numerical correspondence involved, since he pointed out that there were two matches in one half of the *W*, two matches in the other, and two matches in the shortened element *A*.

The eight remaining subjects all produced memory-drawings (after a week no less than after an hour) and reconstructions of types IV and V: there were four drawings of type IV and four of type V, and three reconstructions of type IV and five of type V (four matches each in *A* and *A'*). However, their grasp of the numerical correspondence did not create any conflicts, and this because they did not evaluate the length of the *W* in

85

terms of the boundaries of *A*. One subject (5;5) even told us: '*Here* (*A*) *there were four, and there* (*A'*) *there were four as well. At first I thought that there were more* (in *A*) *because it is longer, but that was only because this one was straight, and over here* (*A'*) *it was like this* (*W*)'. In other words, this subject refused to accept the equivalence 'longer = larger number of segments' from which he would have concluded that 'equal number = equal length' in the case of Figure 9. With the more compact *W* of Figure 11, on the other hand, whose shape sets it off more clearly from that of the line *A*, he saw no contradiction in holding that the same number of elements can be associated with different lengths and, in the absence of this conflict, his memory remained unimpaired.

II. In the case of model II (Figure 11, II), i.e. of the centred *W*, the results were practically the same: of eleven subjects from 4;6 to 6;6 two proved to be of type I, one only of type IIB, six of type IV, and two of type V (exact numerical correspondence). The subjects representing these last two types often substituted an *M* for the *W*, mentioning 'a letter' as well as a mountain or a church.

The introduction of colour correspondence into models I and II did not affect the results in any way: of eight 5-year-olds, one was found to have type I recall, one to have type IIA recall, and six to have type IV and V recall. However, if the coloured *W* was opened out to resemble the *A'* of Figure 9, the reactions were as described in §1: of the eleven 5- to 7-year-old subjects examined in this way, only one produced drawings and reconstructions of type IV; two vacillated between types II and IV, one coming down in favour of type IV during the reconstruction, and the other opting for type IIB; two remained at type I; and seven produced the type II reactions described in §1.

III. If we present the subjects with the squashed *W* (no colours) but accompany the couple *AA'* with another couple of elements BB' in corresponding rows, and if we further draw attention to these numerical correspondences without reference to the lengths, we immediately re-introduce the conflict, with the result that the memory of five- to six-year-old subjects tends, as with Figure 9, to bring the boundaries into coincidence, either by increasing the downstrokes of the *W* (up to twelve elements consisting of six *V*s) or else by extending the figure by horizontal strokes starting from the upper extremities. The only five-year-old subject to reproduce the model correctly (type V) explained his efforts by the following remarkable commentary: 'The two lines (*A* and *A'*) had the same thing (numerical correspondence of the matches) but did not have the same things (lengths evaluated ordinally).'

In other words, though no explicit reference was made to the equality or inequality of the lengths, all our subjects were immediately at grips with this problem. In the case of Figure 9, in which the element A' is wider and hence does not resemble any familiar shapes, numerical correspondence impinges on perception and conflicts with the apparent inequality of the lengths, and it is in the attempt to remove that conflict by the restoration of equality that the memory becomes distorted. In the case of the compact W, its greater spatial separation from A, and its more familiar shape, suppress the conflict and the memory improves—it need only resurrect what has been presented to it. But if the stress is laid on the numerical correspondence as with Figure 11, III, the conflict reappears in young subjects, thanks mainly to the operational schemata to which the figure is assimilated, and which suggests to these subjects that the same number of matches in B and B' and in A and A' must necessarily go hand in hand with the equality of lengths as evaluated by the coincidence of the terminal boundaries of A and A' and of B and B'. Hence, the tendency to introduce such coincidence by means of a mnemonic form of pre-inference which transforms the memory and agrees with the subject's assimilatory schemata. By contrast, the only exact memory produced by a five- to six-year-old was of a purely figurative nature (in contrast to the exact memories of older subjects, who had no conflict to resolve because they know that a broken line can be as long as a straight line even if the terminal boundaries of the two do not coincide). However, our young subject simply took cognizance of this apparently scandalous state of affairs and made no attempt to correct it. His explanation that the two lines 'had the same thing but did not have the same things', indicates that, though the one-to-one correspondence of the segments normally implies the equivalence of the lengths, this normal class satisfying the schemata may co-exist with an abnormal and singular class (in all senses of the term) whose very singularity impinges on the memory. Now, this is just another means of harmonizing the memory with the operational schemata.

§4. *The reappearance of the conflict between numerical correspondences*

If it is indeed the spatial separation no less than the significative character of the element A' (the W) which favours the remembrance of the configurations shown in Figure 11, I and II, by suppression of the conflict between the numerical correspondence (neglected in this case) and the non-coincidence of the spatial boundaries of the elements A and A', then we should be able to revive this conflict and to modify the memory once again, but in the sense described in §1, by replacing the W with a rectangular figure A' without any empirical significance (Figure 12, I and II). And, if it is indeed the numerical correspondence which once again misleads the memory into equalizing the spatial boundaries, it ought to be possible to neutralize this factor, at least in part, by substituting continuous lines for the matches (Figure 12, III).

I. In the case of Figure 12, I, we applied Method I of §1: presentation of the model without any reference to the numerical correspondence,[1] after an hour; followed by recall and reconstruction after a week, etc.

Of fifteen subjects ranging in age from 5;8 to 8;3, only two (7;8 and 8;3) had exact memories of both the numerical and the spatial

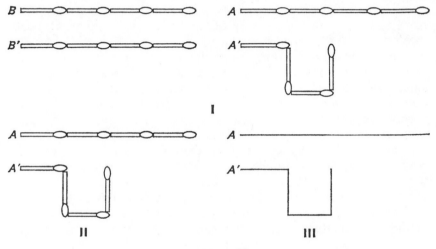

FIGURE 12

relations—these we shall again classify as type V responses. One subject (5;3) also produced the correct response after an hour, but regressed to type III after a week. All the other subjects were of types I to IV, as described in §1.

In type I the element A is suppressed, and A' alone is reconstructed with a larger number of matches. Only one subject produced this type of memory after an hour, but advanced to type II after a week. This type was, however, represented by several subjects when we tested them six months later.

In type II, the rectangular element A' is extended by the addition of further segments to the top or bottom of the figure, such that the boundaries correspond to the exaggerated number of elements thought to constitute A (with or without B and B' of similar lengths—see Figure 13, IIA). In type IIB the element A' has the shape of a T or a Y. In type IIC, finally,

[1] In contrast to the method used with Figure 11, III.

the two elements A and A' form a closed figure A. Type II occurs at the age of five, six, and sometimes even at the age of seven years (B and B' are often omitted).

In type III, the element A' is still extended as far as the boundaries of A, but the number of segments is roughly correct: four matches each for B and B', four for A and five or six for A'. This type of recall occurs as early as 5;3 years.

In type IV, finally, and in (the correct) type V, A is extended beyond the terminal boundary of A', but by means of an arbitrary number of matches.

By and large, the recall of this model corresponds to that of Figure 9. Quite naturally, it, too, gives rise to interpretations based on empirical shapes ('rails' for B and B', a 'track' for A, hats, lorries, garages, etc. for

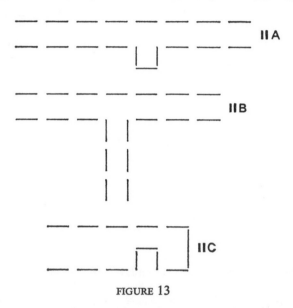

FIGURE 13

A'). All these fall readily into the customary types, except after six months, when the schematizations often give rise to strange forms akin, if anything, to type I.

For the rest, the subjects examined after an hour fell into the following categories: one of type I, five of type II (3 IIA, 1 IIB and 1 IIC), three of type III, three of type IV and three of type V. Recall after a week produced no type I, eight of type II (5 IIA, 1 IIB and 2 IIC), three of type III, one of type IV and three of type V, including one advance from type IV. Except for this last case, there was, therefore, a fair amount of regression between the two sessions. The reconstructions (shortly after recall at the second session) produced the same results, except that the subject of type IV advanced to type V. Finally, of the thirteen subjects we were able to retrace after six months, recall and reconstruction alike gave four of type I, six of type II (3 IIA, 1 IIB and 2 IIC), one of type III, one of type IV and no type V. Moreover, one of the subjects who had been of type V remembered nothing at all.

Clearly, therefore, the over-all results of this test bear a remarkable resemblance to those obtained with the model illustrated by Figure 9.

II. Now, Figure 12, I includes the elements B and B', which hint at numerical correspondences, and we shall now go on to examine Figure 12, II, which bears a closer resemblance to Figure 9. Here, the element A projects horizontally by two matches beyond the element A', i.e. almost as much as in Figure 11, I and more than in Figure 11, II. As a result, the element A' looks even more independent of A than it does in Figure 9. However, the first and third matches of A' are parallel to those of A, which again suggests numerical correspondence as between A and A'. Hence, it is interesting to establish whether Figure 12, II helps to revive the conflict between number and length, or whether, like Figure 11, I and II, it is remembered without the kind of distortions resulting from the equalization of the boundaries.

Among twenty-one subjects[1] ranging in age from 5 to $7\frac{1}{2}$ years, one 5-year-old was found to have a memory of type I (fusion of A and A' into a single figure). During the reconstruction, however, this subject produced a closed figure consisting of one line on top and a parallel line with a rectangular inclusion corresponding to A' at the bottom (type II recall). Another subject also fused A and A', but in the form of a square with horizontal extensions to both upper edges; during the reconstruction, however, he produced two elements: a rectilinear A consisting of three matches, and an A' open to the right side and completed by a horizontal match to ensure the coincidence of the terminal boundaries. A third subject produced a design of type IV (on immediate recall) but after a week reverted to type I (succession of two As).

Eight 5- to 6-year-old subjects were found to have recall of type II, i.e. to extend the element A' by adding a horizontal line (or, during the reconstruction, one or more matches) to the upper right, thus aligning its end point with that of A. One 7-year-old subject added one horizontal element during the test, an hour after the presentation (type intermediate to II and IV) and a second one a week later (type II).

Subjects from 6;5 to 7;5 produced six drawings and reconstructions in which A projected horizontally beyond A' but by the wrong number of elements. Finally, three 6- to 7-year-olds remembered the model correctly.

In addition to these twenty-one subjects, a further ten were examined by a special method: they were asked to copy the model

---

[1] Eight of these subjects were asked to recall the model immediately after presentation instead of after an hour, but this did not affect the results in any way.

(Figure 12, II) immediately, and to produce a further memory-drawing and a reconstruction a week later. All the copies were, of course, correct (one 5-year-old subject began by fusing A and A', but corrected his mistake at once). When it came to recalling the model, however, only four subjects from 6;5 to 7;2 produced the correct response (type V). We failed to discover a single case that could be described as a pure type IV, for though one subject produced a type IV reconstruction ($A = 5$ segments, $A' = 7$ segments extending beyond A), his recall was of type IIA. Two other subjects fell between types IV and II; two more produced reconstructions of type II (coincidence of boundaries), and one was found to be of type I. This shows that copying the model in no way eliminates the conflict and, though it may improve some reactions, in other cases it gives rise to the same distortions as the other methods (no copy drawing).

III. Let us now look at a crucial experiment: presentation of the same model but this time in the form of continuous lines instead of matches, which helps to mask the numerical correspondence and, hence, the conflict between number and the evaluation of lengths by terminal boundaries.

Figure 12, III was used to test ten 5- to 7-year-old subjects, all of whom were asked for memory-drawings after an hour, and, again, after a week. All these subjects extended the line A beyond the element A'. In most cases (eight out of ten) the element A' was drawn correctly. One subject drew a staircase, and another extended the top right-hand corner by means of a small stroke, but refused to continue it as far as the terminal boundary of A, and this despite suggestions by the experimenter, who was trying to test his resistance.

By contrast, of the four subjects we were able to bring back after four months, not a single one had an adequate memory of the model: two had forgotten the element A, one produced a closed figure, and another, whose reproductions after an hour and after a week had been fairly faithful, now made a type II drawing. His reaction suggests that, over and above the conflict between the operational schemata, the drawing was also influenced by a figurative factor: since mental images in general are specially affected by terminal boundaries,[1] it is possible that the child, when recalling two originally parallel lines starting from the same initial boundary, tends to make their end points coincide, even if one of the lines involves a detour.

To verify this assumption we tested four younger subjects, aged from 4 to 5 years, whose operational level was low and who had received no pre-school education. All of them were asked for

[1] See J. Piaget and B. Inhelder: *Mental Imagery in the Child*, Routledge & Kegan Paul, 1971.

91

drawings, first after an hour, and, again, after a week, of what they remembered of Figure 12, III: after an hour, not one of them produced the correct copy and three made drawings of type II; after a week, all four drawings were of type II (two closed figures, one *T*, and one short extension). In other words, even in the absence of numerical correspondence (continuous lines), there is a marked tendency to bring the terminal boundaries into coincidence. This is due to a simple spatial correlation, in which the laws of imaginal representation are quite plainly at work, thanks largely to the general centration of the image on the terminal boundaries.

Let us note in passing that, in the case of these four subjects, the figurative factor, while playing an obvious part, gave rise to mnemonic distortions and not to the faithful reproductions one might have expected of memory-images on which the operational schemata do not exert a great deal of pressure. Hence, it would be tempting to postulate that the more figurative the memory of young subjects, the closer it corresponds to their actual perception of the model. In fact, the image is subject to systematic deformations of its own (rôle of terminal boundaries, etc.), and these distortions may even account for the presence of certain pre-operational spatial schemata —a point to which we shall be returning.

For all that, these special figurative factors only play this rôle (Figure 12, III) at a very elementary level: all ten of the 5- to 7-year-old subjects we have mentioned produced drawings in which the terminal boundaries did not overlap, and this even after a week; at this second level, it is therefore the absence of numerical correspondence between distinct segments (continuous lines) which aids the memory, while the intervention of numerical correspondence (matches) sets up a conflict, which explains why the tendency to equalize the terminal boundaries persists until the age of seven and sometimes even until the age of eight years (Tables 7 and 8).

IV. In order to establish the generality of the tendency to equalize the terminal boundaries either by resolution of the conflict between numerical, and the apparent lack of spatial, correspondence, or else by means of figurative factors centred on the end points alone, we decided to proceed to a brief recognition test. Mnemonic recognition is, of course much more primitive and direct than mnemonic recall or even mnemonic reconstruction (with the materials provided by the experimenter): it is reinforced by renewed perceptive contact. Hence, it is of interest to establish whether or not subjects instructed to select the correct copy of the model they have observed earlier, and to eliminate all those that do not correspond to it, have the same reactions as they produce in the case of recall and reconstruction in the absence of the original model. We accordingly asked fourteen 5- to 7-year-old subjects to choose one of several models, including that of Figure 12, II and some of the main distortions we had observed earlier. The recognition test was given to all these subjects after a week, and to some of them also an hour and, again, four months later.

As expected, many of the recognitions proved to be of a higher type than the corresponding recollections or reconstructions (the reader will remember that in the present series of tests, the results of the last two were very much the same). About one-third of the recognitions were more or less correct, with the element A extending beyond the element A' (types IV and V) while the corresponding recall was still of types I–III; the other two-thirds produced recognitions of the same level (I–III or IV–V) as the corresponding recall.

For all that, recognition was by no means correct in all cases, and indeed gave rise to the same distortions as recall and reconstruction, though to a (quantitatively) lesser extent. After a week, seven of our fourteen subjects (up to the age of 7;11!) chose figures of type II; the remaining seven chose figures of types IV and V. After an hour, the ratio was 3 type II and 4 type IV or V, and after four months it dropped to 2:1 (six sets of segments of equal length, three sets of overlapping segments). It seems clear, therefore, that the process we have been describing affects the whole memory and does not engender distortions specific to mnemonic recall: the same schemata are at work at all mnemonic levels, from recognition upwards.

§5. *Conclusions*

To clarify which improvements and distortions are respectively due to the figurative and the operational aspects of the memory, and quite especially to the relationship between the figurative image and the operational schema in the mnemonic processes studied in this chapter, we shall now try to put some order into the observed facts.

I. At the most elementary level, our subjects ignore the numerical correspondence of the elements A and A', and rely exclusively on spatial correlations. In the most primitive cases, these correlations go hand in hand with a simple lack of differentiation: the most salient feature of the model is seized upon, and the rest neglected (type I), or else the two elements are combined into closed figures of different shapes. But, at a fairly early age, our subjects have learned to distinguish and correlate the elements A and A', either by means of spatial or classificatory dissociation (Figure 11, I and II) or else by means of spatial correspondence (Figure 9 and Figure 12, I and II).

These correlations can involve topological or classificatory schemata, but even in that case, the figurative factors continue to play a dominant rôle. Now, this rôle may lead to distortions as well as to correct recall. In the case of Figure 11, I and II, it is the perceptive dissociation of A and A' which encourages the formation of adequate images; in the case of Figures 9; 12, II; and, especially, 12, III (in which the continuous lines mask the numerical correspondence), it is the boundary factors which play an important and sometimes exclusive rôle in the illusory equalization of the terminal limits.

II. At the next level, the subjects grasp the numerical correspondence (four matches in element A and four in element A'), and their use of operational schema might be expected to assist their memory. But they lack an adequate space-conservation schema, and hence fail to appreciate that an irregular line can be as long as a continuous one: in consequence, they experience a conflict between the numerical equality and the apparent spatial inequality of A and A', and this conflict tends to distort their memory—in this case, under the influence of the operational schemata, or, rather, due to their incoordination.

We can attribute such distortions to a kind of mnemonic 'pre-influence', akin to perceptive pre-inference or even to pre-operational representative inference, and this in the following ways: (1) the lines A and A' are believed to be equal because their segments are in one-to-one correspondence; (2) if they are equal in number, it follows that they must also be equal in length; (3) hence, their extremities must coincide. But when and how is this inference made? In the case of our matchstick models it apparently proceeds by two stages: notional assimilation in the presence of the model, and transposition of the memory-image or mnemonic assimilation.

In the presence of the model, i.e. during direct inspection, assimilation is bound to be purely notional, since no mental image or memory has been formed as yet, and also since the perception runs counter to the expected coincidence of the boundaries: hence, there is a more or less conscious or implicit adoption of the premises (1) and (2), and a conflict with the actual data. If the child were questioned about the lengths at that moment, he would say that A' was shorter than A because the latter extended beyond the former. But while accepting this inevitable consequence (after all, he is still looking at the model) he remains dissatisfied: the one-to-one correspondence suggests that the lines ought to have the same terminal boundary.

Let us now look at the second stage: the construction of the memory-image once the model has disappeared. In a famous passage, Luquet has shown that at the age of five to six years, the child's drawing reflects what he knows of an object rather than what he sees or has seen of it: the child's drawing therefore represents the conclusion (3) from the premises (1) and (2). But is this a purely graphic process? In fact, it is nothing of the kind; first, because recognition leads to the same conclusion (§3, IV); and, second, because the mental image is often a conceptual symbol rather than a symbol of the model itself. Moreover, as our own observations have shown, the conversion of the perceived object into a modified memory-image is partly independent of the drawing that serves to express it. Now, the surprising fact, in the experiments we have described, is that this conversion is, so to speak, immediate, because just as soon as the model is removed from sight (cf. §3, II), our subjects already proceed to equalizations. The only possible explanation we can think of is that as soon as perception ceases to act as a restraint, the two premises (1) and (2) lead to the conclusion (3); not, of course, because the child argues explicitly, and especially not because he argues in spoken or unspoken words, but because he proceeds to a full coordination of the schemata involved. In other words, the one-to-one correspondence of the terms leads to the notional or schematic equalization of the lengths conceived in ordinal terms. However, to advance from this notional approach to an assessment of the real situation i.e. to a recall of what has been observed in fact, the child must have recourse to the memory-image. It is here that the mechanism of mnemonic recall, consisting as it does of both the conservation of schemata and figurative consolidation by means of the memory-image, reveals its potential no less than its limitations. Now, the memory-image is at first an imitative symbol and not an extension of perception, and, being a symbol, it merely represents the object as a concept. It follows that, in his attempts to reconstruct what he has seen but no longer perceives, the subject is reduced to symbolizing as faithfully as he can what assimilations to his schemata he made in the presence of the model: he will accordingly produce the most faithful image possible of what he has seen, but an image that is more faithful to his thought than to his perception, simply because his thought persists while the perception has gone and cannot be replaced by the image.

In short, at the second level of development, it is the operational schemata which are chiefly responsible for the distortions of the memory, and no longer the figurative factors which play a predominant rôle in certain subjects at Stage I (for instance, in the case of Figure 12, III). As soon as these figurative factors lead to a strong enough dissociation of the elements A and A', as in Figure 11, I and II, the numerical and spatial correspondences cease to be in conflict, and the memory improves. However, once the numerical equality is emphasized once again (Figure 11, III), the conflict reappears. Moreover, its suppression (Figure 12, III) confirms the rôle of the inco-ordination of the operational schemata.

But we must still try to find an explanation for this lack of co-ordination. It is not, in fact, thanks to a better grasp of numerical correspondence that the memory remains distorted at the second stage (the original distortion, during the first stage, was due chiefly to figural correlation), but thanks to the lack of co-ordination of the numerical schema with the more advanced schemata of (metric) evaluation and of the conservation of lengths. Now, the explanation of why this evaluation should become ordinal at the age of five to seven years instead of remaining purely metric cannot be sought in the development of the image, but must once again be attributed to the development of the operations themselves. However, ordinal evaluation is chiefly centred on the order of the terminal boundaries, which are thus treated as privileged factors, and since this privilege depends largely on the image, it serves to extend the influence of the figurative factors encountered at Stage I.

III. At the third stage, finally, which does not appear before the age of eight to nine years, there is operational co-ordination between the numerical schemata and the spatial schemata, whereupon the previous conflict is resolved, and the schemata ensure the correct retention and reproduction of memories. As a result, the image becomes a reliable symbol, thus paving the way for the collaboration between the figurative and operational factors of the memory. But it is essential to remember that this final situation, which occurs in all the models we have been discussing, and not merely in those whose structure is such as to obviate conflicts, can only come about thanks to the evolution of the operational schemata; neither perception nor the memory-image sufficed until that point to reproduce the models illustrated by Figure 9, or Figure 12, I and II. Here, the results of the present series of tests agree fully with those of the seriation experiments, in which, as we saw, the model, however simple and in conformity with the laws of 'good form', was also distorted by the subject's schemata, until such time as the latter had developed sufficiently to allow for the proper assimilation.

IV. Despite the differences between the results described in Chapters 1 and 2 and the present findings (see end of §1), the mnemonic mechanisms involved in both are thus identical. However, in the case of seriation, we were dealing with a simple schema, i.e. with one that emerges relatively early in the child's life, and whose figurative symbolism adapts itself without great difficulty or conflict to the stages of operational development: hence, the initial deformations were the direct reflections of the latter, and mnemonic progress was due to their rapid succession. In the case of the correspondence between the lines A and A', on the other hand, the subject is brought face to face with two distinct sets of schemata, one of which develops well in advance of the other. The variety of memory types we have discussed is therefore a reflection of the several attempts to combine these schemata, particularly at those stages where there is still a marked lack of co-ordination. It follows that the memory which, as in the case of seriation, tends to organize all the data it records can only find that organization in illusory solutions, which suppress the conflict but at the same time distort the data. In that case, the memory of a particular event or object will not improve with time; the visual image, which is more concerned with spatial than with numerical relations, can only express these poorly co-ordinated situations with the help of figural symbols obeying the same laws as govern its own function (centration on boundaries, etc.). This explains why it is only at the point where the schemata are ready for co-ordination (towards the age of eight to nine years) that memories of type V persist in subjects tested six months after the presentation of the model.

CHAPTER FIVE

The Remembrance of Transitive Relations[1]

The models we have described in Chapters 1 to 4 all had two aspects likely to attract attention in various ways: a figurative aspect, mainly reflected in the child's memory-drawings, and an operational aspect responsible for the conceptualization of the model in accordance with the available action or operational schemata. The experiments demonstrated clearly that, contrary to what might have been expected, the second aspect plays at least as important a rôle in the memory as the first, from which we concluded that it would be eminently worth while to examine the remembrance of situations in which reasoning plays a more obvious rôle, i.e. in which the figural arrangement is bound up, not simply with a possible operational construction, but with deductive arguments.

As we shall see, the experimental material consisted of three vessels of distinct shape but containing the same amount of liquid. This equivalence could be verified by means of a fourth, empty vessel. The experimenter himself performs the necessary operations, but asks the child, first, to anticipate, and, later, to state, the results. The remembrance of this experiment, one hour, one week, and, again, three to five months later, is therefore bound up with the solution of a problem, and this poses the following preliminary questions: (1) Does the memory of the experimental model remain closely linked to the characteristic schemata of the understanding and solution of the problem? (2) Is the figurative aspect of the memory more obviously subordinate to the operational aspect than it is in the case of seriation?

§1. *Experimental material and procedure*

Two methods were employed.

Method I involved the use of four glasses: A, tall and thin and filled with yellow liquid; B, conical and filled with green liquid; C, short and squat and filled with red liquid; and $B' = B$ so as to enable the child to verify the equivalences. The first three vessels

[1] In collaboration with J. Bliss and O. Maratos.

contain the same amount of liquid. The interrogation extended over four sessions.

During the first session, the child is presented with four glasses, of which *A*, *B* and *C* have previously been filled with the same amount of liquid: (a) The experimenter pours *A* into *B'* and asks the child to establish the equality of the levels in *B* and *B'*. When this has been done, he pours the contents of *B'* back into *A*; (b) the experimenter proceeds in the same way with the vessels *C* and *B'*; (c) the experimenter places the vessels *A* and *C* side by side and asks: 'If I drank this syrup (the red liquid) and you drank that one (the yellow liquid), would one of us have drunk more than the other, or would both of us have drunk the same amount?' The child is asked to explain his answer; (d) the experimenter places *A*, *B* and *C* on the table and removes *B'*. He then asks the child if the three vessels contain the same amount of liquid. If the answer is 'yes', the child is asked to explain

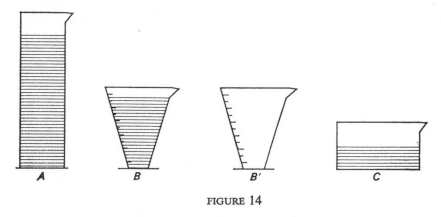

FIGURE 14

his reasons. If the answer is 'no', the child is asked to state which vessel contains the greatest amount of liquid.

The second session is held an hour later, and no vessels are presented. The child is asked: (a) to give a verbal description of what was done during the first session; (b) to make a memory-drawing of the vessels, in the appropriate colours (when drawing the empty vessel *B'*, he is asked whether or not there were two vessels of the same size); (c) to give a second verbal description of what was done during the first session and to mark successive decantations by arrows on his drawing. The order of succession is noted; (d) the child is asked to repeat the questions that were put to him by the experimenter.

The third session is held a week later and consists of three parts: I. The first part is identical to the memory test we have just described; II. In the second part the child is handed all the vessels (with their original contents) and asked to perform all the decantations he observed during the original presentation. If he wishes to mix the liquids he is allowed to do so (the relevance of this operation will become clear in what follows). He is again asked to repeat the questions that were put to him, and to explain the objects of the experiment (the essential thing is to discover whether or not the child makes use of the vessel B' as a mean term); III. In a post-experimental test, the child's operational level is established by means of the vessels $D–H$ (Figure 15) in which, appearances to the contrary, $F > E > D$: (a) the child is asked to estimate which of the vessels D to F contains the most liquid; whereupon (b) the experimenter proceeds to a verification.

F is poured into the graduated vessel H and the child is asked to note the level, whereupon the liquid is poured back into F; (c) E is poured into F and the same procedure is followed. The child is asked which of the two liquids (F = red) or (E = green) reached the highest level, and to remember his answer. F and E are now shown to the child, and he is asked to explain which holds more liquid; (d) the experimenter pours E (green) into G and

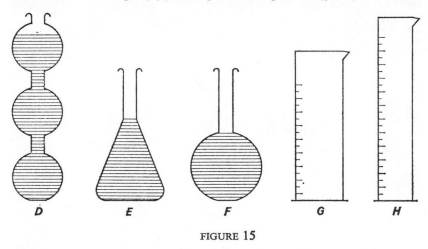

D   E   F   G   H

FIGURE 15

follows the same procedure as with H. Next, he pours D (yellow) into G and back into D and, after placing E beside D, asks the child which vessel contains more liquid; (e) finally, he asks the child to compare D and F and to explain his answer. The correct reply shows that the child has grasped the transitive relation $F > D$, because $F > E$ and $E > D$ (serial transitivity).

A fourth session is held three, four or five months later, and again consists of three parts: I. Simple recall by means of drawings, as in the first session and in part I of the second session. II. Reconstruction as in part II of the second session. III. Verification of operational level as in part III of the third session.

Method II. The second method differs from the first in that the initial material includes two empty vessels B' and B'' instead of only one. During the first session, the experimenter: (a) pours A into B', whence $A = B' = B$, and then pours B′ back into A; (b) he next

100

pours C into B' and the child observes that $C = B' = B$, whereupon B' is poured back into C; (c) the child is asked if $A = C$, and once he has replied, the vessel B' (hidden until then) is brought out. The child is asked whether $B = B' = B''$ if A were poured into B' and C into B''. After he has replied and justified his answer, the equality is demonstrated.

The following sessions are held an hour, a week, and six months later, and the child is asked for drawings, verbal descriptions and reconstructions, but is not given the supplementary operational test. In fact, Method II, which was the one we employed first, had to be abandoned for simplicity's sake; the extra vessel proved to be an unnecessary complication. We shall nevertheless mention the chief results obtained with it, if only to show the generality of our findings.

Method II was used with seventeen 5- to 7-year-old subjects, and Method I with twenty-three 4- to 9-year-old subjects. We shall first look at the operational results obtained with the second group, the better to judge their level of mnemonic performance.

§2. The operational reactions

The best assessment of the grasp of transitivity is provided by the post experimental test (vessels D–H) which formed the third part of the third session (Method I) and involved the seriation $F > E > D$. By their responses, the subjects proved to be at three distinct operational stages. Stage I, which was clearly pre-operational, was characterized by a complete failure to grasp the transitive relations: all subjects at this stage substituted their perceptive impression $D > E > F$. Stage III was characterized by a grasp of transitivity and the correct explanation of the relations involved,[1] thus demonstrating that these subjects were fully capable of handling the operations involved. Between these two stages was a Stage II, in which the amount of liquid was estimated correctly but either without valid explanations, or else with inconclusive arguments. A typical Stage II reply was: '*I am sure that the red one (F) has more in it, but I can't tell you why.*'

Now, the grasp of transitivity at Stage III clearly implies a grasp of the conservation of quantities, thanks to its logical construction and also to the method used to verify the relations. The logical structure of the inference $F > D$ if $F > E$ and $E > D$ naturally rests on the presupposition that the quantities F, E and D do not vary during the course of the argument, no matter what spatial arrangements are used. As for the verification of the inequalities $F > E$ and $E > D$, it involves the middle terms H or G, and these can only be considered as common measures if F, E and D conserve their quantities when poured into H or G.

Conversely, though the conservation of quantities during a single decantation does not imply transitivity, the latter intervenes as soon as

[1] With explicit reference to the vessels H and G as the necessary mean terms.

101

there are two related decantations. For example, if A in x (Ax) is poured into y (Ay) and then into z (Az), the conservation of A involves the transitivity $Ax = Ay$, $Ay = Az$ and hence $Ax = Az$. And this is also true of only two vessels: $Ax = Ay$ and the reverse $Ay = Ax$, whence we have $Ax = Ax$ (in the case of 'empirical reversal', which is first grasped without conservation at about the age of six years, we also have $Ax = Ax$, but neither $Ax = Ay$ nor $Ay = Ax$). Our basic experiment (Figure 14) thus involves several forms of transitivity based on conservation, of which those the child is asked to make explicit are merely the particular cases $A = B'$, $B' = C$, hence $A = C$; or $A = B'$, $B' = B$, and $C = B'$, $B' = B$ and hence $C = B$.

But all this is simple logic and it is quite possible that, from the psychological point of view, the child may lay stress on either transitivity (which

TABLE 10   *Distribution of stages of transitivity (T) and conservation (C) by ages*

| | Stages | | | | | | Numbers | |
| | I | | II | | III | | | |
	T	C	T	C	T	C	T	C
5 years	6	6	0	0	0	0	6	6
6 years	5	5	1	1	0	0	6	6
7 years	2	3	2	2	3	2	7	7
8 years	1	2	1	0	2	4	4	6

TABLE 11   *Correlation of Stages I–III of transitivity (T) and conservation (C)*

	I C	II C	III C
I T	14	0	0
II T	1	2	0
III T	0	1	4

he is forced to do in the post-experimental test when comparing D with F, having first established the two relations $D < E$ and $E < F$ with the help of H and G), or else on conservation: for instance, in the basic experiment some subjects conclude as to $A = C$, without explicit use of the argument $A = B'$, $B' = C$, but simply by stating that '*the glasses A and C contain the same amount of liquid because, when they were in B' it was all the same*'. This makes one wonder whether or not there is any correlation between the grasp of transitivity during the operational test and recourse to conservation in the basic experiment.[1] Tables 10 and 11 set out the

[1] In general, the experimenter, after pouring, say, A into B', asks the child if there is as much drink in B' as there was in A, which provides a direct indication

results, the first by comparing ages with stages, and the second by comparing the relative grasp of transitivity and conservation.

Clearly, the correlation is almost perfect. There are only two exceptions, in both of which transivity is in advance of conservation: if this fact were significant, it would tend to show that the more general framework leads to a structuring of its particular contents.

§3. *Remembrance at pre-operational Stage I*

The reader who has followed the arguments set out in §§1 and 2 will no doubt be thinking that, since our constant preoccupation with operational structures has once again carried the day, our experiments can have none but the most banal results in respect of the memory as such—those subjects who have no grasp of either transitivity or conservation are bound to have the most sketchy memories of the experiments, while those who understand these relations will necessarily remember all they have grasped. Luckily, the facts are much more interesting than that, or else we could have dispensed with most of the material in this chapter. What happens, in fact, is that the youngest of our subjects, who failed to see the point of the experiments through lack of operational ability (grasp of conservation and transitivity), neither expunged them from their memories nor remembered them accurately, but restructured them in accordance with the figurative organization of their memory, although in ways that showed this organization was conditioned (in the logical and not the reflexological sense) by the level of the operational schemata at their disposal.

Thus, subjects with the most elementary type of memory recalled a series of decantations which could not have been performed for logical reasons, and which bore no relation to any actions the child or the experimenter might have performed. Some of these subjects, for instance, imagined that they had seen (for what they produced was, in fact, a visual memory and not a possible reconstruction—'one might have . . .', etc.) the red liquid (C) being poured into the green (B), and the green back into the red. This cross-decantation, without the help of an empty vessel, was explained in two distinct and equally improbable ways: either the process was thought to have been synchronous, i.e. the child believed that the experimenter had poured the green liquid into the red at the same time that he poured the red into the green; or else it was thought to have been successive,

---

of the child's grasp of the principle of conservation, independent of his grasp of transitivity.

regardless of the fact that the vessels were full (and were drawn accordingly).

Before discussing the relevance of these findings to the memory, we shall first of all establish the authenticity of this type of reaction by quoting several responses verbatim:[1]

MAR (5;9; Method II) produced a drawing (one week after presentation of the experiment) of C being poured into B 'at the same time' as B was being poured into C; similarly, he thought that A was poured into B' 'at the same time' as B' was being poured into A. When asked to explain the reason for these manipulations, he replied: '*Because you said that the syrups were not supposed to be in the same glasses.*'

CLA (5;0, Method I) also drew $A \rightarrow B$ and vice versa, explaining that '*the yellow one has been put back here*' (A), followed by $C \rightarrow B$ and vice versa, explaining once again that '*afterwards the red* (C) *and the green* (B) *were put back*'. For him, the cross-decantations were therefore successive: the green was poured into the yellow, and then the yellow back into the green liquid. Do you have any idea of how the yellow came out and got into the green (B)?—*No.*

SER (6;10, Method II, an hour after presentation) drew one-way decantations only. However, a week later, he introduced synchronous cross-decantations, and was quite explicit about it: *The yellow* (A) *was put into the green* (B) *and the green into the yellow* (A).—But didn't the two get mixed up?—*No, they can both be done at the same time.*—Very well, let's try and see.—*Yes, let's.*—Which one are you going to pour out first? *Both together.*

MON (5;6, Method I) said that the yellow was poured into the red, and made his drawing accordingly. But isn't the glass full?—*No, it was done like this, and then the red was put into the yellow glass.* (Successive cross-decantations.)

LUC (5;11, Method I) said that A was poured into B, and B into A 'at the same time'. Why did we do that?—*To find out if they were the same kind of syrup.*—And how can we tell? *Because the glasses were changed.* (Synchronous cross-decantation to verify the equivalence.)

NA (5;0, Method I): *The red one was poured back and put with the yellow.*—And the yellow?—*Was put with the red.*—At the same time?—*Yes.*—The two got mixed up?—*Yes, they got mixed.*—Tell me how.—*The red was here* (C) *and the yellow there* (A).—And then?—*The yellow was put back here, and the red there* (A). During the subsequent reconstruction Na prepared quite seriously to pour C into A: '*First of all, the red was poured into the yellow*', but seeing that this could not be done, he poured C into B' instead.

FLO (5;11, Method I): *The red one was put there* (A).—But wasn't there some yellow in it?—*No, it was put there* (C).—Without mixing the syrups? —*No, they were put back into their own place afterwards.*—Then if we put one syrup into the other, don't they get mixed up?—*Sometimes they do and sometimes they don't.*

[1] M. Boehme discovered the same reactions in several senile and demented subjects.

MIC (5;0, Method I) drew $A \rightarrow C$ and vice versa: Don't the two get mixed up?—*Yes, but the red was taken out.*—Is that possible?—*Yes, the yellow one was put into the red, and the red one into the yellow.*

NOB (5;11, Method II) looking at the vessels (reconstruction): *The green was poured into the red and the red into its place.*—Like this? (the experimenter picks up the bottles).—*Yes.*

TIM (6;11, Method II) drew three vessels and marked $B \rightarrow A$, $A \rightarrow C$ and $C \rightarrow A$. He explained: '*The yellow was put into the red and the red into the yellow.*'

These responses show plainly that without the support of an operational framework, the memory will produce the most improbable data. They also show that these improbabilities do not appear at random, but that they are governed by laws which, in the present case, appertain to memory retention and not to perception. As for the latter, the subjects must obviously have noticed that the decantations were successive and in two directions: for example that A (yellow) was poured into the empty B', followed by the return of B' into A. Now, the subjects we examined did not generally forget the empty vessel, but chose to ignore it, simply because they failed to appreciate its purpose in the argument. Focusing their attention exclusively on the full vessels and remembering that the decantations took place in both directions, they fused them into a single action in accordance with the most economical image.

This fusion into a single action $A \rightleftharpoons B$ can be compared to an act of 'condensation' in the sense in which Freud, describing dream symbols, spoke of the combination of two or more images into a single one. In general, condensation is not specific to dreams. Thus, it often happens that, on returning along a mountain path, we condense the memory of two valleys or two bends into a single image combining the features of both. The cross-decantation $A \rightleftharpoons B$ would thus be a simplification of the memory-image. But, in addition, there is the odd fact that our subjects should think it possible to perform this type of manœuvre in the first place. This possibility is doubtless bound up with the remarkable pre-operational symmetries children of these age groups so often introduce into the causal domain.

As for the absurdity of this kind of representation, it revolves about two sets of factors. The first is that subjects at Stage I have no grasp at all of transitive reactions, and so fail to see the point of the decantations. Hence, they simply 'think' like Mar that the syrups were not supposed to be in the same glasses, so that A had to be poured into B, and vice versa. More important still is the deficient and static nature of their pre-operational mental images, a fact on which we have dwelt at length in another study. Four- to six-year-old subjects readily recall the initial and final stages of a transformation, but not the transformation itself. Hence, though they remember that *A* was poured into *B*, and *B* into *A*, they find it much simpler to imagine direct cross-decantation than to recall the intermediate rôle of the vessel *B'*.

The proof that the dominant process is a simplification of the memory-image is that subjects at this stage presented with an even simpler manipulation will choose the latter in preference to the cross-decantations. Thus, when, as a control experiment, we replaced the 'syrups' with coloured beads and for the rest followed Method I, our subjects continued to think in terms of cross-decantations but with this remarkable addendum; the beads were thought to have been poured out on to the table between two successive decantations:

FER (5;7) said that the white beads were poured into the green vessel, and the green beads into the white. Did they get mixed up?—*A little bit.*—Are you sure?—*No, the green ones were put on the table and then the whites into the green and the greens into the white.*—What for?—*To see if the green ones come to the same thing as the whites* (equalization).

PAT (6;1): *The green ones were put in the red glass and the red into the green.*—How so?—*You put them on the table* (there was no hesitation!) *then you put the green ones into the jar with the red ones and the red ones into the green jar.*

It is surprising that, since they are so ingenious (for there was no justification at all for remembering beads on the table), these subjects should not have had recourse to the empty vessel *B'* which, in fact, appeared in most of the drawings (especially those of the last two subjects).

Cross-decantations can, as we saw, also be associated with a different type of memory, equally false, but much simpler and nevertheless far less common, i.e. the belief that the liquids were mixed together:

AN (4;11, Method I): *You mixed the green and the yellow in the small glass (C).*—Did I really?—*No, there was only a very little of the yellow at the bottom, like this* (points to *B*). He looks at his drawing with an absorbed expression and adds (for *A*): '*I think I should add as much green to where the yellow was, and the red was put together with the green.*' In other words, cross-decantation had made way for a mixture of liquids.

NIN (6;2, Method I): '*A little of the green was put into the yellow.*'

Some of the subjects who invoked cross-decantation without having a grasp of transitivity (for instance Luc) nevertheless realized that the aim of the decantations was the verification of equivalences. However, in the majority of cases they could see no other purpose in the experiment than the wish to change vessels. Those who thought the liquids were mixed showed an even greater lack of understanding, and Nin, for instance, could see no other reason for the experiment than: 'You wanted to drink the green . . . and afterwards you didn't want to drink it.'

The following subjects merely referred to possible decantations, and did not allow their equalizations to be dominated by the idea of transitivity, and this despite the use of one or more empty vessels:

MAN (5;6, Method II) drew five vessels and marked $C \rightarrow B'$, $B \rightarrow B''$ (irrelevant) and $A \rightarrow C$, but without grasping the purpose of the experiment.

VAN (5;7, Method I) at first wanted to mix the yellow and the green liquids, but after counter-suggestion by the experimenter, added the empty vessels B' ($B' \neq B$), whence she arrived at $B \rightarrow B'$ and $B' \rightarrow B$, $C \rightarrow B'$ and $B' \rightarrow C$, $A \rightarrow B'$, $C \rightarrow A$ and $A \rightarrow C$, and finally $B' \rightarrow A$. For all that, she thought the whole experiment was performed 'to play a little game'.

CLA (7;0, Method II) drew five vessels with $B' = B'' = B$ and marked $B \rightarrow B'$, $C \rightarrow B''$, $A \rightarrow B$, $B \rightarrow A$, $B' \rightarrow B$ and $B'' \rightarrow C$, but merely said: 'I'd have to think to show you how it should be done.'

PAS (6;7, Method II) drew five vessels correctly and marked $A \rightarrow B$ and $B' \rightarrow A$, $C \rightarrow B'$, $B \rightarrow B''$ and $B' \rightarrow B$, which, except for BB'', amounted to a series of reciprocal decantations, in which he saw no other purpose than 'to find out whether we can do it like Monsieur' (the experimenter).

GAB (6;4, Method I) drew four vessels and marked $B \rightarrow B'$, $B' \rightarrow B$, $A \rightarrow B'$, $B' \rightarrow A$, $C \rightarrow B$ and $B' \rightarrow C$, adding: 'It was all done to find out if three of them were as tall as each other but the yellow one (A) was the tallest!'

RUD (7;1, Method I, one hour after presentation) drew seven vessels and marked $C \rightarrow D$, $D \rightarrow A$, and $B \rightarrow A$ (which had already received the contents of D). He made no use at all of B', B'' and D', and concluded: 'All three syrups were put into the three glasses, and they were all the same.' After a week he drew only four vessels, three of which were identical in shape and shown to be filled to the same level in green, red and violet (supplementary colour). The yellow liquid in the long thin vessel A was also filled to the same level, but its base was drawn below that of the three others: We were trying to see if everything was still the same.—And was it? —Yes, all four glasses were filled as high as each other.

These subjects had clearly made progress over the preceding ones for none of them remembered impossible decantations. Nevertheless they had forgotten the experimenter's question about the equalization (question d), and this because they had not grasped the purpose of the decantations and thought that the whole experiment was a kind of game. Those subjects, on the other hand, who remembered the question, made use of the equalization as their operational level permitted and assessed the equality of the liquids accordingly, i.e. irrespective of the shape of the vessel; thus Gab concluded that the yellow vessel was the tallest, and Rud, accepting the equivalence, lowered the base of one of the vessels (*A*) so as to bring its level down to that of the rest.

In brief, the type of memory associated with this pre-operational level goes hand in hand, either with a distortion of the data by condensation, or else with partly correct recall but organized in accordance with the schemata corresponding to the subject's intellectual development.

§4. *Remembrance at intermediate Stage II and at operational Stage III*

Table 11 showed that there was excellent correlation between successful responses during the post-experimental test and a grasp of conservation during the main test, with a slight lead of transitivity over conservation. With more advanced subjects, the responses during the main test can be fitted into an intermediate Stage II, in which there is a rudimentary idea of conservation but very little appreciation of transitivity. There is no contradiction in these facts: in the post-experimental test, transitivity is explicit and the conservation of quantities is implicit (inequality), while, in the main test, the subject concentrates on the equivalences and their conservation, before concluding as to their transitivity. Here are some examples:

JUL (6;5, Method I) drew four vessels and marked $A \to B'$ and $B' \to A$, $B \to B'$ and $B' \to B$, and finally $C \to B'$ and $B' \to C$, which was correct, though BB' was unnecessary. Why did we do all this?—*Was it to see if everything was the same?*—And were they?—*Yes*. How could you tell? *I can't remember*. Hence, there was equalization of the liquids in two vessels at a time, which naturally implies transitivity. Nevertheless, the explicit argument was forgotten.

BER (7;10, Method I) marked the same operations and produced the same responses: What precisely were we trying to find out?—*If it was all the same*. At the first test she doubted the conservation of the liquids, except for *A* and *C* '*because you poured the red* (*C*) *into here* (*B'*) *and it was the same as with the yellow one* (*A*)'. But an hour later, she had the impression that '*you added a little water*' to *C*, and a week later she simply recalled the equalities but offered no justification.

BON (8;7, Method I) was an interesting case, because she denied the equality during the actual presentation, and this despite the decantations into *B'*: '*No, this one* (*A*) *has more than that* (*B'*), *and here* (*C*) *there is less.*' But an hour later, she produced the reciprocal decantations AB', $B'A$ followed by CB', $B'C$, and BB', $B'B$. Why did we do that?—*To see if it's the same in that glass* (*B'*)—And was it?—*Yes, the yellow one* (*A*) *was the same as the red one* (*C*).—Can you explain it?—*I don't know how to*. When the experimenter looked surprised at her change of opinion, Bon added that she had '*thought about it*' between the two sessions, and indeed she made the same remarks a week later and also produced the same reconstruction. She did so again after three months.

LOU (7;9, Method I) was an even more curious case. During the presentation, an hour and, again, a week later, she continued to deny that equal amounts of liquid were contained in the different bottles: *The yellow had more because it was bigger.*—And when we put it there (B′)?—*It was the same* (as in the green vessel B).—And when we put it back into its own glass (A)?—*The yellow one had more.* Six months later, Lou still stuck to her original view but had forgotten the empty vessel B′, so much so that she was forced to revert to cross-decantations (C → B and B → C, simultaneously!). But when she herself handled the vessels again, she discovered the correct operations and concluded: *All three are the same, because when the red was poured in here (B′), it was the same as the green, and when the yellow one was put there (B′), it was the same as well.*—And now? (the vessels A, B and C had been refilled with yellow, green and red liquid).— *The three contain the same amount of drink, because the same thing happened here* (in B′).

MAR (6;11, Method I) progressed from Stage II to Stage III in the course of the experiment: during the first session she denied the equalities despite decantations into B′, but then, quite suddenly, she changed her mind (like Bon, but in the laboratory): *'There is a little bit more in here (A); oh, no, it's the same in both (A and B = B′)'.* .... After a week (and after an hour) she reproduced the correct decantations A → B′, C → B′ and back, without feeling any need to add B → B′. She summed up by saying that *'this shows that all of them are equal'.*

Here now are the responses of several subjects who had reached Stage III:

OP (6;11, Method I) drew the four vessels with A → B′ and vice versa, then C → B′ and vice versa. He concluded straight away that the B and B′ were equal: *'It was done to see if there were as many drops in the two glasses'.*

NIC (7;1, Method II) drew four vessels (an hour after the presentation) and marked B → B′, adding: *'That was to find out if they were equal.'* He explained that A was next poured into B′ and back, and C into B′ and back, to find out *'if there was as much syrup as in that one (B′)'.* A week later: same responses.

PAC (7;3, Method II): *We poured (C) into (B′) and (A) into (B′) and saw they were the same as (B).*

These responses show that, unlike subjects at Stage I, those at Stages II and III no longer produce spectacular memory distortions —the only error to persist in certain cases is the addition of the decantation B → B′ and back, which may be called a simple form of mnemonic generalization.

Here, we must distinguish between two mnemonic planes: that of the figurative elements associated with the experimental material, and that of the significations and arguments that endow the decantations with meaning. Now, the figurative elements were generally grasped by subjects at Stage I, but not the meaning of the empty vessels, which explains the many distortions we mentioned or the description of pointless but possible decantations. The figurative elements, however, spring to life and acquire a general significance as soon as the problem and the argument are remembered. But what precisely is the memory of an argument? Evidently the ability to retrace it in full and not merely to recount it parrotwise. In other words, the memory of the argument is based on the conservation of a schema, the conservation itself reducing to the functioning of that schema.

The reactivation of a schema may lead to a simple consolidation (once the schema is in equilibrium) or an advance (once the subject is on the threshold of a new stage): the responses of Bon and Lou are remarkable instances of this point, and recall our findings in respect of seriation (Chapter 1). Bon changed her ideas on conservation within the space of one hour, and it made little difference that she 'thought about it' between the sessions (for what is the difference between a new reflection and the mnemonic recall of an old argument?): and Lou faithfully repeated her mistaken views six months later, until, during her second reconstruction, she suddenly acquired an operational grasp of the problem.

§5. *Memory changes with time as expressed in drawings and manipulative reconstructions*

The last few cases bring us to our central problem: establishing whether or not mnemonic progress results from the development of the schema on which it is founded. Let us say at once that, when it comes to transitivity, the evidence is far less telling than it was in the case of serial configurations. The reason is, first of all, that no configuration can be directly associated with transitivity, and that the opposition between recognition and recall, to which we have attributed the rôle of catalyst (since, having drawn the series, the child may gain the impression that he does not fully recognize the model in his drawing), cannot exert any influence on what, in the case of transitivity, are purely symbolic representations. Moreover, the stages marking the grasp of transitivity are more spaced out and fewer in number than those involved in the grasp of seriation,[1] so much so that, in order to check their progress, the subjects ought to have been re-examined, not after six, but after ten or even twelve

---

[1] The serial configuration described in Chapter 1 involved ten elements and the transitivity test only four. It is possible that the use of a longer chain ($A = B$; $B = C$; $C = D \ldots$; $J = K$, and hence $A = K$) might have resulted in a greater number of partial advances.

months. Now, for a number of reasons, we could merely bring back twenty-three of the subjects tested by Method I, and then only as early as three or four months after the first sessions. That being the case, no appreciable changes could, of course, be expected.

I. A comparison of the drawings produced during the second session (one hour after presentation) with those produced during the third session (one week later), showed that of twelve pre-operational subjects, five had regressed, five had remained stationary, and two had made progress. At the intermediate and operational stages, by contrast, there was not a single case of regression, three advances, and three stationary cases (whose memories were already correct during the second session). The drawings of the experimental material (the vessels) were equally revealing: omission of the empty vessel and distortions of the material by pre-operational subjects increased from eight to ten between the second and third sessions, and the correct reproductions decreased from four to two, while, at the higher levels, there was a slight improvement on the part of those subjects who had not produced fully accurate drawings (B $\neq$ B') during the second session.

II. Remembrance during the fourth session (three to five months after presentation) calls for a preliminary remark: of the twenty-five subjects who were given the post-experimental test, only five had advanced by one stage (or in the case of Van by two stages) since the last session (Figure 15)—they were Mic, Van, Nob, Lou and another subject not previously mentioned. Lou, as we saw, reconstructed the data correctly during the last manipulative reconstruction, i.e. just before she was given the post-experimental test (fourth session): her memory had, therefore, progressed not so much with time as during the actualization of that particular form of the memory which we call reconstruction—a point to which we shall be returning. As for the other three subjects, they showed progressive advances in recall from the first week onwards:

MIC (5;4) whose cross-decantations at 5;0 we have mentioned, drew a black instead of the green vessel after four months and forgot the yellow vessel. For all that, he now grasped the decantation principle he had failed to appreciate at 5;0; he marked decantations of the red liquid and then of the black liquid into the empty vessel and back (equalization).

VAN (6;1) who at 5;7 had drawn a mixture and thought that all the vessels had been emptied into one another, '*to play a little game*', now drew four vessels straight away, including $B = B'$, and then marked $C \rightarrow B'$ and back, and $B \rightarrow B'$ and back. He too had clearly made great progress since the last session.

111

NOB (6;3) who at 5;11 had drawn synchronous cross-decantations and had thought he could recall them even as he started his reconstruction, now drew the decantations quite unsystematically. All his operations were, however, possible ones and there were no mixtures or cross-decantations.

MON (5;9), though showing no progress during the post-experimental test, nevertheless ceased to draw the cross-decantations he had offered at 5;6. His memory of the basic experiment had therefore advanced.

These subjects all showed memory advances comparable to the improvements we noticed in the case of seriation, and which, like the latter, resulted from the development of the underlying operational schema.

Of the other seventeen subjects (no appreciable operational progress during the post-experimental test or in remembering the basic experiment), twelve produced the same memories after three to five months as they had offered during the second or third sessions, and the memory of five had slipped back. Thus, Mod (6;5) drew three vessels only, one empty, and marked $A \rightleftharpoons C$; while at 6;2 he had drawn a mixture: his was the only case of true regression, not so much due to mnemonic de-structuring as to a loss in mnemonic depth. Duc (7;0) emptied A into B' and then used the empty vessel A to measure B and C—an irrelevant step as far as the basic argument is concerned. Three subjects aged 7;0, 8;11 and 9;0, respectively, produced the correct decantations, but added B $\rightarrow$ B' and back, which was pointless. Their responses thus represented an irrelevant extension or uniformization of the memory.

All in all, those subjects who had not changed operational level in the course of three to five months retained their original memories with minor modifications, while those who had made operational progress also improved their memories of the experiment they had observed.

III. We must now look at manipulative reconstructions of the experimental material, i.e. at a type of memory half-way between recognition and recall: reconstruction obviously involves recognition inasmuch as the subject recognizes the vessels and liquids, but it also constitutes a kind of recall, since the decantations are no longer carried out before the subject but must be resurrected from memory (recall by actions and not by images).

Being an intermediate form of mnemonic behaviour, reconstruction naturally comes much more easily to the child than pure recall or recall by drawings: of the twenty-three subjects examined by Method I eleven produced reconstructions that were superior, and twelve produced reconstructions that were of a comparable level to the drawings they had provided a week earlier; the corresponding figures after three to five months were ten and thirteen. There are two reasons for this advance.

The first is that, in the presence of the experimental material, the subject can no longer ignore the empty vessel B', and its very presence suggests that it is part of the general reconstruction. The second reason, which serves to reinforce the first, is that synchronous cross-decantations are impossible in practice, so that the child is forced, willy-nilly, to make use of the empty vessel. There was, however, one exceptional case of a subject picking up two full vessels and preparing to pour them into each other, though, of course, he had to stop just as soon as he began. Nevertheless, when the vessels A, B and C are not filled to the brim, it is possible to mix part of their contents, but as they perform this operation, the subjects are reminded of the actual model much more so than they are in the case of drawings, which explains the advances we have mentioned.

Hence, the importance of comparing the reconstructions offered after a week with those produced during the fourth and last session. Now, subjects re-examined after three to five months included six cases of progress, two regressions, and fifteen unchanged responses. The regressive cases included Mod, and another subject, aged 6;11, who drew a series of unsystematic decantations but, during the first reconstruction (after a week), showed a complete grasp of transitivity, thanks, no doubt, to a temporary flash of insight, for, after five months, his drawings no less than his reconstructions were of the same level as his earlier responses.

As for the six advances, they must all be attributed to the same mnemonic progress that was at work in the case of recall by drawings (see II). In fact, the same subjects did not necessarily make progress in both spheres, except for those whose drawings improved during the last two sessions, and who immediately afterwards produced the equivalent reconstructions. However, Duc, whose drawings, as we saw, were somewhat backward, rediscovered a system of equivalences in his reconstruction (with the help of B' or of $A \rightarrow B'$); and Sab (7;0) who, during the third session, had simply reconstructed his own drawing, now produced a general equalization.

Now, advances in respect of manipulative reconstructions are something quite other than advances in pure recall. The latter takes place in the course of retention or of spontaneous memory conservation and, unless the memory is reactivated during the interval (which seems unlikely), is bound to result from the development of the associated operational schema. In the case of reconstructions, on the other hand, an additional factor comes into play, namely, the act of recognition. In fact, recognition, while constituting recall by action, is also an operational action: the child reasons while he reconstructs and constantly bears the results of his actions in mind. Reconstruction is therefore more closely bound up with the operational schema than pure recall, and though possible advances over previous reconstruction may originate during the retentive phase, they are mainly accomplished in action, and sometimes exclusively so, as we saw in the case of Lou (end of §4).

Generally speaking, therefore, remembrance is the combined result of mnemonic retention and reconstruction; and reconstruction often goes hand in hand with the reactivation of the underlying operational schema.

CHAPTER SIX

Remembering Associative Operations[1]

In this chapter we shall be discussing the remembrance of a series of operations $A + (B + C) = D$ and $(A' + B') + C' = D' (= D)$, and shall determine to what extent it depends on the subject's grasp of associativity (in the logical sense of the term), with the two series $A = A'$, $B = B'$, $C = C'$ and $D = D'$ (Figure 16) before his eyes. This problem differs from the last (transitivity) in that the latter involved additive compositions of the relations (which happened to be associative as well, a point that did not, however, have to be stressed), while the present experiment calls for additive operations with the objects themselves.

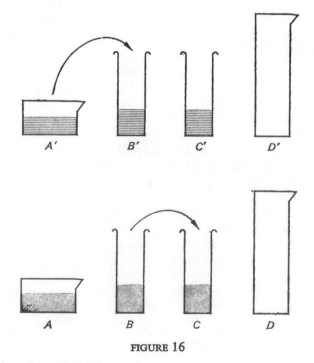

FIGURE 16

[1] In collaboration with P. Mounoud.

The reader may by now have come to take it for granted that our subjects will only remember those aspects of the model which they have fully understood. However, this need not necessarily be so, and, in any case, when we say that a phenomenon is obvious, it does not follow that its explanation is simple or obvious as well. If the memory comprises the entire conservation of the past and its restoration in the present, there is no reason to think that it must confine itself to those aspects of reality that have been understood; it is quite conceivable that a child, having observed a series of peculiar decantations and, above all, having arrived (by two distinct paths) at the unexpected final conclusion that $D = D'$, may remember the general procedure even though he fails to grasp its purpose. If, on the other hand, the memory is inseparable from comprehension, we must still establish in what precise sense the latter affects the former.

According to Woodworth and many others, including particularly C. Florès,[1] the memory manifests itself in the form of recall, recognition, or greater ease in re-learning what has been previously taught (or perceived). Even if we agree with this definition, we still want to know (a) if the reactivation of the past invariably involves the memory, and (b) if everything that has been learned or perceived (no matter for how long) is, in fact, conserved by the memory, and why.

With respect to question (a) we cannot, for instance, argue without further ado that the application of the principle of identity ($A = A'$) involves the memory.[2] With regard to question (b), those authors who treat the memory as an independent 'faculty' for fixing everything that has been perceived or experienced, so as to conserve it with *maximum* efficiency, at least in the subconscious, often explain forgetfulness in terms of utility: though the memory records all relevant data, it rejects whatever has not been understood as so much useless lumber. Now, associativity itself is completely 'useless' in the form in which we are presenting it in the present experiment (though not in the case of displacements, where it provides a useful explanation of 'detours'): it is simply a deductive consequence of the conservation of $A + B + C = D$. In any case, we have to establish whether or not usefulness is a measure of the frequency of use and recall, or whether it refers to the internal workings of the organizing schemata, i.e. of schemata that are conserved independently of the memory.

[1] 'Memory' in P. Fraisse and J. Piaget (eds): *Experimental psychology*, vol. 4, *Learning and Memory*, Routledge & Kegan Paul, 1970.
[2] Young subjects assume that while they themselves preserve their identity as they grow up, plants or crystals do not. They also do not admit that a square turned through an angle of 45°, preserves its identity. See *Études d'Épistémologie génétique*, vol. 24, *Épistémologie et psychologie de l'identité*, Presses Universitaires de France, 1968.

Our second problem is that of temporal succession. In general, memories are recorded in temporal order, and we want to know whether the conservation of memories also involves the conservation of their order of succession, or whether this is reconstructed, after the event, by an inferential process based on the spatial, causal or logical order, etc. The experiment we have chosen involves a series of decantations, and hence, a particular temporal order. Does this factor constitute an additional obstacle, or does it aid the memory? To settle this issue, we also performed a control experiment (Figure 17), once again involving the operation $(A + B) + C = A + (B + C)$, but no temporal sequence other than the order of the manipulations (in contrast to the physical processes illustrated by Figure 16).

We shall also be looking at the re-learning process. Unlike seriation and transitivity, associativity involves structures that cannot

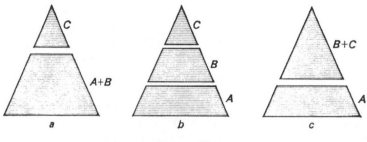

FIGURE 17

easily be fixed in the memory (especially in the case of the model illustrated by Figure 16) and consequently deteriorate with time. For that reason, we brought the original model back immediately after the six-month test, and performed a further memory test a week later. As we shall see, the results proved to be greatly superior not only to those obtained during the six-month test but also to those we were offered a week after the original presentation. In other words, we had come across the third of the manifestations commonly attributed to the memory (the others being recognition and recall), namely accelerated re-learning, Now, in the case of associativity, the problem is far from simple, and, hence, all the more interesting: mnemonic progress associated with re-learning is not, in effect, quantitative or related to the number of elements retained by the memory, but qualitative or organizational. To explain why re-presentations should lead to a better organization of the memory than the original presentation, we cannot simply assume that new 'traces' are added to, or superposed on, the old: rather must we invoke the

117

contrast between the original (or degraded) memories and the un-expectedly revealed features of the new presentation. We are not, therefore, dealing with cumulative associations, but with the assimila-tion of the new presentation, i.e. with the development of the schemata responsible for the assimilation of the first presentation, and with the co-ordination of the new schema with the schema constructed during the original contact with the model. This brings us back to the question of the relationship between the memory and the intelligence, but seen in a new light: the re-learning process.

For a better understanding of what follows, the reader should bear in mind that, while transitivity is an instrument for constructing or discovering new relations ($A < C$ if $A < B$ and $B < C$), associativity is simply the expression of internal coherence or conservation. It is implicit in all forms of conservation in which at least three terms can be distinguished, and these the child employs with perfect assurance: he knows perfectly well, for instance, that if he is handed two rings, one red and one white, together with a white square, the total set remains the same no matter whether it is divided into 'rings and the square' or into 'whites and the red'. But once associativity is taken out of its over-all context (classification or conservation, etc.), as we have done deliberately here the better to present it as an operation or a series of isolated compositions, it becomes stripped of its functional significance for those subjects who are concerned with discovery rather than verification. As a result, there is a retardation in operationality, and a mnemonic problem quite distinct from the one we discussed in the last chapter.

§1. *Methods used*

I. Using the material illustrated in Figure 16, we applied Method I during three (or, with some subjects, during five) sessions.

(A) In the first session, the child is given a brief description of the material, and his attention is drawn quite particularly to the equalities $A = A'$, $B = B'$, $C = C'$ and $D = D'$, and also to the fact that each pair of vessels contains the same amount of liquid.[1] Next, the demonstrator pours the contents of B into C and A' into B' (inequalities) and says to the child: 'If I were to pour these liquids (A and C) into that glass (D), and these (B' and C') into here (D'), would there be the same amount of syrup in these two (D and D') or would one of them contain more or less than the other?' The child is asked to justify his answers.

Next, A and C are poured into D, and the question is repeated so as to elicit a further anticipation: 'And now, if I were to pour these (B' and C')

---

[1] The vessels A–D are filled with red liquid, and the vessels A'–D' with blue liquid.

into that one (D'), will we have the same amount of syrup as here (D) or will one hold more and the other less?'

B' and C' are now poured into D', and the final equality $D = D'$ is pointed out to the child, who is asked to justify it.

(B) During the second session, held a week later, the child is asked to make a memory-drawing of the material and to recall the decantations. Once these memories have been produced, the material is brought out, and the child is asked for a reconstruction of the decantations. During both parts of this session the child is asked the same questions: 'What were you asked to do?' and 'Why are these two (liquids in D and D') equal?'

(C) Some six months later the subject is brought back (if possible) and given the same instructions as in (B).

(D) Some of the subjects are brought back for a fourth session one day after the third (C), and are shown the same material and decantations as during the first session. The same questions are asked.

(E) One week after (D), the subjects are invited to a fifth and last session and asked to produce the same memory-drawings and to answer the same questions as in (B) and (C) (explanations followed by manipulations).

A few subjects were tested by a slightly different method (IA): in addition to the vessels shown in Figure 16 an elongated vessel P was placed between A and B, and a shorter but more capacious vessel Q between B' and C'. A and B were then poured into P; B', C' into Q; C and P into D; and $A' + Q$ into D'.

II. The triangle test illustrated in Figure 17 (Method II) involved the following procedure:

During the first session the demonstrator presents the experimental material, i.e. the three sets a, b and c painted blue, and then three yellow test elements A', B' and C' congruent to the elements A, B and C of the triangular set b.

The subject is now asked if it is possible to cover the figure a with the test elements, and after giving his answer he is asked to check for himself.

Second anticipation: the same procedure for the triangular set c.

Finally, the subject is asked if the test elements A', B' and C' could be used to cover the figures a, b and c and whether or not they can therefore be called equivalent.

During the second session (held a week later) the subject is asked to recall and draw what he saw in the first session, and then for a manipulative reconstruction. To that end, he is handed fifteen elements, representing three copies each of the elements A, B, C, $A + B$ and $B + C$ (Figure 17). The elements are presented in irregular order and the subject proceeds to a reconstruction of the figures a, b and c.

Some subjects were tested by Method IIA. Here, the first session was devoted to purely figurative descriptions, and no reference was made to the underlying argument or the associative operations. The child was shown a piece of cardboard with a figure 2 pasted on, and then a second, identical piece of cardboard, and was asked to look at them carefully and say if they were similar (this serves to fix his attention). If he said that they were not, the first piece of cardboard was brought out again (in fact all our subjects granted the identity straight away). The second session (held a week later) was as in Method II, but of course without anticipations or equalizations.

§2. *Results of Method I (liquids) after a week*

The only remarkable results obtained by Method I, which are in complete conformity with our earlier findings, point to a very close correlation between the memory and intellectual understanding, and to a clear difference between material reconstructions and recall by word of mouth or by drawings.

I. The memory types we encountered fitted into five distinct levels, which, by and large, proved to correspond to differences in age.

At Level I (four to five years) there is a broad grasp of the experimental set-up, reflected in either incomplete drawings of the vessels (two series of two full ones and one empty one, or two series of three full ones) or else in complete but essentially figurative copies (especially with Method IA, in which the subjects often draw two series of five glasses each, but without bothering about P and Q). The vessels in any one series may all be given different shapes, though sometimes two of them are shown to be identical. The decantations are performed in any order and the two series are confused (thus Per [5;11] poured B into C, C into D', B' into C' and C' into D'; A into A' and finally A' into D; while Pa [5;2] poured A into C, B into C, B' into C' and A' into C', completely ignoring the vessels D and D'). The final equalization $D = D'$ (or in the absence of D, $C = C'$) is often mentioned in the course of the verbal description, and also the intention of 'seeing if they are the same', but this does not necessarily mean that these subjects have a grasp of conservation (a point to which we shall be returning), and may merely reflect their appreciation that $D = D'$—thus Fab (5;6) explained: '*It's because these two are both the same size.*'

Level IA marks an advance on Level I, in that the vessels in both series have been ordinated, with the elements A–D and A'–D' (or AC and $A'C'$) equated two at a time. But the decantations remain incomplete and un-co-ordinated. Thus, Fu (5;3) drew A' above A; B' in front of B and D' next to D, explaining that B' was poured into D'; B into D; A' into D' and A into D.

At Level II, by contrast, the decantations are performed in the correct temporal sequence. The vessels are ordinated as at Level IA (for instance, C next to C', B next to B' and A next to A') but do not yet constitute two distinct and corresponding rows. The number of elements is often too small, and this because the subjects are more interested in the decantations and their order than in producing correct figurative copies. The proportions of the vessels, on the other hand, are more generally appreciated. Thus, Car (5;9) offered A into D', followed by B' into D'; and A into D followed by B into D (no C or C').

Level III combines the following two characteristics: (1) the two series

AD and $A'D'$ are shown to be in one-to-one correspondence (but not the series of pairs AA', BB', etc.); and (2) the decantations are complete but unco-ordinated: A into D, followed by B into D and C into D, A' into D' etc., or even (type IIIA): A into B, B into C and C into D, A' into B', etc.

Level IV is characterized by an emerging grasp of particular associations: A into B and B into D, then C separately into D or A separately into D; B into C and C into D. But these associations are identical for both series, which shows that the subject has not yet grasped, or remembered, the meaning of the associative composition $(A + B) + C = A + (B + C)$.

At Level V, finally, there is a full grasp of the latter, and adequate remembrance of the original presentation.

II. Now, the existence of these mnemonic levels points, first of all, to a highly systematic advance of material reconstructions on pure recall. Thus, of the thirty-five subjects examined by Method I, twenty-three had advanced from one level to the next (I to II, II to III, etc.) in respect of their reconstructions, eleven had stayed at the same level (1 at Level II, 6 at Levels III and IV, and 4 at Level V), which was only to be expected from these more advanced subjects; and only one had regressed (a subject at Level IV who, during the reconstruction, forgot the association $(A + B) + C$).

This advance is easily explained by the fact that all the vessels are set out before the subject, who need only arrange them in spatial order to reconstruct what decantations he remembers. The only surprising thing is that the advance should not have been even more striking than it proved to be in fact.

Here are a few examples, beginning with an advance from Level IA to III: Fab (5;6) drew six vessels in a single row: C, A, C', B, A' and B', and suggested decantations of the smaller vessels into the bigger vessels C and C'. During the reconstruction, he systematically poured A, B and C into D, and A', B' and C' into D'.

Bert (6;0) had recall of type II: D, A, B, B', A', D' with decantations of A into D, B into D; and A' and B' into D', while his reconstruction was similar to Fab's (Level III).

Klu (8;1) produced a drawing of type II to III (six vessels) and showed that she had a glimmering of the correspondence $A : A'$, and $B : B'$, and separately of $C : C'$. She poured A and B into C, and then A' and B' into D'. Her reconstruction, on the other hand, showed that she was beginning to grasp the idea of associativity (Level IV): A' into B' and B' into D', followed by C' separately into D'; A into B, B into D, and C into D.

Several other subjects had similar reactions, thus demonstrating that the presence of the vessels served them as a reminder that A–C or A'–C' were not poured into D or D' one at a time, but that some of them were associated in pairs. It is, however, worth stressing that none of our subjects tested by Method I or Method IA, advanced from Level IV (identical associations in the two series $A–D$, and $A'–D'$) to Level V (correct associations $[A + B] + C$ and $A' + [B' + C']$) when going on from pure recall to manipulative reconstruction. In other words, all the subjects who had grasped the final equalization remembered it even while drawing the vessels, etc., while those who had not, also failed to remember it during their reconstructions. Here, we have a further pointer to the close relationship between the memory and the schemata of the intelligence.

III. The second conclusion we can draw from these results is the existence of a remarkable correlation between mnemonic levels and operational stages. This correlation is the more interesting in that it is not directly bound up with the developing grasp of associativity, but bears directly on the conservation of liquids. In fact, at the end of the second session (one week after the presentation) all our subjects were given a supplementary test of their grasp of the conservation of liquids so as to determine their intellectual level. There was no need for a supplementary associativity test, since the memory itself showed whether or not associativity had been grasped.

The thirty-five subjects tested by Method I proved to be of three types in respect of their responses to the supplementary test: clear non-conservation (nine 4- to 5-year-old subjects and several 6-year-olds); intermediate responses (eight subjects, including one or two from 4;5 to 5 years and the rest from 6 to 7 years); and clear grasp of conservation (eighteen subjects, most of them from 7 to 9 years and two or three from 5 to 6 years).

In respect of recall, all subjects without a grasp of conservation were almost exclusively at Level I (two cases at Level II); most subjects at the intermediate stage were at Level II (one transitional case from II to III); and the eighteen subjects who had a grasp of conservation were mostly at Levels III to V (one was at Level II to III but closer to III). It would therefore seem that, in the case of pure recall (i.e. without restimulation by perception of the model), our subjects do not remember the over-all decantations (as distinct from the 'associations' which they appreciate from Level III onwards), unless impelled to do so by the grasp of conservation. In fact, without that grasp, the complete meaning of decantations must remain obscure: either the subjects think, like Fab, that the liquids poured into D and D' must be equivalent, since the vessels are identical, or else they do not anticipate a final equalization. Just as soon, however, as they have mastered the idea of conservation, they also remember the entire set of vessels used in the experiment.

The differences between subjects who have not grasped the idea of conservation (mnemonic Level I) and those at the intermediate stage (type II recall) suggest that the first glimmerings of conservation arouse the subject's interest in the temporal order of the decantations he is asked to remember. Here we have one indication among many that the memory does not automatically lead to the ordination of time unless impelled to do so for causal, logical or other special reasons.

In respect of the reconstructions, which were almost invariably superior to pure recall, since, as we saw, the material was once again placed in front of the subject, it is no longer the ability to repeat the original decantations that distinguishes subjects with a grasp of conservation from those at the two previous operational stages: subjects without a grasp of conservation can have recall of type II, and there were even three cases with recall of type III, and a further three cases who proved to be of type II to III. Moreover, nearly all subjects in the intermediate group proved to have recall of type III (except for two cases half-way between types II and III); and of the eighteen subjects with a firm grasp of conservation, twelve reached (or remained at) Levels IV and V, as against six who remained at Level III.

It follows that, in the case of reconstructions, the new factor introduced by the full grasp of conservation is either an understanding of the associative composition, or, at the age of seven to eight years (most of the six cases at Level III were five to six years old) a centring of the attention on the associations AB or BC.

Now, as we mentioned earlier, though associativity is one of the laws of additive composition when more than two elements are involved, it does not constitute a principle of discovery but only one of regulation or coherence; a subject with a grasp of conservation based on reversible, additive compositions may fail to be aware of the latter while making use of them in practice. Hence, it is only to be expected that they should go unnoticed during the original presentation and that they should not be remembered until after the over-all equalizations. It is all the more interesting to find that the only subjects with a stable grasp of conservation managed to remember one or both of the 'associations' AB or BC.

§3. The results obtained with Method I after six months (recall and reconstruction) and the results of a new presentation followed by a third test of recall

We were able to bring back some of our subjects and to examine them during sessions three to five (Method I) as described in §1.

I. Our first remarkable discovery, which was in full accordance with the preceding analysis, was that there is a more or less general deterioration of the memory in the course of six months: at the end of this period, nine of our thirteen subjects produced inferior descriptions and drawings (drop by one level), three remained at the same level, and only one advanced from Level IA to Level II. The most striking fact was that the two 8- to 9-year-old subjects who had been at Level V one week after the presentation had dropped to Level IV, i.e. they now believed that they could remember identical associations in the two series AD and $A'D'$, thus forgetting the correct associative composition they had offered one week after the presentation.

When compared with the almost general progress in seriation and with the partial but significant advances (because they are linked to operational progress) in transitivity, this deterioration is instructive: since associativity is not a means of discovery, it does not constitute an operational schema by itself, but only an implicit aspect of schemata polarized in other ways. Even those subjects who understood the significance of the associative composition preformed before their eyes, and remembered it a week later, did not therefore have the same reasons to retain this memory for a further six months as they had in the case of seriation or transitivity: the schema on which the memory relies had not become differentiated, nor had there been a construction of a special schema. We may therefore put it that in the particular case of associativity, the deterioration of the memory constitutes a negative counter-proof of our earlier interpretation, i.e. that memory retention is dependent on the presence of operational or action schemata which conserve themselves by virtue of their own function. What is conserved in the present case is, in effect, exclusively bound up with the conservation schemata (or, in pre-operational subjects, with the most elementary action schemata: invariant decantations, etc.) and not with the differentiated schemata needed for the construction of a stable memory—such schemata have not yet been constructed.

II. The second result worth mentioning is equally obvious: after six months, just as one week after the presentation, manipulative reconstructions tend to be superior to drawings or verbal descriptions. Thus, of thirteen cases, six produced superior reconstructions, six produced reconstructions of equal quality, and only one offered a Level III drawing that was slightly superior to his reconstruction (Level II to III).

Nevertheless, a comparison of the reconstructions offered after six months with those offered after a week showed a deterioration comparable to, though less accentuated than, that found in the case of pure recall: seven drops in level and six equalities.

III. The most interesting aspect of these re-examinations was the effect of a new presentation of the vessels and decantations (one day after the previous session) on a further recall by drawings and descriptions (one week later).

Of the thirteen subjects re-examined, two had no previous grasp of conservation and three were at the intermediate level (operational Stage II). Now, after the third and last recall, four of these five showed that they had acquired a grasp of conservation, and only one continued to uphold non-conservation. The progress of the first four may well have been spontaneous, but it is quite possible that the experiments gave them an additional impetus.

For the rest, the results of the new test (one week after the new presentation) were as follows: of the thirteen subjects, three maintained the level they had reached during their first recall (1 type IV and 2 type V), while all the others advanced by at least one level and sometimes by two (from III to V). In other words, after the deterioration mentioned in Sections I and II, a new presentation led to a marked advance in ten out of the eleven subjects below Level V.

To explain these results, we must first of all establish whether or not they are comparable to those associated with the classic re-learning situation. Here, if a subject is set a task involving a series of trials and errors, he may well manage to correct his errors after n attempts under carefully defined conditions; once this performance has been forgotten, and the test is repeated (re-learning), it is often found that $n - m$ trials will produce the same result. The obvious conclusion is that memory 'traces' of the first series of trials smoothed the path for the second. In the particular case of our associativity experiments, the first learning process was terminated when the subject still committed errors while, during the second, that number had decreased or vanished.

Now, the special feature of our experiments was that, before the re-learning situation, there was only a single presentation lasting five minutes in all, and giving rise to recall of level N a week later. After a further six months, that recall had dropped to level $N - Y$. Then, a week after a second (and final) presentation for a further five minutes, came a third recall, which proved to be of Level $N + Z$. How is it possible that so much progress should have been made with so few 'traces'?

In the case of seriation, progress (from the first to the second recall, without a fresh presentation) could be simply explained by mnemonic reliance on a developing schema and by the fact that, during the first recall, the contrast between what the subject managed to put down on paper and his recognition (which, at the very least, revealed a gap between what he had been doing and the forgotten model) served to focus his attention on the developing schema.

Now, in the case of associativity, though the subject lacks a schema of comparable importance (the only schemata found at the age levels under consideration are conservation schemata; differentiated associativity does not emerge until later, and is not fully consolidated until about the age of eleven to twelve years), two similar phenomena nevertheless occur.

The first emerges during material reconstructions, both after a week and, again, after six months. In either case, the subject has just produced a drawing and a verbal description which he may consider satisfactory or not: if, at this point, the vessels are brought out once more and he is asked to reconstruct the actual decantations, he will, as we have seen, make corrections and improvements which, in fact, constitute the beginnings of a schematic construction. This schema, and we cannot stress this fact enough, lacks the functional importance of the schema involved in seriation, and this explains why there should be a deterioration instead of an improvement in recall or reconstruction after six months. For all that, the schema is present throughout, albeit in rudimentary form, and hence capable of affecting the responses.

The second analogous phenomenon appears during the second presentation of the decantations (fourth session): this presentation, one day after the third session (second recall and reconstruction), is not, in fact, a mere repetition, as if the model had been presented twice during the first session. There is the additional, and fundamentally important, fact that the subject, having played an active part in the previous reconstructions (the last one just one day earlier) assimilates the new presentation to his own activity, and thus finds the solution to problems he was previously unable to resolve. In other words, the new presentation makes an essential contribution to the early construction of a schema, and it is the progress of this schema which explains the final progress $N + Z$.

Clearly, therefore, no matter how different its external manifestations or tangible results, the remembrance of associative processes has something in common with the remembrance of seriations and transitive manipulations: in all three cases, the 'traces' responsible for the final advance $N + Z$ are nothing else than an evolving schema —memories can only be conserved if they are attached to that. However, since, in the case under consideration, the schema is still under construction, there is deterioration instead of progress during the last recall of a particular presentation, while a new presentation leads to a general reconstruction which, in turn, entails a systematic advance over prior reconstructions or recall.

§4. *Method II* (*triangles*) *and results after a week*

I. The main importance of the second type of associativity test is that it is relatively simpler than the decantation test: no temporal sequences are involved in the experimental set-up. The reader may think that there is a simpler explanation, namely that an associative composition of areas is more figurative than a decantation, since the latter involves transformations that call for an operational interpretation. In fact, the two explanations come back to the same thing. Thus, each vessel that has been filled or emptied represents a figurative state: the only difference, therefore, between decantation and the association of areas is that, in the latter, the three figures *a, b* and *c* (Figure 17) can be combined in any order, which makes it possible to remember the figurative states independently of the order of the manipulations, while, in the case of the liquids, the state of the vessels *A, B, C* and *D* (Figure 16) is determined by decantations involving a temporal order, which helps to focus attention on the transformations.

Another interesting feature of the new test springs from the contrast between the two methods applied: with Method II, the subjects are asked to justify their conclusions (equivalence of the three areas despite differences in their composition) and with Method IIA they are simply asked to look at the material so as to fix it in their memories. Now, all those who find it hard to believe in the 'assimilation' of data to schemata will be surprised to hear that the results of both procedures proved to be almost identical. This, it may be argued, is simply because Method II is based exclusively on figurative impressions and because the subject's subsequent justifications do not involve the memory. That is certainly a possible interpretation, and we shall be looking into it more fully. But there is another, equally coherent explanation, namely, that the inspection of the figures demanded in Method IIA leads to assimilation to the same schemata (equivalence or non-equivalence of the whole and the sum of its parts; conservation of the whole despite different associations of the corresponding parts *A, B* and *C* of the three figures, etc.) and that the same is true when subjects tested by Method II are asked for their anticipations (first session).

II. After these preliminary remarks, we can go on to distinguish four successive levels of reconstruction and recall reflecting the subjects' average age and, moreover, corresponding in part to the results of the anticipation test administered during the first session (equivalence of the three main areas).

Level I is characterized by the relative inability to differentiate between the whole and its parts,[1] i.e. the three triangles look more or less alike and undivided. Thus Dup (4;10), when tested one week after the presentation, drew three undivided triangles one of which appeared to be slightly flatter than the others. (He explained: '*We saw two figures and hid them under the yellow figures.*')

Level IA differs from Level I in that it involves symbolic sub-division of the figures. Thus Cha (4;6) produced three large triangles, and three sets of extra sides representing internal or external triangular structures (Figure 18A), explaining the original divisions with '*There were lines inside.*' This interesting response shows that, at this level, the idea of additive composition has not yet been grasped; as a result, the child offers a partitive composition of his own (topological surround). Ste (4;1) drew three unequal triangles (remembrance of the parts but reproduced as the whole) and gave a symbolic representation of the divisions by drawing a series of lines underneath his main figures (Figure 18B).

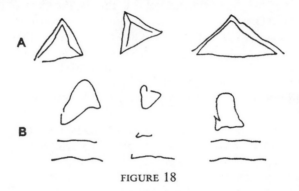

FIGURE 18

At Level II there is progress in respect of the partitive composition: the three triangles are either divided by lines or else represented as discontinuous parts (as in the model). But the parts are identical for the figures *a* and *c* and sometimes even for the three figures *a*, *b* and *c*. Thus Zel (4;6) drew three equal trapezia surmounted (at intervals) by three equal triangles. He, too, had failed to grasp the purpose of the experiment: *We were supposed to put the yellow on the blue.*—What did they look like?—*They were flat below* (= trapezia).

Subjects at Level III remember that the triangles were divided up in distinct ways. Here we can distinguish two sub-levels, without apparent correspondence to the levels of intellectual development. Level IIIA is characterized by drawings showing the wrong number of parts. Thus Fran (6;6) produced two triangles divided into three parts and one triangle divided into two parts, but had obviously grasped at least part of the purpose of the experiment: '*We were trying to see if we could make blue triangles with the yellow bits*'. . . . Subjects of type IIIB, on the other hand,

[1] The whole may be a simple juxtaposition of parts assembled into a 'figural collection'.

128

offer drawings with the correct number of parts, but wrongly put together. Thus Sou (5;1) drew two triangles bisected in identical ways, and one triangle divided into three parts, but merely remembered that *'there were tents and we saw where the lines were'*.

Subjects at Level IV have correct recall: two triangles divided into two in distinct ways, and one triangle divided into three parts.

III. Let us now compare levels of recall I to IV with the subjects' own justifications. The reader will recall that, during the original presentation, the child is asked if he thinks the triangle a can be covered with the three control elements, if the same can be done with the triangle c; and finally if the three areas are equivalent. There are three distinct types of response: α) Refusal to grant the congruence for a and c; β) appreciation of the congruence in one case but not in the other; and γ) appreciation of the congruence in both cases and hence equalization of the three triangles.

Now, at Level I, there are more responses of type α than of type β, and not a single type γ. At Level II, type γ has disappeared, but there is a greater number of types β than of types α. The same thing happens at Level III, except that one subject aged 7;2 and approaching Level IV produced a type γ response. At Level IV, finally, all the subjects offer the correct anticipations (type γ) and some of them also give correct explanations of the associative composition: thus, Por, when only 6;4 (Level III) though wrong in his anticipations, came to the correct conclusion when trying out figure c: *It's the same thing as* (a). —Why?—*It's one large bit* ($A + B$) *together with a single piece* (C).— So?—*They are the same.* At Level IV, Rus (7;2) produced the same arguments, but he did so as part of his anticipations: 'We can put (A) and (B) on that one ($A + B$), and (C) here (figure a). With that one (figure c) we can put (B) and (C) on ($B + C$) and (A) over here.'

IV. All in all, therefore, the quality of these memories (Levels I to IV) accords better with the level of the understanding (anticipations α–γ), than it does with Method I. On the other hand, and evidently for the same reason, the difference in level between recall and material reconstructions is much smaller in the case of triangular areas than it is in the case of decantations (Method I). In fact, of the forty-seven subjects examined, thirty-six, i.e. roughly four-fifths, did not change level when going on from pure recall to reconstruction; two regressed (from Level III to Level II or II–III), and only nine made progress. Nor was their progress spectacular except in five cases (from I to III or from II to III or even to IV). The remaining four subjects made slight progress (from II–III to III or from III–IV to IV). In other words, the visual inspection of the figures during the presentation (first session) and above all the anticipations followed by a verification (covering the figures *a*, *b* and *c* with the control elements A', B' and C' associated in different ways) already constitutes a virtual reproduction. Moreover, since the resulting visual memory-image is bound up with an activity, it follows that the material reconstruction with *A*, *B* and *C* adds very little to what has or has not been grasped during the original presentation and the subsequent recall.

Remarkably enough, Method IIA, in which no anticipations or verifications involving rudimentary manipulations were asked for, produced precisely the same results: of twenty-three subjects, only four made slight progress (IA to II, or II to II–III, etc,) as they proceeded to the reconstruction of the model, while the nineteen remaining subjects offered recall and reconstructions of the same level.

V. We are now ready to look at the main problem: the quasi-identity of the results obtained by such distinct methods as II and IIA. We have been stressing the close connection between figurative memories and the underlying operational schema in the case of associativity no less than in seriation and transitivity, and the reader may have concluded that this is only to be expected, since the very presentation of the experimental material involves a measure of conceptual analysis (except with Method I as used in the simple and *M*-shaped seriation tests). However, with Method IIA as applied in the present experiment, nothing of the kind happens: a purely visual configuration is presented to the subject, who may admittedly grasp the additive compositions, but he is by no means impelled to do so in the way that, say, he is forced to take cognizance of the underlying operations when inspecting a well-ordered series. What, then, is the explanation of the identity of the results obtained by Methods IIA and those obtained by Method II?

We have already seen (in section I of this chapter) that there are two possible answers: either the responses obtained by Method II are purely figurative, or else the visual inspection of the figures involved in Method IIA goes hand in hand with the assimilation of the data to the operational schemata. In the second case, it is the conservation of the latter which is responsible for the same mnemonic recall as occurs with Method II.

(1) It is quite impossible to maintain that the responses elicited by Method II are of an exclusively figurative kind, because they point to an obvious correlation of the qualitative level of the memory and the intellectual level, as determined by the anticipations (see section III of this chapter).

(2) As for the responses elicited by Method IIA, the fact that they reflect the same mnemonic levels (pure recall and manipulative reconstruction) and fit into the same age groups cannot be fortuitous; it shows that the visual presentation alone does not result in a uniform mnemonic imprint but leads to a gradual structuring of reality. And since this process develops quickly and noticeably with age, it cannot be governed by the laws of perception but must be subject to the laws governing either the construction of the drawings or the under-standing. Now, the 'intellectual realism' of young children, as its name suggests, is dominated by notional interpretations, and we have shown elsewhere that the transition from intellectual to visual realism corresponds to the evolution of geometric intuitions, from the topological (cf. the case of Cha at Level IB) to the metrical and projective.[1] As for the evolution of the comprehension of the figures presented, it is reflected as clearly in the results of Method IIA as in those of Method II: at Level IV, for example, Gil (8;5) said of the three triangles: 'They are all the same size, but they aren't cut up in the same way'—a clear intuitive and visual expression of the grasp of associativity.

In short, it is quite wrong to claim that, since the memory is essentially figurative, i.e. a signifying image, it cannot have a con-ceptualized signification: to say, with Gil, that the triangles are 'cut up' in different ways, is tantamount to saying that they constitute so many states resulting from transformations, and it is precisely be-cause these young children have not yet become aware of the latter that their memory is incomplete and distorted. All our memories, no matter how trivial, isolable or individualized, involve a host of spatial, temporal, causal and other relations, and a whole hierarchy of planes of reality (relations between the self and objects), so much so that they cannot be divorced from schemata too complex to be fully grasped. The short examples we have used to illustrate the results of Method IIA are thus highly typical of what happens in everyday mnemonic processes, and make it clear that, whenever we think we have remembered a simple, isolated fact or event, that memory, however particularized, could only have been fixed and con-served as part of an over-all organization, the major part of which is admittedly in constant flux, but also includes a stable nucleus based on the general co-ordination of our actions, and hence on our operational schemata.

VI. With regard to the remembrance of the triangular figures after six months, there was one case of clear progress in reconstruction at

[1] See J. Piaget and B. Inhelder: *The Child's Conception of Space*, Routledge & Kegan Paul, 1967, Chapter II.

8;1 (during the second session this subject had twice offered the combination 1–2 and 3, and once the reconstruction 1, 2, 3; after six months he produced the correct reconstruction). There were several stationary cases among successful (Level IV) or nearly-successful subjects (Level IIIA). As for the remainder, i.e. the great majority of those re-examined, it was extremely difficult to say whether or not they had made progress or regress, since their responses were significantly dominated by a fairly well-developed schematism which took different directions from one subject to the next. Thus, Phi (4;1)

FIGURE 19

produced a figure consisting of arcs, a rectangle and a square (Figure 19): his drawing could be considered a kind of generalization based on the comparison and differentiation of the elements. Another subject (Ber 6;2) drew one of the divided triangles together with a

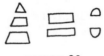

FIGURE 20

rectangle and two semi-circles (Figure 20): his drawing may be described as the generalization of a partition schema. A third subject (Cla 6;6) drew a kind of pyramid topped by a triangle: his was a generalization of the serial composition of the parts (Figure 21).

FIGURE 21

Younger subjects, by contrast, do not invariably or exclusively tend towards schematizations; they are also drawn towards the representation of empirical shapes (mountains, houses, etc.).

In these circumstances, it is exceedingly hard to decide whether or not the reconstructions are superior to the drawings: the drawings can stray far afield from the original shapes, while the material offered for purposes of reconstruction consists of the latter alone. But with those subjects whose drawings recorded the original shape, the advance of the reconstruction on the drawings was clear: one subject at 6;6 whose drawings represented three complete triangles (two small ones of equal size and one big one) produced three clearly divided triangles during his reconstruction, and there were many similar cases.

In sum, we could detect no difference between the responses elicited by Methods II and IIA respectively.

§5. *Recognition of triangles after an hour*

Forty-four new subjects were given the triangle test for the purpose of evaluating their powers of recognition one hour after the original presentation. To that end, a plate with twelve figures, in three columns of four sets of figures each, was presented to them (see Figure 22). The reader will see that No. 11 is the correct replica of the model, and that No. 12, too, is correct except for the re-positioning of the elements *a* and *c*. Nos. 8 and 10 represent a heterogeneous division of *a*, *b* and *c*. Nos. 4, 5 and 7 represent symmetrical shapes, Nos. 1 and 6 are undivided triangles, and Nos. 2–3 include one triangle divided into four parts.

The subjects were asked to look at all the figures carefully, and then to make their choice. Once they had done so, they were asked to select from among the remaining figures those which bore the closest and those which bore the least resemblance to the original, and to continue until all the figures had been chosen. They were then asked to justify or explain their answers. Finally, they were offered all the figures they had chosen as the best copies of the original model, and asked to make a final choice.

The subjects were divided into two groups. Those in Group A were given the recognition test one hour after the original presentation by Method IIA as described in §§1 and 4, and then asked for a memory-drawing and, finally, for a reconstruction. Those in Group B were asked to produce a drawing first, then to take the recognition test, and, finally, to make new drawings and to proceed to a reconstruction. The reason for having the second group was, of course, that it enabled us to analyse possible failures of recognition due to the influence of the schemata proper to pure recall.

The responses were classified by mnemonic level (see §4) and not by age or level of recognition, our main purpose being a detailed comparison of the latter with the stages in the development of the schemata proper to recall.

Level IA (relative lack of differentiation of the whole and its parts and approximate equivalence of the triangles *a*, *b* and *c*): eight 4-year-old subjects made a final choice of Nos. 8–12 as the best figures; in their

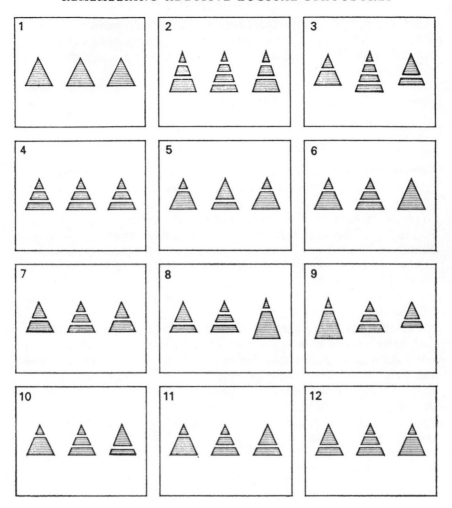

FIGURE 22

initial choice, six subjects also chose Nos. 8–12; one chose No. 5 (symmetry) and another No. 6. No appreciable difference between Groups A and B could be detected.

Level IB (beginnings of more or less symbolic differentiation of the parts): four 4- to 5-year-old subjects made an intial choice of Nos. 10 and 11, and one chose the symmetrical No. 7, but all five (groups A and B) made a final choice of Nos. 3 and 4, which showed that the comparisons involved had helped to degrade their level of recognition.

Level II (clear differentiation of the parts, but *a* symmetrical to *c*). At this level there was a general deterioration of recognition: three subjects in Group A made an initial choice of Nos. 2, 3 or 7, and a final choice of Nos.

4, 7 and 9; three subjects in Group B made an initial choice of Nos. 5, 7 and 8 and a final choice of No. 7. There was a marked tendency to select symmetrical shapes (Nos. 4, 5 and 7).

Level IIIA (triangles divided up in different ways but errors in respect of the number of sections). The initial choice (Groups A and B) was No. 6 (one case) and Nos. 10 and 11 (four cases) and the final choice No. 7 (one case) and No. 8 (four cases), all aged from five to six years.

Level IIIB (almost correct). Eleven subjects (from 5;0 to 6;0 but mostly nearer to 6;0) made Nos. 10, 11 and 12 their initial and final choices.

Level IV (correct). Same reactions (five subjects).[1]

The most striking results of this test were therefore the relatively high quality of the recognitions at Level I, their relative deterioration at Level II and even at Level IB (but it should be remembered that Level II is characterized by symmetrical preferences) and their gradual improvement at Levels III and IV. Hence, one could postulate the existence of two distinct forms of recognition, one which appears first and is superior to recall, and another which is bound up with the schemata proper to recall. One could even put it, as a first approximation, that as soon as these schemata are formed, they tend to encourage the second type of recognition at the expense of the first.

But before we jump to the conclusion that the first type of recognition is purely figurative, while the second has its figurative elements firmly rooted in operational schemata, we must take a closer look at this peculiar state of affairs.

(1) The first thing to note is that Level IA recognitions are both good and inaccurate, in the sense that subjects at this level choose several forms most closely resembling the model, but are often unable to distinguish between them. By contrast, subjects at the subsequent levels grasp partial similarities or equivalences but not the identity of the model with No. 11 (thus one subject aged 4;6 claimed $8 = 9 = 10$);

(2) Even in the absence of such mistaken identifications, the highly systematic hesitations of four- to five-year-old children show that

---

[1] The above responses were those of forty out of the forty-four subjects tested. The remaining four (3;0 to 4;2) could not be classified because they quickly concluded that all the figures were more or less equivalent, and because their reconstructions were either worthless (dispersion of elements over the entire cardboard) or else too inadequate for classification (five sets of three elements). However, these four cases were extremely interesting in that, either before they confused the figures, or else at the end of the test when they were pressed for a final choice, they all selected the symmetrical figures (No. 7 and, quite particularly, No. 2). In other words, lacking adequate recall, these subjects allowed themselves to be guided by simple *Gestalt* laws, while subjects at Level IA allowed their choice to be guided by globally correct memories of the general set-up.

their recognition lacks the force of an impelling impression conserved by the memory as such;[1]

(3) Level IA recognition is, nevertheless, based on the correct memory of the general set-up: these subjects reject Nos. 1–3 and 6 (except for one initial choice of the latter) and quite particularly the symmetrical shapes 2, 4, 5 and 7, on which they might have been expected to focus attention because these shapes conform to the laws of perceptive 'good form';

(4) The fact that, at Level IB, comparisons between the original and final choices tend to have an adverse effect on recognition (greater preference for Nos. 3–4) shows, on the other hand, that these early recognitions are fairly unstable and quite distinct from the later type;

(5) The existence of an intermediate stage (Level II), at which the choice of symmetrical figures predominates, confirms the assumption that the superior recognitions presuppose the existence of a schema similar to that involved in recall, and one that gradually becomes quasi-operational: in that case, it would be because the schema remains incomplete at Level II and also, because their elementary recognition is unstable, that subjects in this age group resort willy-nilly to the most symmetrical forms (which also predominate with Level II recall);

(6) The gradual improvements in recognition at Levels IIIA to IIIB–IV seem to bear out our belief in the growing links between recognition and recall; while shape No. 11 (the model) was only selected by one subject at Level IA, it was chosen by 1 subject out of 10 at Level IB, by 0 out of 12 subjects at Level II, by 2 out of 10 at Level IIIA, and by 17 out of 27 subjects at Levels IIIB and IV.

(7) It is equally significant that we were unable to detect any appreciable difference between Groups A and B: hence it could not possibly have been the prior recall (Group B) that disturbed recognition at the intermediate level (II) but the formation of a new type of schema. Moreover, since the absence of prior recall (by Group A) failed to affect the correct or near-correct recognitions at Levels IIIB and IV, it seems most likely that the latter are based on schemata comparable to those involved in successful recall.

This does not mean that the more elementary forms of recognition do not involve schemata in any way: the shapes selected by subjects at Levels IA and IB (by the latter during the initial choice only) are not purely arbitrary (e.g. 1–3 and 6) or purely symmetrical (4, 5 and 7) but constitute a kind of equivalence class (8, 9, 10 and 12).

[1] It goes without saying that with different experimental material (a greater or smaller choice of figures) the results of the recognition test could have been, or could have appeared to be, quite different.

To attribute this to syncretism or to attention to minor details is unjustified, since syncretism ought to lead to the selection of a much larger class, and the same minor details (a triangle; a trapezium; one or two sections, etc.) recur in most of the figures. Nor is it enough to invoke the figurative 'pregnancy' of the original perception of the model, first, because the purely figurative factor ought to have led to the recognition of the model itself (No. 11) and not of a class of similar shapes, and, second (and above all), because there is no plausible reason to assume the existence of figurative 'traces' which would ensure correct recognition at the age of four years, i.e. before the memory deteriorates again. If the figurative factor as such made its effects felt forcibly from the very start, it ought rather to have encouraged the construction of recall schemata by providing the memory-image with figural symbols which, in their turn, would be consolidated by the nascent schema instead of being distorted by it . . . If, on the other hand, the figurative element involved in elementary recognition is bound up with the schemata, it follows that there must be a more or less stable equilibrium at the perceptive-motor level between figurative or perceptive recognition in general, and assimilation to the schemata at the perceptive-motor level. This equilibrium is upset during progress to the next level, only to become consolidated at those levels where image and concept replace, extend or complete the instruments used at the first level.

We are thus led to assume: (a) that recognition of the model already involves the use of assimilatory schemata; (b) that these schemata function quite differently from the schemata proper to recall; but (c) that they nevertheless constitute a first step in the same direction. Before justifying these three hypotheses, we must first repeat that the interpretation of all processes of development proceeds by way of a thesis (the heterogeneity of the successive stages), an antithesis (the reduction of the higher to the lower or the preformation of the first within the second), and a synthesis transcending them both, thanks to the reconstruction, at successive levels, of similar or convergent structures, each of which extends and enriches the preceding structures while integrating them into itself. This, as we shall see, is precisely what happens in the case under consideration.

(a) Elementary recognition must obviously involve assimilatory schemata, once it leads to a structuring of reality broad enough to include such variants as shapes Nos. 8–12 and precise enough to exclude the rest. In fact, the perceptive explanation involved in comparisons of the figures and even in the structuring of the actual model (No. 11) is a form of accommodation and not a purely passive recording process. Now, all forms of accommodation involve an

137

assimilatory schema, even if the latter is exclusively perceptive. That this schema should suffice to ensure adequate recognition even in the absence of correct recall is only to be expected, seeing that recognition occurs in the presence of both the perceptive model and of objects similar to or different from it.

(b) It goes without saying that the perceptive schemata underlying recognition (and in everyday life bound up with wider action schemata) should differ from the schemata of recall, if only because the latter arise out of the former. The schemata proper to recall, in fact, have two distinct but inseparable aspects: (1) On the one hand, they involve operational or pre-operational assimilation—in our particular case partition or recomposition in accordance with the possible associations. Now, all operations transcend perception and even habitual actions, etc. (2) On the other hand, recall presupposes the existence of a memory-image, i.e. of an internalized form of imitation constituting an extension of accommodation (imitation is a form of accommodation modifying the original schema until the latter is brough into more or less perfect correspondence with the model). But there is a clear difference between the actual accommodation to an object present before the subject's eyes, and extended accommodation by deferred imitation and internalization in the form of an image, i.e. capable of being activated in the absence of the object. Now, in the particular case of recognition, the accommodation schema is conserved in the absence of the object, but there is no reactivation until the object is brought back, whereas in the case of the schema proper to recall, the image itself or the internalized imitation extending the accommodation can be reactivated at will without further contact with the object. This explains why, at the level where recall first emerges and where it still leads to systematic errors (e.g. the symmetrical forms recalled and not simply 'recognized' at Level II), these reactivations and the deformations to which they give rise can lead to distorted recognitions; as he tries to extend the accommodation of the recognitive schema to the representational plane, but deforms it because of inadequate internalization, the subject distorts his accommodation or, more precisely, alters the equilibrium between it and the assimilation, and hence paves the way for a possible distortion of recognition.

(c) However, though there are two distinct planes and forms of accommodation—one perceptivo-motor and the other imitative and extended by inadequate or correct images—there is, nevertheless, a measure of functional and even structural unity between the schemata of recognition and recall. In the functional sphere, both types of accommodation involve assimilatory schemata, but in the structural sphere, an additional factor comes into play: to select Nos. 8–12, and to distinguish them from Nos. 1–7, or even to proceed to the perceptive structuring of the model (No. 11) and to recognize that model more or less clearly afterwards, the child must be able to distinguish and combine some of the parts or elements of the triangles (positively, or negatively in terms of the spaces between them), and must hence have minimal powers of spatial composition even on the perceptivo-motor plane. Here, we have the beginnings of imitative accommodation, but in the form of actions, not of images or motor recall. Now, it is this form of accommodation which, as it becomes stabilized and internalized, leads to mnemonic reactivation in the absence of the object, i.e. to recall with the help of the memory-image. And this figurative recall, in turn, can only arise thanks to the underlying schemata of partition and spatial composition. However, though these schemata transcend the schemata proper to perceptive activity, they are none the less compelled to reconstruct the same relations and compositions as are built up in cruder form by the perceptive activity and the recognitive schemata. Hence, there is a measure of continuity between recall and recognition, both in respect of assimilation no less than of accommodation, as the two sources of perceptive or imaginal figuration; both call for equilibrium between assimilation and accommodation, and while this equilibrium is rather unstable at Levels IA and IB, and momentarily upset at Level II, it is restored on a new plane and with new instruments at Levels IIIB and IV, but in forms that revive and extend those used at the initial level.

PART II

Remembering Multiplicative Logical Structures

In Part II (Chapters 7 to 10) we shall continue the argument of the earlier chapters, but with an analysis of such two-dimensional structures as multiplicative matrices and of the particular case of the intersection of classes. In addition, we shall be looking at structural 'arrangements' involving the co-ordination of combinations and permutations. The chief importance of these configurations is that they bring out the relationship between the figurative factors and the operational schemata in situations that, in some respects, are more complex than those we have been examining so far.

CHAPTER SEVEN

The Remembrance of Double Serial Correspondences[1]

After studying the remembrance of additive seriations (Chapters I to 2), we thought it important to establish the generality of our findings by an analysis of the memory of serial multiplications involving the ordination, in two dimensions, of objects differing in two seriable characteristics, for instance, size and colour. The simplest and at the same time the most comprehensive model is a support (cardboard) on which the elements have been seriated from left to right according to variations in one of these characteristics (e.g. a gradation of colours from light pink to dark red) and from top to bottom according to variations in their other characteristic (e.g. decreases in size). With this type of arrangement (Figure 23), only the two diagonals and the lines parallel to them represent seriations of both characteristics at once (e.g. Nos. 1, 6, 11, 16; 4, 7, 10, 13; 2, 7, 12; 5, 10, 15; 3, 6, 9; 8, 11, 14; 2, 5; 9, 14; 12, 15; 3, 8), while the horizontal rows and vertical columns consist of elements differing in only one of the two characteristics. For the purposes of serial multiplication, the child must bear these semi-equivalences in mind, since he cannot reconstruct or remember the model by means of the diagonals alone.

From the operational point of view, this construction is hardly more difficult than that of a simple seriation,[2] but from the figurative point of view, it involves a more complete spatial composition. Hence, it is of interest to establish whether or not the same type of recall is present in both types of mnemonic organization at the age when successful operations first appear (seven to eight years). Moreover, using the sixteen elements of the model, it is also possible to construct a much more symmetrical *Gestalt* (Figure 24), in which the four large squares occupy the four corners, the four smallest ones

[1] In collaboration with Tuât Vinh-Bang.
[2] See B. Inhelder and J. Piaget: *The Early Growth of Logic in the Child*, Chapter X (in collaboration with A. Morf), Routledge & Kegan Paul, 1964.

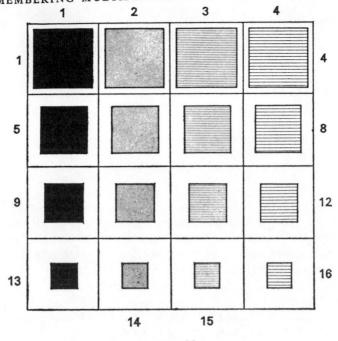

FIGURE 23

are in the centre and the rest occupy the remaining compartments to form the following horizontal rows:

2, 8, 5, 4; 12, 14, 16, 11; 9, 15, 13, 10; and 3, 6, 7, 1.

We wondered whether this *Gestalt*, being more aesthetic than Figure 23, but devoid of all operational significance, would be remembered at the same average age as the serial multiplication, or whether the development of the memory with age would prove to be of quite a different type. Hence, the great importance we attached to this analysis of the remembrance of multiplicative structures.

§1. *Methods used and mnemonic levels*

Our model was a piece of cardboard 28 cm square, divided into sixteen compartments filled with squares of four distinct sizes (5·5 cm square; 4·5 cm square; 3·5 cm square; and 2·5 cm square) and of four colours ranging from deep red to light pink. It was shown to two separate groups of children.

Group A. The subjects were asked to take a good look at the model (for thirty seconds) and then to describe it: 'Tell me all you have seen,' and, if necessary: 'Is that all?' etc. The model was then removed, and the child

144

was asked for a memory-drawing[1] as a test of his immediate recall. Next, he was handed a piece of cardboard measuring 40 × 28 cm and twenty-five squares, including the sixteen used in the model, and asked to make a reconstruction. If he used up all the twenty-five squares, he was handed another cardboard measuring 28 × 28 cm with sixteen empty compartments, together with the sixteen elements of the model, and asked to make a new reconstruction.

A week later, he was asked to recount what he had seen, and no attempt was made to fill any gaps in his story. Then he was asked for a memory-drawing and a new reconstruction, using the same procedure as during the first session. Ditto after six months.

Group B. The model was presented and left on the table. The twenty-five control squares were brought out, and the subject was asked to reconstruct the original model on a piece of cardboard divided into sixteen blocks. For the rest, the same procedure was adopted as with Group A: verbal accounts, memory-drawings, and material reconstructions immediately after the presentation, a week later and, again, after six months.

Before we look at the results, we must first point out that, in the case of Group B, the reconstruction of the model by means of the twenty-five squares already provides some interesting hints as to the manner in which the model is assimilated to the schemata of children at different ages, and hence, probably, as to the way in which it is fixed in the memory. At the lowest level, children pick up one of the twenty-five squares at random, and place it in one of the empty compartments (perceptive correspondence with the model left on the table). This method of purely perceptive trial and error rarely leads to the correct end result. At the next level, there is a more systematic approach, but based on classification rather than on seriation: the subjects combine elements identical or near-identical in respect of size or colour, and put them into correspondence with the model—the final result may be correct. At the third level, there is seriation by means of an anticipatory schema, but based on a single criterion (usually size) and trial and error in respect of the second. At the fourth level there is double seriation based on immediate anticipation following the inspection of the model. This level is not reached until the age of seven to eight years, but the third level also persists until that age, while the first two are confined to five- to six-year-olds.

The verbal accounts of the subjects do not provide any additional information: as with simple seriations (Chapter 2), they involve dichotomies (big and small), trichotomies (big, small and medium) or such descriptions as 'a bit bigger' or 'a bit darker'. These become generalized at about the age of seven to eight years.

---

[1] He was provided with a greater number of coloured crayons than the model itself demands.

Graphic recall fell into the following four types:

Type I. Unsystematic distribution: the subjects simply cover the cardboard with squares of like size (except that their draftsmanship is often so poor that they vacillate between squares and trapezia). Sub-type IA, uses one colour only; sub-type IB uses several colours at random, including some that did not appear in the original model.

Sub-type IC differs from the above in respect of the order in which the paper is filled rather than of the final result (which is equally wrong): subjects of this type begin by drawing squares round the edges of the paper, and then fill in the middle. This might be called a start towards the construction of an over-all configuration, particularly when compared with certain mistaken forms produced by sub-type IA, in which the subject simply offers an alignment of squares of equal size.

Type II. Subjects of this type proceed either by way of partial classifications (big, small, or big, medium and small) using one colour only, or else by arranging certain squares according to two or more colours. However, they also attempt to construct seriations, and these remain partial as well. Here we can distinguish two sub-types: at Level IIA, the seriations are introduced within the classes, but the latter are not placed into corresponding series: thus the red consist of large, medium and small squares, and so do the pink, but the colours themselves are not graded and the sizes not arranged to correspond from one class to the next. Alternatively, the class of big squares may be sub-divided into bigger and smaller squares, or according to colours aligned at random, or, again, according to partial series.

At Level IIB, there is a start towards an over-all organization, in that the classes themselves are placed into series. One subject (6;5), for example, drew two large squares above a row of three slightly smaller squares, a third row of five still smaller squares, and a final row of seven very small squares. Hence, there was no correspondence between the elements, but a seriation of classes as such (all of the same colour).

Type III. With type III we have serial correspondence, term for term, but based on a single criterion—usually size. Such constructions appear from the age of five years onwards, but at first infrequently and incompletely (sub-types A and B): there may be two series of three squares in decreasing order, but in one-to-one correspondence; or else there may be six series, the first four correct (four squares each in decreasing order) and the last two consisting of three squares only, etc. In sub-type IIIA the colours are uniform, and in sub-type IIIB they are different (one colour per row or column) but not in series. Subjects of sub-type IIIC offer four series in correct order of size and in correspondence, but fail to seriate the colours in these series.

Type IV. Subjects of this type anticipate and achieve double seriation. Sub-type IVA still makes figurative mistakes: there may be three corresponding columns of squares in decreasing size and rows of seriated colours (as in the model) and a fourth (correct) column placed beneath column III (possibly for lack of space). Or else the drawing may be correct in all respects, except that the columns (decreasing sizes) are shown as rows, and vice versa.

Sub-type IVB offer the correct solution.

§2. *General results*

I. The existence of these mnemonic types shows first of all that the memory is much more closely bound up with the operational level than it is with the figurative aspects of the model. Here, the model is a *Gestalt*, distinct from that of a simple series but equally good or 'pregnant' in that it consists of two types of ordered sequences, arranged in horizontal and vertical order. Now, subjects with the most primitive type of recall merely retain that this form looked like a square or rectangular conglomerate, with its elements in complete disorder; this is because, lacking a multiplicative schema, they could only perceive (or copy) and retain the figure in the most general way, i.e. without any system (as also happened in the case of seriation, where subjects of type I simply produced an alignment without any attempt at ordination). Next come types II and III, which mark the beginning and subsequent progress of the seriation schemata, but still without multiplicative co-ordination except in purely local forms. Finally, with type IV, we have the correct structuring of recall and re-construction, due to the acquisition of the corresponding operational system, and not to simple figural influences which, as such, would have made themselves felt much earlier. In fact, the correct memories appear at the average age at which operationality is normally attained (seven to eight years), and the latter itself coincides, more or less, with the emergence of Level IV in the operational construction of seriation. In other words, the development of the additive and multiplicative schemata is closely correlated. The accompanying Tables give the distribution of mnemonic types with age, and clearly illustrate that the evolution of the memory is indeed a function of operational development.

II. A comparison of Group A (simple perception of the model during the presentation) and Group B (copy of model by means of twenty-five squares offered for selection) casts an interesting light on the rôle of the operational or pre-operational schemata: the latter act as codes for recording and deciphering the data, but vary with age, since, in the case under consideration, the code itself is gradually transformed until it eventually reaches equilibrium at about the age of seven to eight years.

As we see, copying of the model while it is still before the subject's eyes has a slightly favourable effect on mnemonic retention and accuracy, but only at the age of five to six years, and no longer at seven to eight years. Now, this effect may be caused by one of three sets of factors: (1) It may be due to purely perceptive factors in the sense that, to copy the model there and then, the child must look at it more attentively (or more 'analytically' as *Gestalt* psychologists would put it) than when inspecting it for the sole purpose of remembering it for subsequent reproduction; (2) it may be due to motor or sensori-motor factors, in the sense that the act of reproduction can introduce conditioning processes or associations capable of conserving themselves as such, and hence of facilitating recall and particularly reconstruction; (3) however, copying the model may also help to exercise, and hence to advance, the pre-operational or operational assimilatory schemata, and it is these schemata, consolidated or perfected, thanks to the act of copying the model (reproduction),

TABLE 12 *Distribution of types of response during immediate recall and a week later (by number of responses: drawings and reconstructions)*

Types of response	Group A				Group B			
	I	II	III	IV	I	II	III	IV
5 years (28 and 26)	14	8	6	0	8	10	7	1
6 years (20 and 20)	2	6	8	4	0	5	15	0
7–8 years (24 and 24)	0	0	6	18	0	1	14	9

which subsequently hold greater sway over mnemonic retention, recall and reconstruction than they do with Group A.

Now, we saw (in §1) that the quality of the copy differs from age to age: before the acquisition of multiplicative or even additive seriation schemata, the copy is produced by pure trial and error, whence the frequent mistakes. But as the construction of seriable operations proceeds, the copy can lean on anticipatory schemata and is greatly assisted by the assimilation of the model to these schemata. This demonstrates the paramount importance of the third factor.

Oddly enough, successful copy work in no way improves the memory, not even during immediate recall, which points to the inhibiting rôle of factors (1) and (2). Moreover, the operational method used in constructing the copy is also applied, as such or as a simple extension, in mnemonic recall and reconstruction.

BOUL (5;7), relying on purely perceptive correspondences, nevertheless managed to produce a copy that was correct in respect of both size and colour, except that he confused Nos. 11 and 15 with Nos. 12 and 16, an error he corrected on inspection. Now, on immediate recall, he drew a series of squares all of the same dimension and confused the colours (except for a first column of pink squares only). His reconstruction, with twenty-five squares on unruled cardboard, resulted in a very irregular figure with no attempt at seriation but a search for identical shapes. With sixteen squares and cross-ruled paper, on the other hand, Boul was able to seriate the sizes, but confused the colours (except, once again, for a first column of pink squares). After a week, his drawing was of the same quality (identical sizes and random colours except for the first column) but in his reconstruction, he made no attempt at seriation and simply tried to classify (non-seriated) colours.

NER (5;6), using trial and error and relying on purely perceptive correspondences, produced a correct copy of the model, except for one mistake in respect of size. His memory-drawing (immediately after presentation), on the other hand, was a jumble of squares and a mixture of reds, greens, yellows and blues. His reconstruction was no better.

ZIL (5;1) offered a copy, the first three columns of which were correct in all respects, but the fourth column of which was made up of two large and two very small squares with no regard for colour sequences. On immediate recall, he produced a jumbled series of columns consisting of three squares each: two large ones and one small one, or one large one and two small ones (all red except for a single pink square). His reconstruction was based on the same partial anticipations and the same confusion, except for an attempt to classify the colours (not placed into series).

AN (5;7) used trial and error to copy the sizes correctly, but arrived much more quickly at the correct colours. On immediate recall, she said: '*Red, almost red, pink, a little pinker, then bright pink,*' and drew her copy accordingly. Her recall of the sizes, however, amounted to a small square, followed by five to eight large rectangles. Her reconstruction was of the same kind (columns of five to eight elements).

These brief examples will suffice to show, on the one hand, that successful copy drawing based on perceptive correspondence (factor (1)) is not sufficient to ensure faithful recall, not even immediately after the presentation, and, on the other hand, that if the type of activity associated with copy drawing (factor (2)) affects the memory, it does so only to the extent that it is guided by schemata corresponding to the child's operational level (factor (3)). The reason why subjects in Group A show some progress over those in Group B is therefore that the former engage in an operational exercise, which is something quite other than what happens in the classical learning situation, based as it is on external reinforcement,

III. This leads us to a comparison of the results of immediate recall, and those of recall and reconstruction after a week. Now, in the present experiment, the reconstruction was asked for at once, in the hope that this might reveal striking differences between Group B, which reconstructed the model while looking at the original, and Group A, which did not have that advantage. However, as we saw, the differences were not particularly marked. Unfortunately, the comparison of immediate recall with recall after a week lost some of its value as a result: a reconstruction had intervened between the two. By contrast, the comparison of the immediate reconstruction with that made after a week continued to be of great interest.

In fact, in their drawings, both groups taken together produced three clear cases of regress during the intervening week, twenty-nine stationary cases and three cases of progress. If we consider sub-types as well, Group A produced 1 regression, 12 stationary cases, and 5 advances; Group B produced 4 regressions, 10 stationary cases, and 3 advances. By contrast, the reconstructions of Group A represented 1 regression, 16 stationary cases and 1 advance (or, considering changes of sub-type as well: 4 regressions, 12 equalities and 2 advances). The corresponding figures for Group B were: 0 regression, 13 equalities and 4 advances (or including sub-types: 1 regression, 10 equalities and 6 advances). However, the greater progress of Group B in respect of their reconstructions, merely compensates for the inferiority of this group at the age six to eight years (Table 12). Everything thus happens as if the successive copies and reconstructions of Group B entailed a gradual learning process.

This impression is confirmed by a comparison of the drawings and reconstructions offered during the first sessions. In Group A, the reconstructions were in advance of the drawings in 11 cases, of identical quality in 25 cases, and never of an inferior type. In Group B, on the other hand, the corresponding figures were 12, 18 and 5 (not considering sub-types).

As for remembrance after six months, the two groups taken together produced thirteen reconstructions that were superior to their drawings, sixteen cases of equality and three inferiorities. By contrast, the two groups differed slightly in respect of drawings and reconstructions taken together.

We see that, among the thirty-three subjects brought back after six months, the distribution of memory types varied with age and hence, probably, with the operational level. Once again there was the same relative inferiority at seven to eight years of Group B with respect to Group A.

Changes in type (not sub-type) in the course of these six months were as follows: in Group A, two advances in respect of the reconstruction (one at 5 years from type I to type II, and at 6 years from type II to type III); three regressions (type III to type II at 5 years; type IV to type III at 7 and 8 years (the last in respect of his drawings));[1] and twenty-seven stationary cases (drawings and reconstructions counted separately). In Group B, there were 6 cases of progress, 11 regressions and 15 stationary cases. Progress was made at five years from type I to type II, at six and eight years from type II to type III, and at seven years from type III to type IV. The regressions were: several 5-year-olds who reverted from Stage II to Stage I; one 6-year-old who reverted from type III to type II in his reconstructions and from type III to type I in his drawings, several 6- and 7-year olds who reverted from type III to type II or from type IV to type III, and one 8-year-old who also reverted from type IV to type III, but only in his reconstructions.

All in all, the sixty-four drawings and reconstructions offered by Groups A and B, consisted of eight cases of progress, fourteen

TABLE 13   *Remembrance after six months (in absolute numbers)*

	A				B			
Types	I	II	III	IV	I	II	III	IV
5 years (8 and 5 subjects)	5	6	3	0	3	5	2	0
6 years (4 and 5 subjects)	1	2	5	0	1	3	6	0
7–8 years (5 and 6 subjects)	0	0	4	6	0	2	7	3

regressions, and forty-two stationary cases, which suggests that this type of memory is fairly stable, the more so as most of the regressions were by one level only.

§3. *Remembrance of a symmetrical* Gestalt *composed of the same sixteen elements*

We shall now look at an essential control experiment, namely, the remembrance of a symmetrical *Gestalt* composed of the same elements as the main model, but no longer constructed by a simple

---

[1] This subject, aged 8;3 (and many others as well), showed clearly that mnemonic regression goes hand in hand with the operational schematization of just one of the essential structural aspects: while this schematization leads to double seriation on immediate recall, six months later it merely provides a column of five figures in decreasing size, but also in increasingly bright colours. In other words, it only retains the diagonal of the matrix, a frequent error in subjects attempting to construct a serial matrix with objects having double properties and presented at random.

operation. All we have described in §§1 and 2 tended to show that the remembrance of a double seriation was closely bound up with the underlying operational schemata: the memory seemed once again to rely much more on the latter than on the figurative aspects of the model. To verify this assumption, we used another model, constructed with the same elements as before, but this time in the form of a symmetrical figure,[1] and tried to determine, by the same methods,

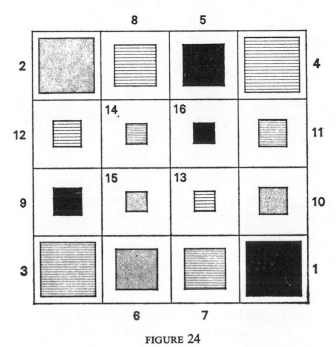

FIGURE 24

In the centre, 14 and 16 between 12 and 11; 15 and 13 between 9 and 10

whether the elements were remembered as well, better, or less well than those of Figure 23.

Now, the results of our control experiment proved conclusively that the remembrance of this type of structure is much more tenuous than that of the double seriation, even in respect of the distribution of squares by size alone. The responses were of five types:

I. The squares were arranged without regard to size and the colours were scattered at random, unless only one single colour was used.

[1] Though it was impossible to arrange the colours in the same symmetrical way as the shapes, they were nevertheless combined in accordance with a law: each dark square was followed by a brighter square and vice versa.

II. Attempt at organization: remembrance of the first row or column, or of the four corners, or of the small squares in the centre.

III. Over-all, but simplified, organization with gaps and errors in the placing of the mean terms.

IV. Correct reproduction of the model in respect of size but not of colour (cf. type III, §1) or vice versa.

V. Correct reproduction of the model in respect of both size and colour (except for some errors in respect of the latter, but, in any case, remembrance of the alternation of colours).

Table 14 shows the distribution of these five types during the first two sessions and after six months (in absolute numbers of drawings and reconstructions, i.e. four or two per subject).

TABLE 14   *Remembrance of a symmetrical* Gestalt (*in absolute numbers*)

	Immediate remembrance after one week					After six months				
	I	II	III	IV	V	I	II	III	IV	V
5 years	15	8	1	0	0	8	3	1	0	0
6 years	11	7	0	0	0	3	7	0	0	0
7– 8 years	4	16	0	0	0	4	6	0	0	0
9–10 years	0	9	5	2	0	0	5	2	0	1
11–12 years	0	4	0	1	7	2	0	0	0	2

The only five-year-old to reach type III did so merely in respect of his reconstruction.

(1) The two most striking results to emerge from the first two sessions were, first, the persistence, until the age of eight years, of type I reactions: the sheet is filled with squares of similar size and of one colour, or of several colours distributed at random; and, second, the belated appearance of types IV (nine years) and V (ten and eleven years), both in respect of the drawings and of the reconstructions.

Type I is the only one to occur in both the double seriation and the symmetrical figure—it reflects a complete lack of organization. However, in the case of double seriations, this type of reaction does not continue beyond the age of five years, because attempts at simple seriation, or at least at classification involving rudimentary series, appear relatively early on in the child's life. Hence, it is all the more remarkable that, in the case of the present *Gestalt* (four large squares in the corners of the model, four small squares in the centre, and two pairs of medium-sized squares placed between the large ones both vertically and horizontally), the figural arrangement should be completely forgotten, not only by the great majority of five- and six-year-old subjects but also by an appreciable number of seven- and even eight-year-olds:

CAR (8;10), for instance, drew sixty squares of the same colour. During her reconstruction (for which she was handed sixteen squares) she constructed three columns of unequal length on the unruled cardboard, the first containing four large and two medium-sized squares, the second containing medium-sized squares only, and the third small squares. With the ruled cardboard, too, she failed to produce a symmetrical form, distributing the elements more or less at random, with the big squares in only two of the corners, and with the small squares all on the right side.

LIN (7;8) offered an immediate memory-drawing of fourteen squares distributed in four vague columns of 3, 5, 4 and 2 elements, and with no horizontal rows. All the elements were identical in size (except for one which was slightly larger than the rest) and there were three colours. After a week, her drawing became even more confused, and her reconstruction was a jumble of sizes and colours.

It is worth noting that one of the few six-year-olds (Mar, 6;7) who did not offer this type of agglomeration (and who, like the rest, had not, of course, taken the double seriation test) produced, on immediate recall, two elegant series of decreasing squares in four sizes, with one colour per series, as if he were trying to recall Figure 23! Other six-year-olds produced long columns of squares (7–13 elements) differing in colour (including blue, etc.): these squares were either equal in size or else formed three columns of large squares plus one column of small squares, etc. Here we have something like a search for, or an implicit need of (though very explicit in the case of Mar!) serial order.

Between type I and types IV and V, there are, again, several intermediate stages, which show that the failure of subjects of type I is not due to a complete lack of interest in the model. Thus, between type I and type II, in which rudimentary attempts at organization are first made, some subjects are quite obviously trying to discover some sort of over-all form: they begin by placing some markers on the periphery in accordance with what they remember of the general structure, but, unable to continue, they fill in the rest at random. Next come types II and III, which show organizational progress pending full success at Levels IV and V:

LIL (9;9) proved to be of type III–IV: her immediate memory-drawing consisted of four large squares placed in the four corners, two pairs of intermediate squares in vertical rows, and two small squares and one medium-sized square in the central region. Her first reconstruction was of similar quality but, after a week, her drawing, no less than her reconstruction, consisted of four large squares in the corners, again separated by medium squares, and small squares in the centre, but the whole figure was made up of ten instead of sixteen elements, and the colours were chosen at random.

MIL (9;10) used sixteen squares, but filled the centre with a mixture of small and medium-sized squares. His colours, however, were correct: '*I think there must be a pink one next to the red.*' His reconstructions were of similar quality (type IV).

DUP (11;0) arrived at the correct distribution of sizes but with some colour inversion (type IV) and BON (11;7) reached Level V: '*The really big ones go into the four corners. Next come the smaller ones then the still smaller ones, and the smallest ones go in the middle.*' But he continued to hesitate about the colours: '*I saw that a dark one was here, and then a bright one, another dark one, and another bright one* (first column). *Here* (fourth column) *it was the other way round*'. At long last, and after some further vacillation, he extended his generalization to the centre.

Clearly, there is a marked contrast between the difficulties children experience with the present model and the relative ease with which they memorize the double seriation at the stage of development where this operation normally emerges.

(2) The twenty-two drawings offered six months after the presentation consisted of five regressions and seventeen stationary cases, while the reconstructions accounted for four regressions, twelve stationary cases and sixteen advances. Significantly enough, and again in contrast to what happened in the case of the serial matrix, the immediate reconstructions and those of a week after the presentation were no better than the drawings: three were inferior, forty-one were of equal quality and only one was superior (a five-year-old who advanced from type I to type III). Even after six months, when we handed our subjects the cross-ruled cardboard and the sixteen squares of the model, there were only six advances on the original reconstructions and eight advances on the drawings. Of these, a single one (9;10) had advanced from type II to type V, while the rest (aged five and six years) had simply advanced from type I to type II, and, remarkably enough, in an operational and not in a *Gestaltist* sense (cf. Mar, 6;7, mentioned earlier): they made attempts at seriation or classification, but not at recapturing the symmetrical form of the model. Thus Gol (5;1) who, during the first sessions, had arranged his squares at random and by steps, now formed small piles of elements and then arranged them in increasing order of size.

During all three sessions, therefore, the symmetrical model was remembered either far less clearly than the serial matrix, or else confused with the latter.

CHAPTER EIGHT

The Remembrance of Double Classifications[1]

In this chapter we shall be looking at the remembrance of a set of red and blue squares and circles presented in the form of a square matrix (not drawn in) whose two upper sections consist of three red circles and five red squares, and whose two lower sections consist of four blue circles and three blue squares (Figure 25). This model provides us not only with a logical structure involving a multiplicative classification, but also with a highly 'pregnant' symmetrical

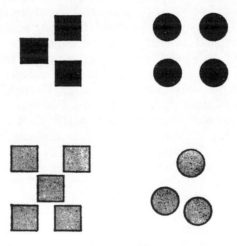

FIGURE 25

configuration the figural aspect of which corresponds closely to the operational structure. Moreover, the circles and squares are made of wood, the better to symbolize that the model represents one over-all class divided into four sub-classes according to colour and shapes.

What we are concerned to establish is whether the figurative factors ensure the formation of correct memories at all ages, i.e.

[1] In collaboration with J. Bliss.

156

irrespective of the subjects' logical or operational development or whether, as in the case of double seriations, the mnemonic levels once again correspond to the levels of operational development.

§1. *Methods and levels*

Two distinct methods were used. In the first, the subjects were not asked for a description, but were simply told to look at the model carefully and to keep it 'in their heads' so that they might later draw everything they remembered. In the second method, the subjects were

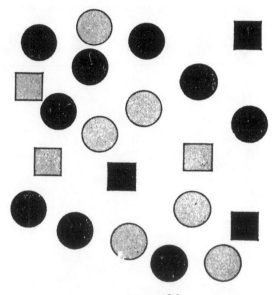

FIGURE 26

asked to describe everything they could see. If the details they produced were too sketchy, they were asked if they were sure that was all they had actually observed. If any said 'yes', no further questions were asked, and the subjects were told, as in the first method, that they would be expected to make a memory-drawing at a later stage. Each of the two methods, moreover, involved two distinct techniques. In the first, the subjects were asked for a memory-drawing an hour after the presentation, and for a further memory-drawing one week later, this time followed by a reconstruction, for which purpose they were handed a larger number of wooden counters than had gone into the original model. In the second technique the reconstruction was dispensed with.

The mnemonic types represented varied with age, i.e. with operationality, and were also affected, though to a much lesser extent, by the figurative aspects of the model:

Type I. This type does not generally occur beyond the age of four to five years. In sub-type IA the counters are either jumbled up or else placed in a line; in sub-type IB the counters form a single class (squares or circles, all of the same colour), or a single element of two colours.

Type II. Here there is classification (generally involving two classes only) but no matrix or a multiplicative system. There are several variations, but these do not represent true sub-levels. Some subjects combine two or more counters with similar properties into one class, while others produce classes of one counter each. Then there are those who offer dichotomies

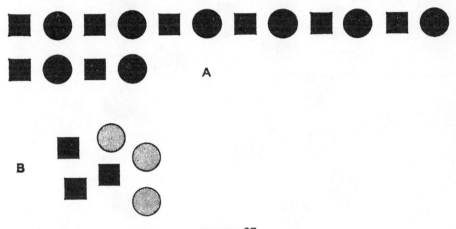

FIGURE 27

based on a single predicate: a blue and a red circle, or two red and two blue circles. Others again offer dichotomies in which the second term differs from the first in respect of two predicates: one (or several) blue circle(s) and one (or several) blue square(s). Finally, there are those who produce trichotomies (a red circle, a blue circle and a red or blue square) but these subjects are exceptional and generally change their minds after six months. They have a rudimentary recall of the multiplication, but since this variation is confined to a very few of the younger subjects (four to five years), it cannot be said to be of a higher level than the dichotomous constructions.

Type III. Except at the age of five years, when this type is far less common than type II, and at the age of eight years, when it is more common, type III seems to represent the same operational level as type II:[1] there are the same variations but, in addition, the matrix is remembered and drawn

[1] That is why the distribution of types II and III is shown both jointly and separately on the Tables (pp. 160–2).

correctly. In the dichotomous drawings (the most frequent case), two of the four compartments of the matrix are filled with the same element or elements as the other two, and in the trichotomies one of the compartments appears to have the same contents as another.

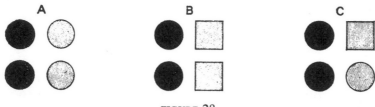

FIGURE 28

Type IV. As with memories of type II, type IV represents a failure to grasp the nature of the matrix, but can be called an advance in that subjects of this type introduce a multiplicative structure: the four classes are

FIGURE 29

remembered correctly, either in the form of one red and one blue circle, and one red and one blue square (often aligned), or else as consisting of several members each, which may be scattered at random or set out in a row.

FIGURE 30

Type V. Here, there is some recall of the matrix or of the existence of four distinct classes, again represented by a single member or by several members. In addition to drawing matrices that correspond to the model, these subjects also produce diagonal distributions, for instance by placing the blue squares in the upper left compartment and the red squares in the lower right. However, since this configuration appears at the same age levels as the vertical–horizontal distribution, there is no point in treating it as a special sub-level.

159

§2. *Responses an hour and a week after presentation*

These different types of mnemonic organization thus correspond, by and large, to the levels observed in the simple classification of red and blue squares and circles, which demonstrates once again that the memory is a function of operational developments. There are, however, two qualifications, The first is the presence of type III, in which the memory conserves the figurative form of the matrix together with the elements of the various compartments, but in which there is no grasp of the multiplicative composition. The second is that the age distributions (see Tables 15 and 16) differ from those associated with the synchronous, as opposed to the successive, formation of (1) additive and (2) multiplicative compositions: the fact that, in the present case, the former seem to emerge before the latter, suggests that they are more easily retained by the memory, whereas in active

TABLE 15   *Recall after a week (all groups combined) (in %, and in brackets, in absolute number of subjects)*

	N	I	II	III	II + III	IV	V	IV + V
4–5 years	(32)	12 (4)	37 (12)	28 (9)	65 (21)	6 (2)	15 (5)	22 (7)
6 years	(30)	3 (1)	50 (15)	36 (11)	86 (26)	3 (1)	6 (2)	10 (3)
7 years	(33)	0	39 (13)	36 (12)	75 (25)	9 (3)	15 (5)	24 (8)
8 years	(17)	0	17 (3)	29 (5)	47 (8)	12 (2)	41 (7)	53 (9)

classifications, i.e. the solution of new problems, the two seem to go together.

Let us now look at the distribution of memory types with age.

The reader will see that there is a clear evolution of type with age, and that approximately (IV) or completely successful (V) solutions are offered by 50–75 per cent of the eight-year-olds, which is precisely what happens in operational tests as well. Hence, we have yet another indication that the memory relies more strongly on the operational schemata than it does on the figurative aspects of the model, except for subjects of type III who remember the configuration (four compartments) but not the multiplicative composition. But type III is not a real exception, because it, too, involves the use of an operational schema, but one that is oversimplified (dichotomy) and in which the matrix involves logico-geometrical as well as perceptive symmetries.

Now, in the Tables, we have combined subjects who were asked for a verbal description of the model with those who were not. In respect of the former, it might be argued that their memories were swayed more strongly by the conceptual analysis associated with their description than by their perception of the model. However, we know that verbal descriptions do not significantly affect the memory of four- to five-year-olds or of eight-year-olds, but that in six- to seven-year-olds the absence of verbal descriptions is reflected in a slight predominance of type III, in which the figurative element seems to counterbalance the operational aspect of the model. Hence, while descriptions seem to enhance the influence of the operational schemata in the intermediate age groups, which is only to be expected, they do so to a slight extent only—even in their absence the schemata will soon afterwards (at the age of seven to nine years) come to prevail over the purely figurative aspects of the memory. At the age of four to five years, on the other hand, the figurative memory of the model is too poor to offset the lack of operational schemata. Hence, at the age of six to seven years, we simply have the situation in which

TABLE 16 *Reconstructions after a week (all groups combined)*

	N	I	II	III	II + III	IV	V	IV + V
4–5 years	(32)	9 (3)	19 (6)	16 (5)	34 (11)	28 (9)	28 (9)	56 (18)
6 years	(30)	0	33 (10)	10 (3)	43 (13)	20 (6)	37 (11)	56 (17)
7 years	(33)	0	15 (5)	30 (10)	45 (15)	18 (6)	36 (12)	54 (18)
8 years	(18)	0	0	22 (4)	22 (4)	28 (5)	50 (9)	77 (14)

the developing schemata collaborate somewhat more closely with the figural data if they are reinforced by a description, and a little less closely if they are not. This explains the predominance of type III in the second case.

The Tables also combine those subjects who produced their first memory-drawing an hour after the presentation with those who did not, and this because the differences proved to have no statistical significance, which was again to be expected in cases of recall based more on the pre-operational or operational schemata than on the purely figurative aspects of the model: as we saw, subjects with type III memories simply remember the general shape of the matrix but not the characteristics of the sub-classes. Hence, we need not be surprised that, of the fifty-eight subjects who were tested an hour and, again, a week after the presentation, forty-four had remained where they were, four had made progress and ten had slipped back slightly (these proportions were more or less identical for subjects who had been asked for descriptions and those who had not).

By contrast, a comparison between material reconstructions and recall after a week revealed the usual advance of the former over the latter:

$$(1) \quad \text{Reconstruction} > \text{Recall:} \quad 31 \text{ subjects}$$
$$(2) \qquad ,, \qquad = \quad ,, \quad : \quad 71 \text{ subjects}$$
$$(3) \qquad ,, \qquad < \quad ,, \quad : \quad 10 \text{ subjects}$$

The ratio of (1) to (3) was therefore 3 : 1, which demonstrates once again that the operational schemata hold sway over the figurative memory-image.

In short, the memory of multiplicative classifications seems to develop in much the same way as the memory of serial configurations, but with this rider: the construction of multiplicative schemata is a little more complex and appears at a slightly later age than that of seriations, and constantly interferes with the construction of simple or dichotomous classificatory schemata. However, in the present case no less than that of seriations, the figurative structure of the model corresponds very closely to its operational structure, a fact that aids the memory but impedes the dissociation of the two structures. It is for this reason that we decided to proceed to an analysis of a situation in which there is a direct conflict between the multiplication of classes and the figurative arrangements. The results will be discussed in §4.

§3. *Remembrance after six months*

Let us first look at the changes in the responses of the eighty-eight subjects we were able to bring back after six months.

If we compare Table 17 with Tables 15 and 16 (§2), we arrive at the remarkable conclusion that, while the memory-drawings of all age

TABLE 17 *Remembrance after six months (all groups combined)*

		N	I	II	III	II + III	IV	V	IV + V
Recall:									
4–5 years	(27)	33 (9)	55 (15)	0	55 (15)	11 (3)	0	11 (3)
6 years	(19)	26 (5)	63 (12)	5 (1)	68 (13)	0	5 (1)	5 (1)
7 years	(30)	0	70 (21)	10 (3)	80 (24)	10 (3)	10 (3)	20 (6)
8 years	(12)	8 (1)	50 (6)	16 (2)	66 (8)	16 (2)	8 (1)	25 (3)
Reconstructions									
4–5 years	(27)	30 (8)	15 (4)	11 (3)	26 (7)	33 (9)	11 (3)	44 (12)
6 years	(19)	5 (1)	26 (5)	5 (1)	31 (6)	26 (5)	37 (7)	63 (12)
7 years	(30)	0	16 (5)	10 (3)	26 (8)	43 (13)	30 (9)	73 (22)
8 years	(12)	0	8 (1)	8 (1)	16 (2)	41 (5)	41 (5)	83 (10)

groups deteriorate, the reconstructions of all age groups (except the four- to five-year-olds) not only make progress as such but are also greatly superior to the drawings. Thus, successful reconstructions were produced by 63 per cent of our six-year-old subjects after six months and by only 56 per cent after a week; the corresponding percentages for seven-year-olds were 73 per cent and 54 per cent, and for eight-year-olds 83 per cent and 77 per cent. Hence, there is clear progress among those age groups who are approaching or have reached the stage of successful operations. The whole question merits closer scrutiny, both in respect of the individual subjects and also of the statistical distribution of the results. Regarding the latter, Table 18 provides three types of useful information. In it, we refer by $R2 > D$ to reconstructions after six months which were superior to the drawings produced at the same time: by $R < D$ to the opposite case,

TABLE 18 *Comparison of drawings and reconstructions after a week and after six months*

	$R > D$	$R = D$	$R < D$	$R2 > R1$	$R2 = R1$	$R2 < R1$	$D2 > D1$	$D2 = D1$	$D2 < D1$
4–5 years	13	9	5	3	7	17	2	5	20
6–8 years	39	21	1	19	30	12	7	30	24
Total	52	30	6	22	37	29	9	35	44

and by $R = D$ to identical responses. Similarly, by $R2 > R1$ we refer to reconstructions after six months that were better than reconstructions after a week, and by $R2 < R1$ to the opposite case. Finally, by $D2 > D1$ we refer to drawings after six months that were better than drawings after a week, and by $D2 < D1$ to the opposite case. The Table does not include sub-types but simply refers to Levels I–V.

The reader will see, first of all, that at the purely pre-operational level (four to five years) there is a general deterioration of the memory after six months: most of the drawings of types IV–V, and one-third of the reconstructions of the same types, have regressed to types II–III and many of the latter have reverted to type I. Moreover, quite a few subjects proved to be of sub-type IA (not represented during the earlier sessions): they could only recall one of the four classes. Despite these regressions, however, the four- to five-year-olds produced thirteen reconstructions superior to their drawings, but this superiority was already apparent during the first sessions and was only to be expected, since, at the time, the material was in full view. All in all, the memories of our four- to five-year-old subjects seemed to be of a mainly figurative kind, which did not prevent seven of these thirty-two subjects from reaching types IV and V during the first sessions, but explains why that number dropped to three after six months.

As for the sixty-one 6- to 8- year-old subjects, their reconstructions proved to be vastly superior to the memory drawings produced at the same time (39 improvements and only 1 regression). Moreover, though their drawings were strikingly inferior to those produced during earlier sessions (24 regressions as against 7 cases of progress), the corresponding reconstructions had advanced in nineteen cases (as against 12 regressions, mostly from type V to type IV, and 30 stationary cases). Here are a few examples:

GIA (7;10) produced a second-session drawing representing two classes and two predicates: red circles and blue squares (type II) and a reconstruction by means of red and blue squares and blue circles (type III). After six months his reconstruction and drawing were both of type II: red and blue circles.

MOD (7;5) produced a second-session drawing and reconstruction of type II: red squares and blue circles. After six months, his memory-drawing was still of type II, but his reconstruction was of a matrix with a first column of red squares on top and red circles below, and a second column of blue squares on top and blue circles below.

TIS (7;4) provided a second-session drawing and reconstruction of a square matrix with red circles in two of the compartments, and red and blue squares in the other two. After six months, his drawing had deteriorated: he still produced a matrix but with red circles in two compartments and blue circles in the other two (regression from III to II). In his reconstruction, however, he produced the complete matrix. When he had finished his drawing, he was asked: Is that all?—*Yes, I think so.* During the reconstruction, he volunteered the following explanation: *Squares on top, circles below; the red ones here* (right-hand column) *and the same for the blue ones* (pointing to the left-hand column).—How did you remember it all?—*It just came to me.*

The most obvious interpretation is that this kind of progress does not concern the memory itself, since it does not affect the type of recall; when they are presented with a choice of counters, these subjects simply engage in a practical exercise, without reference to the past. However, were that the case, these subjects ought to have been able to produce the same reconstructions six months earlier: operations involving the multiplication of classes evolve very slowly (in contrast to seriations whose development comprises several sub-stages).

It is worth noting that two out of three of the six- to seven-year-olds whose reconstructions had advanced in the course of six months belonged to the two groups that had been asked for descriptions, and that no difference could be detected between those who had been asked for a drawing one hour and, again, one week after presentation and those who had only produced a drawing after a week. This difference between these two-thirds and the rest, all of them in age groups where, as we saw, descriptions have an ameliorating effect on the memory even after a week (while nothing comparable occurs with four-to five-year-olds or eight-year-olds, either after a week or after several months), can only be explained by the combination of mnemonic with operational factors. It is to this combination that we must undoubtedly attribute the progress of six- to eight-year-olds, the more so as some of these subjects do not need a description to engage spontaneously in a conceptual analysis which they subsequently extend in conjunction with their remembrance of the reconstruction—thanks to the slight operational progress which subjects in this age group can be expected to make in the course of six months.

§4. *Remembrance of a poor figurative presentation of a logical multiplication*[1]

The remembrance of matrices is facilitated by their good figural form (though, as we saw, not good enough to guarantee correct memory-drawings after six months). Moreover, as one of us has shown elsewhere,[2] children are capable of filling the compartments of a previously constructed matrix (Raven) by figurative and perceptive means well before the appropriate operational structure emerges at the age of five to six years. Hence, our decision to examine the memory of a model whose figural form is exceedingly poor though not absurd (for a symbolic representation can be a good or a poor signifier without changing the signification of the significates).

To that end we presented our subjects with a two-dimensional matrix in which the objects (large = L; small = S; black = B and white = W) were placed not in the empty compartments, as is normally done, but on the perimeters (Figure 31). In that case, the external lines represent the real products LB, LW, SB and SW, and the internal lines the contradictory products LS and BW.

---

[1] In collaboration with E. Schmid-Kitzikis and C. Widmer.
[2] See B. Inhelder: 'De la configuration perceptive aux structures opératoires' in *Le Problème des stades en psychologie de l'enfant*, Presses Universitaires de France, 1955, p. 140. See also B. Inhelder and J. Piaget: *The Early Growth of Logic in the Child*, Routledge & Kegan Paul, 1964.

To remove these contradictions, the rectangles S and L need merely be placed crosswise so that their perimeters no longer coincide (except for the four points of intersection, which we can ignore for the purposes of the present test, since we are concerned with arbitrary symbols and not with geometry). In that case (Figure 32 a), the black (B) and white (W) elements will occupy the same lines but in accordance with another dichotomy: the

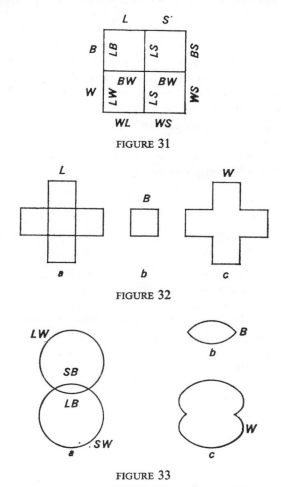

FIGURE 31

FIGURE 32

FIGURE 33

black, for instance, will be assigned to the inner square (Figure 32 b) and the white to the outer cross (Figure 32 c), in such a way that each segment of the general figure (a) will be uniquely LB, LW, SB or SW.

But since this arrangement is rather complicated, we can substitute intersecting circles for the rectangles (Figure 33 a). In that case, the upper circle will contain the L, the lower circle the S, the inner 'lens' (Figure 33 b) the B and the outer perimeter (Figure 33 c) the W: whence the four arcs of

166

circle *LW*, *SB*, *LB* and *SW*. It must, however, be stressed that this structure is not a simple intersection in the operational sense, since there are four instead of only three classes: the intersection only concerns the figurative aspect of the model, i.e. the signifier, while the operational structure is that of a logical multiplication (which admittedly includes intersections, but these are as complete as those of a matrix whose every compartment belongs to a vertical column and a horizontal row: whence we have four instead of three classes).

It is this combination of a simple intersection as the signifying figure with a complete multiplication of classes as the significate which is responsible for the poor figurative form and which makes the present experiment look rather absurd. But having investigated the memory of structures represented by good figural forms, we felt it important to check the results by a brief investigation of the memory of the model represented by Figure 33.

To show that we did not waste our time, we shall state the results at once. The first was, quite obviously, that the new structure is grasped at a later stage of development than is a matrical multiplication of four classes (in their normal figurative forms) or even an intersection (three classes). The second was that remembrance after a week corresponds almost exactly to the subjects' level of understanding, even though, in the case of the present model, the grasp of the multiplicative structure involves familiarity with some of the conventions we have adopted in constructing a model with such deceptive features. The third result was that, when they were reexamined six months later, seven of the thirty-four subjects had made clear progress, and this could not be explained in precisely the same terms as could the mnemonic advances we discovered in our earlier tests.

I. The subjects were seen during four sessions. In the first they were shown forty counters distributed over four arcs of circle, (Figure 33) according to their properties: *LW* (large and white), *SW* (small and white), *SB* (small and black) and *LB* (large and black). The subjects were then asked: (*a*) to draw all the objects with their distinctive properties (*L*, *S*, *W* and *B*); (*b*) to describe the general configuration; and (*c*) to supply criteria of classification. A second group of subjects was presented with eighteen large, small, white or black animals, belonging to eighteen distinct species; this fact, which may enhance the figurative interest of the whole presentation, may also divert attention from the differences in size and colour.

The second session was held one hour later. The subjects were first asked for a verbal description of what happened during the first session (no drawings were called for). Then the material was brought out again (plus two supplementary counters or animals) and the subjects were asked to reconstruct the model. When they had finished, they were asked whether or not they were satisfied with their reconstruction and why (interpretation).

167

The third session was held a week later and began like the second. At the end, the objects were jumbled up, and the subjects were asked for a first classification based on at least one criterion, and for a second based on another criterion (double classification or logical multiplication).

The fourth session was held six months after the presentation, and was similar to the second. For reasons we shall be explaining below, it proved abortive with the second group of subjects (presentation of animals).

II. Forty-eight subjects aged from 5 to 12–14 years were given the counter test, and some fifty in the same age groups were given the animal test. In their original description of the general configuration, these subjects proved not only relatively backward but also showed that they found the counter test easier than the animal test—the latter completely baffled all subjects below the age of ten, four out of eleven 10-year-olds, and six out of twelve 11- to 14-year-olds! The counter test, on the other hand, was described successfully by three subjects aged about 9 years and by sixteen out of eighteen 10- to 14-year-olds. The reason why the correct interpretations do not appear until fairly late in the course of the child's intellectual development is clear: it is due to the ambiguous nature of the model, which is neither an intersection of three classes (grasped during operational tests by 58 per cent of seven- to eight-year-old subjects and by 83 per cent of nine- to ten-year-old subjects) nor a matrical multiplication (the latter is grasped successfully by the age of seven to eight years).

As for the striking contrast between the reactions to the counters and the animals, particularly during the fourth session, when most of the subjects taking the animal test declared that they could remember little more than that animals had been shown to them, it might conceivably have been due to the fact that all the animals were of different species, so that the abstraction of size and colour proved more difficult than it did in the case of homogeneous counters. But since the child himself described these two properties of each element during the presentation of the models, the failure must, in fact, be due to poor mnemonic retention of the multiplicative classification and not to poor perception. Here, the rôle of the classificatory schema can be clearly discerned—its conservation is essential to the memory and, in the particular case of the animal test, is impeded by the complexity of the model.

III. When they were re-examined a week later, only five of the ten subjects who had previously grasped the arrangement of the animals were able to reproduce it correctly, while one subject who had failed to grasp the arrangement during the first session now produced the correct reconstruction. By contrast, eighteen of the nineteen subjects who had grasped the distribution of the counters during the earlier sessions also offered satisfactory reproductions during the third, as did one subject who had apparently failed to express himself properly during the first session. Clearly, therefore, remembrance of the model was bound up with its comprehension, which, as we cannot stress enough, also entails the assimilation of the particular conventions we have adopted.

Now for a few brief words about the memory distortions we observed. The most primitive response was that of a 5;5-year-old who arranged his animals in simple rows without any attempt at classification. Next came classifications based on one criterion only, with the elements placed in two separate or, often, in two concentric circles. Then, there were some subjects who produced intersecting circles but used a dichotomous classification, for instance, distinguishing between L and S but not between S and W. This construction is easily explained: the over-all logical structure comprises two dichotomies, and the additive schemata often prevail over the multiplicative schemata (see §§1 and 2).

If two criteria are used, the resulting figure may still bear little resemblance to the original model: for instance the child may construct two concentric circles with the LW and LB in the upper half and the SW and SB in the lower. Or else he may arrange them as in the model but without the intersections (concentric circles divided horizontally into two halves). He may also offer two unrelated dichotomies.

Now, as we have seen, there is a close correspondence between these different types of memory and the results of the analysis the subject was asked to make during the first session when, in view of the arbitrary figural form and the small number of classes (4) he might perfectly well have had a purely passive and figurative memory of the configuration he was shown.

IV. After six months, we re-examined thirty of the subjects who had taken the counter test and four who had taken the animal test (the rest had forgotten everything). Of these thirty-four subjects, seven had improved their memories, fourteen had regressed, and thirteen produced memories of the same quality.

Of those who had made progress, one subject (5;5) who had taken the animal test and who had drawn two separate circles during the third session, now offered two concentric circles but conserved his original dichotomy based on two criteria only. A nine-year-old and a ten-year-old conserved their original concentric circles but improved the organization of the four classes. One subject (6;5), who had contented himself with two concentric circles and a simple dichotomy (SW and LB) during the third session, now produced two concentric circles divided into four sectors, into which he distributed the four classes. Three subjects (6;4, 11;0 and 11;9), who had produced concentric circles during the third session, now offered two intersecting circles and indicated the distribution of the four classes more or less accurately.

In other words, with the exception of the first, all these subjects probably owed their progress to the impetus of the conflict between the figural form (intersection) and the structural content (four classes) of the model. Either the subject sticks to the idea of concentric circles and does his best to fit the four classes into the sectors, or else, dissatisfied with this arrangement and its arbitrary sub-divisions, he resurrects the intersection and arranges the four classes as best he can.

The thirteen subjects who produced equivalent memories during the third and fourth sessions do not pose any special problem, least of all those who remembered the model correctly. The only possible exceptions were two subjects aged 7;5 and 9;2 respectively, who transformed the concentric circles of their first drawings into two ovals, no doubt because they recalled the lens-shape of the intersecting circles.

The regressions, finally, were represented by: (a) dissociations (concentric circles now separated); (b) simplifications (two concentric circles B and W originally divided into two halves S and L now transformed into single circle with four sectors); (c) the most common case (six subjects): opposition of sectors based on one criterion with a mixture of elements based on the second.

In general, therefore, remembrance of the model after six months inclines towards schematization, which may assume three distinct forms and lead to three distinct results:

(1) There may be a simplifying schematization which tends to focus attention on the schema rather than on the scheme,[1] and often entails loss of information.

(2) There may be a logicizing schematization (i.e. in the direction of the scheme and no longer of the schema) which, if the initial model is not logical, may lead to coherent neo-formations, forcing the subject to modify his memories. In that case, we have a logical deformation of the model.

(3) There can also be a logicizing schematization which conserves and reconstructs what logic there may have been in the original model and which explains the progress revealed during the last session as an attempt to repair what has not been grasped partially or fully during the inspection of the model.

In short, this brief probe into a situation in which the double-classification schema is in conflict with the specially contrived figural arrangement leads to two important conclusions:

(a) The types of mnemonic organization involved are the same as

---

[1] For a definition of the terms 'schema' and 'scheme', see p. 382.

in the case of the matrix described in §§1 and 2: arbitrary figurative arrangements (cf. type I), simple dichotomies (cf. type II), arbitrary multiplicative compositions (type IV) and correct multiplicative compositions (type V). There is also the equivalent of type III, in which the figurative arrangement of the model is remembered, but in the form of simple dichotomies;

(b) It follows that the memory, in this paradoxical case no less than in that of the matrix, is swayed more strongly by the subjects' operational schemata than by the figural form of the model, which, in the present case, is generally 'corrected' by adaptation to these schemata. Moreover, when the double classification schema is obstructed by the complexity of the contents, i.e. by the fact that the sub-classes *LB*, *LW*, *SB* and *SW* comprise a host of heterogeneous sub-divisions (the case of animals as distinct from counters), the memory is degraded because it lacks the support of a simple structure. In all these cases, the control experiment therefore confirms what we have learned during our previous analysis, of which it thus constitutes a kind of *reductio ad absurdum* proof.

CHAPTER NINE

The Remembrance of Class Intersections[1]

Having established that the memory of multiplicative matrices (classes and relations) develops in full accord with the evolution of the underlying operational schemata, we decided to go on to an examination of the remembrance of simple class intersections. It might, of course, be argued that this complementary analysis can add little to what we already know; after all, an intersection is but a particular case of the multiplicative operations associated with the matrices we discussed in the last chapter. However, we were firmly convinced that intersections pose a special and very real problem: an intersection can (and, from our point of view, must) be considered as an isolated and, hence, incomplete operation, while the matrix multiplication (isomorphous to a Cartesian product) is a complete operation.

Our model consisted of a class of blue and another of round buttons placed inside two intersecting circles (Figure 34 I), the intersection containing the common part of these two classes, i.e. the sub-class of blue and round buttons, and the outer sectors containing the sub-classes of blue and non-circular buttons (in the case of our experiment square blue buttons) and of non-blue buttons (in our case red discs).

Now, these three sub-classes are quite obviously part of a multiplicative matrix, identical to the one we discussed in the last chapter (§1) and represented by Figure 34 II: here, the two vertical columns consist of blue and red buttons respectively, and the two horizontal rows of round and square buttons. But in that case, the matrix will represent a complete operation, since all four sub-classes are present, including that of the red squares which do not occur in Figure 34 I. Moreover, the new matrix is a generalization of the operation involved in the construction of intersections, since each of its four compartments contains two classes *at once*: that of blue or red buttons and that of round or square buttons. Figure 34 II, however, can be rearranged so as to represent the incomplete operation illustrated by Figure 34 I, by the simple transformation of its four squares into two rectangles (the round *or* blue buttons) sharing a common square (the round *and* blue buttons) (Figure 34 III).

The distinction between the complete and incomplete operations can be expressed most clearly in terms of the negations they introduce: in Figure

[1] In collaboration with E. Schmid-Kitzikis and A. Bauer.

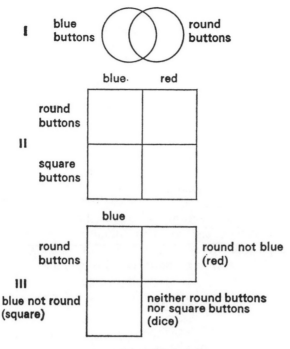

FIGURE 34

34 II, those objects that are neither blue nor round buttons may be square and red buttons, and, in Figure 34 II, they can, in fact, be nothing else. In Figure 34 I (intersecting circles) and Figure 34 III (intersecting rectangles), on the other hand, those objects that are neither blue nor round fall outside the figure: they could, in fact, be anything, including buttons, pebbles, trees or dice.

Now for the psychological problem. In an earlier study of the origins of multiplicative operations,[1] two of us have shown that, as far as the intelligence is concerned, the operations involved in a complete or matrix multiplication (Cartesian product) are easier to perform and appear earlier than those involved in simple intersections. Thus, when working with Raven's matrices, in which an empty compartment has to be filled with various objects, young subjects find it easier to fill one of the empty compartments of Figure 34 II, than to fill the common part of Figure 34 III (and this even when multiplying sub-classes: for example green objects and leaves, whose common part consists of green leaves only). While the complete multiplication is mastered at the age of about seven to eight years,

[1] See J. Piaget and B. Inhelder: *The Early Growth of Logic in the Child*, Routledge & Kegan Paul, 1964, Chapter VI.

simple intersections are not mastered until about the age of nine years. In other words, the general structures are grasped more easily than the isolated operations abstracted from them, and this despite the fact that traditional logical atomists contend that intersections represent simpler operations because they are 'elementary' parts of a complete matrix.

But let us return to the memory. Since all the preceding experiments have tended to show that the memory rests on the schemata of the intelligence, we felt that it would be of great interest to establish whether or not there were any differences between the retention and recall of a complete multiplicative system, as described in the last chapter, and retention of the apparently simpler system represented by Figure 34 I. To that end, we used the same experimental material, except for the red squares, and also placed a number of dice outside the circles, which caused no extra difficulty—on the contrary, their effect, as expected, was to close the class of buttons. Moreover, as a control, we also presented a model consisting of a row of four separate circles (four separate classes) arranged at intervals of 5–10 cm and containing respectively square blue buttons, round blue buttons, round red buttons and dice.

§1. *Method and mnemonic levels*

The model depicted in Figure 34 is presented to subjects in Group A in the form of wire circles containing four red and round buttons (discs) in the common part, flanked by three blue squares on the left, and by six red discs on the right (Figure 35). The whole figure is surrounded by a dozen dice in a variety of colours. During the first session the subjects are asked to look at the model carefully and to describe what they have seen. If their description is too brief, they are asked a series of questions such as: 'Anything else? And what about this one?' etc. The method of presenting the model is therefore identical to the second method described in Chapter 8 (§1). A week later, the subjects are asked for a second description, a memory-drawing and a reconstruction, The same procedure is adopted six months later. A second group of subjects (Group B) is treated in exactly the same way, but, as we have said, in their case the four classes are placed in separate circles.

The two groups of subjects consisted of fifty-seven and fifty-two 4- to 10-year-old children respectively. We shall first discuss Group A, which, as we shall see, responded in much the same way as did children taking the matrix test described in the last chapter.

Type I. Subjects of this type made no attempt at classification and their responses proved too heterogeneous to be fitted into distinct sub-types. The extreme form was represented by Gil (4;6), who drew three adjoining circles and did not know what to put into them; during his reconstruction he filled one of the circles with as many elements as he could squash into it. Mon (5;10) drew just one circle and filled it with all the elements including the dice. And (4;7) drew two intersecting circles, but left the first of these and the common part empty, and crowded all the elements (including the dice) into the remaining part of the second circle. At the other extreme, several

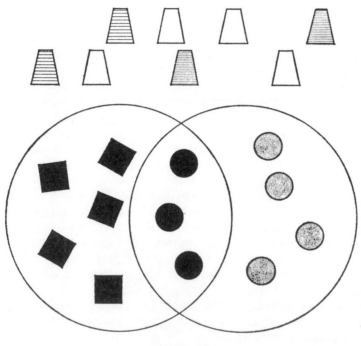

FIGURE 35

subjects drew two separate elements and no circles: for instance a red disc and a blue square (which was not present in the original model).

There were also several transitional types between I and II, who produced rudimentary but incomplete dichotomies: Cri (5;7) drew two circles, one crowded with all the buttons, and the other containing the dice.

Type II. This type differed from the last in that it involved an attempt at classification based on dichotomies: the dice in particular were regularly put to one side. Moreover, it differed from type III in that the intersection was omitted: the two circles either touched or were left out altogether. Subjects of sub-type IIA (for example, Mar

175

6;11) drew two juxtaposed circles, one of which contained one sub-class (blue squares) and the other the remaining buttons (including some in new colours), with the dice placed outside. Subjects of sub-type IIB (six to eight years old) distinguished two of the sub-classes but left out the third; their circles were set apart or else omitted. Subjects of sub-type IIC (seven to eight years old) produced similar reactions, but closer towards type III in that their circles were neither separate nor in intersection, but combined into a ∞-shape.

We may also have to treat as type II the common practice of representing the sub-classes by one element only: thus Cla (6;1) drew one blue disc and one red square flanked by several dice.

Type III. Just as some subjects remembered the general shape of the matrix (Chapter 8) but in the form of simple dichotomies (and with repetition of one of the sub-classes in two sections), so also subjects of sub-type IIIA (seven to eight years old) leave the common part (intersection) empty and place opposite sub-classes in the other parts: red discs and blue discs, or red squares and blue discs, or even red squares (not present in the model) and red discs, etc. Subjects of sub-type IIIB (also seven to eight years old), on the contrary, fill the common part with the same elements as appear in one of the outer segments: blue discs in one of the circles including the common part, and red discs in the other part of the second circle, etc. Subjects of sub-type IIIC, finally, draw symmetrical outer sectors: red discs in the intersection and blue discs in the rest (Die 7;8) or two blue discs in the intersection and red squares in the rest (Isa 10;4), etc.

Type IV. Subjects of this type begin to grasp and hence to remember the intersection of classes as a logical schema. But, as also happened with the matrices treated in Chapter 8, some subjects (eight to ten years old in the present case, and seven to eight years old in the case of the matrices) may remember the logical intersection yet not its figurative representation. Thus, subjects of sub-type IVA (transition between types between III and IV) draw the intersecting circles but do not localize the common sub-class (blue discs) in them; Arc (9;0), for instance, placed the blue squares in the outer part of the left circle, and the blue discs in the inner part and also in the intersection; finally, he placed the red discs in the outer part of the right circle. Subjects of sub-type IVB draw no circles at all, but arrange the sub-classes (including the common one) in the correct order, or else, like Syl (8;3), they draw two separate circles, one containing the blue squares, the other the red discs, and place the blue discs between them. In her reconstruction, however, Syl arrived at the correct figure.

Type V. Here, we have perfect remembrance, both figuratively and logically (one 8-year-old and three 9- to 10-year-olds in respect of recall, and two or three 5- to 6-year-olds in respect of their recon-structions).

Before we analyse these results, we must first examine the cor-responding responses of Group B (four separate circles containing the same classes and sub-classes):

Type I: no classification; identical or single buttons without surrounding circles;

Type II: two kinds of buttons (with a possible mixture in one of the two classes);

Type III: three classes, but no logical intersection;

Type IV: four classes, but no logical intersection;

Type V: four classes, with blue discs placed between blue squares and red discs (with or without surrounding circles, which are not generally drawn in before the age of seven years).

§2. *Responses after one week*

I. Let us, first of all, look at the percentage distribution of the different types of memories in the two groups of subjects in Tables 19 and 20 (absolute numbers shown in brackets).

On comparing these results with those listed in Chapter 8, §2, we see at once that children find it much more difficult to remember intersections than multiplicative matrices. Thus, while types IV and V are almost completely absent up to and including the age of seven years and only represent about a quarter of the eight-year-old subjects in the present case, the same types are represented by 10–24 per cent of the five- to seven-year-old subjects and by half the eight-year-olds in the case of the matrices. In respect of the reconstructions, too, success is achieved at about the age of eight years with the matrices (77 per cent) and only at about the age of nine to ten years with the intersections.

Now why precisely should it prove so much more difficult to remember the latter? The first reason to spring to mind is, naturally, the lack of correspondence between the figurative interpretation and the intrinsic figural attributes of the model. However, this whole question is still shrouded in obscurity.

II. As for the circles (made of wire in the model) which, from a certain level onwards, clearly act as symbols encouraging the com-prehension of the intersection, it is a remarkable fact that they are systematically left out from the drawings of four- to six-year olds, and are not produced spontaneously until about the age of seven or eight years. If their inclusion is suggested to four- to six-year-olds, they will often show mnemonic regress in respect of the contents,

TABLE 19 *Remembrance of intersecting circles*

	Memory-drawings							Reconstructions						
	I	*II*	*III*	*II–III*	*IV*	*V*	*IV–V*	*I*	*II*	*III*	*II–III*	*IV*	*V*	*IV–V*
4–5 years (13)	53 (7)	(4)	(2)	46 (6)	(0)	(0)	0	23 (3)	(3)	(2)	38 (5)	(2)	(3)	38 (5)
6 years (10)	0	(7)	(2)	90 (9)	(1)	0	10 (1)	0	(2)	(4)	60 (6)	(2)	(2)	40 (4)
7 years (10)	0	(5)	(5)	100 (10)	(0)	(0)	(0)	10 (1)	(2)	(4)	60 (6)	(1)	(2)	30 (3)
8 years (11)	9 (1)	(3)	(4)	63 (7)	(2)	(1)	27 (3)	9 (1)	(1)	(5)	55 (6)	(2)	(2)	36 (4)
9–10 years (13)	0	(1)	(5)	46 (6)	(4)	(3)	54 (7)	7 (1)	(2)	(0)	15 (2)	(4)	(6)	77 (10)

TABLE 20 *Results of test with the second group (separate circles placed in a row)*

	Memory-drawings							Reconstructions						
	I	*II*	*III*	*II–III*	*IV*	*V*	*IV–V*	*I*	*II*	*III*	*II–III*	*IV*	*V*	*IV–V*
4–5 years (11)	27 (3)	(2)	(5)	63 (7)	(0)	(1)	9 (1)	0	(1)	(0)	9 (1)	(4)	(6)	90 (10)
6 years (10)	0	(1)	(6)	70 (7)	(1)	(2)	30 (3)	0	(0)	(1)	10 (1)	(4)	(5)	90 (9)
7 years (9)	0	(1)	(4)	55 (5)	(3)	(1)	44 (4)	0	(0)	(1)	11 (1)	(3)	(5)	89 (8)
8 years (11)	0	(1)	(8)	82 (9)	(1)	(1)	17 (2)	0	(0)	(3)	27 (3)	(4)	(4)	72 (8)
9–10 years (11)	0	(1)	(3)	36 (4)	(2)	(5)	63 (7)	0	(3)	(0)	27 (3)	(1)	(7)	72 (8)

and even separate the circles (e.g. produce the ∞-shaped form we have mentioned). It is worth recalling that, in the case of the matrices described in Chapter 8, the model did not have a wire or even a pencil cross, whereas the matrices described in Chapter 7 did have the compartments carefully drawn in (to separate the sixteen elements); now, in the last case, too, the frame was only remembered by subjects who had reached the age of seven, and sometimes of eight, years.

The influence of the intersecting circles is best appreciated from a comparison of the responses of Group A with those of Group B (separate circles arranged in a row): the latter produce plainly superior memory-drawings between the ages of four and seven (inclusive), and spectacularly successful reconstructions (89 per cent and 90 per cent successes at the age of five to seven years). However, since this percentage drops to 72 per cent at the age of eight to ten years, we are bound to conclude that remembrance of the present model is essentially figurative at the age of four to seven years, to deteriorate as soon as the intersection problem comes to the fore (at the age of eight to ten years). In this connection, it should also be noted that the memory-drawings of the two groups of subjects (intersecting or separate circles) are more or less identical at the age of eight to ten years (41 per cent of type IV and V in both cases). Hence, it is difficult to assert that it is easier to remember the complete multiplication (matrix) simply because it lacks a symbolic framework.

Coming now to the intrinsic figural qualities, it might be argued that the arrangement of the four sub-classes in a square matrix is more 'pregnant' than that of two intersecting classes (three sub-classes only), and this simply because the matrix contains two axes of symmetry, and the intersection only one. But why should two axes be better than one? We saw, in Chapter 7, how much more difficult it is to remember a symmetrical *Gestalt* in the form of a square than it is to remember a double seriation. Moreover, in double classification (complete multiplication) the figure is not fully symmetrical: the squares are opposed to the discs and the blues to the reds in two dimensions, so that there is a two-dimensional overlap, and this arrangement can hardly be said to have a greater figural 'pregnancy' than a one-dimensional intersection.

It would seem, therefore, that the decisive factor does not lie in the figurative qualities alone, but that it must also be sought in the conceptual structure (whose figurative aspect constitutes an important symbol of the significate): the class multiplication is 'complete' and, hence, satisfying, while the simple intersection contains three sub-classes instead of four, i.e. it has a hiatus whose effects we have still to determine. Let us first of all point out that children (often up to the age of ten years) will frequently think they can remember seeing red squares in addition to the other three sub-classes or in the place of one of them (in their drawings but not in their reconstructions). And, indeed, why should the red squares have been omitted except for purely arbitrary reasons? We may take it, therefore, that a complete model is more satisfying than an incomplete one, for the memory no less than for the intelligence, and that its figural attributes are 'pregnant' (as in the square matrix), to the extent that they express this completeness. The intersecting circles will therefore act as impediments inasmuch as they accentuate the existence of a hiatus, while the simple alignment of separate circles does not: it represents each class or sub-class as an independent whole.

Nor is that all. It is characteristic of the incompleteness of the intersection that it implies a negation. Thus, while the blue discs in the common sector are both round and blue, the other sectors represent negations as well as affirmations: the remaining blue elements are blue but *not* round and the remaining round elements, round but *not* blue. In the complete multiplication involved in the matrix, on the other hand, each sub-class has two attributes at once: in that case, the negation disappears and the model can be described in complementary terms as in the 'non negational' logic of the Dutch logician Griss. From the psychological point of view, the hiatus presents a considerable obstacle, since it is the wholly positive character of the complete structure which explains its conceptual and figurative pregnancy.

III. Let us now compare the memory-drawings of our subjects with their reconstructions. In both groups, the reconstructions were clearly the better of the two, and in a far greater number of children than in the case of matrix multiplications. The reader will recall that, with the latter, three subjects produced better reconstructions than memory-drawings, and one subject produced the opposite response. In the present case the corresponding figures were as shown in Table 21 ($R > D$ signifies reconstructions superior to drawings).

In other words, there were seven advances to one regression in the case of the intersections, and fourteen advances to one regression in the case of the separate circles. Stationary cases accounted for 45 per cent of Group A and 43 per cent of Group B (as against 71 per cent in the case of the matrices).

The difference is easily explained in the light of our preceding remarks. With the matrices, children who had not grasped the underlying principle tended to produce better classifications in the presence of the material than they did without. With the intersection, this process was accentuated further because the possible sub-classes

TABLE 21   *Comparison of recall and reconstructions (after a week)*

	$R > D$	$R = D$	$R < D$
Intersecting circles	27	26	4
Separate circles in a row	28	23	2

were incomplete and the omissions quite arbitrary. The result was a considerable advance in the figurative memory of four- to seven-year-olds. That this advance was, in fact, a form of retreat is shown by the fact that eight-year-olds produced less satisfactory reconstructions of the intersection than they did of the matrices; only in the case of the separate circles set out in a row was their reconstructive memory improved by the greater figurative simplicity of the model.

§3. *Responses after six months*

The reader will remember that while the recall by four- to five-year-olds of four-class multiplicative structures deteriorated with time, six- to eight-year-olds improved their reconstructions in the course of six months. Moreover, though on immediate recall or recall after a week, the original four classes were reduced to three, the number was later brought back to four by those subjects who had made some progress, and reduced to two by those who had reverted to types II and III. It is no doubt the lack of 'pregnancy' and stability of three-class structures which explains why the correct reconstruction of matrices should precede that of intersections, why young children should find it so difficult to remember the latter, and why, after six months, there should be a systematic deterioration in the remembrance of intersections, at least in subjects from four to eight and a half years of age (the case of subjects from 8;6 to ten years will be discussed under III).

I. In order to look more closely into the matter, we gave a group of five- to eight-year-olds a recognition test six months (or more precisely five to ten months) after the original presentation, but naturally after first demanding a memory-drawing and allowing a week to elapse after that, lest the drawing have too great an influence on the powers of recognition. In the test, we showed our subjects eleven colour photographs of the buttons and dice, two of which corresponded to the original models (intersecting circles or separate circles in a row) and the remaining nine of which represented the most common mistakes of younger subjects (Figure 36).

181

The subjects were then asked to point out the photographs that bore the closest and those that bore the least resemblance to the model, and to justify their choice.

Now, all our twenty-eight subjects from 5 to 8;2 years (fourteen in each group) made relatively good choices, which suggests that their very low level of graphic recall was not so much due to a deterioration of their figurative memories, as such, as to their inability to confer any meaning on these incomplete structures.

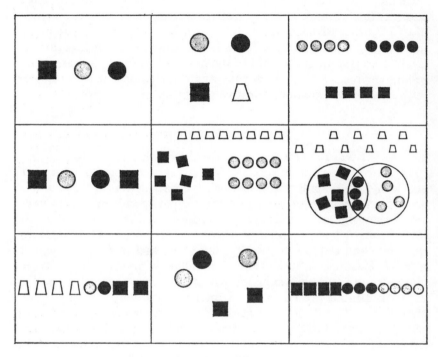

FIGURE 36

In particular, twelve of the fourteen subjects in Group A (intersection circles) chose the correct photographs, and eleven did so to the exclusion of all others (these subjects were all in the age group 6 +). Moreover, thirteen of these fourteen only chose photographs with wire circles.

By contrast, of the fourteen subjects in Group B (buttons and dice in separate circles) only seven recognized the model, and only eight chose photographs incorporating the symbolic circles, and of these eight, four first chose the intersecting-circle model (which they had never been shown) before finally selecting the correct figure.

This difference between the two groups shows very clearly that the intersecting circles tend to have a strong perceptive effect and are therefore more easily recognized (all seven- to eight-year-old subjects in Group A picked them out without hesitation). If they omit the circles from their drawings, they must, therefore, do so for quite special reasons.

Here are a few examples from Group A. MYR (5) selected the correct model. Why? *I knew, because the others were different. In that one* (No. 6) *the counters are correct* (but) *they are in a row and* (in the model) *they weren't.*—And the worst picture?—*That one* (No. 9) *because it hasn't any dice, and this one* (No. 2) *because it has only one die.* During the test of her recall, Myr had drawn nothing but discs (= a single class = type I) and, in particular, had omitted the circles.

GIA (6): *This one* (No. 6, correct) *because there were round ones.*—And what about this one (No. 2)?—*No, that's no good; there were just two of them and they were big.*—And which one is the worst?—*That one* (No. 1) *because it hasn't got the other counters or any of the dice.* Gia's recall, too, was of type I (a single counter and one die).

LIS (6;4) proved to be a highly instructive case. Her recall was of type II: three red and three blue discs in two separate rows, and some dice in addition. During the recognition test, however, she unhesitatingly selected the correct figure, explaining that '*it's almost the same as I drew*'.

MAN (6;6), who had drawn two classes inside two circles, chose both models (separate and intersecting circles) during the recognition test. Why?—*Because they were like this and like that.*

MAD (7;10) had drawn one large circle, on the circumference of which he had placed a large number of round buttons in all sorts of colours. During the recognition test, he nevertheless chose the correct model straight away. The worst model was No. 7 '*because they are all in a row and some of them are missing*'.

As for Group B, seven out of the fourteen subjects chose cards without circles as well as No. 6, but, of the seven who selected the correct model, four had chosen another one first, and one that resembled nothing they had ever been shown:

MAR (6;6) vacillated between five cards: *The rest are no good.*—And if you had to choose just one?—*I'd pick that one* (No. 6: intersection) *because it has all kinds* (= classes). *And that one as well; these two have everything.* His drawing had been of three disjoint circles, one empty and the other two containing the same class (blue discs).

STE (7;6) produced a memory-drawing of two classes, but during the recognition test he first chose No. 6 '*because it has more of the dice*' and then No. 5 because it had the same number!

Clearly, the intersecting circles have no significance at this level and are remembered for purely figurative reasons. But their figurative impact is so strong that they are far more easily remembered and recognized than are the separate circles.

183

II. Turning now to mnemonic recall, we find that our twenty-eight 5- to 8;2-year-olds fell into the categories shown in Table 22.

Classification proved to be extremely difficult for the four subjects of types III and IV. Group A did not offer a single intersecting circle, except for one subject, aged 7;11, who drew three intersecting circles followed by another set of eight, and placed the buttons, divided into two classes (small and large discs), outside. We accordingly classified him as type III. The doubtful subject of type IV, on the other hand, merely drew one circle containing one blue and one red disc, with a blue square placed between them, which would have been fairly good had he not substituted green and yellow discs for the dice. In Group B, one of the subjects of type IV, aged 6;6 years, drew a triangular arrangement (no circles) consisting of a blue square, a blue disc and a red disc, and changed the die into a snail which, he pointed out, was 'on the outside of the drawing'. Remarkably enough, this subject also expressed his surprise that 'there were no red squares',

TABLE 22 *Types of recall after six months*

	I	II	III	IV	V
Group A	7	5	1 (?)	1 (?)	0
Group B	3	9	0	2	0

which clearly shows how spurious he found a multiplication of classes containing three terms instead of the normal four.

The other subject of type IV (another six-year-old) drew two dice followed by a blue square, a red disc, a red square and a blue square, thus producing a complete multiplication without verbal explanations, but the more obvious in that the first square was red before he changed it to blue!

All the remaining subjects drew only one class, or an arbitrary mixture of elements (type I), or else a dichotomy (type II). There were also one or two drawings representing three classes but without intersections (for example, two red discs, two blue discs, one round and one square brown figure), which we classified as type II because they represented dichotomies, though accompanied by 'fillers' as at Stage I (the 7;5-year-old who offered this drawing said quite simply: 'There were several colours, so I'll put in another one', and promptly added the brown figures). All in all, therefore, these memory-drawings were much poorer than the corresponding recognitions, and this, clearly, because of a failure to grasp the significance of the intersections. This explains why the recall of the intersecting circles shown to Group A was poor, both after a week and after six months, while their recognitions were superior to those of Group B. And this is also why the best subjects in Group B came up with the complete multiplication. The symbolic circles were remembered by only three subjects in Group B and by six in group A; five of them drew these circles as separate figures and one in the correct way but without any contents. One-third of the subjects relied on single elements (and of these, two in three omitted the surrounding circles), and, in order to reconcile this presentation with their awareness that the model had contained a larger number of elements, they added one or more figures of the same shape but in different colours, which served to efface all traces of the multiplicative structure.

In short, after six months, even more so than after a week, the remembrance of the intersection differed strikingly from that of the complete multiplication (Chapter 8) and this for two connected reasons. The first is that in a collection of blue (B), red (R), circular (C) and square (Q) objects, the four classes CB, CR, QB and QR form a complete system, while the three classes CB, CR and QB seem incomplete because of the absence of the red squares QR. The second reason, which, if anything, is even more important than the first, is that in the multiplication $(C + Q) \times (B + R)$, the four sub-classes CB, CR, QB and QR are separate and symmetrical, whereas the system CB, CR, and QB (no QR) lacks symmetry and the class of the blues ($QB + CB$) is no longer separate from the class of the discs ($CB + CR$). This shows once again how great a sway the operational schemata hold over the memory.

III. With our 8;6 to ten-year-old subjects we used the same procedure in respect of graphic recall, but instead of the recognition test, the results of which had proved conclusive enough with the five- to eight-year-olds, we simply asked them for a reconstruction immediately after recall, just as we had done several months earlier. As a result, we were able to compare the quality of reconstructions produced at an interval of six to twelve months, which struck us as being important, since, in the case of multiplicative matrices (Chapter 8) the reconstructions had evolved quite differently from recall (many cases of progress in the former and regressions in the latter). Moreover, we realized that recognition and reconstruction tests were quite incompatible in the present case, since one of them reinforces the other. That is precisely why we decided to confine the recognition test to five- to eight-year-olds, on the grounds that, if successful (which was the case), the results would apply *a fortiori* to subjects from 8;6 to ten years, because, if they failed, five- to eight-year-olds would do even worse.

Unfortunately, we could only bring back fourteen of our 8;6 to ten-year-olds (most of the rest had left Geneva in the meantime). Ten of these were of Group A and four of Group B, but though the number was small, it served our purpose well enough.

There was first of all an advance (8½ years) in Group A: one week after the presentation, this subject had drawn two circles arranged as a ∞, one containing four red discs and the other four blue squares, with five dice on the outside (his reconstruction was identical except that the circles were separated). After seven months, his drawing and reconstruction alike consisted of two touching circles, one containing five red discs and the other five blue discs and six blue squares, and there were also some ten discs of different colours. His response showed that, even if the rôle of the circles is not grasped, the classes can nevertheless be represented in the correct way.

In Group B, there was another advance, but only in respect of the drawing—this subject (9;0) had produced a correct reconstruction during the first test. His original drawing had been of three separate circles containing a single blue disc, a red square and another red square, with a number of dice outside. Several months later, his reconstruction was still excellent, and his drawing, too, was correct except for one mistake: he started with three separate circles, one containing ten dice in nine different colours, the second ten blue squares, and the third ten red discs, but, after inspection, observed that he had 'forgotten' something (the four holes for sewing the buttons on). He now added a fourth circle, containing ten blue discs which he could no longer squash in beside the blue squares.

A further five subjects, who represented a mixture of progress and regress, nevertheless introduced some highly interesting schematizations. The first (a girl precisely ten years old six months after the presentation) had originally drawn a long row of four sets of elements all in a straight line (no circles): red discs, red squares, blue discs and blue squares; the dice appeared in a separate straight line. Six months later, she produced a large oval (but with three large bumps for arcs) containing the dice and the red and blue discs. Her original reconstruction had contained dice, two large circles surrounding red discs and blue squares respectively, three smaller circles surrounding the same elements, with blue buttons (square and round) scattered outside: her over-all arrangement was thus completely chaotic, but she had rightly omitted the red squares. Six months later, her reconstruction consisted of two pairs of superposed circles (= 'they ran round both lots' = memory of the intersection, but schematized into complete superpositions), the first pair containing dice and blue and red squares, and the second pair the same elements plus several red discs (the absence of red squares was remembered correctly). A nine-year-old subject produced an original drawing of two intersecting circles containing blue discs in the common part and in one of the outer sectors, and red discs in the other (two classes in all). Eight months later, he drew two separate circles, one containing blue discs and the other red squares (non-existent in the model), but he also introduced a third class, which, though constructed of yellow ovals (placed between the circles), showed that he had made some progress.

In his reconstruction (correct during the second session) he looked in vain for these ovals among the material, and then made do with the two other classes. A third subject, aged ten years, who, one week after the presentation had drawn two intersecting circles with the common part empty, and the remainder containing blue squares and red discs respectively, proceeded in much the same way seven months later, but added the blue discs, thus showing that he, too, had made progress. By contrast, his reconstruction, which had been correct after a week, now consisted of (a) blue squares; (b) blue and red discs; and (c) a common part containing red discs and blue squares. A fourth subject, aged 8½ years (Group B), who had originally produced a drawing of two classes without circles (blue discs and one red disc plus the dice), now offered three classes (scarlet discs, dark red discs and yellow discs, plus the dice). His reconstructions were correct both after a week and also after seven months, except that the circles were missing.

Finally, one 9-year-old (Group A) produced a first drawing and reconstruction of intersecting circles, with the first sector containing blue discs and squares, the common sector blue discs, and the other sector blue and red discs. Eight months later his drawing was of inferior quality (four classes) but his reconstruction was based on an improved schematization: two empty, intersecting circles surrounded by sets of blue squares, blue discs and red discs. In other words, though his circles were pointless, he had clearly separated the three classes.

Next came four subjects who, after six to ten months, proved to be a mixture of stationary responses (generally in respect of their reconstructions) and regress (generally in respect of their drawings). One 9-year-old subject produced the correct reconstructions both after a week and after six months; his original drawing, too, was correct, but six months later he filled the intersection with blue squares, and the outer sectors with red squares and red discs (symmetrical arrangement but no intersection of classes). One subject, aged 8;10 years, made a first drawing of three classes (but including a red square and omitting the intersecting circles); seven months later he produced two classes only. His reconstructions on both occasions were identical (type IV). Another subject (8;6) also produced a type IV reconstruction, but in his drawings he omitted the intersecting circles (with the common part empty) in favour of separate circles (three classes). Another eight-year-old, on the other hand, supplied two equivalent drawings (two classes) while his reconstructions reverted from type V to type III. Except for the last subject, therefore, who was, moreover, one of the youngest in his age group, all the regressions we have just described were confined to the drawings.

Finally, there were three regressions in respect of both the drawings and the reconstructions. One subject (8;10) produced a first drawing of two separate circles containing three classes, but with the blue discs placed between the circles. After eight months he could only remember two superposed circles and the dice, but not the buttons. His reconstruction, which had been correct one week after the presentation, was still correct eight months later, but only in respect of the position of the classes: he now omitted the circles. One subject in Group B (9;6) who had produced a correct drawing and a correct reconstruction after a week, retained the three classes eight months later as well, but the blue discs had turned green and now appeared outside the circles; his reconstruction was of the same type. The third subject (9;7) offered an original drawing of two classes only (plus the dice) and the correct reconstruction; seven months later, his reconstruction and drawing both contained four circles with the elements jumbled up inside.

All in all, therefore, eight out of these fourteen cases produced better reconstructions than drawings after six months, five produced reproductions and drawings of the same level, and one produced a drawing superior to his reconstruction. These findings compare most unfavourably with the progress in the reconstruction of matrices (Chapter 8). For all that, 8;6 to ten-year-olds conserved their memories of the intersection of classes much better than do five- to eight-year-olds: two cases of progress, five combinations of partial progress and slight regress; four stationary cases with partial regress, and three cases of general but equally limited regress. The responses of the older subjects thus point to much the same thing as those of the younger group: on the one hand, the symbolic meaning of the intersecting circles is not properly grasped and, hence, badly remembered; on the other hand, the construction of the intersection as such (with or without the circles) is a much more incomplete and partly artificial operation than the construction of the Cartesian product (or complete multiplication) whence the clear difference in the mnemonic reactions to these two structures, particularly in the reconstructive sphere.

CHAPTER TEN

The Remembrance of an Arrangement[1]

The operation often described as an 'arrangement' is the permutation of n things taken all or r at a time. It is therefore not a multiplicative operation in the same sense as those described in Chapters 7 to 9, though it may be called a multiplication in the broader sense because it involves a squaring operation. In fact a permutation is a seriation of all the possible seriations or ordinations of the elements. Our main reason for examining the memory of such structures is therefore that they involve a higher operational level than the multiplication of classes or relations (and serial ones in particular). Thus, while simple, or first power, multiplications can be performed by children as soon as they have reached the level of so-called 'concrete' operations (seven to eight years), i.e. of operations based on step-by-step 'groupings', permutations call for a grasp of higher structures based on hypothetico-deductive, or 'formal', thought, i.e. on propositional operations with a combinatorial function, and these are not normally grasped until the age of eleven to twelve years. Hence, we thought it important to establish whether or not the memory of such structures (perceived but not constructed by the subjects themselves) obeys the same laws as that governing the structures we have been discussing, i.e. whether or not it, too, does not become perfected until the corresponding operation can be performed.

§1. *Method and memory levels*

The models chosen were the simplest possible: arrangements of three elements, taken two at a time. In fact, they were so simple that, had we not made a prior study of the development of the operations involved in combinations and permutations,[2] we might easily have concluded that the remembrance of these configurations was bound to be quite uncomplicated.

[1] In collaboration with C. Widmer.
[2] J. Piaget and B. Inhelder: *La Genèse de l'idée du hasard chez l'enfant*, Presses Universitaires de France, 1951, Chapter IX (English translation in preparation).

We used two distinct models, the first comprising the nine possible arrangements of three geometrical shapes taken two at a time (Figure 37, I): a square, a circle and a triangle, and the second of the nine permutations of a train set: a locomotive (*L*) a truck (*T*) and a carriage (*C*), again taken two at a time (Figure 37, II). Figure 37, I was shown to thirty-two children aged from four to 12;11 years,

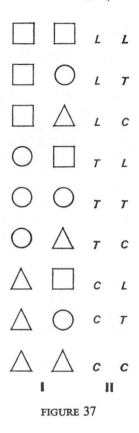

FIGURE 37

and Figure 37, II to twenty-eight different subjects of the same ages.

During the presentation, the child was asked for a brief description of the model and for his views about its orderly structure: 'Do you think it's all a mix-up or is there some order in it?' etc. The child was then asked to make a memory-drawing. A second memory-drawing was demanded a week later, followed by a reconstruction (for which purpose the child was handed a larger number of figures or railway trucks than were present in the original model). The same procedure was adopted six months later.

The following mnemonic types or levels were observed:

Type I. The elements are not arranged in pairs. Two sub-types can be distinguished. In the first (IA), the whole page or part of the page is filled with random elements. Thus, And (4;7) drew thirty-five circles, some in a straight line, together with eight squares and seven triangles scattered all over the paper. In sub-type IB the set consists of single elements only. Thus, Step (4;11) drew one circle, one square and one triangle. Here, as with matrices and intersections, this type represents a relatively faithful memory of the configuration coupled to a complete failure to grasp its significance. No wonder, therefore, that types I and IB only occur among very young or intellectually backward children.

If children of type IB are pressed for a further contribution, they will generally produce such empirical figures as a house, a tunnel, a fireman's helmet, etc., and if they are urged to pronounce on the order of the elements, they will often declare that the model was *'neatly arranged because it was nice'*.

Type II. This type introduces pairs of elements, but without any attempt to distinguish between them. The subject seems to have two aims: to proceed by pairs as in the model, and to cram the sheet with figures. The result is a jumble of pairs repeated at frequent intervals and without any order—there is no attempt to avoid repetitions, let alone to apply an exhaustive method. Moreover, identical pairs are invariably omitted. Thus, the second session drawing of Mar (4;11) consisted of twenty-one pairs including fifteen repetitions: 1 pair of squares (drawn first and probably by chance); 6 squares + circles; 6 triangles + circles; 5 circles + squares; 2 circles + triangles; and 1 triangle + square. The repeated couples were not in sequence and were apparently selected at random, and the inversions were purely accidental. In addition, there were two other subjects who substituted random triplets for the pairs.

Type III. Subjects of this type have the following two aims: to construct distinct pairs without repetition, and to multiply these pairs, especially by inversion. When one of these two tendencies is expressed without the other, we have sub-type IIIA. Thus, Joe (7;5) finished up with six distinct pairs, three of which were identical but none of which was an inversion; while Mag (7;0) produced eight pairs, four of which were inversions of the immediately preceding figure (4 pairs of pairs). When the two tendencies are combined, i.e. when there are systematic inversions and no repetitions, we have sub-type IIIB, which is fairly close to the correct solution. Thus, Ber (8;10) produced five pairs and Ped (8;7) produced six, both attempting to use a systematic approach: inversion of pairs, or six pairs, three of which began with a circle and two of which were inversions.

There is also a sub-type IIIB in which the combination of trial-and-error with a rudimentary system leads to the complete reconstruction of the nine pairs. But it is easy to distinguish this kind of success, based partly on chance, from the correct memories associated with type IV, in that, in the former, the pairs are not arranged in successive groups of three, all beginning with the same element. For example, Phi (9;8) constructed nine pairs beginning with T, L; T, C; L, C; T, C and L, T. In other words, his construction, though complete, was not based on an exhaustive system.

Type IV. Here we have the correct memory: nine pairs, consisting of three successions of three figures, all beginning with the same element. In sub-type IVA, the succession is imperfect (the second elements of the pairs do not follow in the same order as the first); in sub-type IVB it is perfect.

§2. *General results*

The fifty-eight subjects we examined proved to be of the types shown in Table 23.

The table not only shows that there is a clear correlation of type with age, but also that the correct memory does not appear until the level of propositional or 'formal' operations is reached: success was achieved by one 9½-year-old, by two 10-year-olds and by four

TABLE 23 *The remembrance of arrangements (immediate recall, in absolute numbers)*

	N	IA	IB	II	IIIA	IIIB	IIIC	IVA	IVB	I–II	III	IV
4 years (6)		2	2	2	0	0	0	0	0	6	0	0
5 years (7)		2	2	2	0	1	0	0	0	6	1	0
6 years (6)		0	1	0	5	0	0	0	0	1	5	0
7 years (12)		0	0	2	5	4	1	0	0	2	10	0
8 years (9)		0	0	1	0	6	2	0	0	1	8	0
9 years (5)		0	1	0	0	2	1	0	1	1	3	1
10 years (6)		0	0	0	0	2	2	1	1	0	4	2
11–12 years (7)		0	0	0	1	2	0	0	4	0	3	4

11- to 12-year-olds. Now, the model, which the subjects were merely asked to inspect and to describe, but not, of course, to construct themselves was, figuratively speaking, extremely simple and regular: three objects *A*, *B* and *C* repeated three times on the left side of the drawing and followed by the same three elements in rotation: (*A*)*A*, (*A*)*B*, (*A*)*C*, (*B*)*A*, (*B*)*B*, (*B*)*C*, and (*C*)*A*, (*C*)*B*, (*C*)*C*. One might therefore have expected that, particularly after having been asked for a description and an opinion about the order of succession, our subjects would have remembered this configuration, thanks to its configurative impact alone, and without recourse to the underlying operational law. However, we found once again that, before they can encode a structure sufficiently well to retain and decode it later, children must be in possession of a code corresponding to the operation itself. In other words, before they can remember an arrangement, they must be able to construct it themselves.

In this respect, the comparison of immediate recall with recall a

192

week later proved highly instructive, as did a comparison of the second memory-drawings with the reconstructions.

The second drawings included only four improvements on the first, so that there was no need to provide a special Table. Admittedly, two or three subjects, who had originally relied on single elements, now crammed the whole sheet with elements, and vice versa, but this in no way changed their levels (IA or IB). By contrast, the following four subjects all produced much more interesting responses:

(1) One subject (5;2) who had drawn numerous pairs during the first session (type II) now filled the page with single elements. His reconstruction was of the same type (IA);

(2) One subject (9;8) had used trial and error to produce a type IIIB memory during the first session (eight pairs in disorder). This rudimentary attempt at ordination enabled him, during the second session, to arrive, again by trial and error, at nine pairs, still in disorder (IIIC). His reconstruction, however, remained of type IIIB.

(3) One subject (10;9) had produced a type IIIC drawing during the first session, but being on the threshold of operationality, he reached type IV during the second session, both in respect of recall and reconstruction;

(4) One subject (8;4) produced a first memory-drawing that might have been based on a perfect system: in the first column, he put three squares, three circles and three triangles; in the second column, he placed another square, a circle and a triangle behind the first-column squares. Next to the first circle he also drew a square, and the experimenter was fully confident that he would continue in the same way to end up with a (precocious) type IV drawing. But he stopped in his tracks, as if lacking the appropriate memory-image, and only completed the series at the experimenter's prompting. During the second session (drawing and reconstruction) he began with three pairs of squares, followed by three circles and three triangles correctly associated with their partners. In other words, this subject lacked a precise memory of the system and had only half-correct memory-images—hence, his three pairs of squares.

A comparison of the second-session drawings, with the reconstructions that followed immediately afterwards, revealed no more than six changes among the sixty subjects we saw. Once again, we have to ignore some transitions from type IB to type IIA, since young children are always tempted to use more than three elements when they are shown some thirty figures (including rectangles which were not part of the original model). However, some of the reconstructions consisted of single elements, which never happened with the multiplicative structures discussed in the earlier chapters. The six changes were as follows:

(1–2) Two subjects (6;8 and 7;5) whose second drawing had been type III advanced to type IIIB in their reconstructions (distinct couples constructed by inversion).

(3) One subject (8;1) advanced from type II to type IIIA.

(4–6) By contrast, three subjects (7, 8 and 9 years) regressed from type IIIC to type IIIB, which shows clearly that the success achieved at the higher stage (nine complete pairs, but in disorder and constructed by trial and error) was purely fortuitous: there was no system coherent enough to ensure the correct reproduction of the model even in situations involving material actions (reconstructions).

No wonder, therefore, that changes as between the second drawing and the reconstruction were both rare (one case in ten) and non-polarized: three slight advances and three slight regressions. Now we know that there is clear progress between recall and reconstruction whenever the subject can avail himself of the appropriate pre-operational or operational schemata. In the case of permutations and combinations, however, the schemata do not emerge until the age of about ten to twelve years, whence the systematic predominance of types I to III in children between the ages of four and nine to ten years. It is the absence of these schemata which explains why there was no progress between recall and reconstruction in the present case, and particularly why there were no advances from IIIC to IV.

To sum up: the memory (recall and reconstruction) of an arrangement of three elements taken two at a time is reliable in only those subjects who have reached the age level at which the corresponding operations emerge. At the age of four and five years, the memory remains purely figurative in respect of both the individual elements and the pairs, and completely disorganised in respect of their succession. Between the age of six and nine years, there is a first attempt to structure the memory, but in a completely empirical way, and without any directive system: whence the predominance of type III, and the gradual advances from IIIA to IIIC. Only at the age of ten to twelve years do the correct memories appear in 33–57 per cent of our subjects. This trend once again points to a very close relationship between the organization of the memory of a static figure and the operations needed for its construction or reconstruction.

§3. *The memory after six months*[1]

Of our fifty-eight subjects, we were able to retrace forty-nine after six months (or, more precisely, after five to seven months). They were asked (by a new examiner) to state in a few words what they remembered of the model, and also to make a memory-drawing. Those subjects who had originally worked with the train set needed

---

[1] In collaboration with C. Challande.

no special prompting, but the rest had to be urged on, though only by such vague hints as: 'Can you recall the large blue one? Or that things were glued to the card?' One subject refused to respond, which, incidentally, does not prove that he had completely forgotten the model. Of the remaining forty-eight subjects, twenty-two had been shown the geometrical figures, and twenty-two the train set.

Let us begin by listing some of the special features we noted. Nine subjects had forgotten one element and two had forgotten two elements (most of these subjects had worked with the train set, the figurative details of which are subject to quicker mnemonic deterioration than those of the geometrical shapes). Five 6-year-olds added ovals or rectangles to the original geometrical figures. Several subjects, especially from eleven years onwards, produced triplets instead of pairs (seventeen out of the nineteen subjects who had been of type II a week after the presentation), and many of the younger ones extended their trains with additional trucks or carriages.

There were four advances in recall since the earlier sessions: one 5;1-year-old progressed from type IB to type IIIA and another of the same age produced a more systematic drawing than he had done six months earlier (pairs of identical figures instead of a mere jumble), and two subjects aged eight and eleven years advanced from type III to type IVA.

Next, there were twenty-four stationary cases (precisely half the number of subjects examined), including seven who could not have made progress since they were at Stage IV to begin with. Of the other seventeen, two were of type I, three of type II and twelve of type III. As for the twenty remaining subjects, eight had regressed (from Stages II and IIIA, but not from Stage IV) and twelve had made semi-regress, mainly due to their use of triplets.

We were struck by the ease with which all our subjects could recall some of the regular features of the model, immediately after presentation no less than some six months later. Admittedly, the operations involved in these arrangements belong to the propositional or hypothetico-deductive level, so that it is only natural that correct memories should not appear until the age of about eleven to twelve years, and, in certain precocious cases, until the age of nine or ten years. And it is a remarkable fact that, seven subjects in nine (77 per cent) having reached the age of $10\frac{1}{2}$ to twelve years six months after the presentation, should have had the correct (type IV) memories. For all that, subjects aged from seven to ten years, though unable to recall all the arrangements, were nevertheless able to remember an appreciable number of the regularities immediately after the presentation, and even several months later, which again shows how strongly the operational schemata influence the memory, often completing and guiding the figurative aspect. Thus, the substitution of triplets for pairs (seventeen cases) is a purely figurative error: in schematic terms, the triplets are a perfectly natural generalization of the arrangement, once the memory has become blunted.

PART III

The Remembrance of Causal Structures

In respect of the relationship of the memory to the intelligence, which constitutes the exclusive object of this book, it is true to say that our everyday memories bear either on static configurations, possibly resulting from actions or operations that we may remember as well, or else on causally interrelated states. In Parts I and II, we have been looking at the remembrance of the former; in what follows we shall be examining the remembrance of the latter. While we know very little about the detailed development of causal structures, we do know that causality appears first as a system of actions and later as a system of operations 'attributed' to the objects and not simply 'applied' to their description. This raises the question of whether the remembrance of causal structures obeys the same laws as do logico-arithmetical structures, or whether the two are quite distinct. The answer will be found in Chapters 11 to 14.

CHAPTER ELEVEN

Remembering a Causal Process Represented by Levers[1]

For the present experiment we have used two models which resemble each other in the static state, but represent two distinct causal mechanisms. The first model, which we shall call B (blue match-box), is rigid and held in position by a slide; when the handle a is pushed up, the whole model moves in a vertical direction (see Figure 38, II). Model R (topped by a red match-box), on the other hand, is fixed to the board by a central bolt, and its three segments are connected by two screws: when the handle a is pushed up, the segments b and c move down (Figure 38, IV).

§1. *Method and problems*

With the two models before him, the child is asked to provide a static description: 'What do we have on this board?' Next, he is told to move the two rods up (the direction is indicated by a gesture) and to note what happens. He is then told to pull the two rods down (new gesture), and again to watch the results carefully. Once he has done so, his attention is distracted for a minute, the material is hidden, and he is asked to describe and draw everything he remembers of the experiment. A week later, he is asked for a second description and memory-drawing, with a minimum of prompting by the examiner, who provides a number of wooden slats with which the child can illustrate his commentary. The same procedure is followed six months later.

We were again interested to discover if the responses could be fitted into distinct mnemonic types according to age, and if there was a direct relationship between these types and the child's level of understanding, or whether his memory was largely confined to the reproduction of what perceptive data he had been able to absorb. Some readers may object that this problem has been solved long since, but this is far from being the case, not only in respect of the memory

[1] In collaboration with P. Mounoud.

in general, but also in respect of the remembrance of causal processes in particular. In the case of the former, we are again confronted with the problematical nature of the encoding process, and above all with the question of whether or not the code varies with age, and hence with the level of the relevant schemata. As for the remembrance

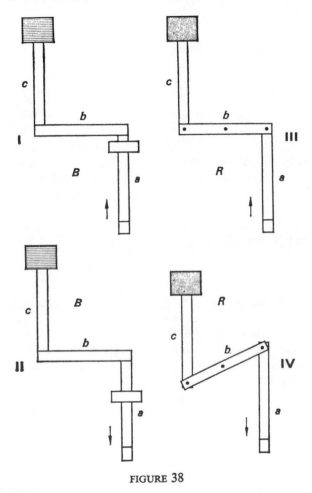

FIGURE 38

of causal processes, if the memory were confined to recoding, retaining and recalling perceptions, and hence involved no intellectual transformations, then it would rest exclusively on the 'observables'. Now, in the domain of mechanical or physical relationships represented by the next few models, the observable is the purely descriptive, no doubt associated with an increasingly searching analysis, but never transcending the data. In short, all the memory would retain in that case would be the regular or 'lawful' sequence of events, i.e. the set of observable and repeatable relations that lead from the bare fact to a natural law ('pure legality'). On the other hand, if the subject chiefly remembers what he has 'understood', he will, while observing and remembering the facts and the laws (however elementary) also remember, and this from the very outset, his own interpretation or 'explanation' of the latter. If by 'causality' we refer to an explanation of observed relations or phenomena in terms of their 'mode of production', then even the most blurred memories of our several models must contain a causal element, linked more or less closely to their descriptive or 'lawful' aspects.

Now, the main question our present experiment is designed to answer is whether the child's remembrance is purely descriptive or whether it is, at all times, affected by his causal interpretation; or, again, if an elementary stage of mnemonic retention centred purely on the 'lawful' aspect is followed by a stage at which the causal connections are taken into account as well. Let us add at once that in the experiments described in Chapters 13 and 14, the causal mechanism is external to the child's own actions, so that we shall be able to establish whether or not he organizes his memory according to his explanations, and, above all, according to his awareness of the underlying problem. In the present experiment, by contrast, the causal mechanism seems more transparent (a fact we have still to examine) and the child performs the action himself: in that case, we can determine whether he remembers no more of his action than that it was a succession of events (which would be tantamount to reducing his memory to an associationist schema, and causality to the Human concept of an initial 'conjunction' without a necessary 'connection') or whether his memory is governed by his level of causal comprehension.

Though it proved difficult to examine the level of causal understanding and the level of mnemonic recall separately, the verbal descriptions, drawings and commentaries, both during the presentation and a week later, did, in fact, tell us a great deal about both.

We found, first of all, that what the memory retains is chiefly what the subject has understood. Three principal stages could be distinguished. In the first, the subject recalls a direct and over-all connection between his actions and their results: you push the handle, and one of the pieces of wood moves up, while the other one moves down; you pull the handle, and the second piece of wood goes up, while the first goes down. The subject clearly remembers the general shape of the two models B and R and often a series of details as well, but he fails to grasp the 'reason why' and cannot even describe the articulations (three segments, bolt in R, etc.), so that he sums up the contrast

201

between B and R, by asserting that R is 'skew' while B is straight. At the second stage, the details of the articulations are reproduced correctly in the drawings and the descriptions and their spatio-temporal relations are explained, but the 'reason why' has not yet been understood: the subject still believes that there is a direct causal link between his actions and their results. At stage III, finally, the child's drawing and description alike show that he now seeks the 'reason why' in the interaction of the segments (the 'nail' holds segment b back, etc.) and no longer merely in terms of his own powers to alter the spatial arrangement.

§2. *Stage I*

This stage was represented by fourteen subjects between the ages of 4;6 and 5;11 years. In their drawings, the moving parts of the model were figured by a single vertical stroke (Figure 39, I) or by a straight bend (II). One subject (4;10) tried to picture three distinct segments

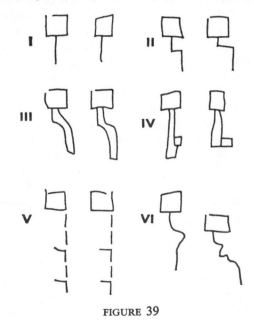

FIGURE 39

(Stage II) in his second drawing, but only managed two (Figure 39, IV); on immediate recall he merely drew a continuous figure (Figure 39, III). Another subject (4;7) also made an attempt in the right direction by producing a series of broken lines (V), and a boy aged 4;6 years, after first producing shape II, added a symbolic representation of the motions of B and R (Figure 39, VI), explaining that 'the

202

red one twisted a bit'. Only one subject drew the slide, but failed to attach any significance to it.

Now the errors in these representations, which might be attributed to poor draftsmanship, are, in fact, highly symbolic of what these subjects remember about the general behaviour of the model. It was all summed up by Gen (5;7), who produced Figure 39, V and explained: 'In that one (B) we pushed and then it all went up, and here (R) we also pushed but it all came down'; and by Par (4;9), who put it even more eloquently: 'There (B) we went up and came down again, and here (R) we went down first and then we went up.' Now, these formulations pose two fundamental problems: (1) where to draw the line between the subject's own action ('we pushed') and the interactions of the different parts of the object (the handle a, the fixed or mobile central segment b, and the terminal segment c) to which Gen referred as 'it' ('it all went up'); (2) is the nexus remembered by Gen, one of pure succession (Hume's conjunction), and does the term 'and then' in 'we pushed and then it all went up' have the same meaning as the 'then' linking the two distinct temporal actions in 'we went down first and then we went up'? Or is there some recall of the causal nexus (as in the expression 'X was heavy and then (= hence) he weighed more than Y')? In fact, the two problems are partly interrelated: if the child fails to distinguish between his own actions and the motion of the object or its parts, it goes without saying that the specifically causal character of his own action will be extended to all processes he can remember, whereas, if he can distinguish between his own actions and the internal connections of the object, it remains an open question whether he confers a causal connotation on the latter as well, or whether they remain purely descriptive (a question that does not arise until Stage II).

Now, the general character of the descriptions or commentaries offered by children at Stage I, shows precisely that they have failed to distinguish their own actions from the object and its articulations. When Par said: 'we went down' or 'we went up' or 'we came down again', etc. he did not think that his own action was confined to the handle a, but believed that it had been directly responsible for moving the whole model. Again, when Gen said 'we pushed and then it all went up', he clearly distinguished 'it' from the action itself, but only as one distinguishes between cause and effect, and not as if this 'it' were the seat of a whole series of causes and effects which, while admittedly extending his own action, were nevertheless quite distinct from it.

The comments of other subjects provide further illustration of this point. Thus, Nar (4;11) produced a drawing of shape I (Figure 39) and explained: *'We pushed and it had to give'* as if the folding motion of R had been the direct result of his own exertions and not of the articulations. Nar also said of *B*: '*It had to go straight up*', once again as if his own action had forced the object to move in this particular way. Hul (5;10) summed it all up by saying (immediately after the presentation): '*There were some small bits of wood and when we went up they went up as well; when we moved they moved.*' A week later, he explained: '*There were some small bits of wood and two bits of cardboard (the two match-boxes) one red and one blue, and as soon as we pushed, the match-boxes started to move.*'

In short, what these children remember is what they have understood, namely, that their own movement is transmitted to the entire model including the match-box on top. Now, because this transmission serves them as a sufficient explanation, they have no grounds for dissociating their own contribution from that of the object's articulation, whence the global (i.e. non-differentiated) character of their descriptions and drawings.

This approach is clearly reflected in the words these children use to describe their own actions as well as the motion of the boxes. In fact, of the sixteen subjects below the age of six years (fourteen at Stage I and two at Stage II), ten used the same verb (or verbal syntagma) to describe their own actions and the movement of the boxes: 'go up', 'drop', 'move', 'stop', 'go like this'. By contrast, of the thirty subjects aged 6 years +, only a single one expressed himself in this way.

We should add, however, that it is possible to distinguish two sub-types within Stage I (subject to verification with a large enough number of subjects). Subjects of sub-type IA centre their memories on the motion of the match-boxes and do not bother about the rest, which explains why they describe the differences between models *B* and *R* by such simple opposites as 'go up' and 'go down'; 'go up' and 'fold up'; 'go up' and 'twist'. Subjects of sub-type IB apparently pay heed to all the features of the presentation but treat the two models as being identical except in respect of the results: 'It all went in one direction and we made it come down,' said Fra at the age of 5;11 years (cf. Gen).

As for the problem posed by the succession or legality and the connection of causality, the content of these elementary memories is, in fact, profoundly causal, in that it bears, and bears exclusively, on the production of the only phenomenon that interests these children from the outset, namely, the motion of the apparatus. The articulations and the 'reason why' do not seem to matter, because the motion seems the obvious result of what the child himself has impressed and transmitted to the 'bits of wood' and the match-boxes. He can, of course, see straight away, and undoubtedly considers this an interesting fact, that the motion of *B* is 'straight up' while that of *R* 'twists a bit', or 'goes down', etc., a process that children in the older age groups are anxious to explain, but about which the younger subjects are quite satisfied to say with Par that 'we pushed and it all went up', because that is precisely what their action resulted in, and that, as far as they are concerned, is that.

The reader may consider this an oversimplified explanation, one that endows children with very elementary ideas or poor mnemonic contents. However, these initial notions are not nearly as simple as they appear to be, and can in no way be interpreted in the manner of Hume or Maine de Biran. In our experiment, which was designed exclusively to test the memory of children, we could not, of course, stop to test their grasp of causality as well. However, when, in another study (with the collaboration of G. Voyat) we questioned subjects of the same age group about their grasp of transitive motions (a ball thrown by the subject or propelled by a spring and transmitting its own motion to a series of other balls), we discovered that whenever the initial motion is due to the child's own action, subjects at the most elementary level treat the initial and the transmitted motions as one and the same thing; however, where the initial motion is due to a spring or to the release of the first ball down a slope, etc., the transmitted motion is no longer considered to be identical with the original one. If these facts are granted, it follows that our present subjects who, at Stage I, attribute the motions of B and R exclusively to their own actions, are not nearly as simple-minded as they seem; they are only simple in that they fail to ask themselves why the transmitted motions should produce different effects in B and R. Now, it is characteristic of the growth of causal understanding that each explanation throws up new problems, which, in turn, call for fresh explanations. This, as we shall see, is precisely what happens at Stage II. The main thing to remember for the moment is that the subject retains what he has understood during the presentation and nothing else, except, perhaps, for a few figurative details (the colour of the match-boxes, etc.) which play no meaningful part in either his descriptions or his drawings.

§3. Stages II and III

The fourteen subjects aged between 5;7 and 7;8 years whom we classified as being of type IIA (including six intermediate cases of type I–II) all tried to account for the different effects of B and R by an analysis of the articulations. While they, too, failed to grasp the causal sequences in detail, they nevertheless all tried to explain the spatio-temporal connections. For the rest, their memory-drawings and descriptions showed that they had simply transferred the causal explanation from themselves, now treated as mere initiators of the motion, to the object and its articulations. At level IIA children grasp the idea of causal transmission in respect of Model B, but not in respect of Model R: the latter still faces them with an insoluble causal problem.

The new approach is used from the very outset, i.e. as soon as the data are presented. Sometimes it goes hand in hand with clear signs of surprise, in other words with the sudden recognition of a problem that was not appreciated at Stage I: Cri (5;7), for example, moved the handle of B, watching carefully all the while but never interrupting his action; on moving R, on the other hand, he was visibly surprised, and stopped for a moment before continuing more slowly. Par (5;7) also pushed B continuously; with R she began to push the handle but started to pull it as soon as the match-box began to descend and then pushed up again—while pulling she did not even bother to look at the match-box of model B, but kept staring when the match-box on top of R started to come up again as soon as she removed her hand.

However, the most striking feature of the memory-drawings of all but one of the subjects at Level IIA was that, a week after presentation no less than on immediate recall, they drew in all three segments (represented by double lines) and often the 'nails' and the slide as well (the one exception was a girl who contented herself with single lines, as in Figure 39, II). Not that they always drew the joints correctly—far from it (and this precisely because, unlike subjects at Stage III, they fail to grasp the detailed phases of the causal sequences), but they did pay heed to them during the presentation and remembered them well, which serves to underline the novelty of their approach, i.e. the attempt to explain the differences between B and R in terms of the articulations. A typical case was Kel (5;9), who produced four drawings of the initial (Figure 40, I and II) and final state (Figure 40, III and IV) of the two models—his three segments of R were discontinuous (Figure 40, II) and folded (Figure 40 IV). 'They look a bit like an N', Kel explained. He also drew a nail at the junction of segments a and b (Figure 40 IV) and another just on top of the figure. During immediate recall, he said: 'Over there was a small nail and the stick touched it, but over there (Figure 40 III) the nail was missing.' On the other hand, the two match-boxes were often mixed up, and there were other indications, too, that the figurative details are neglected by children who focus their attention on the joints, but still fail to understand their function fully.

During verbal recall, too, descriptions in terms of the child's own actions characteristically disappear as greater attention is paid to the articulations, which again points clearly, not to a decline of causality in favour of 'legality', but to a gradual transfer of the effects of the child's own actions to the objects, corresponding to a better grasp of the 'lawful' sequence of events. In fact (though this is difficult to prove), it is to the extent that he makes this transfer that the child's analysis of the articulations becomes more searching, and his grasp of the lawful processes improves. Thus, Bae (6;4) said: 'There were some bits of wood, a few nails, some small boxes, and when we pushed these two (the handles *a*), they all (segments *a*, *b*, and *c*) started moving, and then we pulled them all back. Here (*R*) it was different . . . it all changed: first it was like this (Figure 40 II) and then it was like that (zigzag). Here (*B*) it all stayed the same.' Dan (6;11) explained: 'We pushed, and then that one (*B*) just went up. The other one (*R*) went down like this because there was something that made it,' etc.

Quite obviously, all these subjects drew a clear mnemonic distinction between their own action of pushing the handle on the one hand,

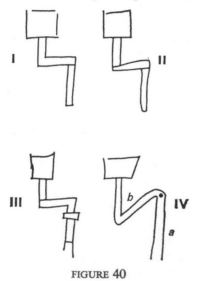

FIGURE 40

and the articulations of the model. The latter thus represent the causal factor inherent in the object, which is obvious with model *B*, all of whose parts move in the same direction, but mysterious and inexplicable in model *R*, though nevertheless taken into account, since 'there was something that made it (*R*) go down'. Were we to examine the grasp of the internal causality of *R* for its own sake, we should undoubtedly discover a number of surprising features, but let us content ourselves here with stating quite simply that the causal nexus is recognized but not yet understood, which is precisely what distinguishes Stage II from Stage III.

Subjects at Levels IIB and III (sixteen cases from 7;4 to 12;2 years) do, in fact, manage (more or less) to arrive at a causal answer to the questions why model *B* should behave so differently from model *R*. But, curiously enough, though all their memory-drawings contain nails or screws to explain the articulations of R, their verbal descriptions are limited to a recitation of the actual events (that is precisely why we distinguish a Sub-stage IIB among seven- to ten-year-olds). It is only when these children complete their memory-drawings by a symbolic reconstruction with the help of battens that they (unlike children at Sub-stage IIA) gain a rough grasp of the causal factors involved. Thus, Lur (9;9) gave an accurate description of the displacements of B and R (type IIA), but during her reconstruction she also produced the following argument: 'That one (R) was made differently there were screws. The screws could turn with the bits of wood.' Similarly, Cla (9;6) explained: 'Here (in B) the two screws and the nail were missing . . . In that one (R) it was the nail (screw) which made it turn, and it all went like that (N-shape) when we pushed.' From about the age of ten years, however, the causal factor is grasped at once (Stage III). Thus Rus (9;9) said spontaneously in his first description that B went up as a whole because it was glued together, while 'here (B) there was a screw'. During his second recall he added: 'That one (B) was all screwed together and here (R) there was a screw in the middle', and he indicated how the joints moved. Ain (9;10; first recall) said: 'The nail (screw) makes the wood move over here, but over there it makes it go down.' But a week later, she hesitated when drawing the fixing bolt and one of the screws responsible for the rotation: 'That screw bothers me; I don't know whether it should go here or there, because when I pushed it ought to have . . . but then it went up. It was like this (correct drawing), and it could turn . . . etc.' Wal (11;3) produced a correct drawing of 'a nail which kept it (joint b) to the board and a screw (junction of a and b) which made it turn . . . it moved quite freely' (pointing to the two ends of b).

In short, these subjects, unlike those at Level IIA, all have a vague grasp of the causal mechanism, though they do not yet express it except during their symbolic reconstructions, and this precisely because they fail to understand it fully. Then, at Level III, they introduce the causal mechanism explicitly, both in their verbal descriptions and in their memory-drawings.

§4. *The memory after six months*

We were able to retrace and question thirty-six of our subjects six months after presentation. None of them had made mnemonic progress and there were several regressions, but there was a remarkable correlation between the retention of the data (and particularly between their schematization) and the level of intellectual development.

Ten subjects at Stage I made either identical drawings of *B* and *R* as in Figure 39, I and II (four cases) or else drew squares and rectangles joined by vertical or horizontal strokes, or in simple juxtaposition (six cases). Their descriptions seemed to justify our distinction between a Sub-stage IA centred on the motion of the match-boxes and a Sub-stage IB in which the motion of the entire model is taken into account. Some subjects at Stage IA had forgotten everything but the match-boxes: *It was all about those boxes, they were placed side by side.—*What colours?—*A red one, a yellow one, a blue one and a dark green one* (Pat, 4;7–5;5). *There were several boxes.—*And what did you do?—*I did nothing; I just looked.—* Who did it then?—*You did.—*What?—*Move the match-boxes—*How? *I don't really know, by the wooden whatsits* (Ros, 4;6–5;2). 'There were some bits which we could move' (Syl, 5;6–6;20. Subjects of Sub-stage IB confined themselves to describing the action: '*When it was pushed it all went up and then it came down again.*' (Val 5;6–5;10). Pas (5;10–6;2) distinguished *B* from *R*: '*You pushed and the boxes moved. There was also a blue one that had to be pushed as well but it didn't move so far.*'

The twelve subjects at Sub-stage IIA (5;7–7;6 years during the presentation and 5;11–7;10 during the last session) fell into two distinct groups (I–II and pure II). The first showed unmistakable signs of systematic memory deterioration; clearly the transfer of causality from their own actions to the object had plunged them into a deep conflict: '*I can't remember any more; I think there were some small pieces of wood and two things at the top, a red one and a blue one*' (Pat, 6;2–7;0). Of the others (six subjects) all but two drew three more or less identical segments (cf. Figure 39, II) for *B* and *R* (cf. Figure 39, III and VI), accompanied by such schematized descriptions as: '*When we pulled, the one went up and the other one went down*' (And, 6;11–7;7) or: '*Here it kept twisting; in the other one it just went up*' (Dan 6;11–7;8). However, only two of these twelve drawings (after six months) contained nails or screws to mark the articulations of *R*, which is in full accord with what we have said about subjects at this stage in §3, i.e. that they fail to grasp the causal factor in *R*. One of these two subjects was Kel, whose initial drawing we have mentioned earlier (Figure 40). That drawing suggested that he had arrived at the correct explanation, but six months later he placed the nail above the junction of segments *b* and *c* (see Figure 38) in an attempt to explain why *R* did not keep moving in a vertical direction: '*There was that small nail so it couldn't go any higher*' (the reader may remember that Kel was already beginning to think along these lines during first recall).

Nine subjects out of fourteen at Levels IIB and III included the screws in their drawings, and two mentioned them but failed to put them down on paper. Except for three subjects who did not recall the model correctly,[1] this entire group had remembered that the two models had moved in

---

[1] Two of these three subjects produced figures with five or even seven segments, which suggests that their emerging interest in mechanical questions (at the age of eight to nine years) went hand in hand with what may seem the introduction of pointless complications, but are, in fact, attempts to express the complexities of the articulations.

distinct ways: '*In the one it was all hinged up with screws, in the other it was all fixed, so when we pushed it went straight up*' (Wal, 11;3–11;7). Even those subjects who had forgotten the details, remembered the general idea: '*Here* (in *R*) *it was all different, because there was a screw that turned; I can't remember the rest very well*' (Mar 8;11–9;2). Cla (9;5) explained that '*the sticks were fixed in a certain way; they were all joined together*', and his drawing showed that he knew the screw was responsible for the bending of *R*.

Despite the neglect of the figurative details, these memories after six months were therefore in fairly close correlation with the degree of causal understanding. Thus, one remarkable feature, among others, was that, at Stage I, nine children out of ten failed to differentiate model *B* from model *R* in their drawings, whereas at Stage IIA four drawings out of twelve did reflect this difference. At Levels IIB and III the ratio had risen to 11 : 14, and two of the three subjects who had failed to distinguish *B* from *R* in their drawings said in their verbal descriptions that *R* 'looked different' (e.g. Fra 9;2).

§5. *Conclusion*

The above remarks may have served to make clear the similarities and differences between the remembrance of a causal process on the one hand and the remembrance of operational structures on the other. In both cases, the child's memory reflects his level of understanding, i.e. the manner in which he structures the data he has recorded in terms of a code that varies with the schemata available to him. Though this happens as obviously in the sphere of causality as it does in the case of logico-mathematical structures, there is one important difference between them, and this difference undoubtedly explains the slight divergence we have observed in the recall of subjects at Stage II and Stage III respectively. In the case of logico-mathematical structures, the subject is presented with a configuration which, though constructed by an adult, is remembered in much the same way as one he might have constructed by his own actions (seriations, correspondences, etc.). In the present experiment, on the other hand, the model was presented but not activated, by an adult. What the memory reflects in that case is the subject's interpretation of the causal links in the object and not the way in which he himself would have constructed it. Now, this difference is fundamental, because a logico-mathematical operation is equivalent to a transformation of the object by the subject (series, sets, etc.), whereas causality is an operation attributed to the object itself, though only after the subject has passed through a (pre-causal) stage in which he fails to separate his own action from that of the object. It is during this early phase of pre-causal non-differentiation that the subject's grasp of causality is given its clearest expression. But as causality is gradually objectified and detached from his own action, the child at Level IIA who postulates it but does not yet understand it, and even the child at Levels IIB and III who (in the case of the present model) comes to understand it better, still centre their description on the observed results rather than on the causal mechanism. Now, in the logical sphere, the results and the operations are identical because the time factor can be ignored, whereas in the causal sphere, there is a clear difference between describing the results and retracing the events that led up to them, because, in the second case, the time factor is crucial. That is why we must distinguish (in the present case but not, or very much less so, in the case of seriations, etc.) between what the child draws and describes and what he has actually remembered. To that end, it is essential to put a series of discreet questions or to demand a symbolic reconstruction, for in these alone can the child manifest his actual remembrance of causality, i.e. his remembrance of his own interpretation of the sequences he has observed, and not merely his remembrance of the results.

Now, lest these remarks may seem to place a restriction on what the memory of causal processes can tell us, we hasten to add that, quite possibly, they apply to the present model only, i.e. to a model whose segments cannot be taken to pieces and reassembled for closer inspection (as no doubt they ought to have been—but that is another problem). To assess the memory of causal connections in general, we must therefore look at a situation in which several independently moving bodies act on one another in a clearly visible manner and give rise to a comprehensible succession of causes and effects. This is what we shall be doing in Chapter 12. Afterwards, we shall look at a situation in which the causal factor is not grasped by children below the age of eleven to twelve years (Chapter 13), and, finally, we shall examine the remembrance of a situation in which the essential factor is the child's growing appreciation of the underlying problem (Chapter 14).

CHAPTER TWELVE

The Remembrance of a Transmitted Motion[1]

In the last chapter, we considered the transmission of a motion, but one initiated by the child himself and one in which the moving bodies were contiguous. The situation we shall now consider involves the motion of three balls. The first of these *A* (a red ball) is released by a mechanical device from the top of a slope. It then hits the wooden plug *P1*, whch is fixed to the slope (a fact to which the child's attention is drawn) and transmits the motion to a second (green) ball *B*, which, in turn, hits the stopper *Pa* made of Plasticine. The Plasticine is removed, whereupon the ball *B* hits the second (fixed) plug *P2*

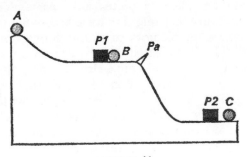

FIGURE 41

behind which lies a third ball *C*, but at some distance from the plug. The ball *C* therefore remains immobile.

This situation is of special interest, first, because, while the motion of *A* is transmitted to *B*, that of *B* is not transmitted to *C*, and, second, because neither the examiner nor the child initiates any of the motions directly: the examiner simply releases *A* and removes an obstacle to allow the continued motion of *B*. Now, we know that younger subjects explain the motion of a ball (or of water) down a slope by asserting that 'there was nothing to hold it back'—the slope itself

---

[1] In collaboration with C. Fot.

does not enter into their explanation until a later stage. Hence the special interest of the present model.

§1. *Method and mnemonic levels*

The child is asked, first of all, for a detailed description (while still looking at the model) of each of the successive events. Next, the model is removed and the child is asked for a second description followed by a drawing, and then for a commentary on the drawing. The same procedure is adopted a week later, and again after an interval of four to six months, when the child is also asked for a general justification and for an explanation of the reason why the second ball stayed in place (if this fact was mentioned by him). On this basis we examined thirteen subjects from 4;6 to 5;11 years; ten 6-year-olds; nine 7-year-olds, eight 8-year-olds; eight 9-year-olds and six 10-year-olds.

Normally, it is rather difficult to distinguish between mnemonic levels, but in the present case we could do so quite easily, not only in respect of the causal contents of the memory but also in respect of its general accuracy.

In respect of the contents, we were able to establish a Level I which continues until the age of six years (and in five cases until the age of seven years). It is characterized, in the youngest subjects, by explanations in which the action of the experimenter ('*You made it roll down*') is combined with the proper motion of the ball ('*it rolled down*', '*it slid down*', '*it dropped down*' or '*it fell down*'), descriptions which, as we know, involve a measure of psychomorphism. From their explanations we can safely deduce that these subjects have failed to grasp the transmission of the motion of *A*, via the plug, to *B*, or the non-transmission of the motion of *B* to *C* (admittedly two advanced subjects aged 4;9 and 4;11 years respectively, said that *A* pushed *B*, but only during the final session!). By contrast, their explanatory schema is centred (in sixteen out of seventeen or eighteen cases) on the fact that the Plasticine was removed so as to allow *B* to continue down the slope!

Level II begins at the age of six years (seven cases out of ten, but also two 4-year-olds, and one 5;11-year-old) and was represented by four out of nine 7-year-olds, three out of eight 8-year-olds, four out of eight 9-year-olds, and one out of six 10-year-olds. It is characterized by the affirmation of the transmission of the motion of *A* to *B* across the first plug, and a failure to grasp that the motion of *B* is not transmitted to *C* once the Plasticine has been removed (this fact is, moreover, frequently forgotten, at least in the beginning, because it has lost the causal importance it enjoyed at Level I). The transmission of the motion of *A* to *B* is not explained, or else attributed to the motion of the (fixed) plug *P1*, which renders the immobility of *C* inexplicable, except by the absence of a gradient (which is sometimes adduced).

213

Level III was represented by one 6-year-old (out of ten), by one 7-year-old (out of nine), by five 8-year-olds (out of eight), four 9-year-olds (out of eight) and by five 10-year-olds (out of six). Children at this level contend that the last ball stays put because there is a gap between *P2* or *C*, or because *P2* is too large or too heavy, or there is some other special reason (one subject at Level II/III claimed that the jolt was not big enough).

As for the accuracy of the memory, Level I is mainly characterized by the failure or reluctance to seriate successive events: in the descriptions no less than in the drawings of these children, the balls follow no set paths and often occupy impossible positions. Moreover, the descriptions are too vague or based on simple enumerations, again without regard to the order of events. With subjects at Level II, there is a first glimmering of the orderly sequence of events, though a remarkably large number of subjects still distort the data (e.g. drawing a steep slope for *B* and no slope at all for *C*). Level III, though not sharply divided from Level II, is characterized by relatively greater, though not always complete, mnemonic accuracy.

§2. *Level I*

The main causal idea of subjects at this level (which we know from several current studies of causality)[1] is that a moving body (water, balls, etc.) is set in motion whenever there is nothing to impede its progress. Hence it is not so much the slope which these subjects consider as the sole or main cause of the motion, as a mixture of spontaneity on the part of the object (the water slides down; the ball slides or runs down, etc.) and its passive submission to the transmitted motion. True, some subjects at Level I will tell you that the ball rolled or was dropped down a slope, but in their case the slope has a purely descriptive function. The chief cause of the motion these subjects invoke is the removal of the obstacle (the Plasticine). One subject (Dan, 7;10) even went so far as to state (four months after presentation, when he also produced a two-level drawing with the slope missing) that the ball *A* 'started for the Plasticine because you took the first plug away' (his drawing included a plug in front of *A*), and that the ball *C* 'stayed put because there was nothing to hold it back'. This subject obviously wanted to say that, in the absence of an obstacle, there was nothing that could be removed to initiate a motion of *C*; but he also added that 'it was all flat', a remark characteristic of Level II.

As for the transmission of the motion of *A* to *B* across the plug *P1*, it is ignored by all subjects at this level, though they would not hesitate to admit it in other situations, for instance, when a ball *A* is released or thrown by the subject himself and collides with an

[1] To be published in *Études d'épistémologie génétique*.

214

immobile ball B, or even when a ball A propels a ball E across three immobile balls B, C and D (E being in contact with D). In the present case, on the contrary, subjects at Level I will at best make the following concession: 'You let go of A, and then the other one (B) ran down, but the blue one (C) stayed put' (Man, 4;10); or: 'The red one rolled down and the green one made for the plasticine' (Ag, 5;1), which represents a partial grasp of the order of events, but does not express the idea of propulsion, for instance in the manner of a subject at Stage II: 'One of the balls pushed the other one' (Pac, at 5;5). True, Man's 'and then' may have had a causal significance (cf. Chapter 11, §2) but the entire context of his remarks (and of those of other subjects at Stage I) shows that he invoked a mixture of spontaneity and submissive behaviour on the part of the balls: 'These whatsits (plugs and Plasticine) moved the balls', was how one subject (4;10) summed it all up. Admittedly children at this level will accept the idea of transmitted motion in the case of projectiles thrown by hand or released by a spring, but since, in the present case, they keep harping on the removal of the plasticine or plugs as the sole cause of the motion, we may take it that they have failed to grasp the fact that a motion can be transmitted across an immobile object—an idea that is expressed more or less overtly by most six- to seven-year-olds.

In respect of the memory itself, Level I begins with drawings in which all the elements are in direct contact, and with such general formulations as: 'All of them rolled down.' This is for instance how Oli (4;9) put it during the first session. A week later, he added a house (= the plug) to his original three balls and, after six months, he pictured four balls and a slab of Plasticine. His final description was: 'There was some Plasticine and the balls were given a push.' Commenting on his drawing, he said: 'The red one started to roll down, and so did the green, the blue and the black ball. The Plasticine stopped them all.' Pat (4;10) lined up three balls, the Plasticine and the two plugs, and gave the following description on immediate recall: 'You brought down one ball and then the other one left; then you removed the Plasticine and pushed the other one, but the blue one stayed put.' She gave the same description a week after presentation, but six months later her drawing showed a slope with the red ball on top, the Plasticine in the centre, the blue ball (B) lower down and a plug right at the bottom: 'You removed the Plasticine and the red ball moved towards the blue one, then you took away the plug, and the blue one went down but the red one stayed put.' Much the same responses were obtained from several five-year-olds, while others referred to the slope. Thus, Mic (5;8) said (one week after the presentation): 'There was some Plasticine and a large lump of wood; when the Plasticine had gone, the green one began to roll down.' Tier (6;0) drew the slope and the plugs but placed the balls to one side; 'One ball, another one: then you fixed the Plasticine, brought the red one down, and the green one left at the same time (!). Then you took the Plasticine away and the green started again.' Flo (7;6) drew a slope with the red ball on top, followed by a plug, a green ball at some distance from the plug but close to the Plasticine, another plug and a green ball: 'When you took the Plasticine away, the two balls started to roll down and changed places; the green one was here (past the first plug) and the red one there (below the last plug).' The plugs, therefore, played no relevant part in her original story, but a week later logic had gained the upper hand: 'The first one went up to the second one and that is why you had to remove the wood.' Four months later, her schematization was better still: her drawing showed a steep slope with a red ball at the top held back by the Plasticine, another red ball in the centre held back by another piece of Plasticine, and a green ball right at the bottom: 'You removed the Plasticine and the red went down there; then you removed the other bit of Plasticine and the red one carried on. The green one stayed put because that bit (the trajectory) was flat and *because there was no Plasticine to take away* (!)' (cf. Dan's explanation above).

We see that from the age of four to seven years the memory-drawings and descriptions of subjects at this level reflect a failure to grasp the sequence of events and the transmission of the motions across the plugs, and, above all, a systematic distortion of the data so that they fit into the pattern of the subject's over-all interpretation of causality.

§3. *Level II*

Let us look, first of all, at a response characteristic of the transition from Level I to Level II. Eri (6;2) said on immediate recall: 'The ball dropped down, then the other one pushed against the Plasticine, then you took the Plasticine away and it (the ball) kept rolling down again.' His drawing showed a slope with an enormous bump at the level of the Plasticine. A week later, the slope had improved and so had the description: 'There was this ball, then the Plasticine and then another ball behind it; next came a piece of wood and then the ball went down—you pushed and it came down.' Six months later this subject advanced to the frontiers of Level II: 'The ball pushed against the wood, and then the other ball started to roll down.' The following subjects were typical of Level II proper and, interestingly enough, often forgot the Plasticine: Yve (6;8) drew a twisting slope with the two plugs in the correct position: 'You made the one roll down and that got the other one started and then you made that one (*B*) roll down, but this one (*C*) stayed put.' He offered the same description and drawing a week later, but after six months he had reverted to Level I; the plugs had gone and all that was left was the Plasticine, which 'you took away'. Did (6;11) offered the following commentary: 'You let go of the red one, and it pushed the other one, etc.' (her drawing was correct except for a duplication of *B* and the plug behind it). As for *C*, 'you couldn't get it to move'. Phil (7;1) omitted the Plasticine from his otherwise correct drawing, and said during the first session and also a week later: 'One ball (*A*) dropped down and that made the other one (*B*) drop down as well, but it didn't budge the third one (*C*).' Cla (8;1), commenting on her drawing of the balls at the moment of impact with the plugs and Plasticine, said: 'The red ball pushed the green one . . . the green one came down and didn't push the other one (*C*).' After six months: *idem*, but 'the last one (*C*) went down . . . oh, no, it didn't because it didn't have enough go' (!). Mar (9;2) said nothing at all about the motion of (*C*) during the first two sessions and simplified the problem six months later: 'That one (*A*) slid down and knocked against the middle one (*B*), and that one knocked against (*C*), and all of them finished up at the bottom.' His first drawing showed the balls in front and behind the plugs (moment of impact), but six months later the plugs had gone, except for one at the very end of the trajectory.

These brief examples may suffice to show how closely the level of causal comprehension corresponds to the mnemonic level. There is no need to return to the former: these subjects quite obviously have no difficulty in accepting the transmission of the motion of *A* to *B* across the plug *P1* which they express in unequivocal terms (pushing, knocking, hitting, etc.); on the other hand, it is equally clear that they understand nothing about the immobility of *C* under conditions that strike them as being similar to those of *A* and *B*—whence their silence or their attempts to account for the facts by levelling the slope, etc. As for the memory itself, though part of its progress is undoubtedly due to the fact that the mental development of these subjects is in advance of those at Level I (for instance, in respect of the ordination of the events), it is, nevertheless, profoundly affected by the new approach to causality, which alone lends meaning to the ordination. On the one hand, the appreciation that motions can be transmitted helps to consolidate the memory and even introduces an intelligible order of succession; on the other hand, it leads to distortions, such as the (common) omission of the Plasticine or its transformation into a rigid plug. Moreover, the number of plugs is increased by some subjects (e.g. by Did) and reduced to zero by others, in an attempt to remove what are considered so many obstacles to the motion. The failure to explain the immobility of the last ball (*C*) leads to further and quite different memory distortions: unable to understand the function of the gap between *C* and the plug, these subjects will often omit the gap altogether, or exaggerate the contrast between the last horizontal section of the slope and the preceding gradient, etc. Thus, Cat (9;11) drew an even gradient during the first two sessions, which increased the mysterious behaviour of *C*; several months later, however, she produced a decreasingly steep slope ending in a long horizontal stretch and explained: 'The last ball didn't roll down because it was all flat.' Other subjects, unable to resolve the problem, simply eliminated it from their memories: they either made the third ball roll down like the rest (Mar), added an extra obstacle (a new plug in front of *C*), or placed *C* in front instead of behind the last plug; sometimes the experimenter himself was said to have removed plug and Plasticine alike.

In short, with subjects at Level II the grasp of the order of succession as a function of the transmission of the motion goes hand in hand with a series of omissions or distortions, either because the spectacular effects of the transmission cause them to overlook the rôle of the Plasticine, or else because of their failure to explain the immobility of *C*.

§4. *Level III*

The causal explanations proffered at this, the last, level are an extension of those produced at Level II: the immobility of *C* is attributed to the immobility of the plug and no longer to the absence of a slope or some insoluble mystery. The correct explanation—the gap between *P2* and *C*—was given by one 6-year-old, one 7-year-old, three 8-year-olds, two 9-year-olds, and by most older subjects. For all that, subjects at Level III, too, offer insufficient explanations, but explanations that invariably introduce the transmission factor. Thus, Ren (8;6) attributed the immobility of *C* to the fact that the plug *P2* was 'bigger' than the plug *P1*, and hence unable to transmit the motion (he drew *C* in contact with *P2*); and Jac (9;2), who also eliminated the gap, simply said that *C* had stayed put without further explanation, though six months later he attributed the strange behaviour of *C* to the fact that *P2* was too heavy and made of a different material from *P1*. Lag (10;4), who did draw a gap between *P2* and *C*, attributed the immobility of *C* to the fact that *P2* was 'fixed very tight', thus implying that the transmission of the motion across *P1* had been due to the displacement of the latter. Finally, Lis (9;11) was remarkable in that she attributed the transmission of the motion *A* to *B* to the 'jolting' of *P1*, and the immobility of *C* to the lack of a slope. However, four months later, she added that 'it isn't really logical because the other one (trajectory B) was just as straight (horizontal). That bothers me; I don't seem to understand it at all.' She then suggested that $P2$ might not have been 'right' for receiving a 'big jolt', but again failed to remark on the gap between $P2$ and C, even though she had clearly shown it on her drawing.

Greater appreciation of the causal factor quite naturally leads to better recall of the model, especially in respect of the gap between $P2$ and C, which, more often than not, is completely ignored at Level II. At Level III it was remembered by fourteen subjects out of seventeen (first drawing), by thirteen subjects out of sixteen (second drawing) and by eleven subjects out of thirteen (after four to six months). The memory after four to six months often gives rise to significant schematizations. Thus, Tri (10;5), who during the first two sessions had simply declared that C 'did not budge', though she had drawn in the gap during the second (not the first) session, forgot the plug $P2$ and the correct position of C four months later, and explained: 'It stayed put because it wasn't resting against the Plasticine.' By contrast, Dan (6;0, a very advanced subject) said during the first two sessions that C stayed put because 'it isn't against the wood so it can't leave'. Six months later his memory had greatly deteriorated: now, there was only one ball and, spaced out along the trajectory, four bits of Plasticine which, he claimed, were removed one at a time—in other words, he had regressed from Level III to Level I.

Apart from such deformations by generalization, the memories produced by subjects at Level III are much more adequate than those presented at Level II. This raises the problem of whether mnemonic progress entails progress in causal comprehension, as might happen when the remembrance of the gap between $P2$ and C goes hand in hand with the correct explanation of the immobility of C; or whether, on the contrary, progress in the causal sphere entails greater mnemonic precision, or again whether the two kinds of progress are independent of (though naturally reinforcing) each other, and simply reflect the child's general development.

However, the child's general development cannot serve us as an explanation unless its mechanisms are clearly defined, so that it is between the first two alternatives that we must look for the answer. To that end, we must not only consider the differences between the three levels, but must also compare the results of immediate recall with those obtained after a week and again after four to six months.

§5. *The development of the memory during three successive sessions*

Mnemonic changes from the first session to the second session (one week later) and above all from the second to the last session (four to six months later) can be described in terms of progress and regress, or in terms of general tendencies, of which the most striking is a marked increase in interpretative comments during the last session.

I. In respect of progress and regress, we can draw up Table 24, in which $W > I$ signifies progress over immediate recall (I) during the first week and $M > W$ progress during the next four to six months.

The changes between the first and second sessions pose no problems, except in the case of one 5;10-year-old who did not reach Level II until the second session. As for the changes in the course of four to six months, they took the following form. At Level I, there

TABLE 24 *Mnemonic progress and regress*

	$W > I$	$W = I$	$W < I$	$M > W$	$M = W$	$M < W$
Level I	1	13	1	2	4	7
Level II	1	21	1	3	8	11
Level III	0	16	0	4	5	6

was a marked improvement in the drawings—the Plasticine, previously omitted (from the drawings but not from the descriptions), was now clearly marked in. At Level II, as we saw (§1), two subjects (4;9 and 4;11) mentioned the transmission of the motion during the last session ('one ball pushed the other one' or 'made the other one slide down,' when it hit the first plug). The second of these subjects also produced an almost correct memory-drawing, whereas, in the first two drawings, he had failed to place the balls on the slope and had omitted the plugs. The third child to make progress at Level II (Eri, 6;2) also failed to mention the transmission of the motion until the last session. The four cases of progress at Level III were two subjects aged 8;6 and 8;9 years respectively, who failed to recall the connection between the gap and the immobility of C until the final session (their three drawings showed an increasingly wide gap!) and the two subjects aged 9;11 and 10;4 we mentioned earlier, who only searched for and found an explanation of the immobility of C (inadequate impetus or rigid plug) during the third session.

As for the regressions, they were generally due to simple mnemonic deterioration which, it should be stressed, was slightly more pronounced in subjects with a poorer grasp of causality: 54 per cent and 50 per cent respectively at Levels I and II, and 40 per cent at Level III. At Level III, there was also one regression in respect of causal understanding (i.e. Dan (6;0), who reverted to Level I); in addition, one 9;5-year-old produced a final drawing in which the plug was placed beyond, not in front of, C (thus schematizing its immobility), and one case of simplification, in which the third ball was made to roll down the slope like the rest.

II. This brings us to the most striking and most general characteristic of mnemonic developments over an interval of several months, namely, the marked reinforcement of the interpretative, as opposed to the purely figurative, aspects of the memory. Thus, a comparison of the original drawings of six- to ten-year-olds with those they produced four to six months later shows the following modification of the relationship between the ball A, the plug $P1$ and the ball B: during the first session there were forty figuratively correct drawings and one interpretative distortion, but by the last session the number of correct drawings had decreased from forty to twenty-three, while the number of distortions had increased from one to nineteen. Now, these deteriorations in no way reflect a simple 'loss of memory' in the associationist sense, since our subjects did not so much ignore the relationship between the three elements as reinterpret it, with, as we saw, $3 + 4$ most spectacular advances (at Levels II and III). As for the relationship between the ball B and the Plasticine, there was little deterioration from the first to the last session, but many cases of forgetfulness, especially at the beginning of Level II, where, as we saw, this relationship loses the causal importance it has at Level I (at least, for one or two subjects, who likened the Plasticine to a plug whose real function they had only just discovered). As for the relationship between the ball B, the plug $P2$ and the ball C, the figurative recall of subjects at Level II, which is often accurate during the first two sessions, deteriorates in the course of four to six months, for a reason we have already mentioned (failure to grasp the rôle of the gap). But this deterioration is not always reflected in the omission of the gap—it often involves other distortions intended to render the situation more intelligible (plug placed behind C or left out). By contrast, subjects at Level III pay increasing attention to the relationship between the gap and the behaviour of C.

All in all, the development of the memory from the first to the last session appears as a massive transition from accurate figurative recall to a form of recall in which the figurative element is schematized and subordinated to the causal interpretation. This kind of situation throws a great deal of fresh light on the mechanisms of the memory.

§6. *Conclusion*

To return to the problem we raised at the end of §4, the results of the present test show quite clearly that intellectual progress plays the same part in structuring the memory of causal processes as it does in the case of logico-mathematical structures. This may have appeared doubtful in the case of the lever experiment (Chapter 11), since there the stages in the development of causal understanding were neither as clear-cut nor as plainly based on new acquisitions as they are in the present model. However, we find, in both cases, that, provided the stages of intellectual development are distinct enough, the successive mnemonic levels are perfectly distinct as well.

In respect of the relationship between the child's power of understanding and his memory, therefore, though it is quite impossible to decide to what extent the first supports and guides the second, or vice versa, our analysis of the changes between the first two sessions and the last session shows that there are four distinct reactions:

(1) The data are badly remembered and poorly interpreted: this is the case of mnemonic deformation (often with time) due to gaps in the memory and a failure to grasp the underlying relations (Level I). In that case, it seems undeniable that a better understanding of these relations would have improved the memory, and, in the only case in which gaps in the memory seemed to be responsible for a degradation of the powers of understanding (Dan, who at the age of precisely six years reverted from Level III to Level I), it would seem that the precocious intellect of this subject was so fragile precisely because it was so precocious.

(2) The data are badly remembered but correctly interpreted: this happens with numerous mnemonic deformations meant to introduce greater coherence. Clearly, in that case, it is the activity of the intellect which imposes schematizations or simplifications on the memory, with a corresponding loss in figurative accuracy.

(3) The data are well remembered but badly interpreted; this is the rarest case; the child remembers the gap between the plug $P2$ and the ball C and also that C remains immobile after B has collided with $P2$, but simply leaves it at that. In that case, the memory is purely figurative and the intellect plays no part in it. But this, as we said, is an uncommon response, and it often happens that, failing to understand why C remains in its place, the subject will 'remember' that it was in direct contact with $P2$, and hence that it ought to have moved down the slope (which brings us back to case 2).

(4) The data are well remembered and well interpreted: this is the inconclusive case, or rather the case that would have been inconclusive in the absence of the first three. But the first three cases do exist, and

it is clear that, as children grow older, they pass on to this type of response simply because their intellects have developed in the meantime. But, as we pointed out earlier, a general form of development that accounts for the progress of the memory as well as that of the understanding does not, in fact, account for anything at all: while we can see why the intellectual construction of causality should progress with age, it is hard to see how a mnemonic faculty detached from the intellect and functioning on its own account, i.e. figuratively, could progress in the same way, since all of us, let alone the senile, have great difficulty in retaining all the figural details of all the memories we accumulate all the time.

By and large, therefore, the memory in the strict sense needs the constant support of the schemata of the intelligence—in the case of causality no less than in that of logical or mathematical structures. The seven clear advances at Levels II and III over four to six months are reminiscent of those we have met in the construction of operational schemata, and the general correlation of mnemonic improvements with the construction of causal schemata is as close as it proved to be in the case of logical or arithmetical schemata.

Final remark. A current study on the transmission of the motion of a ball A to a ball C across several plugs B seems to show that, if the plug B is immobile, children at Level I fail to grasp the transitivity of AC. If, however, the plug moves just a fraction after the impact of A, children will accept the idea of a transmission in much the same way as they accept the idea of instrumental actions. This explains why, in the present experiment, some young subjects accepted the idea of the transmission of the motion of A with the help of the plug PI. But just as soon as the experimenter stressed the fact that the block was fixed, he obtained the reactions mentioned in §§1 and 2 (Table 24).

CHAPTER THIRTEEN

Remembrance of an Incomprehensible Causal Process[1]

A causal situation such as a transitive motion, which is grasped fairly quickly by children between the ages of four to ten years, represents a privileged case of the relationship between the understanding and the memory, and is therefore suspect. To be quite certain of our conclusions we must examine the remembrance of a situation that is completely incomprehensible to children in the same age groups. Now, 'incomprehensible' is a relative term: very young or ignorant subjects think that there is nothing they cannot understand. However, far from being a disadvantage, this proves a great help in our case. As for the more advanced subjects, they invariably centre their attention on the 'lawful' succession of events—they refuse to accept oversimplified explanations and are not yet capable of appreciating the more intricate causal arguments. This raises the question of whether or not the memory of 'lawful' successions and relationships deteriorates more quickly with time in the absence of a satisfactory causal explanation than it does in its presence. Finally, the new experiment will enable us to look at the emergence of causal explanations proper and of their effects on the memory.

§1. *Method and levels*

The child is shown a cardboard tray with two barometer tubes, *T1* and *T2*, and two flat dishes, *D1* and *D2*, half-filled with blue and red liquid respectively. Each of the dishes contains a candle. This arrangement will be referred to as the initial situation *Si*.

The child is asked to describe the material, and his attention is drawn to the equality of the levels in *D1* and *D2* and to the fact that the vessels are half-filled.

Then, after telling the child to pay attention, the experimenter plunges the tube *T1* into the dish *D1*, lights the candle in *D2* and covers it with the tube *T2*. The result will be referred to as the final

[1] In collaboration with R. Maier.

situation, *Sf* (Figure 42). (If *T1* is plunged into *D1* very quickly and upside down, the air in it cannot escape and the level of the blue liquid in *D1* will be forced up. By contrast, if the candle in *D2* is allowed to burn for two to three seconds, at which point it is extinguished for lack of oxygen, the combustion product (CO_2) being soluble in water, the red liquid, which was at first forced up in the dish like the blue liquid, will be able to enter *T2* and the level in *D2* will drop. Since many other factors, e.g. heat, must also be taken

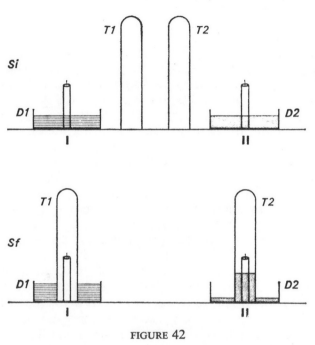

FIGURE 42

into consideration, the explanation of the phenomenon is highly complex.)

The material is now removed and the subject is asked to describe what he has seen. No supplementary questions are put to him, but as soon as he has finished, he is asked for a drawing, and if possible for two drawings corresponding to *Si* and *Sf*. Next, he is asked for a second description with his drawings still before him, and, in particular, for an opinion as to whether or not the levels of the red and blue liquids were equal during the initial and final situations. Young children whose drawing ability is too poor, and all doubtful cases, are handed a sheet on which the vessels but not the levels of the liquids in *Si* and *Sf* are marked, and are simply told to fill in the levels.

The same procedure is adopted after a week and, again, after six months.

In respect of their grasp of causality, the subjects could all be fitted into one of three distinct categories or levels. Until about the age of seven years, they showed no signs of genuine intellectual astonishment at the sequence of events—true, there was an element of surprise, but of the kind children produce when confronted with an unexpected effect, not with an inexplicable mystery. In fact, they all employed the double explanatory schema characteristic of children at this level: they combined their idea of the near-omnipotence of adults with the spontaneous behaviour of moving bodies into such formulations as: 'You lit the match and that made the water come.' From the age of six to ten years, on the other hand, the child often prefers to eschew all explanations and to focus his attention on the regular succession of events—as a result, causality begins to be objectivized and the child starts to look for the answer in the articulations of the model (instead of relying on the general spontaneity of things). Once the nature of these articulations is fully grasped (at Level III), there is a sudden flood of interpretations involving such factors as heat, air, steam, etc. The search for the correct explanation sometimes revolves round a question that is easily answered by adults, but greatly bothers young children: for instance, how is it possible that the water should enter $T2$ when its rim is pressed tight against the bottom of $D2$ (the seal is, of course, imperfect).

In respect of the memory itself, i.e. of the accurate recall of the relationships involved, we can also distinguish three levels; the first two are quite plainly related to Levels I and II in the comprehension of causality, whereas the emergence of the third level is associated with various special features, including the search for the 'reason why' the liquid should rise in $T2$ but not in $T1$. The first level is characterized by a defective or non-existent differentiation between the two models in Sf, and especially by a systematic difficulty (which persists until the age of 5;11) in distinguishing between the initial and final situations, which indicates a defective temporal organization of the memory and at the same time reflects the inability of younger subjects to differentiate between effects produced by human intervention and those due to the behaviour of objects.

The second level extends from the age of six to eight years (but also included one 9;8-year-old) and sees a gradual differentiation between the two models as well as between Si and Sf, and improved recall of the relationships involved. However, with one notable exception, none of these children seemed to realize that the liquid rose in $D1$ for the simple reason that it dropped in $T1$. Since the perceptive and spatial recognition of liquid levels is a simple matter for four- to five-year-olds (who, as we saw, invoked it when denying the conservation of liquids in the decantation experiments) we must interpret this systematic failure as a residual inability to correlate the situations Si and Sf: children at this level differentiate between them but cannot yet combine them into an over-all system, perhaps due to their failure to grasp causality or the fact that the total quantity of liquid in $T1$ and $D1$ is constant.

At Level III, by contrast, this fact is recalled, and the memory is thus relatively complete, though with one qualification (whence it is possible to distinguish between Sub-levels IIIA and IIIB): it is only gradually that the subject remembers the rise of the liquid in $D2$ and in $D1$ before it enters $T2$ and drops again in $D2$. Level III thus represents a relatively complete correlation between Si and Sf, together with a re-emergence of the search for an explanation. However, since the latter cannot yet be found, we must go on to examine what becomes of the memory (excellent at this level during the first two sessions) after an interval of six months—success or failure then may be due to either growing awareness of the problem (still unresolved in subjective no less than in objective terms) or to the adoption of an (often mistaken) explanatory schema.

§2. Level I

The grasp of causality characteristic of this level is clearly reflected in this conversation with Pat (4;6): *How did you manage to do that with the glass?*—How do you think I did?—*You lit the candle and that made the water come.* And a week later: *You put in a glass* ($T2$) *and then lit the candle* (reversal of the temporal order). *'That' put out the candle and the water came up* (in $D2$). But what precisely is the meaning of 'that' in this description? It may be called a descriptive term, but one designating a concept and not just the events: it describes an all-explanatory force due simultaneously to the actions of the experimenter and the spontaneity of the objects. In these conditions, the order of events matters little, and though Pat was able to recall the dishes, the candles, the tubes and the liquids, he was incapable, on immediate recall, to distinguish the initial from the final state—his drawings of Si and Sf were practically identical: the liquids had risen in both tubes and occupied the same level in the two dishes. Asked whether Si represented the beginning or the end of the experiment, Pat replied: *The end . . . no, the start.*—Was there a lot of water in both dishes?—*No, that one was red and the other blue*, etc. His drawings of the two situations were identical as well: Is that one (Si) the start?—*No, the end.*—And this one (Sf)?—*That came at the beginning.*—Not the other way round?—*Yes, the other way round.*—Tell me again!—*We put the glass in the water and then it rose. I haven't put enough water in this time.* And he quickly added the same amount of water to both tubes. His reactions were exactly the same a week later. After six months, he explained 'that one went out when there was water in it'. His drawings of the two models were still identical; there was a small amount of water in both tubes (same level) but none in the dishes.

Pat's case was typical of all subjects at Level I, though there were several variations in respect of the causal explanation. Thus, Mic thought that 'the glasses were put on top (of the candles), then we lit them, and when we put them out all the smoke went down and the water came up'. His drawings of the two models were identical, but a week later he raised the level of *T2* (*Sf*) by way of a final correction, thus moving on to Stage II. Six months later, however, he had reverted to the original (identical) drawings. Fra (4;8) reacted like Mic, but during the last session he mentioned that the final levels of the two models were different; for all that, he produced identical drawings. He had nevertheless made some progress during these six months, in that he no longer confined himself to drawing two series of blue and red elements in juxtaposition. Such progress, which was also shown by another subject, may well represent the first stage in awareness of the underlying problem. Ala (5;1) recalled (during the first two sessions) that one candle was lit but not the other: 'Then you put the glass on top and the candle went out.' In his drawing, the levels of *D1* and *D2* were nevertheless identical (the tubes were empty) and he failed to distinguish between *Si* and *Sf*. Six months later, however, he recalled the rising level: 'It brought the water up and then it put out the candle.' Even so, his drawings and descriptions of *D1* and *D2* remained identical. Other subjects with similar responses claimed that the level had risen as a result of the steam, or because the candle was lit, or again (Mar, 5;8) because of the smoke (Mar also asserted that both candles had been lit). Cat (5;6) took a first step towards differentiating between I and II and between *Si* and *Sf*, thus heralding Level II, though still in a most primitive way, both in respect of her memory (both candles were lit) and also of her grasp of causality: the candle in II 'went out and then the water rose up red', while in I 'you put in the flame', whereupon the candle went out and 'the water went down and became very small'.

In short, the various type I reactions are very much of a kind: all these subjects recall a number of set sequences: one (or two) candles were lit, a tube was put over them, the water rose, etc. All of them realized that there were two distinct situations, namely, *Si* and *Sf*. However, assuming the existence of a process and recalling it as a series of actions in time is something quite different from reconstructing the order of events or even from producing a *post hoc* reconstruction of the differences between the initial and the final situation. Now, this is precisely what subjects at this stage are unable to do—once they have recalled the final situation, they can no longer detach their minds from it, with the result that they describe and draw *Si* as being identical or nearly identical with *Sf*.

This failure in ordination explains the other characteristic of these subjects' memories, which at first seems much more surprising: the relative lack of distinction between models I and II. Several children, in fact, believed that both candles had been lit and even those who did not, produced identical descriptions and drawings of I and II, with the liquid up to the same level in both tubes. These strange errors suggest that the subject, struck by the process but unable to reconstruct its several stages, generalizes the final state of I (unlit candle) and of II, and likens *Si* to *Sf* after the event.

Such grave mnemonic defects must quite obviously reflect a systematic difficulty in temporal ordination (e.g. the belief that the candle was lit after it had been covered by the tube, etc.). Quite obviously the seriation of the events in time would have been more successful in a more comprehensible situation: thus, in the case of transmitted motions (Chapter 12) not a single subject placed the balls on top of the slope in their drawings of the final state. It follows that the memory gaps in the present case are, in fact, so many gaps in the grasp of causality. The case of Cat was typical in this respect: to state quite unconcernedly that the extinction of the candle was followed by a rise in the level of *T2* and by a drop in the level of *T1*, and to be oblivious to the fact that the water in I dropped precisely because the candle in it was unlit, and the level in II rose because the candle in it was lit, is a sign both of a mistaken idea of causality and of an equally strange memory lapse. Now, if we are right in thinking that the causal understanding of children at this stage amounts to assuming that everything is possible, thanks to the omnipotence of the experimenter and the caprice of the objects, then we need not be surprised at their causal explanations, or to find that, lacking intelligible schemata, they are incapable of reconstructing the temporal order of events. The apparent incoherence of these Level I reactions thus bears witness to what is, in fact, a high degree of inner coherence.

§3. *Level II*

As the reader will appreciate, the transition from Level I to the correct memories (Level III) is anything but sudden. In fact, throughout Level II we find a gradual succession of improvements, beginning with the more primitive reactions of several 5;11- to 6;3-year-olds, and continuing with the more advanced reactions of several 6;0- to 8;1-year-olds, and even of two 8;9- and 9;8-year-olds.

In their approach to causality, the new factor is the obvious astonishment of these subjects as the experiment proceeds. Now, this astonishment quite obviously leads them on to a closer analysis of the underlying relationships and of the spatio-temporal and 'lawful' articulations of the model, which, in turn, paves the way for the improved organization of their memories.

Let us begin with an intermediate case. Arc (5;11), in his drawings as well as in his descriptions, distinguished between the initial and final states, but failed to distinguish between models I and II and though, on immediate recall, he said: 'We lit one candle but the other one was out', a week later he claimed that both candles had been lit, though with different effects: 'Then we put in the other one, but it stayed the same.' However, when questioned, he corrected his drawing by eliminating the flame from I. Six months later, he recalled the different states of the candles, but had forgotten the rise in level: his drawings of I and II were therefore identical except for the flame in I, and he no longer distinguished between Si and Sf.

Level II proper begins at the age of 6;0 years: Fra (6;0), for example, clearly expressed her astonishment during the presentation. She produced two drawings and unhesitatingly pointed out which one corresponded to Si and which to Sf: in the first, the levels of $D1$ and $D2$ were equal, but in the second, the level of $T2$ had risen and the level of $D2$ had dropped. For the rest, $T1$ was empty of liquid, while the final level of $D1$ was the same as the initial level (the reader will recall that the rise in $D1$ is not recalled before Stage III). A week later, her description and drawings were still mainly correct and though, after six months, her memory showed some deterioration, she continued to mark the differences between models I and II: 'You lit a match and that put more (liquid) into the other one' (crossed causality). While drawing, she added: 'You lit a match but I've forgotten where to put it,' and, finally: 'You took two bottles and you put more (liquid) into the red one' (her drawing, in fact, consisted of just two 'bottles' in which the tubes and the dishes were fused into one).

Dor (6;3), having examined the experimental set-up with an air of astonishment, produced two correct drawings of Si and Sf, and though she had noted that one candle had been lit but not the other, she forgot the drop in the final level of $D2$ and the rise in the final level of $D1$. A week later, she began in the same way, but then recalled that the level in $T2$ had risen, and specified that this had only happened in the model with the lit candle, but refused to give any further explanation: 'I don't know why.' Bog (6;7), on the other hand, attributed the rise in level in *T2* to the 'steam' which had also put out the candle. Sim (7;2) produced a correct drawing of *T2* and *D2* during *Si* and *Sf*, with a rise in the level of *T* and a drop in *D*, but denied, on immediate recall, that *T1* had been immersed in *D1*; a week later, he first drew *T1* in the correct place but afterwards rubbed it out and placed it by the side of *D1*, no doubt accentuating his memory of the contrast between I and II. Pel (7;0) gave a correct description (except again for the level of *D1* in *Sf*) and explained the rise in level as follows: *When the candle went out, that caused some pressure.—*What exactly is pressure?*—There is a lot of air, and some extra air here (T2), I think, and that sucked up the water. The candle went out because there was more air.*

Level II is thus chiefly characterized by the attempt at co-ordination of the temporal relationships: the order of events is no longer treated with indifference, as at Level I, and is often remembered down to the details (initial drop of liquid in *T2* before its massive rise), and there is a growing co-ordination of the spatial relationships: a drop in the level of *D2* during the rise in the level of *T2*, etc. The attention is focused on model II, and the entire process is remembered with growing accuracy, even though the subject may not have noticed, and in any case does not recall, the rise in the level of *D1* as *T1* is plunged into it. This, in the case of seven- to eight-old-year subjects, is the only difference between Levels II and III.

However, six months later there is a remarkable difference between the reactions of subjects at Level II and those at Level III. At Level I, the memory remains essentially figurative, except, as we saw, in two cases who made slight progress in the course of six months, no doubt because they began to take cognizance of the underlying problem. At Level III, the memory after six months is either correct, or else centred on the problem as such, and the configuration becomes more or less distorted. At Level II, neither of these two reactions occurs; instead, there is a systematic and general degradation of the memory. Thus, Sim (7;2) and Cor (7;5) remembered nothing at all, while Eli (6;2) and Pie (7;0) only recalled the two tubes and the red and blue liquids (Eli mentioned these in her description but failed to introduce them into her drawing). Pat (6;10) spoke of two candles in the two dishes (*D1* and *D2*), the one lit, and the other one (in a dish containing half as much liquid as the first) not, but he forgot the tubes *T1* and *T2*, which showed that he had completely suppressed the problem. Mar (8;1) remembered *D1* and *D2* as being identical, but replaced the two candles with one lit match, which went out when one of the tubes was placed over it: he thus transformed the problem into a spectacle that held no mysteries for him. Ria (7;11) also drew the two tubes *T1* and *T2* (no dishes) each filled half-way with liquid and each containing a candle, one lit and the other not: 'When you put the glass (*T2*) here it went out.'

The highly systematic degradation of the memory by these subjects, in respect of the configuration (in contrast to subjects at Level I) no less than of the problem (in contrast to subjects at Level III), seems to be closely linked to their level of causal understanding. Rejecting the facile explanations of subjects at Level I and devoid of even the most rudimentary grasp of causality (Level III), these subjects confine themselves to the most exact and 'lawful' explanations available to them. One might therefore have supposed their memories to be all the better (as, indeed, they are on immediate recall, and one week after the presentation) and hence all the more durable. In fact, their reactions after six months show quite unequivocally that, in full accord with what we have learned about the remembrance of operational situations, failure to construct causality as such, renders their mnemonic organization unstable. In other words, mnemonic accuracy in the present case would seem to depend more on success at arriving at a casual explanation than on the correctness of the 'lawful' descriptions.

§4. *Level III*

At this level, causal explanations become rather more common. Thus, Jac (7;9) attributed the rise of the liquid to the vapour produced by the candle; Vio (9;2) contended (like Pel) that the rise in level of *T2* was due to the air which, moreover, helped to put out the candle, but she had nothing at all to say about the disappearance of the liquid from *T1*. Rao (9;5), on the other hand, contended that the air pushed the water out of *T1*, and attributed the rise in level of *T2* to heat, 'because that gets hot, and then it went like this and sucked it all up'. Moreover, the liquid produces air as it rises: 'The water went up, and that made too much air and so the candle went out'. Dom (9;11) argued correctly that the candle went out because there was no air, but added that 'there was pressure, because the smoke of the candle made the water rise up; it was hot and the heat forced it up'. Cri (11 years) also explained that 'the water rose because of the heat'. As for the tube *T1*, many of these subjects believed, correctly, that it was the air in it which forced the water up inside.

This last point, which, in fact, is the only one capable of serving as a causal interpretation at this level, no doubt explains why some of these subjects begin to wonder how it is that the liquid should enter *T2* but not *T1* when both were pressed equally hard against the bottom of the two dishes. Bern (10;5) said that 'it rose before the glass was almost at the bottom'; Pau (10;7), on the contrary, contended that, once the tube was put in position the smoke lifted it up. The smoke?— *Yes, it was the steam.*

In short, the process of objectivizing causality, begun at Level II, leads, at Level III, to a dialectical confrontation between the 'lawful' and the causal relations: once he has discovered a constant relationship, the child feels a need to explain it, and all explanations based on the internal connections of the model call, in their turn, for a closer observation of the new relations. As a result, there is an improvement in the organization of the memory as such and an enrichment of its contents: whence the recall that the rise in the level of $D1$ went hand in hand with an apparent drop in the level of $T1$, a fact that almost completely eludes most six- to seven-year-old subjects, who, by virtue of that very fact, must be assigned to Level II. The greater accuracy of the memory is certainly bound up with a better grasp of the conservation of matter which, in the case of the decantations, occurs precisely at about the age of six to seven years (as we established with several subjects at Stage II). However, in the present case, the child must remember more than just one conservation; he must also consider a causal transformation: the liquid displaced by the immersion of $T1$ produces a rise of level in $D1$, thanks to the simultaneous action of pressure and conservation. This is no doubt why it is not until the appearance of the explanations characteristic of Stage III that this process is observed and remembered in detail.

As for remembrance six months after the presentation, it either reflects a high degree of mnemonic accuracy, or else reveals a striking contrast between the remembrance of the central phenomenon, i.e. the rise of the liquid in the tube covering the lit candle, and the paucity of the drawings. Thus, though some of these subjects depict process II, they often forget process I, i.e. the rise in the level of $D1$, and this despite the fact that they were able to explain it better than anything else. However, the majority produced very poor drawings even of process II. Thus, Alf (8;7), who had tried to repeat the experiment at home during the first two sessions, merely drew four identical cylinders, two empty and two containing candles and the same amount of liquid. Pointing to one, he said: 'The water was put into that one, then it went up and the candle went out.' Cel (9;6) drew two large cubes, one filled with blue liquid and nothing else, and the other containing an empty tube completely immersed in red liquid: 'You put the glass into the red one and the water rose'. In short, what sticks in the memory of these subjects is the strange fact that the water rises, sometimes coupled to an excessive schematization which tends to suppress the figurative details, or else to a correct drawing of process II with omission of process I. Four subjects nevertheless remembered and drew the whole experiment fairly well. Thus, Pie (9;5) offered the following commentary: 'There was a lit candle and we put the thing on top, and it rose up to here inside, and when we put another tube in the blue it rose up on the outside.' Fra (9;0) omitted the drop in level of II in her drawing, but mentioned it in her verbal description, which was more highly structured than it had been during the second session.

§5. *Conclusions*

When we first decided to study this particular problem, we were particularly concerned to establish whether or not the memory of an inexplicable causal process was comparable to that of phenomena which, like the transmissions of motions (Chapter 12), become rapidly and completely intelligible to the child. Let us now sum up our conclusions:

(1) To begin with, the spatio-temporal structure and figurative aspect of the model presented in this chapter was no more complicated than that of the slope-and-ball experiment (Chapter 12): this is proved by the fact that successful recall (Level III) of the present model (one week after presentation) comes on average at the age of eight to nine years (six subjects out of seven achieved it at the age of eight years), while, with the slope-and-ball experiment, it does not appear until about the age of nine to ten years. In other words, the final element (the level of Tl during Si) is remembered at an earlier age than the end result of the slope-and-ball experiment (the gap between the last plug and the last ball).

(2) The fact that the remembrance of the present model is so good from the age of eight to nine years, on immediate recall no less than a week later, is, as we saw, due to progress, not in the ability to explain the underlying processes (which were quite beyond the grasp of our subjects) but in the general construction of causal schemata and the increasingly trenchant analysis of the latter, thanks to which there is an ever-better recall of the articulations involved. In fact, as they advance from the psychomorphic or biomorphic conception of causality (Level I) to an objectivized conception based on a search for connections between the parts of the object itself, children become increasingly aware of, and remember, a whole set of relationships that completely eludes the younger ones amongst them. In particular, the astonishment of older children when they see the liquid rising in one of the tubes is a powerful impetus to exploration and memorization, and explains their rapid mnemonic progress.

(3) However, six months later, the picture has changed completely:

while the memory of the slope-and-ball experiment advanced over six months in nine cases out of fifty (two in respect of the plugs, and seven in respect of the structure of the causal process), remained stationary in seventeen cases, and regressed in twenty-four cases, the memory of the present model made no clear advances at all: there were three cases of slight progress (improvements in the representation of Si and Sf at Level I, and in the general description at Level III), three stationary cases, and twenty-seven regressions.[1] The reasons for this difference are quite obvious. Wherever improvements do occur, as in the case of such operational structures of a logical type as seriations, or such causal structures as transitive motions, they are invariably due to the fact that the subject can avail himself of (developing) organizational or explanatory schemata which are exercised outside the experimental situation, and, becoming more perfect, lead quite spontaneously to a restructuring of certain memories. In the present case, on the contrary, the child is faced with a problem quite beyond his powers of understanding, and hence cannot invoke any schemata of this type.

(4) As for the degradation of the memory after six months (chiefly at Level II but also in several subjects at Level III), it is due to a similar mechanism. But it remains an odd fact that a phenomenon older children find so puzzling that they feel compelled to seek an explanation, however far-fetched? should be forgotten so quickly, and their original explanations should be forgotten as well. This is probably because the original explanations were not structured enough to be preserved as an organized system. Adducing a causal interpretation is tantamount to attributing such operations to the object as are isomorphic with those the subject himself can perform, thanks to his own logico-mathematical (including spatial) structures. But before this level of elaboration is reached, explaining the behaviour of an object means attributing to the objects what actions the subject himself can perform, i.e. endowing them with anthropomorphic attributes, and this precisely because the subject has not yet reached the level of operational decentration, the *sine qua non* of the objectivation of causality. Now, in the case of an inexplicable process, such as the rise in the level of our tube, the grasp of causality must perforce have remained at a pre-operational level: hence the assertions that the heat sucks up the liquid, that the air attracts or expels the water, that the movement of the liquids depends on, or produces, the movement of the air, combined in all sorts of

---

[1] The actual percentages were: (1) in the slope-and-ball experiment: clear progress 18 per cent; identical responses 34 per cent; regressions 48 per cent; and (2) in the present experiment: clear progress 0 per cent; slight progress 9 per cent; stationary cases 9 per cent; regressions 81 per cent.

contradictory ways. It follows that there can be no operational system, no schema to sustain the memory over an interval of several months. This explains why Alf (8;7) could offer no better explanation of the rise in level he had watched six months earlier than: 'We poured out the water, the candle stayed lit, then we poured it into the other glass, and then I think it went out.' Quite obviously so unschematic an approach is bound to go hand in hand with a singularly impoverished figurative memory, and not with one that is merely simplified, as happened in the case of the ball-and-slope experiment.

(5) It is nevertheless true that, though many younger subjects may, after six months, completely forget the rise in the level of $T2$, which failed to astonish them in the first place, all subjects at Level III and even some at Level II remember it very well as a surprising event, and this quite irrespective of its precise context. But here we must distinguish two factors: the memory of an organized structure, including the configuration embodying that structure, which is precisely what is lacking, and the remembrance of a problem in conflict with the child's habitual schemata. Now, awareness of a problem can have direct effects on the memory, inasmuch as it calls attention to a lacuna or intellectual conflict that engages the child's attention or encourages him to make new efforts (cf. Alf who, at the age of eight years, repeated the experiment at home). But this effect still depends on a grasp of causality, for, before he can even become aware of a problem, the child must have reached a certain level of intellectual development. Hence, though the memory of an inexplicable phenomenon presents quite other, and negative, characteristics than that of an organized and explicable system, it can nevertheless have a positive aspect: it can recall puzzling or problematical events as such. This is what we shall be discussing at greater length in the next chapter.

Meanwhile, we may take it that, in the present case, there is a truly impressive correlation between the grasp of causality and the mnemonic level after six months. At Level I, where there is a complete absence of intellectual astonishment plus verbal explanations for everything, the memory after six months is essentially figurative, but has also markedly deteriorated except in respect of two minor local improvements (in Sf). At Level III, which is characterized by full awareness of the problem and some attempts at a rational explanation, the memory after six months may be faithful or degraded in purely figurative respects, with a centration on the problem itself, and hence more or less schematized in respect of the data. Between these two extremes, subjects at Level II reject the precausal explanations characteristic of Level I but have not yet reached the early phase of causal structuring characteristic of Level III, and hence confine themselves to 'lawful' descriptions precise enough to ensure satisfactory retention during immediate recall and also during recall a week later. But in that case, and this is a fact well worth stressing, the memory after six months suffers *maximum* deterioration, no doubt because the child's inability to find a causal explanation is reflected in a lack of mnemonic organization, whereas if the memory were of a predominantly figurative nature (memory-'images'), the correct 'lawful' description devoid of causal constructions would undoubtedly have led to a greater stabilization of the memory, at least in respect of the general configuration of the model.

CHAPTER FOURTEEN

The Remembrance and Growing Appreciation of a Causal Problem[1]

The model used in the present study (Figure 43) is a simple spatial or physico-spatial configuration, and hence resembles the models we have used to investigate the remembrance of transitive and associative relations (Chapters 5 and 6). However, the behaviour of the liquids in the two U-tubes can also be given a causal, in addition to a logical or spatial, significance. This poses the problem of whether or not the remembrance of the model depends to some extent on the explicative structuring of the memory.

Though the reason for the equality of the levels in tube A is not generally grasped before the age of eleven to twelve years, and the

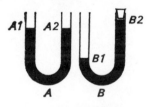

FIGURE 43

rôle of air pressure in B (the stoppered tube) not until about the age of fourteen to fifteen years, the obvious difference between the respective levels in the two tubes may persuade younger subjects to attach a causal significance to the stopper in B. What we shall therefore be trying to discover in this chapter is whether the gradual awareness of this causal problem affects the memory, even when the correct explanation is beyond the subject's grasp, and in what way. To that end, we shall first look at the spontaneous recall of the static set-up (§§1–4). Next (§5), we shall analyse the results of three special methods designed to increase awareness of the causal element: in the first of these (Method II) the examiner helps the child to fill the tubes A and B; in the next (Method III) he also asks a question

[1]In collaboration with G. Voyat.

238

about the conservation of the liquids while filling the tubes (which does not involve the causality of the phenomenon in *B*, but may arouse the subject's interest in the supplementary problem of the equality or inequality of the levels); in the last (Method IV) the causal problem is introduced explicitly. In fact, Methods II–IV serve us simply as control experiments; our main problem is still to discover whether, when faced with a static set-up and not told anything about the way in which it was constructed, the child will merely remember the spatial configuration, or whether his remembrance of it will be influenced by the discovery or realization that the model poses a causal problem.

§1. *Method I and mnemonic levels*

Method I was applied during four sessions.

The first session (presentation and immediate recall) consists of four parts:

(1) In the first, the experimenter informs the subject that the screen before him hides something that he must look at carefully so that he can describe and draw it afterwards;

(2) The experimenter removes the screen to reveal two glass tubes (Figure 43) which have been glued to a card in a vertical position. The presentation lasts 45 seconds precisely and there are no manipulations;

(3) After the presentation, the subject is asked to describe what he has seen;

(4) As soon as he has done that, and not an hour later as in the other experiments, he is asked for a memory-drawing.

The subject is then dismissed and, again in contrast to what happened in the other experiment, he is not told that he will be recalled a week and six months later.

The second session is held a week later. This time the tubes are not brought out and the subject is asked for another description and memory-drawing. When he has finished, he is asked a number of questions intended to establish whether or not he thinks his new drawing is identical to, or worse than, the last, and whether he has noticed any mistakes.

The third session is held six months later and is similar to the second. A fourth session is held one week after the third, and is devoted to recognition based on a choice from twelve models.

We saw a total of fifty-two subjects, including eleven 4-year-olds, eleven 5-year-olds, ten 6-year-olds, eight 7-year-olds and twelve 10- to 14-year-olds; forty-six of them were able to come back after six months.

We were able to distinguish five successive mnemonic levels, and several sub-stages of which it was impossible to say whether or not they were in chronological succession (see Figure 44).

Stage I is characterized by a lack of differentiation between the tubes *A* and *B* and their contents, and hence by the absence of references to the liquids or their levels. Subjects of Sub-stage I*A* simply draw two Us (to

239

which they often refer as such) and fail to distinguish between container and content; those at Sub-stage IB draw double curves but their two Us are empty and identical in shape; at Sub-stage IC, there is an apparent attempt to represent different levels in A and B, which would have been comparable to a Stage IV response had not all these subjects (aged four to five years) referred explicitly to the letters U and J instead of to the liquids and their levels.

Stage II is associated with the explicit differentiation between container (tubes) and content (liquids and levels), but not between the four levels $(A1 = A2 / B1 = B2)$. At Sub-stage IIA the tubes are represented by

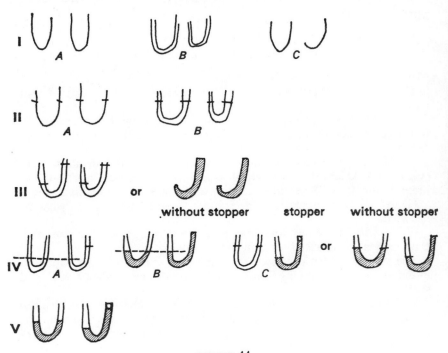

FIGURE 44

single lines (and the levels by horizontal strokes) and at Sub-stage IIB by double lines, though the improvement may well have been mere differences in drawing ability.

At Stage III, the levels in B1 and B2 are clearly distinguished, but not the levels in A and B $(A1 = B1$ and $A2 = B2)$.

Stage IV sees the beginning of attempts to distinguish between A and B. At Sub-stage IVA, $A1 = A2 = B1$, but $B2 > B1$, though not up to the edge of the tube. With Sub-stage IVB, $A1 = A2 = B1$ as well, but $B2$ comes up to the edge of the tube and there is no stopper. With Sub-stage IVC, $A1 = A2$, $B1 < A2$ and $B2 > B1$, but $B2$ does not reach to the edge of the tube, or if it does, the stopper is omitted again (in other words,

240

these subjects remember everything but the presence of the only object capable of explaining the differences in levels).

With Stage V, finally, there is correct recall of the two models.

§2. *Comparison of immediate recall with recall after a week*

I. Let us first of all look at the distribution of types I–V with age in Table 25 (see p. 242) (in absolute numbers of subjects; percentages in brackets).

The close correlation of mnemonic type with age points to a gradual centration of the memory on the levels of the liquids in *A1–B2*, and this despite the fact that the whole situation is quite beyond the grasp of most of these subjects.

As for the development of the memory from recall immediately after presentation to recall a week later, we notice two facts: on the one hand, there is an over-all decrease in the number of subjects of types I and V and a corresponding increase in the number of subjects of types II–IV; on the other hand, two 7-year-olds have advanced from type IV to V, and several others from type I to types II–III.

II. For a more detailed analysis, we must also look at the total number of advances and regressions by age (Table 26).

We see that, of sixty subjects, ten had made clear progress. Up to the age of six years, advances were made by three subjects out of twenty-two (1 in 7); at the age of eight to fifteen years, by 0 subjects out of twenty; and at the age of six to seven years by seven subjects

TABLE 26 *Changes from the first to the second session (in number of subjects in square brackets; percentages in round brackets)*

Ages	4 [11]	5 [11]	6 [10]	7 [8]	8 [8]	10–15 years [12]
Regression	1 (9)	1 (9)	1 (10)	0 (0)	1 (12)	4 (33)
Progress	2 (18)	1 (9)	3 (30)	4 (50)	0 (0)	0 (0)
Stationary	8 (72)	9 (82)	6 (60)	4 (50)	7 (87)	8 (66)

out of eighteen (1 : 2 : 5). Regress, by contrast, was shown by only five of the twenty-two 4- to 5-year-olds, and by five of the twenty 8- to 14-year-olds, and dropped to a mere one out of eighteen in the case of 6- to 7-year-olds. These regressions were from Stage II to Stage I (two cases), from Stage IV to Stage III (one case), from Stage V to Stage IV (two cases), and from Stage V to Stage III (three cases). As for the advances, four were from Stage I to Stage II, one

TABLE 25 *Types of reaction on immediate recall and after a week*

	N subjects	Immediate					One week later				
		I	*II*	*III*	*IV*	*V*	*I*	*II*	*III*	*IV*	*V*
4 years	11	7 (66)	4 (34)	0 (0)	0 (0)	0 (0)	6 (54)	5 (46)	0	0 (0)	0 (0)
5 years	11	5 (46)	2 (18)	2 (18)	2 (18)	0 (0)	4 (36)	3 (26)	2 (19)	2 (14)	0 (0)
6 years	10	1 (10)	3 (30)	1 (10)	5 (50)	0 (0)	1 (10)	3 (30)	1 (10)	5 (50)	0 (0)
7 years	8	3 (38)	1 (12)	0 (0)	3 (38)	1 (12)	1 (12)	2 (24)	1 (12)	1 (22)	3 (40)
8 years	8	0 (0)	1 (12)	1 (12)	5 (64)	1 (12)	0 (0)	1 (12)	2 (24)	5 (64)	0 (0)
10–15 years	12	0 (0)	0 (0)	0 (0)	4 (33)	8 (67)	0 (0)	0 (0)	0 (0)	7 (58)	5 (42)
4–5 years	22	12 (54)	6 (27)	2 (9)	2 (9)	0 (0)	10 (45)	8 (36)	2 (9)	2 (9)	0 (0)
6–7 years	18	4 (22)	4 (22)	1 (5)	8 (44)	1 (5)	2 (11)	5 (27)	2 (11)	6 (33)	3 (16)
8–15 years	20	0 (0)	1 (5)	1 (5)	9 (45)	9 (45)	0 (0)	1 (5)	2 (10)	12 (60)	5 (25)
Total	60	16 (26)	11 (18)	4 (6)	19 (31)	10 (16)	12 (20)	14 (23)	6 (10)	20 (33)	8 (13)

242

from Stage I to Stage III, three from Stage III to Stage IV, one from Stage III to Stage V, and one from Stage IV to Stage V.

These results face us with two problems: we want to know, first, why subjects capable of much better recall should alter their memories of the model so soon after its presentation, and, second, how subsequent progress is possible in these circumstances.

With regard to the distortion of the model on immediate recall, we saw earlier (Chapter 6) that when several subjects below the age of six to seven years were shown one continuous and one broken line whose end points did not coincide, they unhesitatingly lined the end points up in their drawings immediately after the presentation. The response in the U-tube experiment was of a similar kind, except that ten of our subjects corrected their error subsequently. This might suggest that some of these errors were due to sloppy draftsmanship or lack of attention etc., in short to what we might expect of children who are not particularly interested in what they are shown and react to it in a cavalier manner.

However, to dispose of this interpretation, and to show that such distortions are due to the memory itself, let us mention a reaction by one of our collaborators. While writing in a mountain chalet, he saw the proprietor place a metal jug on the ground, which he took to be an electric kettle, the more so as he distinctly saw a flex in the proprietor's hand. Now, a moment later, he remembered that there was no electricity in the place, and that the jug could not possibly have been an electric kettle. When he went down to look, he found that there was no flex, nor anything vaguely reminiscent of one, and yet he had *seen* one and was even certain of that fact. There was only one explanation, and a very simple one at that: because he invariably associated kettles with electricity, his mistaken perception of the jug was immediately translated into a memory-image of a kettle and flex (cf. the mnemonic inference discussed in Chapter 5). Here we have an excellent example of a memory distortion on immediate recall, followed by a correction a moment later. Such distortions are, moreover, quite common in our attitude to familiar objects; we think we have seen the scissors in their usual place though they have been moved, etc.

Now, if we grant that direct recall may be mistaken even in adults, we must grant *a fortiori* that children can distort their memories by means of similar schematizations: for instance by equalizing three or four of the levels in the U-tubes, or by identifying A with B, etc.

III. However, while we can explain the occurrence of such distortions, we must still discover the mechanism on which subsequent progress is based, the more so as the particular causal situation we are investigating does not involve a simple operational schema whose general progress (outside the experimental situation) has an ameliorating effect on the memory. In these circumstances, it seems exceedingly difficult to explain how it is that a model whose spatial relationships the subject is simply asked to observe should be remembered more accurately after a week than it was a few minutes after presentation.

Now, among our sixty subjects, only three, aged from ten to eleven years, expressed their surprise at the fact that the levels of *B1* and *B2* should have been different, when those of *A1* and *A2* were equal. However, interestingly enough, they did not notice this problem when examining the tubes, but only when making their first drawing a few minutes later. 'This level (*B1*) bothers me', said one of the eleven-year-olds, 'because it isn't the same as the other one . . . It must be because of the cork.' A week later, he produced the same (correct) drawing and added: 'I still can't understand it.' This child quite naturally paid special attention to those details he found the most puzzling or problematical. But what is so remarkable about all these cases is that the problem should have struck them during the drawing test and not during the actual perception of the model.

The explanation can only be that, on perceiving the model, they feel a measure of dissatisfaction which, though they are not conscious of it, persists in their memory and hence impels them to seek an answer to the question that puzzled them most: why the levels should be equal in the absence of a stopper and unequal in its presence. Indeed, even younger subjects will often round off incomplete relationships simply because such relationships tend to set up a state of mental disequilibrium.

In fact, as we descend to the next lower level, we find that one subject advanced from *A1* = *A2* = *B1* and *B1* > *B2* (with stopper) to type V (correct levels). Now, the very fact that this subject had noticed the dissimilarity between the levels in the tubes *A* and *B* may very well have triggered off a search for a solution. Moreover, having noticed the asymmetrical levels in *B*, but not the stopper during the first session, and the symmetrical levels in *A*, this child must have been left with a feeling of dissatisfaction that caused him to reinforce his vague memory of the stopper which he had omitted from his first drawing.

On examining the drawings produced a week after the presentation and the answers to the question of whether the subjects were more or less satisfied with them than they were with their previous drawings, we found, first of all, that most of the younger subjects failed to make a precise comparison between the two. Thus, Alb, (5;0), offered a first-session drawing of two curved, and a second-session drawing of two straight, tubes, and said that 'they were the same'. Man, another five-year-old, gave the same reply, though in his first drawing he had marked $B2 > B1$, and in his second $B2 = B1$. San (6;11) on the other hand, changed from $A1 = A2 = B1$ (with $B1 < B2$) to $A1 = A2 > B1$ and had the impression that he had done much better without quite knowing why. Las (7;4) showed the same progress in drawing the levels but, interestingly enough, only remarked on another improvement: 'This one is better, I had forgotten the cork.' (This suggests that remembrance of the stopper in B and of its absence in A leads to $B1 < A2 (= A1)$. Bla (7;2) marked $A2 = B1$ in her first drawing and later corrected this to $A2 > B1$, exclaiming 'Oh, I have made a mistake.' In her second drawing the difference was greatly accentuated, and $B1$ had dropped right to the bottom of the tube. Per (8;4) thought he had improved his second drawing by making $B1 > A2$, when his first drawing had shown $A1 = A2 = B1$. Bec (8;3) produced a first drawing of $A1 > A2 > B1$ and a second drawing of $A1 = A2$; $A2 > B1$, and thought that the second was better, though he was unable to remember the first.

Only subjects of type V, in their first no less than in their second drawings, seem quite certain of success. Thus, Roc (14;3) said: 'I remember perfectly well', and Ron (14;10) explained: 'It isn't quite the same drawing but it's right enough.' Neb (11;4) had forgotten his first drawing but felt satisfied with the second: 'One of the tubes was filled the same on both sides, but not the other.'

IV. Altogether, except for subjects at Stage V, who invest the configuration with a general significance which, as it were, impels them towards awareness of the problem (equality *v.* inequality of levels), it would seem that the first drawings are simply the expression of memories in the process of organization: these drawings satisfy, or fail to satisfy, their authors to the extent that they do, or do not, lead to the correct recognition of the model, and if they do not, the memory continues to develop. Now, even without reflexive or retrospective awareness of the problem, this development must perforce be guided by a schema, since, in order to recognize that the second memory-drawing ($M2$) is more satisfactory than the first ($M1$), the child must refer back to the model, and if the latter has not been assimilated to a schema, it cannot be known or rediscovered except with the help of the memory $M1$, which is precisely the one the child has found to be unsatisfactory. Hence, we must take it that, in all cases of verifiable mnemonic progress, the model cannot be identified by the memory $M1$ alone. Now, the inspection of the model for forty-five seconds may well have enabled the child to take note of the equalities or inequalities of the levels: vague impressions

245

which the memory tries to round off, or precise impressions which the memory tries to resurrect. In both cases, what is involved is an assimilation to schemata (equalization or asymmetry) and it is to these that we must look if we wish to explain the development of the memory from *M1* to *M2*.

§3. *Recall after six months*

We were able to bring back forty-six of our sixty subjects six months after the presentation, all of whom we asked for memory-drawings and verbal descriptions of what they had seen during the first session. The results were both highly instructive and quite different from those obtained during the second session.

I. To begin with, there was a strong concentration of types III and IV, which would indicate mnemonic progress by the younger subjects and mnemonic regress by the older ones. However, eight of our subjects produced such highly elaborate schematizations of the model (for instance two bottles instead of the two U-tubes) that they had to be graded purely by their remembrance of the levels in the two tubes.

Let us first look at the distribution of types with age (Table 27).

TABLE 27   *Memory-drawings after six months, in absolute numbers of subjects (percentages in brackets)*

	N	I	II	III	IV	V
4 years	4	1 (25)	3 (75)	0	0	0
5 years	10	3 (30)	2 (20)	2 (20)	3 (30)	0
6 years	10	1 (10)	1 (10)	5 (50)	3 (30)	0
7 years	7	1 (14)	2 (28)	2 (28)	2 (28)	0
8 years	6	0	0	5 (83)	1 (17)	0
10–15 years	9	1 (12)	0	3 (33)	5 (55)	0
4–5 years	14	4 (28)	5 (35)	2 (14)	3 (21)	0
6–7 years	17	2 (11)	3 (17)	7 (41)	5 (30)	0
8–15 years	15	1	0	8 (60)	6 (40)	0
Total	46	7 (15)	8 (17)	17 (37)	14 (31)	0

We see that types I and II have decreased appreciably in number, that type V has disappeared completely, thus increasing the relative frequency of type IV, and, above all, that type III has increased from

6 per cent (first session) and 10 per cent (second session) to 37 per cent. In other words, what most of these subjects remember above all after six months is a difference in the levels, but they forget the difference between the tubes A and B; in other words, they liken the 'normal' levels in the former ($A1 = A2$) to the 'problematic' levels in the latter. This is a highly instructive response, particularly when we consider it in conjunction with the fact that the proportion of types I and II reactions combined (no difference in the levels of the two tubes) has dropped to 32 per cent (from 45 per cent at the first session and 43 per cent at the second session) while types III and IV responses combined have risen to 63 per cent (from 53 per cent and 56 per cent). The memory would thus seem to have attached itself more closely, though still most inadequately, to the problematic issue, even though that issue is not yet consciously recognized.

Now for progress and regress with age, see Table 28. There was first of all one advance by a four-year-old from type I to type II (this

TABLE 28 *Mnemonic changes from the second session (one week) to the third session (six months after presentation)*

Ages	4	5	6	7	8	10–15	Totals
Regression	0	0	2	3	3	7	15
Progress	1 (0)	2 (2)	2 (2)	0	1 (1)	0	6
Stationary	3	8	6	4	2	2	25

(In brackets: changes from the first session (immediate recall) to the third session.)

subject, however, had already produced a type II drawing on immediate recall). Next, there were two advances by five-year-olds, one progressing from type I to type II by the second session, and from type II to type III by the third session, and the other progressing from type II (first two sessions) to type III. Two 6-year-olds also advanced from type II to type III, and one 8-year-old advanced from type II (first two sessions) to type IV.

As we can see, most of these advances were by four- to six-year-olds, among whom there were few regressions, in contrast to the seven- to fifteen-year-olds, with whom regress was common (thirteen cases) and who produced just one advance only (an eight-year-old). This distribution seems to point to two things: first, that the younger subjects, who had either failed to mark in, or else had equated, the levels in the tubes, were nevertheless troubled by the implicit problem and showed this increasingly during the spontaneous organization of their memories; and, second, that the older subjects, who had paid greater heed to the levels during the initial sessions, had failed to understand the problem they themselves had recognized, and hence were unable to retain for six months what they could not assimilate in the first instance.

The mnemonic changes from the second to the third sessions are thus comparable, though not equivalent to the mnemonic changes from the first to the second session. In the last case, the advances (chiefly at the age of six to seven years) seem to be due mainly to the fact that the problem is increasingly forced on the subjects' attention, whence the relative frequency of types IV and V memories, while the regress of seven- to fifteen-year-olds and the relative frequency of types III and IV are explained by the failure to find a solution to that problem (cf. the similar trend in the experiments described in Chapter 13). Now, what is common to both situations is the predominance of the schema (equality and partial inequality of the levels) and neglect of the figurative details (the tubes), the memory of which deteriorates markedly in the course of six months, simply because these details cannot be fitted into a comprehensible context. We shall discover that much the same thing happens in the case of recognition.

§4. *Recognition by selection*

One week after the third session, we were able to bring back forty-two of our subjects, this time for a recognition test based on the selection of the original model from twelve shapes: three of type I, three of type II, one of type III, three of type IV (including one that was nearly of type V but had two stoppers), one of type V (correct), plus one schematization presented by several subjects during the third session[1] (see Figure 45). When the first selection had been made, the subjects were shown several other shapes, and were asked to state whether or not these were correct as well, and why. Finally, they were asked to make another selection from the complete collection of shapes (final choice).

As a general rule, recognition is much simpler than recall because it involves the rediscovery of a perception and not its reproduction by means of a drawing. The great importance of the present test is that it shows that there are exceptions to this rule, and that recognition may evolve in much the same way as recall. Let us first of all tabulate the responses of the various age groups (see Table 29). We see, first of all, that the final choice of these subjects differs considerably from the first: there were five slight improvements, four

[1] This schematization (No. IIIA of Figure 45), chosen by four subjects, was classified as type II in one case, and as type III in three cases, depending on the subjects' commentaries and previous drawings.

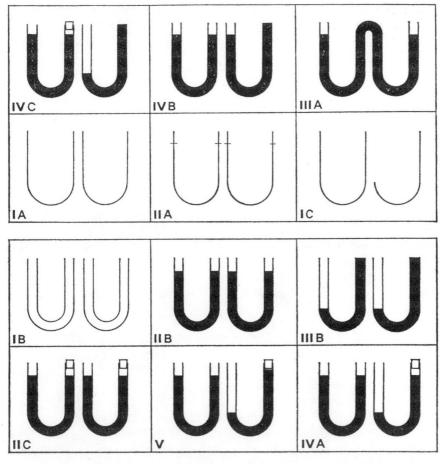

FIGURE 45

regressions, and thirty-three stationary cases. In other words, recognition of the present model depends on the subject's intellectual level and never leads to massive responses of type V: such responses, in fact, account for only 19–21 per cent of the choices, which, though representing notable progress over recall after six months (complete absence of type V), is a poor advance over the initial type V responses (immediate recall 16 per cent; recall after a week 13 per cent).

This dependence of recognition on the intellectual level is also reflected in the evolution of responses with age: four- to five-year-olds produced 49–58 per cent type I–II recognitions as against 32 per cent type IV–V recognitions; the corresponding figures for six- to seven-year-olds were 37 per cent and 49 per cent, and by the

249

TABLE 29 Recognition in absolute number of subjects (percentages in brackets)

	N	Initial choice					Final choice				
		I	II	III	IV	V	I	II	III	IV	V
4 years	3	1	1	0	1	0	0	2	0	1	0
5 years	9	3	1	2	2	1	3	2	1	1	2
6 years	10	1	3	1	5	0	1	3	1	5	0
7 years	6	1	0	2	1	2	1	1	1	1	2
8 years	6	0	2	0	2	2	0	2	0	2	2
10–15 years	8	0	1	0	4	3	0	2	0	3	3
4–5 years	12	4 (33)	2 (16)	2 (16)	3 (25)	1 (8)	3 (25)	4 (33)	1 (8)	2 (16)	2 (16)
6–7 years	16	2 (12)	3 (19)	3 (19)	6 (37)	2 (12)	2 (12)	3 (19)	3 (19)	6 (37)	2 (12)
8–15 years	14	0 (0)	3 (21)	0 (0)	6 (43)	5 (35)	0 (0)	4 (29)	0 (0)	5 (35)	5 (35)
Total	42	6 (14)	8 (19)	5 (12)	15 (35)	8 (19)	5 (12)	11 (26)	4 (9)	13 (31)	9 (21)

250

age of eight to fifteen years, type I has disappeared completely, and type II has dropped to 21–29 per cent, while types IV–V account for 70–78 per cent of the choices.

But what is most remarkable about Table 29 is the considerable drop in the number of type III responses (unequal levels in $A1$ and $A2$, and in $B1$ and $B2$, but with $A1 = B1$ and $A2 = B2$): in other words, after six months the largest group of subjects recalled that there were two equal and two unequal levels, but, failing to understand the reason why, had forgotten details, and came up with the simplest solution $(A1 < A2) = (B1 < B2)$. However, when presented with a card showing all the different solutions they had previously offered, their choice tended either towards general equalities (types I–II) or towards more accurately structured equalities and inequalities (types IV–V), with the result that the compromise solution of type III was virtually abandoned.

More generally, Table 29 shows that recognition (initial and final choices) is much closer to immediate recall or recall after a week than it is to recall after six months, and this despite the fact that the last test of recall preceded the recognition test by only one week. This finding, coupled with the preceding one, shows: (a) that recognition is quite distinct from recall (or else the responses on recall after six months would have governed the recognitory choices), and (b) that the two are nevertheless based on the same schemata, because recognition, too, develops with age and resembles recall during the first two sessions. In order to make this point in full, we would have to construct six separate tables, since there were two recognition tests (initial test I and final test II) and three tests of recall (A = immediate; B = one week after presentation; and C = six months after presentation). To simplify matters, we have therefore adopted the following procedure. Let $R > D$ represent the case where the recognitions RI and RII are superior to the drawings A, B and C (and $D > R$ the opposite case); and let $R \geqslant D$ represent the case where R is partially superior to A, B and C (for example, RI and $RII > A$ and B, but $R = C$), and $R \leqslant D$ the opposite case. The responses of our forty-two subjects were as follows:

$R < D$	$R \leqslant D$	$R = D$	$R \geqslant D$	$R > D$
8 (19%)	5 (12%)	12 (28%)	9 (21%)	8 (19%)

While equivalences accounted for less than one-third of the total responses, the advances and regressions were fairly well balanced, and this in all three age groups (4–5 years; 6–7 years; and 8–15 years); however, the four supernumerary cases of $R \geqslant D$ (9 $R \geqslant D$, but only 5 $R \leqslant D$) were all eight- to fifteen-year-olds. These facts lend strong support to the claim that recognition involves the same

251

schemata as recall. True, had the number of models offered for selection been reduced from twelve to five, i.e. to one per type, or had the children been shown real tubes filled to different heights with coloured liquids instead of figures on cardboard, the results would doubtless have been even more convincing, but in any case these reactions show, at the very least, that the recognition of an incomprehensible model is not significantly better than its recall, and this clearly because the details of the configuration strike the child as being quite arbitrary.[1]

§5. *Methods II to IV*
(*designed to increase awareness of the problem*)

The results of Method I show that the memory of the present model depends, essentially, not on the solution of the causal problem (since that solution is not available to children below the age of fourteen to fifteen years) but on the discovery of the fact that a problem is involved. Now, this discovery may be speeded up if the examiner stresses the inequality of the levels in the tube *B*, not, of course, by verbal explanations—which would be self-defeating—but by showing the child that the tubes *A* and *B* (with a stopper in *B*) are filled with equal amounts of liquid from two identical beakers. In Method II, once this operation has been performed, the child is simply asked for a memory-drawing of the two tubes and their contents. In Method III, he is also asked to draw the original flask, the two beakers with their (equal) contents and the tubes *A* and *B*, whereupon the experimenter puts a number of questions about the conservation of the liquids. In Method IV, finally, the child is asked questions not only about the conservation of the liquids (as in Method III) but also about the causal factor, i.e. about the reasons for the inequality of the levels in *A* and *B*.

Method II. The experimenter produces two identical beakers I and II and explains that one is his and the other one that of the child. He fills the first to the three-quarter mark from a flask and asks the child to watch while he fills the other one to the same level ('until there is the same amount of drink in both of them'). Next, he pours the contents of I into the tube *A* and the contents of II into the (tilted) tube *B*, and adjusts the stopper until the required levels are obtained; after this has been done, he attaches the tube to a piece of cardboard to the right of *A*. The subject is then asked to look carefully at the cardboard (for forty-five seconds) so that he can describe and draw it from memory as soon as the cardboard is removed (immediate

---

[1] With rotating triangles (Chapter 15), however, the child finds it much easier to recognize than to recall the model.

TABLE 30 *Types of memory obtained by Method II (in absolute number of subjects N with percentages in brackets)*

	N	Immediate recall					Recall after a week				
		I	II	III	IV	V	I	II	III	IV	V
4 years	6	5 (83)	1 (16)	0	0	0	6 (100)	0	0	0	0
5 years	11	5 (45)	0	1 (10)	5 (45)	0	3 (27)	0	2 (19)	6 (54)	0
6 years	7	2 (28)	1 (14)	1 (14)	3 (43)	0	0	3 (43)	1 (14)	3 (43)	0
7 years	10	2 (20)	2 (20)	0	5 (50)	1 (10)	1 (10)	3 (30)	0	6 (60)	0
8 years	5	0	0	1 (20)	0	4 (80)	0	0	3 (60)	0	2 (40)
9 years	8	0	0	0	3 (37)	5 (62)	0	0	1 (12)	1 (12)	6 (75)
10–15 years	11	0	0	0	3 (27)	8 (72)	0	0	0	4 (36)	7 (63)
4–5 years	17	10 (60)	1 (5)	1 (5)	5 (30)	0	9 (50)	0	2 (15)	6 (35)	0
6–7 years	17	4 (25)	3 (15)	1 (5)	8 (50)	1 (5)	1 (5)	6 (35)	1 (5)	9 (55)	0
8–15 years	24	0	0	1 (4)	6 (25)	17 (70)	0	0	4 (16)	5 (20)	15 (63)
Total	58	14 (24)	4 (6)	3 (5)	19 (32)	18 (31)	10 (17)	6 (10)	7 (12)	20 (34)	15 (25)

recall).[1] He is asked to do the same again, first, after a week, and then after six months. The results are shown in Table 30.

The reader will see that the correlation of mnemonic level with age is better than it was with Method I. This tends to show that the responses obtained during the additional tests are much more closely bound up with the subjects' operational development, and this because the presentation of the two tubes is preceded by a manipulation designed to emphasize the differences in level. Now the manipulation could have produced two distinct effects: it could have led to a sudden improvement of the memory due to the fixation of a greater amount of information, or else to a gradual improvement due to the child's growing awareness that a problem was involved. In fact, we find that, at the age of four to five years, Method II evoked no better responses than Method I: there were 60 per cent and 50 per cent type I responses as against 54 per cent and 45 per cent, and five and

TABLE 31   *Regress and progress during one week (Method II) (absolute number of subjects in square brackets; percentages in round brackets)*

Ages	4 [6]	5 [11]	6 [7]	7 [10]	8 [5]	9 [8]	10–15 [11]	Total
Regression	1 (16)	1 (9)	1 (14)	1 (10)	2 (40)	1 (12)	2 (18)	9
Progress	0	3 (27)	2 (28)	1 (10)	0	1 (12)	0	7
Stationary	5 (83)	7 (63)	4 (57)	8 (80)	3 (60)	6 (75)	9 (81)	42

six subjects of type IV as against two and two. At the age of six to seven years, the average responses to the two tests were more or less the same, as well, and there was even one regression from type V after a week (none with Method I). By contrast, at the age of eight years, there was an appreciable advance in recall (70 per cent and 63 per cent type V responses as against 45 per cent and 25 per cent obtained by Method I). It would seem, therefore, that as soon as the conservation of liquids during the decantations is grasped, the manipulative presentation drives home the existence of a problem: hence, it is because of awareness of the latter and not as a result of its solution (which comes much later) that the child's interest is aroused and his memory improves.

An analysis of the changes from the first to the second session (one week after presentation) is equally instructive (Table 31).

The reader will see, first of all, that Method II leads to no greater progress during one week than did Method I, which is only natural,

[1] If the child is dissatisfied with his first attempt, he is allowed to correct it (cf. Method I).

since retention in this case depends on awareness of the problem and not on its solution. But he will also see that the main advances occurred in the age group five to six years and not in the age group six to seven years: two 5-year-olds advanced from type I to types III and IV (and another from type I to type II) and one 6-year-old advanced from type I to type III (the single advance by a seven-year-old was from type I to type II): the seven advances, therefore, included five cases who marked in the levels they had forgotten on immediate recall. This shows that their progress could not possibly have been due to their awareness that a problem was being posed (as happened with six- to seven-year-olds tested by Method I) but must have resulted from improved recall of the data as such.

Method III. In this method, the presentation itself is the same as in Method II, but during immediate recall the subjects' grasp of the conservation of liquids is assessed by means of the following, neutral, questions: (a) The examiner asks whether tubes *A* and *B* contained the same amount of syrup, and in case of a negative reply, (*b*) why the amounts of syrup, equal in the beakers I and II, should have become unequal in *A* and *B*. Clearly, what these questions are designed to evoke is not an answer to the causal problem (the inequality of the levels in the two tubes) but simply a justification of the non-conservation, as affirmed by the subjects themselves.

A week later (second session) the subjects are asked to recall and draw, not merely the tubes (as in Methods I and II) but everything else they remember of the presentation, e.g. the beakers, the filling flask, etc. (the examiner does not mention any of these objects by name, nor does he specify the order in which they were presented). Depending on what the child draws, the examiner puts a number of supplementary questions: if the child draws the tubes (or the beakers) he is asked where the syrup came from; if he draws the flask (or the beakers) he is asked where the syrup was poured into, etc. Finally, he is questioned about the conservation of the liquids.

During a third session (one week or one month after the second) the child is given a recognition test (as described in §4 for Method I but omitted from Method II). This test therefore takes place, on average, fourteen days after the original presentation and not after six months and a week, as in Method I.

The results of the first two sessions (recall) were as shown in Table 32. Clearly, these results are appreciably better than those obtained with Method I, and more or less comparable to those obtained with Method II.

From immediate recall to recall after a week, there were seven regressions, four advances, and thirty-two stationary cases (forty-three subjects in all). Recognition will be discussed separately.

TABLE 32 Types of memory obtained with Method III

	N	Immediate recall					Recall after one week				
		I	II	III	IV	V	I	II	III	IV	V
4 years	4	4 (100)	0	0	0	0	4 (100)	0	0	0	0
5 years	8	3 (37)	1 (12)	3 (37)	1 (12)	0	3 (37)	2 (25)	2 (25)	1 (12)	0
6 years	9	0	1 (11)	2 (22)	3 (33)	3 (33)	0	2 (22)	2 (22)	2 (22)	3 (33)
7 years	11	0	2 (18)	3 (27)	4 (36)	2 (18)	0	2 (18)	4 (36)	5 (45)	0
8 years	9	0	0	0	4 (44)	5 (55)	0	0	0	5 (55)	4 (44)
9 years	2	0	0	0	1	1	0	0	0	1	1
4–5 years	12	7 (58)	1 (8)	3 (25)	1 (8)	0	7 (98)	2 (16)	2 (16)	1 (8)	0
6–7 years	20	0	3 (15)	5 (25)	7 (25)	5 (25)	0	4 (20)	6 (30)	7 (35)	3 (15)
8–9 years	11	0	0	0	5 (45)	6 (55)	0	0	0	6 (55)	5 (45)
Total	43	7 (16)	4 (9)	8 (18)	13 (30)	11 (25)	7 (16)	6 (14)	8 (18)	14 (32)	8 (18)

Method IV. This method was similar to Method III at the beginning, but the first memory-drawing was followed by a 'tutorial' that took the following form: (*a*) The tubes *A* and *B* (attached to the cardboard) were brought out again and the child was asked to describe them in detail. The examination continued until such time as the child remarked on the equality of the levels in *A* and their inequality in *B*, and on the presence of the stopper (he was also expected to observe that the 'syrup' was *inside* the tubes); (*b*) next, the demonstrator put the following questions (anticipation): 'What will happen if I remove the cork? What will happen if I put it here (in *A*)?'; (*c*) the demonstrator then asked (grasp of causality): 'Was there something odd about the tubes? Why do you think it happened like this? What do you think I myself did during the experiment?'; and (*d*) the demonstrator asked (grasp of conservation): 'Is there as much syrup in *A* as there is in *B*? And why is (or isn't) there?' The tubes were then hidden from sight and the child was told to make a second memory-drawing and to carry on until he was fully satisfied. He was also asked to reproduce his very first drawing, and the one that satisfied him most in the end.

A week later (second session) came another test of recall (description and drawings) followed by a recognition test (third session).

Method IV was applied to only twenty-five 5- to 9-year-old subjects. It served as a control to establish whether, once all the elements of the model had been specified and described by the child, and hence transformed into problems in respect of both causality and conservation of matter, they would be remembered properly after a week. Now, this is precisely what proved to be the case. Table 33 shows the types of drawings produced on direct recall by children divided into three age groups, and (in square brackets) their recall of these first drawings (not of the model itself) after the 'tutorial'. As for recall of the model itself immediately after the tutorial, there was no point in listing it separately, since no changes at all were observed between immediate recall and recall a week later.

We see, first of all, that 80–85 per cent of all these subjects had correct memories of the model a week after the tutorial (and since the responses were identical on both occasions, immediately after the tutorial as well). This suggests that children in all these age groups would have had far better memories of the model, even without special prompting, had they only been interested enough to observe it more closely. It may be objected that, as with so many of our experiments, the initial inspection involved the child's perception or intelligence and not his memory, which only enters the scene with retention of the observed material and plays no part during its incorporation. However, even without being reminded that the

TABLE 33 *Types of memory obtained with Method IV*

	N	Immediate (before the 'tutorial')					After one week				
		I	II	III	IV	V	I	II	III	IV	V
5 years	[7]	2 [1]	1 [1]	4 [5]	0	0	0	0	1 (15%)	0	6 (85%)
6–7 years	[13]	2 [0]	0 [1]	4 [6]	4 [3]	3 [3]	0	0	1 (7%)	1 (7%)	11 (85%)
8–9 years	[5]	2 [1]	0 [0]	1 [1]	1 [2]	1 [1]	0	0	1 (20%)	0	4 (80%)

decoding process depends on the code and that the real problem is the character of the latter, the reader will appreciate that there is no difference between what the subject 'learns' from the attentive examination of the model which Method IV compels him to make, and what he could have learned by perceptive exploration alone, which, as we know, is quite sufficient for subjects of type V. Now, the careful perceptive exploration of a complex configuration cannot but involve the memory; in order to record the sequence of letters *a*, *b*, *c*, *d* and *e* (or four levels in a tube and a cork) the child must do more than merely perceive them in turn; he must also proceed to their correlation and, as a result, he cannot simply forget *a* as he passes on to *b*, or *ab* as he passes on to *cd*, etc. In short, the memory is at work as soon as perception is other than purely instantaneous. Hence, it would be highly artificial were we to try to make a distinction, in the fixation of the memory, between the pure recording of the data and their retention. And it would be equally artificial to try to draw a line between what is supposed to be the memory pure and simple and the intelligent or schematized correlation of its potential contents: we firmly believe in the unity of the act of data recording and the organization of the memory.

No special features were observed in respect of direct recall before the 'tutorial' (but after the manipulations common to Methods II to IV). It is, however, all the more interesting to note that, after the tutorial, the subject's recall of his first drawing (square brackets in Table 33) was generally of a slightly higher type than it had been before the tutorial, except for one 6-year-old who reverted from type IV to type III. In other words, those subjects whose first recall was relatively poor, could not recall their first drawings without adding corrections based on their own observations during the second presentation. This proves that there is no such thing as an automatic or integral conservation of memories, and that the memory of a memory modifies the latter unbeknown to the subject, in accordance with what he has experienced or learned in the interval.

Remembrance after six months (Methods II to IV). Of the fifty-eight subjects tested by Method II, forty-six could be retraced after six months; similarly, we were able to bring back thirty-three of the forty-three subjects tested by Method III, and seventeen of the twenty-seven subjects tested by Method IV. They fell into the categories shown in Table 34.

The reader will note the interesting fact that though all these methods, specially designed to draw attention to the unusual features of the levels in the tubes *A* and *B*, produced marked mnemonic improvements during the first and second sessions, they failed to produce lasting effects on the memory: six months later there was again a predominance of types II and IV (as with Method I; cf. Table 27), though admittedly, accompanied by a relative decrease in the number of types I and II and the persistence of types V.

Now for a comparison of memories one week after presentation with memories six months later ($W > M$ designates regress; $W < M$ progress).

It should first of all be noted that though the oldest group made little progress with Methods II–III, their apparent failure was due to the fact that all but three of the subjects in this group were already of types IV and V (the three exceptions were of type III and remained

TABLE 34   *Remembrance after six months (Methods II–IV)*

	N (subjects)	I	II	III	IV	V
Method II:						
4–5 years	12	3	1	8	0	0
6–7 years	14	0	0	11	3	0
8–15 years	20	0	0	8	10	2
Method III:						
4–5 years	9	3	1	5	0	0
6–7 years	14	0	1	7	4	2
8–9 years	10	0	1	4	5	0
Method IV:						
4–5 years	6	0	0	4	2	0
6–7 years	5	0	0	1	3	1
8–9 years	6	0	0	3	2	1
	96	6 (6)	4 (4)	51 (53)	29 (30)	6 (6)

stationary). As for Method IV, the reader will recall that one week after the presentation, 85 per cent of the subjects aged five years or more were also of type V, whence their almost total lack of progress after six months (except for one 5-year-old who advanced from type III to type IV, and one 8-year-old who advanced from type IV to type V).

It nevertheless remains a fact that, with Method I, the regressions accounted for fifteen cases out of forty-six, the stationary cases for a further twenty-five, and progress for only six—the proportion was reversed with Method II (twenty-six regressions and thirteen stationary cases). Regressions also outnumbered the stationary cases in subjects tested by Method III, and massively so in those tested by

Method IV. All these facts combine to show that, though greater awareness of the problem can improve the memory appreciably for up to a week or even more, durable remembrance is not possible unless it is based on true understanding, and this Methods II to IV failed to, and indeed did not even try to, stimulate, since the intention was merely to produce a better figural analysis, and closer attention to the underlying conservation (III) and causal problem (IV).

However, on comparing the above results with those obtained in the tube-and-candle test (Chapter 13), which was equally incomprehensible to children before the age of fourteen to fifteen years, we find seventeen cases of progress in the present case as against none in the candle test (three slight improvements in respect of some details), 27 stationary cases as against three, and fifty-two regressions

TABLE 35 *Comparison of memories after a week and after six months (Methods II–IV)*

	Method II			Method III			Method IV		
	$M > W$	$M = W$	$M < W$	$M > W$	$M = W$	$M < W$	$M > W$	$M = W$	$M < W$
4–5 years	7	4	1	3	3	3	4	1	1
6–7 years	6	2	6	4	5	5	4	1	0
8–15 years	13	7	0	7	3	0	4	1	1
Totals	26	13	7	14	11	8	12	3	2

out of ninety-six, as against twenty-seven regressions out of thirty-three. The advances were essentially from types I and II to types III and IV, though two subjects tested by Methods III and IV advanced from type IV to type V (the four other subjects of type V were stationary cases). That progress with Methods II to IV (18 per cent) was only slightly greater than with Method I (six subjects; 13 per cent) lends even greater importance to the fact that it occurred in 24 per cent (eight out of thirty-three) of the subjects tested by Method III, in which the conservation problem was stressed (this also happened with Method IV, but we saw why progress there was impossible).

Recognition after two weeks. The subjects tested by Methods III and IV were given a recognition test, based on a choice from among twelve models, similar to that described in §4 for Method I, but two weeks instead of six months after the initial presentation. In the event,

261

the results obtained by all three methods were practically identical: in contrast to other experiments there was no massive advance of recognition over recall, and this precisely because in the present case recognition is based on the same schemata as recall, and, moreover, on schemata involving awareness of the problem and not of the figurative data alone. At the most, there was a slight advance of recognition over recall at the age of four to five years, but simply because this is the age when recall proves most difficult.

Here, then, is the relationship between recognition (R) and recall (D = drawing and description) in subjects tested by Methods III and IV (total number of subjects: 53):

$R < D$	$R \leqslant D$	$R = D$	$R \geqslant D$	$R > D$
14 (26%)	6 (11%)	5 (10%)	12 (23%)	16 (30%)

These results are very similar to those obtained by Method I, except for a slight superiority of the $R > D$ with respect to the $R = D$, doubtless due to the more detailed presentation of the model.

§6. Conclusions

The results obtained by Methods II, III and IV clearly corroborate those obtained by Method I, our chief technique. All four methods are based on the presentation of a phenomenon incomprehensible to children below the age of thirteen to fifteen years but a phenomenon which, depending on their operational level, may either pose a problem or else be devoid of all cognitive interest. The model itself, however, is simple to perceive (Figure 43) and may therefore appear simple to remember as well. However, as the results of even Method I show quite plainly, recognition no less than recall of the model depends on the realization that it poses a problem and, hence, on the child's operational schemata: either he fails to see the problem and hence deforms his memory of the two tubes by omitting the levels (type I) or by producing the most likely levels (type II–III), or else he is struck by the strange features of the model, which he is unable, or not fully able, to assimilate to his operational schemata, and hence remembers as such, i.e. as being incompatible with his schemata.

The novel feature introduced by Methods II–IV is that they reinforce awareness of the problem, either by providing new information (tubes A and B filled with identical amounts of liquid; Method II) or else by explicitly raising the question (implicit in Method II) of conservation in connection with the determination of the levels in the tubes (Method III), or, finally, by drawing the child's attention to all aspects of the phenomenon and by posing the problem of causality itself (insoluble for children aged four to nine years). Classical theorists would argue that all this is tantamount to increasing (at least in respect of Methods II and III) the number and complexity of the elements to be remembered, which, in the present case, means drawing the child's attention to the inequality of the levels in B and their equality in A, thus triggering off an operational or assimilatory effort that tends to improve the memory instead of filling it with disparate contents. In information theory, where the information rate of a written language is expressed in terms of redundancies and not in terms of the number of material elements, this result would be quite obvious, were it not for a factor that is often overlooked: in the development of the memory, progress and regress do not depend simply on the encoding and decoding process—the code itself seems to improve with the formation of operational structures.[1] In our particular case, the new information with which the subject is provided leads to results that vary appreciably with age: while Method IV shows that all age groups are capable of excellent mnemonic retention of the model with the help of a little tuition, Methods II and III show that the supply of additional information improves mnemonic retention inasmuch as it provides greater awareness of the problem, which, in turn, depends on the child's operational development.

However, Methods II to IV also show that alertness to a problem is not enough to ensure as durable a memory as real comprehension of the problem would have done: in fact, of the ninety-six subjects re-examined six months after presentation, fifty-two had regressed to types III and IV and merely remembered that the levels in the two tubes were unequal. In particular, between the ages of eight to ten years, there was not a single case of progress, and regressions were abundant, simply because children in these groups lack the intellectual means to solve the causal problem. By contrast, there were seventeen advances (18 per cent) which were made especially among the six- to seven-year-olds; this rate even went up to 24 per cent with children tested by Method III, in which the problem of the conservation or non-conservation of liquids is stressed but no solution is offered. Now, the idea of conservation is first grasped at about the age of $6\frac{1}{2}$ years, and poses a problem even earlier. Hence, it is not impossible that awareness of the latter (as opposed to awareness of the causal problem as such) should play a

---

[1] In other words, the information rate depends as much on the level of the code as it does on the redundancies themselves: what is redundant in a superior code is by no means redundant in an inferior code. This is why pouring the liquid into tubes from equal vessels, posing the conservation problem, etc., means supplying distinct units of information (positive or zero), and thus introducing redundancies that depend on the subjects' levels and codes.

part in improving the schematizations: six- to seven-year-olds (and even some five-year-olds) who equate the levels in the two tubes, may well feel a measure of dissatisfaction with their drawings, and gain the impression that 'things were different'. Now, this (notional) judgment might have helped to modify the (figural) symbolism of the memory during the recognition test (two weeks after presentation with Methods III and IV), though six of the 6- to 7-year-olds tested by Method II (no recognition test) also made appreciable mnemonic progress. In short, as far as progress from the idea of equal levels (type II and implicit in type I) to the idea of equal quantities of liquid (types III and IV) is concerned, it is clear that, from the age when the conservation of liquids is first constructed, it is awareness of this partial problem which is responsible for the mnemonic advances we have been describing.

PART IV

The Remembrance of Spatial Structures

The reason why we have left the remembrance of spatial configurations and transformations to the end of this book is that these geometrical structures help to elucidate the relationship between the figurative aspects of the memory and the associated operational schemata, and thus help to answer a number of questions we have had to leave open.

CHAPTER FIFTEEN

The Remembrance of a Geometrical
Transformation (Rotation)[1]

The present experiment is similar in principle to those involving the remembrance of transitive and associative relations (Chapters 5 and 6): the child is shown a series of operations, is asked to anticipate the results and, immediately afterwards, is invited to recall or reconstruct what he has seen. However, in the earlier cases, the actions themselves were quite simple, and the sole problem was their combination. Hence, there was nothing in the relations between these actions and their results to appeal to imagination or to stimulate the powers of figurative recall. In the present case (Figure 46), on the other hand, the action, i.e. the rotation of a triangle through 180°, and its results, i.e. the reversal of the position and direction of three arrows (blue, green and red) are intimately related and might therefore be expected to give rise to correct visual memories even in the absence of operational understanding.

This poses two distinct problems: the remembrance of the rotation as a schematized action, and the remembrance of the initial and final states as mere configurations or as the mere starting and end points of an operational transformation.

Now, remembrance of an operation is something quite other than the conservation of the underlying operational schema. The subject may or may not have grasped the rotational operation: depending on his level of development he may have acquired certain schemata which conserve themselves in everyday life, i.e. independently of the memory in the strict sense. On the other hand, the performance of that operation can be given concrete expression in a particular application, repeatable or not, such as the rotation of a triangle, in which case it may be remembered as a perceptive, concrete and differentiated act. Our main task will therefore be to establish whether this remembrance is independent of the subject's grasp of the operation (and hence of his operational level), which was not so in the case of transitive and associative relations, but might well

[1] In collaboration with J. Bliss.

happen with a purely spatial operation, i.e. with one that corresponds more closely to the figurative aspects.

Considered as a simple rotation, the present operation is easily grasped even by two-year-old children.[1] However, considered as an operation, and not merely as an action, it cannot be dissociated from

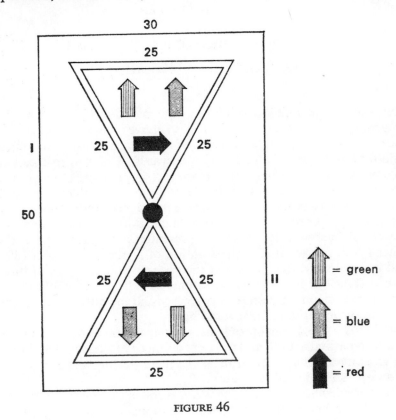

FIGURE 46

its results: after all, it is the transition from the initial state I to the final state II which constitutes the operation. But even when the child fails to see the operation as the reason for the transformation of I into II, or to remember it as such, he might be expected to have

---

[1] It should, however, be stressed that though the rotation is easily understood as such, its different stages, i.e. the phases between its initial and final states, elude most children below the age of seven to eight years (see *Mental Imagery in the Child*, Routledge & Kegan Paul, 1971, Chapters III and IV). This raises the question of whether or not the remembrance of the operation is independent of its comprehension. It is, moreover, perfectly legitimate to distinguish between the remembrance of the operation as a continuous transformation (and not simply as a displacement) and the remembrance of the initial and final states.

visual recall of states I and II as successive configurations unconnected by the rotation, or else connected by them but in a completely incomprehensible way. In what follows, we shall try to discover whether this is indeed the case.

§1. *Method*

The subjects were presented with two equilateral triangles (of side 25 cm) made of transparent plastic, the upper one free to rotate about its (lower) apex, and the lower immobile. Each triangle was provided with a green, a blue and a red arrow (Figure 46) and, during the rotation of the upper triangle, its three arrows came to occupy the precise positions of the three arrows in the lower triangle, a fact the child could easily discover for himself, since the triangles were transparent, and since corresponding arrows had identical colours.

It should be mentioned that, when we first devised this test, we used four, instead of only three, arrows, and we shall be quoting some responses to that model (in which a vertical arrow ran up (or down) from the central apex and the horizontal arrow was placed between the lower extremities of the blue and green arrows). However, when we replaced the arrows with other figures, we discovered that all the child could remember was the existence of four to six objects. It was for this reason that we decided to reduce the number of arrows to three, lest the memory become overburdened with irrelevant problems.

During the first session, the model was brought out and the subjects were asked to anticipate the result of the rotation: 'If I turn this triangle round until it covers the one at the bottom, where will the blue arrow go? And the green one? Or the red?' Once the rotation had been performed, and the coincidence of the arrows noted by the child, the upper triangle was restored to its original position, and the child was told to look at the model carefully and to remember all he had seen.

The second session was held an hour later, and the child was asked for a verbal description and for a drawing of the two triangles with the arrows marked in.

The third session (a week later) began like the second. Thereafter, the child was asked for a reconstruction, for which purpose he was provided with two triangles and a number of arrows. The examiner then proceeded to a further determination of the child's operational grasp of the rotation by means of an old experiment: a landscape studded with objects was rotated, and the child was told to remember its original position and orientation.[1] A first indication of his operational level had already been provided by his anticipations during the first session, but for reasons that will appear later, we thought it important to examine his responses to the landscape model as well.

The fourth session was held several months later and again included a memory-drawing and a reconstruction.

[1] See J. Piaget and B. Inhelder: *The Child's Conception of Space*, Routledge & Kegan Paul, 1956, Fig. 27.

§2. *Mnemonic levels an hour and a week after presentation*

In contrast to those experiments in which we were able to correlate mnemonic levels with operational stages, the present experiment called for a separate examination of the two, for though they were isomorphous and hence comprised the same phases and order of succession, they were not necessarily synchronous. In fact, anticipating the positions of the arrows before the rotation (first session) is tantamount to deducing them from the perceptible elements; while recalling the initial and final states calls for a total reconstruction (in the child's mind) or for a partial one (with the material provided by the examiner). The two tasks are similar, whence the similarity of the stages or levels, but they are not identical, whence the phase differences.

The two are not identical (even though the similarity of the levels shows that, by and large, remembrance of the model involves its comprehension) because with spatial transformations, the memory itself is not as homogeneous as in the experiments described in Chapters 1 to 10. On the one hand, the remembrance of spatial transformations involves a mixture of data, and though this is doubtless true of all memories, it poses a specially acute problem in the present case. On the other hand, because the transformation is spatial, the memory can be more or less figurative or bear more strongly on the connections as such (positions, orientations and directions). Now, young subjects, whose idea of space is not structured in terms of a system of co-ordinates, tend to inspect an object or a picture from all sides (from right to left or even upside down, etc.): hence, they find it much easier than older subjects to express the rotation and change of position of the upper triangle in purely figurative terms, i.e. without understanding the transformations as such.

In what follows, we shall thus have to tackle three more or less distinct problems—operational comprehension, remembrance of transformations (involving a partial reconstruction) and the figurative memory. To begin with, we found that the forty-eight 5- to 9-year-olds to whom we showed the three-arrow model, and the thirty-four 5- to 9-year-olds to whom we showed the four-arrow model (the results were qualitatively identical, but because the two models were distinct, we thought it best to treat the two groups of subjects separately, if only for statistical purposes), could all be fitted into four mnemonic types or levels, established by means of three criteria. The first, which would not have been sufficient in itself had it not been corroborated by the other two, was the logical analysis of the factors involved in the grasp of the rotation, i.e. of the symmetrical or reciprocal relations between the upper and the lower triangle, and also the positions (above and below, left and right), the orientations (vertical or horizontal) and the directions (upwards or downwards, to the left or to the right) of the arrows with respect to the triangles. The second criterion was the evolution of the memory (drawings and reconstructions) with age, which, in the event, proved to be closely dependent on the grasp of the various symmetries. The third and last criterion was based on the fact that the memory-drawings after six months proved to be surprisingly schematized, and as they became increasingly independent of the figurative factors and revealed their schematic nature, they helped us to a better understanding of the intentions expressed in the initial drawings; in particular they confirmed the part played by the symmetries or reciprocities.

I. Let us begin with a catalogue of the latter, compiled on the assumption—as we shall see, to be borne out by the facts—that the mnemonic levels, here as elsewhere, correspond closely to the levels of the understanding:

(1) The red arrow, which lies underneath the blue and green arrows in triangle I, comes to lie on top of these two in triangle II;

(2) The red arrow changes direction: while it points to the right in I, it points to the left in II;

(3) The blue and green arrows also change direction: they point upwards in I and downwards in II;

(4) These two arrows also change their relative positions: while the green one is to the left of the blue in I, it is to its right in II;

(5) The orientations of the three arrows remain unchanged, i.e. the verticals remain vertical and the horizontals remain horizontal.

Now, at Level I, the child ignores the first four of these reciprocities: he often draws and reconstructs the triangles in a way that suggests he has not remembered the motion. Hence, if he apparently respects the fifth, he does not do so because he has understood it, but simply because the orientations are constant; children at the beginning of Stage II, on the other hand, who take the motion of the arrows, though not yet of the upper triangle, into account, quite often neglect reciprocity No. 5.

At Level II, as we have just said, the subject considers the motion, though only of the arrows and not yet of the rotating triangle as a whole: whence the disregard of reciprocity No.1.

Level III marks the discovery of the motion of the triangle as a whole, though the responses still fluctuate between simple rabatment (folding of the upper triangle so that it comes to coincide with the lower one), a mixture of rabatment and rotation, and simplified rotation.

At Level IV, finally, the complete rotation is taken into account, often with slight changes of the basic configuration, though not of the vertical or horizontal directions of the arrows.

Level I: failure to consider the motion. At this, the most elementary level, the memory is purely static and the child disregards all motions. Not, of course, that he has completely forgotten them (see the discussion of the memory after six months); it is just that the figurative expression of the memory-image carries no traces of them.

The first level can be sub-divided into three sub-levels:

Sub-level IA sees a simple alignment or agglomeration of arrows, and the subject is careful to reproduce triangle II as an exact replica

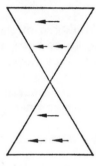

FIGURE 47

of triangle I (but with random variations that are not intended to express the motion; thus, the identity of the colours is often ignored);

At Sub-level IB, the colours are identical and so is the arrangement of the arrows in I and II; in particular, all the arrows may be vertical or horizontal (Figure 47);

At Sub-level IC, the triangles are copied faithfully, but the positioning of the arrows in I and II is still identical.

Here are a few examples:

HEL (5;4) drew three pairs of arrows each along the right side of the upper and lower triangles, but without colour correspondence (IA). During her reconstruction, she at first produced a similar arrangement, though with precise colour correspondence (IB). Then, after a (spontaneous) anticipation of the rotation, she placed a red arrow horizontally above the green and the blue arrows in I, and repeated the same arrangement in II (IB–IC).

DAR (5;4) drew the two triangles as separate trapezia, with the arrows pointing the same way in both (type IC). His reconstruction was similar.

DEC (5;6) first drew two triangles joined at the base (i.e. a lozenge):

the arrows in I and II were all horizontal, one ran in the opposite direction to the other two. His drawing a week later showed some slight progress: the three arrows had become vertical, and though one of them again ran in the opposite direction to the other two, its direction was reversed in triangle II (which, moreover, had become a square).

FAB (5;0) started with two triangles, one inside the other, and containing three pairs of vertical arrows near the vertices. Later, during the same session, he reproduced the triangles correctly, but again made all the arrows vertical, though this time he placed just one in each vertex. A week later, the arrows were still vertical but their directions in I and II were opposite.

In other words, though their memories of the rotation contain motor or operative elements, these subjects have all failed to grasp the operational mechanism involved.[1] What these reactions make clear above all is that the figurative memory does not suffice to

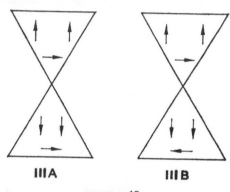

IIIA   IIIB

FIGURE 48

express the results of the rotation, and that even if the child remembers one of the triangles (generally the lower one) correctly, he makes the other identical or similar, thus completely ignoring the motion of the upper one. On the other hand, those subjects (e.g. Dec and Fab) who remember the motion rather than the static, figurative aspect, generally reverse the direction of the arrows (Level II). However, there are many cases of regression as well.

Level II: rotation of the arrows but not yet of the triangles. With subjects at Level II, remembrance of the rotation leads to figurative modifications of the triangles. However, since they have not yet grasped the operational mechanism they apply the rotation to isolated arrows only, and not yet to the triangles as a whole: as a

---

[1] The reader will recall the distinction between the terms 'operative' (= actions and operations), 'figurative' (= perception, imitation and image) and 'operational' (= reversible operations).

result, reciprocity (1) is still ignored, while reciprocities (2)–(5) may be taken into account. In this connection, it is worth stressing that, though reciprocity (5) involves the conservation of the vertical or horizontal orientation of the arrows (in contrast to their directions) and hence seems the simplest of the five reciprocities, it is nevertheless ignored at the beginning of Level II because, if the subject does not grasp the mechanism of the rotation, and transforms the arrows one by one, he has no reason for altering the directions and leaving the orientations unchanged.

Level II can be divided into four sub-levels (IIA–IID) according to whether one, two, three or four of the reciprocities (2)–(5) are respected:

PIE (5;4) produced a drawing (one hour after the presentation) of triangle I with a red, horizontal arrow on top of the vertical green and blue arrows (as in model II); in his drawing of triangle II, the red arrow

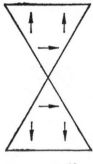

FIGURE 49

had become vertical and the two arrows beneath it had turned horizontal and now pointed in opposite directions. A week later he drew and reconstructed the arrows in precisely the same way, though, significantly enough, both triangles now pointed upwards.

SIL (5;5) drew triangle II correctly, but failed to change the direction of the horizontal arrow; the vertical arrows, too, pointed in the same direction as in I, but had been changed over from left to right (IIB). A week later, he had forgotten this change-over; he now reversed the direction of the vertical and horizontal arrows (IIC). His reconstruction, on the other hand, involved the rotation of the triangle as a whole (reciprocity No. 1), with a reversal of the direction of the horizontal arrow and also of the vertical arrows, though without right–left inversion of the latter (Level IIIC).

BRU (6;11) drew triangles I and II in the shape of II, except that he omitted the left–right inversion of the vertical arrows (IIB). His drawing and reconstruction a week later were of the same type.

VAN (7;2) began in the same way as Bru, but reversed the direction of the vertical arrows in II, again without left–right inversion (the red arrow remained unchanged). He produced the same drawing and a corresponding reconstruction a week later (IIB).

There is no need to quote any further examples, since the sub-divisions of Level II are not so much of interest in themselves, as in respect of their common characteristics, i.e. the replacement of the over-all or 'global' rotation (in the physicist's rather than Decroly's sense) by local and unco-ordinated rotations of individual arrows or of the blue–green pair considered in isolation.

Level III: general rotation of the triangle and adoption of reciprocity (1) but failure to co-ordinate other local reciprocities. At this level there is an attempt to rotate the figure as a whole (reciprocity No. 1). In three cases which we have not treated as special sub-levels (because they involved a ruse rather than a mnemonic or operational reconstruction) the child drew the two triangles and then stood the drawing on its head to see what it looked like upside down. As for the more 'honest' procedures, they could be divided into three sub-levels (Figure 48):

IIIA, simple rabatment with change of the directions and the vertical positions but not of the lateral positions of the arrows;

IIIB, mixture of rabatment and rotation; and

IIIC, simplified rotation.

PER (6;8) produced a drawing involving a mixture of rabatment and rotation (IIIB): the green and blue arrows retained their lateral positions (left–right) and moved beneath the red arrow, which had changed direction as well. During his reconstruction all the transformations were taken into account though in simplified form: the three arrows now had a vertical orientation (IIIC).

AUB (6;1) produced a first drawing based on reciprocities (1) and (3)–(5), but left the direction of the red arrow unchanged (IIIB). A week later, his drawing was based on a general rabatment (IIIA), but his reconstruction was again of type IIIB, though slightly different from his first drawing: the red arrow was now inverted, while the green and blue arrows, though changing direction and position with respect to the red, conserved their original laterality.

Level IIIC leads on to Level IV, but differs from it, and particularly from Level IVA, in that all the arrows are either vertical or horizontal.

Level IV: complete rotation (with due regard to all five reciprocities). At Level IV, we have correct memories, based on a full grasp of the rotation. Even so, it is possible to distinguish three sub-levels: IVA, in which there is a change of the basic configuration and due regard to the two types of orientation; IVB, in which only the colours

275

of the arrows are changed; and IVC in which all the details are remembered.

II. It follows that these mnemonic levels are isomorphous, both in their characteristics and in their order of succession, with a hierarchy of operational stages (though we must still examine the correlation of the two in individual subjects). In the first place, the way in which the reciprocities (1)–(5) combine into a hierarchy bears witness to the subject's comprehension no less than to his powers of recall, though in respect of the latter, we must distinguish between the figuratively correct reproduction of the arrows in the first triangle, and accurate recall or reconstruction of the changes produced in that triangle by the rotation. Now, had our mnemonic levels been based solely on the static, figurative aspect, they would have been distributed at random through the various age groups, and, above all, would not necessarily have followed one another in succession. Only if we base the levels on the remembrance of the transformations, do we find that they constitute a coherent order, isomorphous with that of the levels of understanding. Moreover, this order corresponds, by and large, to the child's general development with age, as Table 36 shows quite clearly (particularly in respect of recall and of the reconstructions produced one week after the presentation).

We see, first of all, that the memory-images are far from perfect at the age of eight years, when Level III responses still exceed Level IV responses, and even at the age of nine years, when Level IV responses are only just beginning to hold their own: of our seventeen 8- to 9-year-olds only two offered slightly imperfect anticipations during the first session, and the remaining fifteen were completely successful. Clearly, therefore, their mnemonic levels were not identical with the levels of operational understanding (anticipations, etc.), but they were nevertheless isomorphous. On the other hand, the distribution of the memory-images by age was highly reminiscent of the evolution of anticipatory kinetic images (which involves the anticipation of representative images but no anticipatory deduction, which latter would have been purely operational). Thus, when, in earlier experiments, we rotated a square, two sides of which were of different colours, we found[1] that the rotation through 180° was represented correctly by 22 per cent of our five-year-old subjects, by 25 per cent of our six-year-olds, and by 35 per cent, 40 per cent and 60 per cent of our seven-, eight- and nine-year-olds respectively, the proportion rising to 73 per cent with ten- to twelve-year-olds. The explanation was in a combination of the rotation with circumduction;

[1] See J. Piaget and B. Inhelder: *Mental Imagery in the Child*, Routledge & Kegan Paul, 1971, Chapter IV, Table 40.

TABLE 36 *Distribution of subjects by age*

Ages	N	(After one hour)				(After one week)				Reconstruction			
		I	II	III	IV	I	II	III	IV	I	II	III	IV
5 years	(11)	7	3	1	0	4	5	2	0	4	3	4	0
6 years	(10)	2	3	4	1	4	4	2	0	4	4	2	0
7 years	(10)	4	5	1	0	5	4	1	0	3	1	2	4
8 years	(9)	1	3	2	3	0	3	5	1	0	3	6	0
9 years	(8)	1	1	3	3	2	2	1	3	1	2	2	3
5 years	(11)	7	3	1	0	4	5	2	0	4	3	4	0
6–7 years	(20)	6	8	5	1	9	8	3	0	7	5	4	4
8–9 years	(17)	2	4	5	6	2	5	6	4	1	5	8	3

277

and this also happened in the present case, but followed (at Sub-levels IIIA and IIIB) by the substitution of a rabatment for the rotation: 'If we fold it over,' said Jor (6;11), 'you will see that it all fits' type IIIA).

The reader will also have gathered from Table 36 that the responses to the three tests varied considerably, which calls for a closer comparison of the recollections produced after a week with the reconstructions produced at the same time, and of the recollections produced after an hour with those produced after a week.

III. Table 37 compares reconstructions (R) (for which purpose the child was handed the two triangles and a series of loose arrows) with memory-drawing after a week (D); $D > R$ means that D was at least one level higher than R, and $D < R$ the opposite case, while the

TABLE 37 *Comparison of reconstructions R and memory-drawings D one week after presentation*

	$D > R$	$D \geqslant R$	$D = R$	$D \leqslant R$	$D < R$
5 years	0	2	4 (8)	2	3
6 years	0	1	5 (9)	3	1
7 years	0	0	4 (4)	0	6
8 years	2	0	7 (7)	0	0
9 years	0	0	7 (7)	0	1
Level I	0	1	8 (10)	1	4
Level II	1	0	9 (11)	2	6
Level III	0	1	7 (10)	2	1
Level IV	1	1	3 (4)	0	0
Total	2	3	27 (35)	5	11

sign $\geqslant$ refers to differences in sub-level (since the latter were uncertain we have thought it best to add them to the equalities and to show the combined results in brackets).

We see that the reconstructions are well in advance of the drawings at Levels I and II (up to the age of seven years), and that by the time the child reaches Levels III and IV (at the age of eight to nine years), the gap has been closed (predominance of $D = R$, and equilibrium between the inequalities $>$ and $<$). This fact by itself shows clearly that, with our particular model, recall involves a mental reconstruction, and one, moreover, that is equivalent, though with partial interiorization, to the active reconstruction R. Now, why should this be so? Quite simply because, in the case of rotating triangles, the transformation and its results are so closely bound up with the figure that the memory-image and the memory of the logical understanding of the model come to support each other, so much so that the child can eventually dispense with the help of material aids. By contrast, in the case of transitive and associative relations (Chapters 5–6), in which the memory was equally supported by the understanding of the transformations, the figural image of the vessels was not directly bound up with the memory of the transitivity or associativity of the decantations, and the operational combination was simply superimposed on the material data. In these circumstances, the subjects quite naturally found it helpful to repeat the manipulations for themselves. However, the reader will also recall that, in the case of the divided triangles discussed in Chapter 6, §4, a mere nine subjects out of forty-seven (as against sixteen out of forty-eight in the present case) showed progress as they proceeded from recall to a reconstruction. Of these nine subjects, six were at Level I–II, and had made a great deal of general progress, and three were at Level III–IV and had merely advanced to $R \geqslant D$: the situation was therefore comparable to the present one, and for the same reason: the close link between the figurative image and the transformation.

Let us also note that the initial (four-arrow) model used in the present series of experiments was of greater figurative complexity than, but demanded the same operational understanding as, the three-arrow model. It evoked the following responses from twenty-eight subjects one week after the presentation:

$1 \ (D > R); \ 2 \ (D \geqslant R); \ 20 \ (D = R); \ 2 \ (D \leqslant R)$ and $3 \ (D < R)$.

The five $(D \leqslant R)$ and $(D < R)$ were all five- to seven-year-olds.

The results were therefore identical with those obtained from the three-arrow test, though not, as we shall see, in respect of the figurative accuracy of the memory.

IV. A comparison of the memory-drawings produced one hour and one week after the presentation, respectively, led to quite unexpected results, which, though not of great importance in themselves, nevertheless throw fresh light on the relationship between the figurative aspect of the memory-image and the memory of the child's own interpretation of the transformations. To appreciate the relevance of these data, we must first compare the results of the preliminary test (four arrows) with those of the main experiment (three arrows).

It should be noted, first of all, that, despite the greater figurative complexity of the original model, the levels observed in the two proved to be identical and appeared at the same ages (Table 38).

Let us now compare the memory-drawings produced one hour after presentation (*DH*) with those produced a week later (*DW*) (forty-eight subjects with the three-arrow model and twenty-seven

TABLE 38   *Types of reactions to the four-arrow model*

Levels	(N)	I	II	III	IV
5 years	(9)	6	0	3	0
6 years	(11)	3	2	3	3
7 years	(8)	2	1	3	2
8 years	(5)	0	0	2	3

subjects with the four-arrow model—not all our subjects took tests *DH* and *DW*):

	(N)	DH > DW	DH > DW	DH = DW	DH < DW	DH < DW
3 arrows	(48)	13	6	24 (32)	2	5
4 arrows	(28)	3	2	14 (20)	4	7

In other words, there was a clear—and quite unforeseen—reversal of the situation as the child passed on from the three-arrow to the four-arrow model: one would have expected to find that the more complex the model the more quickly it would have been forgotten, and that the better the logical schematization the better the memory of the original interpretation. Now, the facts proved to be far less straightforward than that.

By way of illustration, we shall now look at a few cases of mnemonic deterioration (three-arrow model):

PER (6;0) produced a fairly good arrangement of the arrows (one hour after presentation) and remembered two co-ordinated reciprocities (two directions but no change-over of the two verticals). A week later, he drew three vertical arrows (figural simplification), which meant that he remembered one reciprocity only (reversion from Level III to Level II).

ELI (6;1) also produced a fairly correct arrangement of the arrows one hour after presentation: he changed the order and position of the two vertical arrows but had failed to reverse the direction of the horizontal one; a week later he simplified his drawing with three horizontal arrows, whose direction he again failed to reverse (regression from Level III to Level I).

AND (6;3) was found to be at Level IV when we examined him an hour after the presentation; a week later, he drew the two triangles side by side

(Figure 50). Though he conserved the orientation of the arrows in I, he was completely at a loss with II (regress to Level I).

CHAN (8;9) also proved to be at Level IV one hour after the presentation. A week later she drew the odd arrow in a vertical position, and made the other two horizontal and pointing towards each other. In triangle II, she rightly reversed the direction of the vertical, and correctly changed the

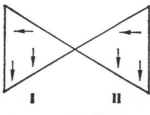

FIGURE 50

order of the horizontal arrows, though she now pointed them to the outside (regression to Level III).

In brief, the regressive responses to the three-arrow model were due, not to a loss in understanding, but to gaps in the figurative memory: because they oversimplified their drawings (Per and Eli) or reconstructed them arbitrarily, these subjects were unable to arrive at the correct number of inversions or reciprocities.

Conversely, the advances observed one week after the presentation were all due to a better understanding of the transformations.

If we now look at the advances with the four-arrow model (the regressions proved to be comparable to those we have just mentioned) we find a curiously reversed situation, though once again for purely figurative reasons; the drawings offered one hour after the presentation were generally so complicated that the simplifications introduced a week later were bound to be so many improvements:

MU (6;3) had originally scattered the four arrows about at random; a week later he arranged them correctly (advance from Level II to Level III).

TIA (6;9) originally drew five arrows (two of which were horizontal); a week later she correctly reduced the number to four.

GAB (7;2) originally fitted the four arrows into a cross, but offered the correct arrangement a week later.

Other subjects arranged the vertical pair of arrows in opposite directions, etc.

In short, most of these advances were due to the application of the original intellectual schemata to simplified drawings, whence the improved schematizations.

All these facts once again serve to raise the problem of the relationship between the figurative aspect of the memory-image and the

281

memory of the child's own comprehension of the model, which is, of course, based on his intellectual schemata.

§3. *Memory-drawings and reconstructions six months after presentation*

Six months later we were able to bring back thirty-six of our forty-eight subjects (eight 5-year-olds; seven 6-year-olds; eight 7-year-olds; seven 8-year-olds and six 9-year-olds). The model was not presented again, and the children were simply asked for another memory-drawing followed by a material reconstruction of the model and a commentary on 'what had happened' six months earlier.

We arrived at two striking conclusions: on the one hand we found a deterioration in the remembrance of the figurative elements, especially among younger subjects; and, on the other hand, we discovered that a rotation schema was employed even by five- to seven-year-olds whose drawings an hour and a week after the presentation were dominated by attempts to provide a purely figurative reconstruction. The figurative deterioration during the subsequent six months was reflected in a variety of ways: in many cases, the triangles were completely forgotten or their number was reduced to one; in other cases they were replaced by a large square, by a cross, by four little triangles, etc.; up to Levels III or even IV, the number of arrows was often increased or reduced, etc. As far as the operative schema was concerned, however, all but one of our thirty-six subjects remembered that the figure had been rotated, and tried to recall precisely in what way, with varying success.

This double transformation of the memory made it exceedingly difficult for us to fit these drawings and reconstructions into the sub-levels described in §2. On the other hand, it proved relatively easy to distinguish the four major levels we have specified, and this despite marked changes in the details: at Level II the rotation is expressed by transformations of individual arrows; at Level III there is a general rotation cum rabatment of the triangle (which is now drawn in a recognizable form); at Level IV the rotation is correctly reproduced even though the configuration may be slightly altered.

The most important feature in Table 39 is that it shows how closely mnemonic regress is bound up with the growing influence of the operative schema. There was a marked decrease in the number of Level I responses, which, during the six-month interval, had dropped from 31 per cent and 25 per cent to 13 per cent (*DM* and *RM*), together with a marked increase in the number of Level II responses (from 31–34 per cent and 27 per cent, respectively, to 44 per cent). In

TABLE 39 *Percentage of subjects who presented drawings an hour after presentation (DH); drawings a week after presentation (DW); reconstructions a week after presentation (RW); drawings six months after presentation (DM); and final reconstructions six months after presentation (RM) (absolute numbers out of 48 and 36 in brackets)*

Levels	DH	DW	RW	DM	RM
I	31 (15)	31 (15)	25 (12)	13 (5)	13 (5)
II	31 (15)	37 (18)	27 (13)	44 (16)	44 (16)
III	23 (11)	23 (11)	33 (16)	31 (11)	31 (11)
IV	14 (7)	8 (4)	14 (7)	11 (4)	11 (4)

other words, the younger subjects who had originally failed to treat their arrows as mobile objects, now dealt with them as such. At Level III (31 per cent), on the other hand, there was little difference between the reconstructions *RW* and *RM*, but further progress over the initial drawings (*DH* and *DW* = 23 per cent). At Level IV, finally, there was no progress at all, due, no doubt, to figurative distortion.

Here, first of all, are two Level I responses:

LIL (5;4) drew three vertical arrows in a row, followed by another row of vertical arrows of contrasting colours. During her reconstruction, she produced two triangles, one empty and the other resting on its side and containing two vertical arrows (not aligned), together with two oblique arrows parallel to one of the sides.

AN (5;4) scattered six arrows vertically over each of his triangles. During the reconstruction he claimed that he had never been shown any triangles, but nevertheless combined two into a recumbent lozenge. He then placed a vertical arrow over their common base, flanked by two vertical arrows.

All these Level I drawings and reconstructions were thus totally static and showed that the memory of the initial configuration had completely deteriorated. Let us now look at some Level II responses, in which the figurative deterioration is almost as marked, but in which the rotation of the individual arrows is clearly taken into account, though the triangle itself (when marked in) is not rotated, and reciprocity (1) is ignored:

PIE (5;4) pointed the four top arrows N., W., S., E., and repeated the same pattern underneath, except that he changed the two vertical (red) arrows into horizontal ones, and the two horizontal (blue) arrows into vertical ones. His reconstruction was similar, but he now enclosed the arrows in two superposed triangles both pointing upwards. Pie said '*the arrows have shifted'*, but he had obviously forgotten the rotation of the upper triangle.

CHA (5;5) offered a similar reconstruction, but in his prior drawing (*DM*) he had omitted the triangles, simply drawing four top arrows, two of which were parallel, oblique and pointing in opposite directions, and two of which were vertical, and also pointed in opposite directions; underneath he repeated the same pattern, but reversed the directions of the arrows. He explained that *'they could be turned round'*.

KOR (5;10) fitted four arrows of different colours into a cross, and then, by means of gestures, tried to indicate that the cross had been rotated through 90°, so that the two verticals were transformed into horizontals and vice versa: *'We turned them round.'* During his reconstruction, he correctly joined the apices of the triangles but with the latter lying on their sides, and again fitted four arrows into a cross, though this time he rotated the green arrow through an angle of 180°.

MOU (6;5) drew two separate triangles in I (random positions) and two others in II (*idem*) and explained: *'We changed their places.'* However, his arrows remained outside the triangles, and the horizontals were simply transformed into verticals. His reconstruction was of a similar kind.

CRI (6;8) drew six arrows, two of which were vertical and in the centre of the drawing, and four of which were relegated to the four corners of the sheet (no triangular or other frame). Two of these arrows pointed outwards and two pointed inwards. When she had finished, she said that *'we turned the arrows round'*, and quickly changed the directions of all except the two vertical ones. Her reconstruction was similar, but included two empty triangles, joined at their apices and lying on their sides.

PAT (7;5) drew a single triangle round four arrows in square formation, and then reversed their direction. During the reconstruction, he produced two separate triangles with the same orientation. He placed a square made up of four arrows in the upper triangle, and reversed the direction of the arrows in the lower one.

MAR (7;2) drew two triangles, one inside the other. In the inscribed triangle he combined four arrows into a cross, explaining that they kept turning. During the reconstruction, he separated the triangles, and again combined the arrows in I into a cross, which he turned through 90° in II.

GEO (8;3) drew a small circle round which he arranged three arrows and then gestured a rotation of 90°. During his reconstruction, he produced two pairs of triangles joined at their apices. Each of the triangles in I contained one vertical arrow; a horizontal arrow started at the junction of the apices, and was therefore external to the triangles. Each of the second pair of triangles (II) contained one external (horizontal) arrow, and the lower triangle also contained a vertical arrow: hence, there was a rotation of 90° (with conservation of colours).

These examples must suffice to illustrate both the great figural variety of these Level II responses, due to figurative deterioration of the memory, and also the common principle on which they are based, i.e. the rotation of the arrows as such and not of the figure as a whole.

Hence, these responses are equivalent to the Level II reactions we obtained one hour and one week after the presentation, though, during the earlier sessions, greater attention was paid to the figurative details (which doubtless explains the equal distribution of Levels I and II) while with mnemonic regress during the next six months, these details become overshadowed by the rotation schema and are therefore neglected.

At Level III, on the other hand, the over-all motion is taken into account, beginning with simple rabatments:

NAD (5;4) who was found to be at Level I an hour and a week after the presentation, now produced two correct triangles, with the blue vertical arrow in I flanked by two oblique red and green arrows running downwards; II was an exact rabatment of I with the blue arrow in the centre (reversed direction) flanked by one red arrow running upwards. Her reconstruction was of the same type, except that the central blue arrow was now above the other two in I and beneath them in II (perfect rabatment, but no rotation).

VIN (6;6) produced a similar reconstruction: in I, the blue arrow was above the green and the red; in II it was beneath them (rabatment without change-over from left to right of the green and red arrows, but with reversal of their directions), whereas in his prior drawing (two correct triangles and three vertical arrows) the blue arrow had appeared beneath the others in I as well as in II.

AOR (7;2) drew two pairs of triangles joined at their apices. Each of the first pair had two vertical arrows pointing upwards and lying beneath a green horizontal arrow pointing to the left; in the second pair, I was an exact rabatment of the first pair, and II a rabatment of that rabatment, i.e. a copy of the first pair. And this was not by chance, since Aor said quite explicitly: '*We turned it over and then it was the same thing!*'

CLA (8;0) drew a pair of triangles reflecting a rabatment which, she claimed, represented the situation '*before we started to turn it round*'. To show what happened 'afterwards', she simply copied triangle II of the first pair. During the reconstruction, she also produced a simple rabatment.

MAR (9;2) offered a simple rabatment in his drawing as well as in his reconstruction.

BUR (9;2), who had proved to be at Level IV one week after the presentation, now produced a mixture of rabatment and rotation (observing all the reciprocities except the reversal of the direction of the red horizontal arrow).

The majority of these subjects at Stage III therefore remembered the over-all motion of the triangle, which they at first reduced to the simplest form, i.e. to a rabatment. The figurative details had again deteriorated, but were generally restored with the help of three arrows (in contrast to what happens at Level II), in such a way that they reflected reciprocity No. 1 but not the change-over from left to right.

Here, finally, are some Level IV responses:

SIL (5;5), despite her age, produced a drawing half-way between a rabatment and a rotation: the blue and green arrows were changed over from left to right in II, but their (horizontal) direction was left unaltered. During the reconstruction, on the other hand, the rotation was represented correctly though in simplified form (two horizontal arrows flanking a vertical one). In her response an hour and a week after the presentation, Sil had been at Levels II and III respectively (see §2).

MIC (7;6) had proved to be at Levels III (drawing) and IV (reconstruction), an hour and a week after presentation. Six months later, he produced a Level IV drawing and a Level IV reconstruction, but with a figural modification: in I, two vertical arrows appeared on top of each other, and between them a horizontal arrow pointing to the right; in II the verticals were changed over, and the directions reversed: the horizontal arrow now pointed to the left. The over-all presentation was therefore correct, but the details had been neglected.

ALB (9;4) offered the correct rotation with the vertical arrows changed into oblique ones. His drawing and reconstruction were identical, except that there was some hesitation during the former: having started with a pair of triangles (with the correct rotation of I to II), Alb was uncertain about what he had to put into the second pair.

ACK (9;4) produced the correct rotation.

While all these subjects proved to be at the same level as they had been one hour and one week after presentation, or else showed partial (Mic) or general (Sil) progress, others reverted from Level IV to Level III, due to confusion of the rabatment with the rotation. But apart from these reversions, doubtless due to interference of the figurative with the operative factors, the kinematic schema generally prevailed over the figural aspect of the memory. In other words, the figural aspect would seem to have a somewhat inhibiting effect on the remembrance of the general sense of the presentation, but, with the passage of time, the latter comes to take precedence over the former, whence the progress up to and including Level III. However, whenever the memory-image of the configurations I and II becomes too patchy, it is impossible to decide whether the over-all motions of the triangle are the result of rabatments or rotations (and sometimes even of rotations of 90° or 180°: see Level III), which explains why the general progress from Level I to Level III is not continued by a systematic advance from Level III to Level IV, and why there are some reversions from rotation (IV) to simple rabatment (III).

§4. *Recognition after nine to ten months*

Nine to ten months after the presentation, i.e. three to four months after the last test, we brought back thirty-three of our previous subjects for a recognition test.

They were shown the eight configurations depicted in Figure 51: the original model plus the most common misrepresentations produced during the last session. The subjects were then asked to copy the one most like the 'game' we had played with them. When they had made a spontaneous choice, we suggested other solutions, and asked them to justify their acceptance or rejection of these. Next we asked them to make a final choice.

The first of the two most striking results of this test was that recognition was well in advance of recall and reconstruction; in particular, only one of our thirty-three subjects chose solutions 3, 4 and 5, which had been fairly common errors during the previous session. Moreover, many six-year-olds and even quite a few five-year-olds came up with the correct solution.

The second striking result (which bears out our interpretation (§3) of the relative lack of progress to Level IV) was that most subjects found it extremely difficult to decide between rabatment (solution 8) and rotation (solution 6): the original (spontaneous) choice of subjects in all age groups was thirteen rabatments and thirteen rotations, and the final choice eleven rabatments and fourteen rotations. In other words, these subjects all tend to endow the figures with an over-all 'turning' motion, but, lacking an adequate figurative image of the left-right relations of the green and blue arrows and of the change of direction of the red arrow, they reduce this motion to a rabatment as readily as they treat it as a rotation.

For the rest, several of the spontaneous choices of subjects up to and including the age of eight years comprised solutions 7, 2 and 5, which were, however, absent from the final choices of all subjects above the age of seven years (operational level). Moreover, if we compare the level of recognition (based on the best spontaneous or final choice) to the level of recall during any of the previous sessions (again choosing the best response) and to the level of the reconstructions offered a week after the presentation (six months later, the reconstructions proved to be more or less identical with the memory-drawings), we arrive at the picture shown in Table 40.

Table 40 shows that, despite the long interval between the original presentation and the recognition test, the latter gave rise to vastly superior responses. The reasons are obvious, but it should nevertheless be noted that, with the present model, recognition is not the result of an immediate *déjà vu* impression but rests on the support of figurative cum operative schemata. Remarkably enough, though most of the choices of five-year-olds were based on static considerations ('that one looks the most like'), some children in this age group made explicit reference to the motion ('it was like that after we turned it round'), and these responses increased greatly in importance with.

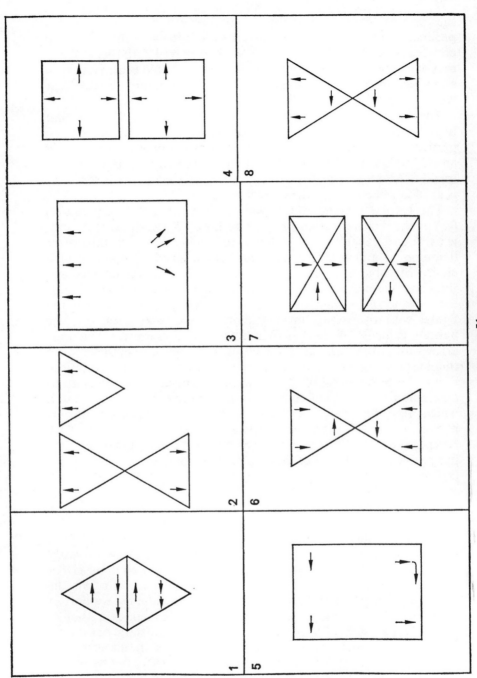

FIGURE 51

288

age. Most eight- to nine-year-olds, in particular, made a spontaneous choice of solutions 6 and 8 'because it turned round', and, if they came down in favour of rabatment, it was only because they thought that it represented the most probable motion: 'Yes, I chose No. 8 because when we turned it round (gesture of rabatment) we got the same thing (as the model).'

This unexpected ability to recognize the model nine to ten months after the original presentation persuaded us to administer a recognition test one hour after presentation to a special group of twenty-five 4;10–9;11-year-old subjects. Each of them was shown the original model (Figure 46) and asked to predict the position of the arrows once the upper triangle was turned through 180°. Each anticipation was expected to include a reference to the position and

TABLE 40 *Comparison of recognition (Rg) with memory-drawings after a week (DW), memory-drawings after six months (DM), and reconstructions after a week (RW)*

	$Rg > DM$	$Rg > DM$	$Rg = DM$	$Rg < DM$	$Rg > DW$	$Rg > DW$	$Rg = DW$	$Rg < DW$	$Rg > RW$	$Rg > RW$	$Rg = RW$	$Rg < RW$
5 years	4	1	2	1	6	0	2	0	5	0	3	0
6–7 years	6	4	2	0	8	2	1	1	6	0	4	2
8–9 years	8	1	4	0	8	0	4	1	9	0	3	1
Total	18	6	8	1	22	2	7	2	20	0	10	3

orientation of every one of the arrows. Next, the subject was asked to perform the rotation for himself. Triangle I was now returned to its original position, and the child was asked to have a good look at the model so that he could describe it immediately afterwards. An hour later, he was given the recognition test: spontaneous choice followed by a final choice after a number of counter-suggestions. The results, compared with those of the main recognition test, were as shown in Table 41.

There is thus a remarkable correspondence between the responses to the two tests, and this despite the fact that they were separated by an interval of nine to ten months and that they involved two quite different groups of subjects. In both cases, the choice of the correct model (No. 6) predominated, and though rabatments (No. 8) were quite common as well, the remaining solutions were chosen infrequently or not at all.

TABLE 41 *Recognition an hour and 9–10 months after presentation*

	Spontaneous choice*								Final choice							
	1	2	3	4	5	6	7	8	1	2	3	4	5	6	7	8
One hour (25 subjects)	0	1	0	0	1	14	0	9	1	1	0	0	0	13	0	10
9–12 months (33 subjects)	0	2	0	0	4	13	2	12	2	2	0	1	0	14	3	11

* One of the subjects who chose No. 5 and four of the subjects who chose No. 6 nine to ten months after the presentation, contended that No. 8 was as good; conversely, four of the twelve subjects who chose No. 8 claimed that No. 6 would have done just as well.

§5. *The figurative memory-image, the remembrance of transformations and the corresponding operational level*

From what we have just been saying, it should be clear that the mnemonic responses of our subjects are based on two components that normally reinforce each other but may become dissociated to introduce new difficulties or even mnemonic regress. There is, first of all, the figurative aspect of the memory-image, which generally obeys the same laws as the mental image: schematization, simplification, pseudo-conservation (cf. the choice of circumduction instead of rotation), etc. Far more important is the remembrance of the transformations, which is bound up with the operative schemata and hence with the subject's operational level.

The latter, which we have been ignoring so far, can be assessed in two distinct ways: by the anticipation of the position and orientation of the arrows before the rotation is actually performed, and by a post-experimental test, in which the subject is shown a landscape crossed by a twisting road and a river. Two buildings joined by a path, several hills and three trees serve as the reference points. A man is positioned in one of five selected positions, and the child is asked to place another man in the same position and looking in the same direction on the identical landscape but turned through an angle of 180°.[1] All in all, the subject must answer five questions involving the position and five questions involving the direction of the figure by simple reasoning.

The anticipation of the position and orientation of the arrows before the rotation of the upper triangle (I) is but another problem

[1] See J. Piaget and B. Inhelder: *The Child's Conception of Space*, Routledge & Kegan Paul, 1956, Chapter XIV.

in operational reasoning, though one that is greatly helped by the fact that arrows of the same colour as those in (I) and pointing in the right directions are marked in on the lower triangle (II). Hence, the child need merely anticipate whether or not the green arrow in I will come to coincide with the green arrow in II, and what its orientation will be, etc. That this simple anticipation nevertheless poses a problem is proved by the fact that some subjects fail to cope with the three positions or only succeed with one orientation out of three (that of the vertical arrow). However, the solution is clearly much simpler than that of the landscape test.

Now, a comparison of the anticipations of the position, etc. of the arrows with the mnemonic levels as determined from recall and reconstruction shows two things quite clearly: on the one hand, there is a measure of correspondence between the two, and, on the other hand, the anticipations come much easier to the child than does the

TABLE 42 *Comparison of remembrance and anticipation*

Mnemonic levels	I (36)	II (44)	III (36)	IV (27)
Anticipations:				
− −	14	7	3	0
+ −	9	24	7	2
+ +	13	13	26	25

organization of his memory, and hence provide the operational framework he needs in order to remember the transformations.

As for the correspondence of the anticipations with the mnemonic levels, it is difficult to establish a satisfactory gradation of the former because there are two types of successful solution: three positions and three orientations. Let us note first of all that the orientations are easier to anticipate than the positions (of forty-eight subjects, seven were more successful with the latter, sixteen with the former, and twenty-five produced equivalent responses). Nevertheless, the reactions can be fitted into three categories: 3 correct solutions of both factors (++), 3 correct solutions in respect of either the positions or the orientations with 0, 1 or 2 correct solutions of the other factor(+ −), and less than 3 correct solutions in all (− −). On this basis we have a comparison as shown in Table 42.[1] There is a clear advance in anticipation with mnemonic level; moreover successful anticipations are more common than successful recollections or reconstructions (13, 13 and 26 at Levels I to III).

[1] The figures in the Tables are based on the three tests with forty-eight subjects: recall after an hour, recall after a week and reconstruction.

The reactions to the landscape test are even more difficult to evaluate, since the model involves five distinct positions and orientations, instead of only three. Nevertheless, we can fit the responses into four classes: (1) less than three correct responses in each category; (2) three or more correct responses in each category; (3) four or five correct responses in each category; and (5) five correct responses in each category. Our forty-four subjects responded as shown in Table 42(A).

There is thus a close link between the four mnemonic levels and the distribution of the complementary classes $<(3 + 3)$ and $\geqslant(3 + 3)$. The sub-classes $\geqslant(4 + 4)$ and $=(5 + 5)$ have a more irregular distribution, but this very fact proves that the correlation of

TABLE 42 (A) *Comparison of mnemonic levels and operational reactions*

Mnemonic levels	I (27)	II (44)	III (36)	IV (23)
Operational reactions:				
$<(3 + 3)$	14 (51%)	16 (36%)	9 (25%)	3 (17%)
$\geqslant(3 + 3)$	13 (49%)	28 (64%)	27 (75%)	20 (83%)
$\geqslant(4 + 4)$	7	7	23	15
$=(5 + 5)$	7	3	5	8

mnemonic with operational levels is not very strict: thus, $7 + 3 = 10$ subjects at Levels I and II (recall and reconstruction) were nevertheless able to solve the landscape test successfully $(5 + 5)$.

For the rest, there is a fairly good correlation between the correct anticipation of the positions and orientations of the arrows $(+A)$ and partial success $[\geqslant(3 + 3)]$ in the landscape test $(+L)$:

$$
\begin{array}{cccc}
+A + L & +A - L & -A + L & -A - L \\
21 & 4 & 5 & 17
\end{array}
$$

From all these results we may take it that, though the remembrance of the transformations depends on the operational stage the subject has attained, it nevertheless introduces additional difficulties due, *inter alia*, to the subject's need to incorporate what he remembers of his own interpretation of the model into a figurative image corresponding to the transformations he has grasped.

Our analysis of the remembrance of rotations thus leads us to conclusions which, at first sight, might appear rather paradoxical. The chief psychological difference between a geometrical operation (rotation) and a logico-mathematical structure (seriation, transitive or associative relations, etc.), is that the former, unlike the latter, can be expressed by an image corresponding so closely to its object that 'geometrical intuition' has long been considered a predominantly demonstrative faculty, albeit one of considerable heuristic importance. One might therefore have expected to find that the remembrance of rotations would be as easy as, if not easier than, the remembrance of seriations or transitive relations (the remembrance of associative relations is more difficult, for reasons we have already stated: it is an instrument of coherence, not of discovery). In fact, however, of the forty-eight subjects who took the three-arrow test, and of the thirty-three subjects who took the four-arrow test, quite a few produced type IVA responses, i.e. they had grasped the purpose of the test but did not have an exact image of the model, while no more than six of our 6- to 9- year-olds produced nine type IVB responses, i.e. the correct image (six of these an hour after the presentation or during the reconstruction, and three a week after the presentation). In other words, the level of success in the remembrance of rotations is much closer to that of the remembrance of the (largely contingent) geometric figures we shall be discussing in Chapters 19 and 20 than to that of seriations and transitive relations.

Now, the reasons have been mentioned several times in §§2 and 3. In the case of seriations or transitive relations, the image is almost wholly determined by the subject's operational level, and the memory organizes its figurative aspect in accordance with the underlying schemata. Rotations, on the other hand, involve the transformation of an object and not an arrangement of a set of objects and, moreover, a transformation that depends on that object no less than on the actions of the subject (because the experiment is both physical and logico-mathematical). The image of the object is therefore no longer a simple reflection of the subject's operational level, but has a degree of independence and in consequence acts as a resistance. Hence, the memory no longer depends on the operative schemata with their own mode of conservation, and on the figurative image as the symbol of the concrete expression of these schemata by a particular event; it also depends on the figurative aspect of the object, and therefore on the image and, because of the relative independence and resistance of the latter, on the memory of the subject's own interpretation of the model. In fact, we have had quite a few hints of this resistance on the part of the image: the substitution of circumduction for rotation, and the simplification of the usual schematizations. Hence, there are good reasons why the precise remembrance of rotations should appear relatively late in the child's life, and for everything we have said elsewhere[1] about the belated appearance of

[1] J. Piaget and B. Inhelder: *Mental Imagery in the Child*, Routledge & Kegan Paul, 1971.

293

spatial images (with general successes at the age of nine to ten years). Of course, once they have been differentiated, thanks to the mutual contributions of the operation and the image, the underlying schemata (rotation, circumduction and rabatment) and the figurative aspects of the model become fully transparent to the intelligence, and the remembrance of the transformations becomes comparable to that of all other operational processes. The result is the conservation of schemata obeying their own laws, and full retention of memory-images based on that conservation.

CHAPTER SIXTEEN

The Remembrance of Horizontal Levels[1]

We know that the idea of horizontality and verticality (for example, the ability to predict the inclination of the surface of a liquid in a jar about to be tilted in specified ways) is not acquired by children before the age of nine to ten years. By contrast, the *perception* of horizontality, though, of course, modified at the age of nine to ten years by the growing influence of operational procedures,[2] provides much younger subjects with a rough but adequate idea of the relation between the horizontal and their own line of vision and bodily position.

Our analysis proceeded by two distinct stages. We began with a presentation of three objects: a bottle lying on its side and partly filled with red liquid, a small motor car with its bottom half painted red, and a bottle standing on its head and three-quarters full of red liquid. Now, of our fourteen 5- to 7-year-old subjects, at least four 6-year-olds and two 7-year-olds thought that they had seen a bottle standing on its head with the liquid vertically against one of its walls. By contrast, of the twenty subjects to whom we had merely shown a drawing of the bottle lying on its side and a drawing of the motor car, fifteen provided the correct solutions, and only five reacted in much the same manner as the first group. These preliminary results raised two questions: (1) how is the memory reorganized so as to restore the normal position of a bottle (i.e. standing on its base) but with the liquid covering its wall (cf. Figure 52 *A*); and (2) how can the memory fly in the face of perception and, in accordance with pre-operational notions, ignore the physical demands of horizontality? In order to settle the second point we presented sixty-six subjects with a drawing of a bottle inclined at an angle of 45° and one-third filled with red liquid, and then asked some of them for a memory-drawing one hour and one week after the presentation, and others for a memory-drawing one week after the presentation only; in what follows, we shall

---

[1] In collaboration with J. Bliss.
[2] Inasmuch as operational thought equips the child with a frame of reference and hence guides his perception. See J. Piaget: *The Mechanisms of Perception*, Routledge & Kegan Paul, 1969, p. 196.

see that their responses were bound up much more closely with the development of their pre-operational and operational notions than with their perception.

§1. *The recumbent bottle*

The experimental material consisted of a bottle half-filled with coloured liquid (Figure 52 *A*), the horizontal level of which could easily be determined by reference to a continuous base line and to the coloured bottom half of a miniature car. Originally, a second bottle (*B*), standing on its head, was placed in a line with the other two objects, but we later decided to dispense with it. The main purpose of this experiment was to establish whether the child would remember these objects as they were presented to him, or whether, realizing

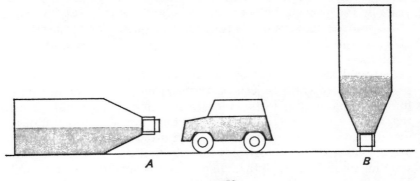

A B

FIGURE 52

that bottles are normally upright, he would 'normalize' his memory of the model. Let us stress that we were purely concerned with his memory: all we asked our subjects to do was to describe what they had actually seen. However, if they changed the position of the bottles in their memories, we also wanted to know if they at least recalled that the surface of the liquid had been horizontal. Now, we have just mentioned that the idea of horizontality, and more generally of the system of natural co-ordinates, is not grasped by children below the age of nine to ten years: when five- to seven-year olds are told that the vessel before them is about to be inclined, and are then asked to predict the position of the level (by marking it on the drawing of an inclined bottle), they generally ignore all external reference points and produce levels running in all directions (including the vertical), as if the liquid were bound to maintain its original position inside the bottle.

Numerous studies of people giving evidence in court have shown that, in the case of vague memories, witnesses tend to come up with the most probable solutions. Now, if the most probable is the most common, then there is little doubt but that the probability of a liquid at rest having a horizontal surface is close to 1. However, if the child remembers his assimilations of an event rather than the event itself, as all our previous observations suggest he does, then his remembrance of such static forms as those represented by Figure 52 is likely to be dominated by pre-operational structures which, while being erroneous from the empirical point of view, nevertheless reflect the child's operational level.

Method. During the first session, the drawing of the two bottles and the car is presented without comment and the child is asked to memorize it.

During the second session, held an hour later, he is asked for a memory-drawing and no other questions are put to him.

The third session is held a week later and begins with a new memory-drawing. Next, the child is asked a number of questions intended to assess his operational level. If his drawing is correct, he is shown several erroneous drawings, and asked to tell whether the levels depicted on them are possible and why (or why not).

Five-year-old subjects. Of the eight subjects in this group, one produced an unusable drawing (he transformed the bottle into a 'rocket') and of the remaining seven, only three drew recumbent bottles with levels correctly drawn in. The other four produced upright bottles:

SIL (5;8) drew one inverted bottle with the liquid adhering vertically to its left wall, and one recumbent bottle with a horizontal band. All he said was that the bottle was '*half-full of syrup*'. When pressed to draw all he had

FIGURE 53

seen, he produced Figure 53. A week later, he repeated the same drawing but with the liquid adhering to the right wall of the bottle: *Is that right?—* Yes—What did you do to remember it?—*I thought in my head.*

MIC (5;3) drew two upright bottles with the liquid pressed vertically against one wall. He was then shown a motor car with a horizontal band, but continued to maintain that the band in the bottle was vertical. Next, he was shown a drawing of a recumbent bottle with the liquid parallel to the base: '*No, that's not what you showed me.*'

PIE (5;4) drew the motor car correctly and also bottle *B* (Figure 52) but stood bottle *A* on its head, with the liquid against one of the walls. Is that what you saw just now?—*Yes.* He produced the same drawing a week later.

PAT (5;6) said one week after the presentation (he had been unable to attend the earlier session): '*It's easy; all I have to do is to draw two bottles and a car. I remember it all, because I thought about it.*' His car had a horizontal band, as did the liquid in the second bottle, but the first bottle was upright and the liquid in it had a vertical level.

HEL (5;7) produced a correct drawing of one of the bottles, but filled the other one to the brim. A week later, she drew both bottles correctly, and was then shown several erroneous drawings: of these, she accepted a recumbent bottle with the liquid pressed vertically against the base, and even thought that it was possible to have a bottle standing on its head with the liquid in the upper part. When she was shown a drawing of an upright bottle with the liquid pressed vertically against one of the walls, she said: '*Yes, that's possible, but it might also have been quite full.*'

All these children were clearly under the impression that they were drawing what they had actually seen. Thus, when Mic was shown an erroneous drawing, he did not say that it was impossible, but simply: 'No, that's not what you showed me.' Had we not been familiar with the operational reactions of children at that age, we might easily have concluded that they all thought we had been pulling their legs and were expecting them to reproduce the joke in their drawings. However, not only did all of them think that they were drawing what they had been shown, but they also thought that all the positions we showed them were possible in real life: thus An (5;6), who produced a correct drawing, accepted all the others as well, though she did hesitate when it came to the upright bottle with a vertical level.

Six- to seven-year-old subjects. Of our seven 6-year-olds, one drew two full bottles, no doubt for the same reasons as Hel; another drew two full and upright bottles an hour after the presentation and two recumbent bottles a week later; three offered the correct drawings; and the remaining two drew upright bottles with the liquid pressed vertically against one wall:

DEM (6;3) drew the recumbent bottle correctly, but reproduced the upright bottle in the form of a parallelepiped with the liquid pressed vertically against the left wall. He was then shown the correct drawing of bottle *B* (Figure 52): Didn't you see that one?—*No.*—Could it have been like this (liquid in upper part of the bottle)?—*Yes, the syrup could go like that.*
TA, on the other hand, produced a correct drawing of both bottles: Are you sure that's right?—*It's just as I saw it.*

Bottle A and the motor car. Next, we tested the reactions of twenty 5- to 7-year-old children to a drawing from which bottle *B* had been omitted. Of these, fifteen offered the correct responses (including one who drew a red spot which, as it turned out, was meant as a symbol of horizontality). The five remaining subjects, all of them five-year-olds, produced one upright bottle with the liquid pressed vertically against the wall (as in Figure 53); one recumbent bottle with the liquid pressed vertically against the top (Figure 54 I); one inclined bottle with the liquid against the side and

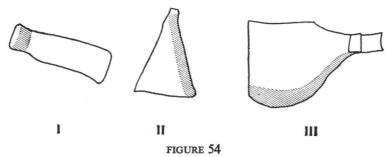

I   II   III

FIGURE 54

the top (Figure 54 II); one recumbent bottle with the liquid running first in a horizontal direction and then following the rise of the neck (Figure 54 III); and one bottle with an inclined base.

The results were, thus, plainly superior to those obtained with the complete model (I), which suggests that the reason why so few subjects remembered the recumbent bottle (*A*) was that they were confused by the presence of the inverted bottle (*B*): thinking that *A* must have been in the same position as *B*, and having seen that the liquid in it covered the lower wall, they gave *A* an upright position and, accordingly the liquid in it a vertical level.

On the other hand, once the upright bottle was omitted from the presentation, it appeared in only one drawing out of twenty, and the oblique bottles in only two. However, five subjects (i.e. 25 per cent) drew in vertical or inclined levels, with the liquid covering the base or one of the walls. This relative frequency of erroneous responses suggests once again that the memory of spatial orientations is influenced by the child's notional structures and not merely by his perception of the model. In order to show that this is indeed the case, we went on to present our subjects with only a single object, namely, a bottle inclined at an angle of 45°.

§ 2. *The inclined bottle*

A drawing of an inclined bottle (Figure 55) was shown to sixty-six 5- to 9-year-old subjects, divided into two groups, the first of which

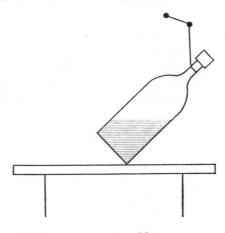

FIGURE 55

was seen again an hour and a week after the presentation. The subjects in it could be fitted into the following mnemonic types:

Type I: The bottle is drawn in an upright or inclined position, with the liquid covering one of its walls (cf. Figure 55 and Figure 54, II).
Type II: The bottle is drawn in an inclined position, but the surface of the liquid is drawn parallel to the bottom, i.e. at an angle of 90° to the axis of the bottle.
Type III: The bottle is inclined and so is the surface of the liquid.
Type IV: The bottle is upright but the surface of the liquid is inclined at an angle of 30°–40°.
Type V: The problem is suppressed, either because the bottle itself is drawn in a horizontal position or else because it is inclined or erect, but full.
Type VI: Correct remembrance.

The correlation of types with age was as shown in Table 43.
The responses shown in Table 44 were obtained from the second group (which we saw one week after presentation only).
The reader will see that, in both groups, correct memories (type VI) are produced by only about 33⅓ per cent of the eight-year-olds (nine-year-olds do slightly better), while mistakes (type I-IV) are made by some 75 per cent of all five- to seven-year-olds. There was no significant difference between the responses elicited from the first group an hour and a week after presentation: twenty-one stationary cases, four advances and four regressions and one indeterminate case (full bottle during one of the sessions). Similarly, the two groups considered together produced more or less the same reactions.
Remarkably enough, we could have expected the same responses

300

TABLE 43 Remembrance by the first group

	N	One hour							One week						
		I	II	III	IV	(I–IV)	V	VI	I	II	III	IV	(I–IV)	V	VI
5 years	(8)	2	1	3	0	(6)	1	1	3	1	1	0	(5)	2	1
6 years	(7)	0	3	2	0	(5)	1	1	1	2	3	0	(6)	1	0
7 years	(9)	0	1	4	2	(7)	1	1	0	1	5	2	(8)	0	1
8 years	(7)	0	0	4	1	(5)	0	2	0	0	3	0	(3)	1	3

TABLE 44 Remembrance by the second group and of both groups combined

	N	Second group (one week)							N	Both groups (one week)						
		I	II	III	IV	(I–IV)	V	VI		I	II	III	IV	(I–IV)	V	VI
5 years	(6)	0	3	1	1	(5)	0	1	(14)	3	4	2	1	(10)	2	2
6 years	(7)	0	2	4	0	(6)	0	1	(14)	1	4	7	0	(12)	1	1
7 years	(7)	0	3	1	2	(6)	0	1	(16)	0	4	6	4	(14)	0	2
8 years	(9)	0	2	3	0	(5)	1	3	(15)	0	2	6	0	(8)	1	5
9 years	(6)	0	1	1	1	(3)	0	3	(6)	0	1	1	1	(3)	0	3
Total										4	15	22	6	(47)	4	13

301

(except for the rare cases of type V) had we simply shown our subjects an empty bottle and asked them to imagine or deduce the angle of the liquid. In other words, the development of these memories corresponds to that of the child's notions in the course of deductive anticipations rather than to that of his perceptions. At the age of five to six years, there is a general preponderance of types I and II, which correspond to the first stage in the child's notional development (the liquid preserving the position it would have had had the bottle been vertical); at the age of seven to eight years there is a preponderance of types III–IV, corresponding to the second notional stage (liquids inclined at arbitrary levels);[1] and reactions of type VI do not appear before the age of eight to nine years, corresponding to the third stage of notional development.

Hence, there is a clear parallel between these reactions and those described in §1: in both cases a transformative deduction takes the place of simple retention of the perceived data. The subjects discussed in §1 (Figure 53) remembered the liquid as adhering to one of the walls of the bottle, but forgot the recumbent position of the latter, and hence concluded that, in a vertical bottle, the liquid would continue to stick to the right wall. In the present case, the subjects remembered that the bottle was inclined, but forgot the inclination of the surface and deduced it from what they thought would happen if an upright or recumbent bottle were turned through an angle of 45°. In either case, the memory played the part of interpreter and not simply of recorder, and we must now try to discover at which level of elaboration this interpretation or deduction occurs: during perception, during retention, or only during recall?

However, let us first look at what happened to these memories after an interval of six months, when we were able to bring back fifty-five of our original subjects. All of them remembered a half-filled bottle, and their responses could be fitted into the six types we have described. Again, there was no difference between the group we saw an hour and a week after presentation, and the group we saw one week after presentation only, except that the latter comprised a slightly larger number of type VI responses—chiefly due to progress by nine-year-olds who were not represented in the first group. The responses of the two groups combined, then, are shown in Table 45.

A comparison of these results with those obtained a week after the original presentation shows at once that while the correct responses (type VI) have decreased among five- to six-year-olds, they have increased from ten out of thirty-seven to sixteen out of thirty-three among seven- to nine-year-olds, which points to partial progress.

[1] Though generally adhering to the walls of the parallelepiped bottles, as we established during operational tests.

Moreover, the general distribution of types has remained more or less the same after six months as it was after a week, especially in respect of the relative frequency of type III (inclined surface in a bottle suspended at an angle). At the same time, type V has increased in frequency among five- to six-year-olds (from 10 per cent to 40 per cent), thanks mainly to their tendency to restore the bottle to a vertical position (cf. §1).

When it comes to a detailed analysis of cases of progress and regress, the six types we have distinguished must be reduced to three —any attempt to establish a hierarchy in respect of types III, IV and even in respect of types I and II (between which there exists a number of intermediate levels) would be quite arbitrary. In what follows, we shall therefore make do with the following levels: 1 ($= I + II$); 2 ($= III$ to V); and 3 ($= VI$). If $M > W$ refers to progress from

TABLE 45   *Remembrance after six months*

Types of memory	N	I	II	III	IV	(I–IV)	V	VI
5 years	(10)	2	1	2	0	(5)	5	0
6 years	(12)	1	2	4	0	(7)	4	1
7 years	(13)	0	1	6	1	(8)	0	5
8 years	(14)	0	3	4	1	(8)	0	6
9 years	(6)	0	0	1	0	(1)	0	5
Total	(55)	3	7	17	2	(29)	9	17

level 1 to 2 or from level 2 to 3 in the course of six months, and $W > M$ to the opposite case, we have:

$W > M$	$W = M$	$W < M$
6	32	17

Regress ($W > M$) was common among all younger subjects. The responses of two children proved particularly interesting. One of them, a five-year-old, drew a horizontal bottle (type V),[1] but reverted to type II after six months (recumbent bottle and vertical level). The other, a six-year-old, was of type IV an hour after the presentation and showed that he had reverted to type II a week and, again, six months later (whence $W = M$). These responses underline the fact that the excellent initial memories of these subjects do not go hand in hand with operational understanding. There were also three regressions among the seven- and eight-year-olds—two reverted

[1] Another subject of the same age and type could not be retraced after six months.

from level 2 to level 1 and one from type VI (level 3) to type III, which again shows that their initial understanding (or perhaps their purely figurative memory) was inadequate.

Stationary cases occurred at all levels and in all age groups. As for the seventeen advances, they included several five-year-olds (progress from I to III or IV), but proved particularly interesting in the case of seven- to nine-year-olds, i.e. of children at the age when spatial co-ordinates in two or three dimensions are first constructed. The most common advance was from type III to type VI, and by means of counter-suggestions ('One of your friends remembered it this way [drawing of an oblique level]'), we were able to establish the degree of understanding on which these memories were based: *'That's wrong, because when the bottle was at a slant, the level remained straight'*, etc. However, other nine-year-olds showed that their memories had grown more precise because they were taking new data into consideration, and not because they had acquired a more balanced grasp of the processes involved. Thus, Mat (9;11) first drew an oblique level, and then corrected it, but when asked 'Is that right now?', she wavered ('*I really don't know*'), and then accepted our counter-suggestion; for all that, the two subjects in this category had made clear mnemonic progress.

These transitional cases, coupled with the more stable advances, show to what extent mnemonic progress in the present case is bound up with the underlying operational schema. It is worth stressing that, though these seventeen advances out of fifty-five (eleven advances out of thirty-three 7- to 9-year-olds) are reminiscent of the nineteen advances made by sixty 6- to 8-year-olds in the multiplication of classes, progress in the latter case was purely in the domain of the reconstructions (with regress in recall), whereas the present advances represent progress in recall itself, i.e. in respect of the memory-image, and this, no doubt, because of the spatial nature of the model.

§3. *Conclusions*

The facts described in this chapter have a direct bearing on two of the main problems discussed in several sections of this book, namely, the relationship between memory fixation and perception or conception, and the relationship between mnemonic retention and deductive reconstruction.

I. The first of these problems is a particularly delicate one. It might be thought (and the reader himself must have done so quite often) that, since the memory only begins where perception leaves off, the question of what the subject feeds into his memory in no way involves the memory as such, but falls exclusively into the province of perception and the intelligence, so that the only purely mnemonic problem to be solved is how the subject retains and later recalls (or recognizes and reconstructs) what has been encoded in his memory. If that were indeed the case, then the memory of children would function precisely like that of adults, except that children would, of course, choose to retain different things. Now, this hypothesis is, in fact, a highly questionable one, for it is just as, or even more, likely that the mode (and not simply the quantity or fidelity) of mnemonic conservation is partly dependent on the organization of the memory at the moment of its fixation and vice versa: thus, in Chapters 1 and 2 we saw that the remembrance of serial configurations can make progress in the course of six months; similarly, in the present case, several subjects altered their memories of the initial data within an hour or a week, albeit inadequately, and we may take it that, in both cases, this strange mode of conservation was due to the organization of the memory at the point of its fixation.

But how can we possibly distinguish between the organization of the memory as such and that of the preceding schemata, or of the conceptions and perceptions that determine what precisely the subject puts into his memory? When the subject himself is allowed to watch the actual transformation, the dividing line is exceedingly difficult to draw, but in such cases as serial configurations or the present experiment, in which the child is simply presented with a static model, a comparison of the objective data with his recollections helps us to determine: (1) what the subject actually saw; (2) what he has failed to notice; and (3) the way in which what he saw has become changed by his assimilatory schemata.

In the particular case of the bottle A (Figure 52), the subject saw and usually remembered: (a) a bottle; (b) a layer of coloured liquid covering the entire side of the bottle; but (c) he may or may not have noticed that the bottle was lying on its side. In the case of Figure 55, he saw: (a) a bottle; (b) that it was inclined; but (c) he may not have noticed the horizontal level of the liquid. But what he certainly did not see was a column of liquid with a vertical or oblique level. From these data, we take it that what the subject fed into his memory was: (a) and (b) but not necessarily (c), and that if he thinks he can remember a column of liquid with a vertical or inclined surface, it is because he has assimilated the physical data to his intellectual schemata.

In that case, there are two possibilities. The subject may have noticed characteristic (c), and produces the correct memory of the recumbent bottle with the liquid covering its entire length, or the inclined bottle with the liquid forming a horizontal surface; there has been no modification of the data he has perceived and it is only during the operational test that we can determine his acceptance or rejection of the possibility that liquids may be suspended in air, or rise at an angle, etc. Alternatively, he may have failed to notice (c) and has simply recorded (a) and (b): in that case, he may, as early as an hour after the presentation, come to believe that he has seen a bottle in the normal (upright) position, and this by reference to the empirical frequencies he has established before the organization of his memory; but he may also believe that he saw a vertical column of water, because he remembers that the liquid covered the side of the bottle. Similarly, he may believe that he saw an inclined bottle, but with the liquid running perpendicular or at an acute angle to the axis of the bottle, etc. These are features that he could not possibly have observed in the model itself, and which he must therefore have added to the original data, but not during the fixation of his memory, when this particular interpretation would have been contradicted by his perception of the model. The first of these features (upright bottle, etc.) need not surprise us, because it represents the most probable state of the bottle as the child has observed it before proceeding to the organization of that memory. The other feature, however, is the direct consequence of the subject's pre-operational schemata, which he subsequently discards.

However, the essential point to bear in mind is that the memory has been modified after, and as a direct result of, its organization, which involves the assimilation of the data to the existing schemata. This provides us with proof that the mnemonic organization at its point of fixation partly determines the conservation of memories, both in their fidelity and in the number of elements retained, and above all in their qualitative mode, i.e. in the tendency to introduce transformations which, if unreasonable, are subject to subsequent corrections, as happened in the case of seriations no less than with the present model, where, as we saw (§2), eleven out of thirty-three 7- to 9-year-olds made mnemonic progress in the course of six months.

II. However, the second problem posed by the present investigation is, if anything, even more crucial: we have to establish whether the mnemonic transformations we have been discussing, and indeed whether those features of the model that are recalled faithfully, are produced during retention as such, or whether all of them result from reconstructions at the moment of recall. In the case of the rotation of triangles (Chapter 15) the reader might have gained the impression that all memories, including the correct ones, were due to a re-anticipation or reconstruction during recall. This is, indeed, the view Janet would have taken, but Penfield has shown more recently that memory-images can be conserved as such (unlike schemata which pose quite a different problem). Now, with the rotation of triangles, as in so many other cases, it is impossible to dissociate the respective contributions of mnemonic conservation and reconstruction, because what we have here are memories of transformations performed by the subject himself or in his presence.

In this respect, too, the present results seem to be decisive. We have to explain how precisely the subject arrives at the inference that (upright bottle) X (liquid covering one wall) = (vertical column of liquid); or (inclined bottle) X (liquid occupying its lower third) = (surface parallel or at an angle to the bottom of the bottle). This inference could not possibly have been drawn during the fixation of the memory, when it would have been contradicted by the perceptive data: now the child remembers these data perfectly well (at least in respect of a and b); thus, when we showed Mic a drawing on which the liquid adhered to the bottom of an inclined bottle, he said at once: 'No, that's not what you showed me.' Moreover, this inference could not have been the result of a process of (explicit or implicit) reasoning during recall, because no transitions are involved except in the case of correct responses following mistaken recollections. Had the child been shown a bottle that was successively suspended at different angles and had he been told to remember the inclinations and positions of the surface of the liquid, then, assuredly, he would have had to make considerable use of deduction, re-anticipation and reconstruction at the point of recall. In the event, however, he simply recalls, say, an elongated bottle with the liquid covering its wall, and yet he unhesitatingly draws an upright bottle, because that is what he thinks he saw: he feels no need to ask himself how the liquid surface will behave if the angle of the bottle is changed, and this simply because in his memory-image, the bottle is upright and the liquid covers its wall. The question of inference would thus not even arise, were it not that the vertical column of liquid was never perceived during the presentation and must therefore have been inferred at a later date. But when?

If it cannot have taken place during the fixation of the memory, nor at the point of recall, the inference must have been drawn during the retention of the memory-image, much as happens in the case of those 'pre-inferences' which Helmholtz had the genius (*dixit* Pavlov) to attribute to perception, and the authentic existence of which, though long in doubt, has finally been recognized. By the side of pure memory conservation and of pure reconstruction, at the point of recall, there is, in fact, room for a third interpretation: conservation coupled to reconstructions, including those of an inferential type. In our particular case, the inference is very simple and results directly from a

307

simplification of the data in accordance with their most probable state, which leads the child to remember an upright bottle and then to co-ordinate this position with his memory that the liquid covered one of the walls of the bottle. Now, this quasi-immediate co-ordination is facilitated by the schemata of spatial co-ordination (topological step-by-step co-ordination coupled with ignorance of the system of co-ordinates and, hence, with neglect of the horizontal).

The great importance of these inferences, drawn in the course of mnemonic transformations, is, therefore, that they are capable of converging with the reconstructions or re-elaborations produced at the point of recall. In the case of seriations, for example, mnemonic advances in the course of six months were, as we saw, due to spontaneous development of the operational schema on which, of course, the memory-image is based; and the transformation of the memory under the influence of a schema presupposes the existence of pre-inferences similar to those whose existence we were led to suppose in the case of the inverted bottles. Now, the pre-inferences modifying the structure of a serial configuration are identical with those the subject would have had to use had he been told to reconstruct the series at the moment of recall.

In the case of the seventeen mnemonic advances described in §2 of this chapter, the pre-inferences were obviously due to the development of the operational schema of spatial co-ordinates, but the new inference, that all liquids must have a horizontal level (and this inference is new precisely because the memory of the model was quite different six months earlier), must necessarily involve the memory itself, for, once this schema has become general, and there is no longer any reason for treating it as the exclusive result of a deduction drawn at the moment of recall, no such deduction would be expected from subjects 'recalling' inclined or vertical levels.

In general, we can therefore say that mnemonic conservation takes place on three planes: pure retention of certain data without modification; conservation with inferential and other transformations, and reconstruction at the point of recall. However, we have just postulated a measure of convergence between the second and the third of these planes, and we have just seen that the conservation and transformation of memories is partly determined by the organization of the memory at the moment of its fixation. Hence, the mechanism of the memory reflects a profound functional unity that can only be explained by the fact that the figurative aspects of the memory, i.e. the memory-images, are brought into harmony with a general schematization whose mainspring is the conservation of the schemata of the intelligence.

308

CHAPTER SEVENTEEN

Remembrance of Three Triangles of Different Shape and Equal Area

Having examined the remembrance of configurations involving rotations and natural co-ordinates, we thought it essential to go on to the remembrance of shapes and spatial magnitudes organized into a system, and subject to a conservation law. However, we saw earlier (Chapter 3) how difficult it is to express conservation problems in terms of memory-images—conservation is not a configuration but a rational relationship involving the transformation of states or configurations. If the transformation is performed by the child himself or in his presence, there is a fair chance that his memory will be purely conceptual or logical, so that success or failure will depend solely on his operational schemata. It is, of course, possible to avoid this difficulty, as we tried to do in Chapter 3, by presenting equal magnitudes in different configurations (e.g. three sets of six counters arranged in different ways) on the assumption (which was proved correct) that the remembrance of these distributions must depend on the subject's operational level as well as on his conservation schemata. However, when it comes to the spatial magnitudes (areas) that we are about to discuss, the subject cannot possibly judge them equal unless he makes precise measurements or applies elementary transformations (division and recombination), which he only remembers in part, since all he has been asked to do is to recall the results in terms of shapes and dimensions, etc.

The present model comprised three rectangles made of thin card-board and measuring 4×16 cm each, and the subject's attention was drawn to the fact that these rectangles were equal in size. Next, one of the rectangles was divided into two parts measuring 4×8 cm and then glued together sideways to form a square. The second rectangle was cut up into two parts measuring 2×16 cm each, and then glued together lengthwise into a rectangle measuring 2×32 cm. The whole operation was performed in front of the child, and the three shapes were set out in the following order: upright rectangle measuring 4×16 cm square; and recumbent rectangle measuring 2×32 cm.

The child was then asked whether the areas were still equal, and his reply was noted without any comment. The model was removed after that, and the child was asked for a description and a drawing on squared paper (the examiner noting whether or not the child made use of this additional aid).

We wanted to find out whether, and to what extent, the memory-image of these three shapes was a direct reflection of the perceptive data, whether it became distorted with age, or whether the child made an attempt to equalize the areas based on his grasp of their conservation. Now, this problem is quite different from that involved in numerical correspondences (Chapter 3) or, more generally, in the relations between an operational schema (e.g. seriation) and the remembrance of the configuration resulting from the application of that schema. Hence, we shall not postulate the existence, in the present case, of a specific and isolable factor, such as the grasp of the conservation of areas, which could influence the perception and remembrance of areas in much the same way as the conservation of equivalent sets modifies the remembrance of rows of counters (Chapter 3) or as seriation leads to the structuring of the configurations described in Chapters 1 and 2. There is, in fact, no such thing as a 'conservative' operation: conservation is but one of several aspects of any operational system, all of which call for a combination of transformations (of the characteristics a, b, c, etc.) with the conservation of some of their interconnections (sum or product, etc.). Now, in the present case, the operation involves a modification of the dimensions, but in such a way that a decrease in a is compensated by an increase in b and the fact that the product ab remains constant. In the model under consideration (and in geometric figures in general), the dimensions a and b are physical properties of the object, and so are the results of the divisions and recombinations; they are not structural characteristics imposed by the operation as such: a rectangle has a long and a short side even if there is no one to acknowledge that fact, whereas two numerical sets cannot be said to have, say, six elements each, unless some subject has first constructed the additive series of integers. It follows that, in order to remember the three figures presented to him (the upright rectangle A, the square B, and the recumbent rectangle C), the subject need merely inspect them, and has no need to evaluate the product of the length a and the width b. But how precisely does he inspect these figures and fix them in his memory?

Now, from many experiments involving the conservation of physical magnitudes (e.g. the conservation of matter, mass, etc., in a ball of clay that has been drawn out into the shape of a sausage), we know that young subjects fail to notice the two-dimensional transformation and centre their attention on one dimension only, whence there is non-conservation because, when the ball is elongated without losing thickness, it must, of course, contain more clay than it did originally. In particular, by concentrating our questions, not on the data the child has perceived, but on his anticipatory image of the results of the transformation, two of us[1] were able to show that the drawings of the youngest children do, in fact, represent elongations without loss of thickness. Now, since the anticipatory image is closely bound up with the memory-image, we are entitled to ask whether recall or even recognition of our transformed figures is affected by the child's grasp of the conservation of areas. But even if it is, this does not mean that conservation as such can modify the memory. Our own hypothesis is that the various schemata responsible for the gradual co-ordination of dimensional changes are responsible for the quality of the memory no less than for constructions more or less favourable to the conservation of areas. Hence, if there should be a connection between the conservation of areas and mnemonic types, it is not because the former acts directly on the latter, but rather because both are rooted in the same perceptive, representative, mnemonic and conceptual organization, whose schemata intervene on the mnemonic as well as on the operational plane. This is precisely why we have kept stressing the effects of schemata, and not of operations proper, on the memory: assimilatory schemata constitute the common source of all mnemonic codes and of all operational structures. The present experiment was designed precisely as a further test of this general hypothesis.

§1. *The development of memory-drawings with age*

It proved extremely difficult to fit the responses to our model into distinct mnemonic types, since what the child sees is not a configuration, however simple, but three distinct figures whose order or position is of little importance. We did, however, discover that the graphic image was subject to continuous transformations with age, so that we felt entitled to speak of levels, though not, of course, in the strictest sense.

Level I. The drawings of four-year-olds quite naturally reflect a complete failure to grasp the conservations of areas, or rather to appreciate the problem: what these subjects recall is essentially a series of three figures of similar shape but of different lengths. A typical example was Gra (4;8), who, having drawn the three initial (equal) rectangles, went on to sketch a very short rectangle (*B*), a longer rectangle (*A*), and an even longer one (*C*), all standing on their shorter side and differing in length

[1] J. Piaget and B. Inhelder: *Mental Imagery in the Child*, Routledge & Kegan Paul, 1971, pp. 270–6.

by equal amounts, but more or less identical in width (as in the original rectangles). This pattern was repeated by quite a few other subjects, some of whom combined a slight increase in width with a rapid increase in length, so much so that the rectangle C became three times as long and one-and-a-half times as wide as the smallest one (B). Other subjects, with less developed drawing skills, made do with three strokes of unequal or practically equal length (but precisely because they could not draw properly, and not because they were trying to solve a conservation problem). Bea (4;8) drew three sausages, the biggest of which was six times as long and twice as wide as the smallest. In short, these subjects endeavour to depict three distinct lengths, but, unable to proceed to a further dimensional analysis, which alone would help them to account for the differences in shape, they simply expand the width of the rectangles at the same time as they expand its length.

Level II. Seriations of rectangles similar in shape but differing in length were produced by one or two five-years-olds, but the majority of the latter, and also of the six-year-olds, paid much more attention to the shape than they did to the size, though most of them thought that $B < A < C$. Thus, Mic (5;5) was careful to draw in the edges of the two halves of B and C, to show that they had been pasted together. On his immediate memory-drawing, the square B had the same width as the rectangle A, and the rectangle C was very much longer than A and disproportionately narrow. A week later, Mic made C twice as long but practically the same width as B, so that the area of C became $2A$. Fel (5;7) drew much too large a square, and much too short a rectangle C, which showed that he was more concerned with expressing the differences in shape than the differences in size. Beg (5;9) finished up with B almost twice the size of A, while Car (5;10) made it three to four times smaller, and C the same length as A but twice as narrow. Man (6;2) made C at least ten times as long and almost twice as wide as A, and produced a square B that was considerably smaller in area than C. In short, all these subjects were mainly concerned with expressing the changes in shape resulting from the division of the original rectangles, but ignored the dimensions and, hence, the conservation of areas.

Level III. Some six-year-olds and many seven-year-olds produced a third type of memory-image, but one that had close links with the last: they began to remember the dimensions, and no longer relied on the seriation of lengths followed by the differentiation of shapes. However, the attempt to achieve dimensional accuracy took a curious form, and one that had an interesting bearing on the construction of the conservation schema: the subjects concentrate on a single dimension, and arrive at the other by guess-work, or rather by relying on their memory of the over-all shape. As for the dimension that they evaluate correctly, it must be stressed that the drawings were made on (8 mm) squared paper; now, while children below the age of eight years do not engage in spontaneous measurements, based on their own construction of units,[1] ready-made

[1] J. Piaget, A. Szeminska and B. Inhelder: *La géométrie spontanée de l'enfant*, Chapter I.

units are promptly employed by seven-year-olds. Thus, while our subjects at Levels I and II ignored the possibilities offered by the squared paper (except for a few six-year-olds), seven-year-olds took full advantage of it, and this precisely because they wished to arrive at the best possible estimates of the dimensions. From the use they make of the squared paper, it is therefore quite simple to determine whether or not they are striving for accuracy and whether they do so in respect of one or both dimensions. At Level III, as we have just said, only one dimension is taken into consideration. Thus, Dan (6;10), having drawn the rectangle A, added the rectangle C, which she constructed by doubling the number of squares representing the length of A. The resulting rectangle was twice as long as A (correct) but not nearly wide enough; again, her square had the same width as A but was much too long. Cla (7;2) drew three rectangles measuring 3×4 small squares each, and went on to construct B from two sections measuring two units in width, but arrived at the length by guess-work (approximately three units); the rectangle C measured 2×4 units in length (correct) and was therefore twice as long as A, but its width measured roughly one unit instead of $1\frac{1}{2}$. Nic (7;11) also made C twice as long as A but too wide; she constructed the square by pure guess-work and gave it an area much greater than that of A. Cyr (8;0) constructed his square of two halves, each the width of A but too long; his rectangle C was twice as long as A but much too narrow, etc.

Level IV. The memory-drawings of children at this level, like those at Level III, are based on accurate remembrance of the division and recombination of the original rectangles; in addition, however, they reflect a desire to take both dimensions into account. Thus, Cir (8;4) drew three initial rectangles measuring 9×2 units. By the side of one (A), he drew two rectangles, each meant to represent $\frac{1}{2}A$ and measuring 2×5 units, and then added a piece to the original rectangle to increase its dimensions to 2×10 units; next, he combined the same two halves into a rectangle measuring 4×5 units ($= B$). Finally, by the side of another of the original rectangles, he drew two halves measuring 1×9 units, and then joined them together lengthwise, which would have made $C = 1 \times 18$, had he not reached the edge of the paper and thus been forced to stop at 16. Bla (9;3) drew an A measuring 4×14 units, a B measuring $(4 + 4) \times 7$ units, and a C measuring $(14 + 4) \times 2$ units. The reader will see that, no matter what their representation of A, subjects at this level clearly recall that B and C were formed of the two halves of A joined together sideways or lengthwise, and that they pay careful attention to both dimensions. Thus, even if they sacrifice the square shape of B for the sake of dimensional accuracy, they arrive (without calculation but by the exact reproduction of the original manipulations) at the equality of the areas $A = B = C$, which, moreover, children at this level generally state quite explicitly (except, oddly enough, for Bla, who contended that his nearly square B 'took up more space').

The approximate distribution of these four types, with age, is set out in Table 46.

TABLE 46 *Types of reaction with age*

	N	I	II	III	IV
4 years	(6)	6	0	0	0
5 years	(7)	2	5	0	0
6 years	(9)	0	5	4	0
7 years	(5)	0	1	4	0
8 years	(7)	0	1	4	2
9–11 years	(7)	0	0	3	4

Clearly, therefore, the above four types correspond to the levels of the child's intellectual development.

§2. *Recognition one week and six months after presentation*

After their second memory-drawing, the subjects were asked to pick out the three original figures from a pile of seven carboard models: $A = 4 \times 16$; $B = 8 \times 8$; $C = 2 \times 32$; $D = 2 \times 16$; $E = 4 \times 22$; $F = 8 \times 11\frac{1}{2}$ and $G = 2 \times 22$ cm. The results are given in Table 47,

TABLE 47 *Recognition by age*

	N	A					B				C					
		A	D	E	F	G	A	B	F	G	A	C	D	E	F	G
4 years	(5)	1	1	2	1	0	0	3	1	1	0	4	0	0	1	0
5 years	(7)	6	0	0	0	1	0	3	3	1	0	4	1	0	0	2
6 years	(9)	9	0	0	0	0	1	5	3	0	0	5	0	1	0	3
7 years	(5)	2	1	1	1	0	0	5	0	0	0	2	1	1	0	1
8 years	(7)	7	0	0	0	0	0	7	0	0	1	3	1	0	0	2
9–10 years	(7)	7	0	0	0	0	0	6	1	0	0	7	0	0	0	0
Total	(40)	32	2	3	2	1	1	29	8	2	1	25	3	2	1	8

which shows that while quite a few of the younger subjects had good powers of recognition, they nevertheless thought that several other models would do equally well. Moreover, of these forty subjects, a mere thirteen picked out the three original figures: all of them were seven to ten years old, except for one 4-year-old who relied on seriation of the elements (the shortest, a medium-sized element chosen at random, and the longest).

A comparison of the recognitions of these subjects with their memory-drawings brings out two interesting points. To begin with, the former seem to be in advance of the latter in subjects of type I. We should not, however, be too impressed by the recognitive powers of four-year-olds, since, though all of them picked out the shortest element (*B*) and the longest (*C*), they hesitated between *A*, *D*, *E* and *F* when it came to the selection of the middle term. Nevertheless, most of them remembered *B* and *C* correctly, and from the age of five years onwards, six out of seven subjects also recognized *A*. This relative advance of recognition on recall of type I, and even of type II, shows clearly that recognition is something quite other than the remembrance of the perceived data. Thus, when we tested the reactions of a comparable group of subjects to a clay ball that had been drawn out into the shape of a sausage, and found that they centred their attention on the elongation and neglected the loss of thickness, we did not think that they had failed to perceive the latter as well as the former, but concluded that they had simply failed to take it into account conceptually. A similar process is at work in type I recall, in which (unlike in recognition) the schematism is directed towards the seriation of lengths, and all the other perceptual features are ignored.

Second, we see that shape *A* is recognized more readily than are shapes *B* and *C*; that shape *B* is often confused with shape *F* (which is slightly longer than the square but has the same width); and that shape *C* is often confused with shape *G*. Now, these are also the most common errors to crop up in the memory-drawings. Hence, we are bound to conclude either that recognition is more closely bound up with the memory-drawings than with the actual models, or else that recognition, though easier and more advanced than recall, is based on the same schemata as the latter. In fact, when we administered a recognition test to a special group of nine subjects, whom we brought back one hour after presentation for the sole purpose of testing their powers of recognition (cf. Chapter 15, §4), we found that the recognitions of the two groups were comparable, which suggests very strongly that recall and recognition have a common schematism. This is true of even the most elementary responses, since the relatively good powers of recognition of four- to five-year-olds are partly due to the same seriation of lengths as guided their memory-drawings.

Recognition several months after the presentation (the test was administered at various periods ranging from three to eight months with no significant changes in the results) produced similar results. Of the ten 5- to 6-year-olds we re-examined (we were unable to retrace a single four-year-old), five had regressed and the other five had remained at the same level. By contrast, the seventeen 7- to

11-year-olds produced four regressions, three advances and ten stationary cases.

§3. *Remembrance several months after the presentation*

The twenty-seven subjects we were able to retrace three to eight months after the presentation were interviewed by another member of our team[1] (which doubtless had an unfavourable effect on the quality of their memories).

Two of the three 5-year-olds had remained at Level II and one had regressed to Level I: he simply drew three straight lines arranged in increasing order of size. Of the seven 6-year-olds, three had remained at Level II, three at Level III, and one had regressed from Level II to Level I (simple seriation). The memory-drawings of the five 7-year-olds showed that most of them had remained at their original level, though one of them (Level II) showed by his verbal description that he had advanced towards the conservation of areas: 'We have to count the squares (on the ruled paper),' he said, but merely arrived at the ratio 1 : 2 for one of the figures and for one of the dimensions. Another subject mentioned that the original rectangles had been cut in half and then joined lengthwise or sideways, but failed to apply this principle to his drawing. A third tried to establish the equality of the areas by counting the ruled units, but arrived at 5×10 and 6×8, followed by 5×10, 7×8 and 6×9. Of the six 8-year-olds, one advanced from Level II to Level III (8×2, 16×1 and 8×2), two regressed from III to II, and the rest remained at their old level, as did most of the nine- to ten-year-olds (Levels III and IV).

What is so interesting about these responses is not so much the number of regressions and the relative lack of progress as the light they throw on the general schema of the memory and on its general development with age. Thus, all three of the 5-year-olds, three out of the seven 6-year-olds, two out of the five 7-year-olds, and one out of the six 8-year-olds had no spontaneous recall of the fact that the original rectangles had been cut up: 'The lady changed them around,' was how one 6;7-year-old put it. When these subjects were reminded of the actual manipulation, they usually cut off a piece from the end of the figures, and it was only later that they proceeded to the longitudinal division; thus, one 6-year-old divided the original rectangle into three long and thin rectangles, while many others divided it into two parts but failed to join these into a rectangle twice the length of the original one. Later still (at the age of about seven to eight years), the predominant reaction was to halve the original figure and to join the resulting parts lengthwise into an elongated rectangle,

[1] Muriel Depotex.

316

which appeared well before the square. Finally, and only at the age of eight to nine years, there was remembrance of the two reconstructions; Rem (8;4–9;0) said: 'The lady divided them, and then we had a longer one and a square' (correct drawings); and Luc (8;6–9;2) said: *There were some rectangles which you cut in two and turned into a square; but when they were cut the other way* (lengthwise) *we got a long strip* (correct drawings).—How long?—*The same number of pieces* (squares on the paper which he had counted carefully).

Clearly, recall after three to eight months reflects the development of the general schema with age; at first, the subject is receptive to only the final lengths or shapes, and neglects the actual transformations. Next, he concentrates on the transformations and is thus led to treat them as quantitative changes, though chiefly in respect of one dimension only, namely the length.[1] Finally, he remembers the quantitative, two-dimensional, variations of B and C (and no longer simply of C), whence his recall, not only of the conservation of areas, but also of the reasons for the latter.

§4. *Recall of shapes and the conservation of areas*

Returning now to the memory immediately after the presentation and a week later, we find that all our subjects had some recall of the details and significance of the manipulations they had observed: three equal rectangles, one of which remained unchanged (A), and two of which were divided longitudinally and laterally, and subsequently joined into a square (B) or a thin, elongated rectangle (C). However, on examining their reconstructions of B and C, and on assessing their objective grasp of the fact that $A = B = C$, we discovered that the reactions of the various age groups were pronouncedly heterogeneous: while younger subjects do not even pose the problem, the growing interest of older subjects in the dimensional relations ensures that the grasp of the equality $A = B = C$ increases regularly with age. Table 48 is based on separate computations of the grasp of the equalities $A = B$ and $A = C$ on immediate recall and on recall a week after the presentation, i.e. on four drawings per subject (expressed in percentage with absolute numbers in brackets).

Needless to say, Table 48 is no more than approximate (since, if, for example, A was made up of 4×7 square units, and C of 2×15,

---

[1] This does not mean that, when Level III subjects construct the long rectangle by joining the ends of the two longitudinal halves of the shorter one, they completely neglect its width (which they evaluate more or less well by guess-work): they simply forget that they must also construct a square out of the two transverse halves of the rectangle. Now, the very fact that they remember the elongated rectangle before they do the square, suggests that children pay heed to the length before they consider the width.

instead of 2×14 units, we felt justified in attributing the mistake to a counting error, and relied on the child's intentions rather than on his finished product). However, these percentages do express an objective fact, namely that, with gradual co-ordination of the dimensions (first of all in a vague and general way, as the child advances from recall of type I to recall of type II, and later in an analytic and even metric way as he advances from type III to type IV) the subject gradually arrives at the equalization of the three areas. But does he do so deliberately, and is he even conscious of it, or does the co-ordination of the dimensions represent the driving force, both of the operations and also of mnemonic structuring? Quite probably the second alternative is the correct one: first, because the co-ordination of the dimensions constitutes the actual operation, the conservation of areas being no more than an invariant; and, second, because remembrance is based on the image of the figures

TABLE 48 *Percentage of equalities per number of drawings*

4–5 years (52)	6 years (36)	7 years (20)	8 years (28)	9–10 years (28)
2% (1)	8% (3)	15% (3)	50% (14)	75% (21)

A, B and *C* and not on the conceptual grasp of the equality of their areas.

It remains a fact, however, that the conservation of areas is taken into account at about the age of eight to nine years, i.e. at an age when, as the Tables show, the effective co-ordination of dimensions first occurs. For though this co-ordination comes earlier (at the age of six-and-a-half–seven years) in the case of additive structures (the removal of two partial areas equal to two whole areas, without further changes), it cannot be effected until the age of eight to nine years in the case of multiplicative structures (co-ordination of two dimensions following changes of the over-all shape and involving compensation for the increase of one dimension by the decrease of the other). The main reasons for this delay are, first that an area is a quantity the child has first to construct for himself; and, second, that the child suffers from a fairly lasting inability to differentiate between area and perimeter. As a result, his description of the equality and conservation of areas remains highly equivocal (for lack of a sufficiently differentiated vocabulary and also because we deliberately refrained from asking leading questions). Hence, only the child's drawings and his own commentaries on them are significant.

By contrast, the descriptions produced after three to eight months proved highly instructive, because, as we saw, non-conservation in that case was mainly reflected in forgetfulness of the transformations (division and reassembly), and progress in the grasp of conservation was reflected in the remembrance of the recompositions, first of all in respect of the lengths (rectangle *C*) and finally in respect of the widths (square *B*).

In sum, the relationship between the organization of the memory and conservation of areas seems to be as follows: remembrance reflects a gradual structuring process, which can be observed in all tests of the conservation of two or three spatial dimensions; centration on one dimension only, followed by its co-ordination with one or both of the others. In the present case, this is expressed quite generally in the succession of types I (seriation of lengths) and II (general shape), and then, more analytically or even metrically, in the succession of types III (careful determination or measurement of a single dimension) and IV (*idem* in respect of the two dimensions). Now this gradual co-ordination constitutes the common schematism of all spatial operations, and leads to the conservation of areas and to the spontaneous organization of the memory of shapes *A*, *B* and *C*, thus entitling us to claim that there is a correlation between the memory and the idea of conservation. But it would be exaggerated to claim that a conscious intention to maintain the principle of conservation modifies the structure of the memory (which may, of course, happen, but only occasionally); the essential point is, and remains, the common schematism, which is both a factor in the structuring of the memory, when the problem is the recall of shapes that have been transformed in the child's presence, and a factor in the grasp of the principle of conservation, when the problem is to decide which elements vary and which remain invariant in the course of these transformations (which, in that case, are investigated as such, whereas the present test was chiefly designed to test the child's recall of the results).

CHAPTER EIGHTEEN

Remembrance of the Positions and Orientations of a Moving Body[1]

In Chapter 15, the moving bodies (arrows) were carried along by the rotation of their support; in the present experiment, on the other hand, the moving bodies (four snails) described independent motions (along a ribbon in the shape of a figure 8). However, lest the child's memory be overtaxed by reconstructions or re-anticipations, we did not ask him to remember the movement of the snails but merely to remember four positions: two inside the figure and two on its outside. We had previously used the same model to study the anticipatory image, and were hence familiar with the relevant schemata of four- to eight-year-old subjects.[2] In the present case, however, we were not concerned with anticipation but exclusively with the memory (recall, reconstruction and recognition).

Our main problem, therefore, was once again to determine the relationship between the subject's memory and his schemata (positional order and orientation). If he reconstructs the model in terms of the motion of a single element and leaves that element on the same side of the ribbon from which it started, his memory will be a function of the positional order. However, if he does not understand the motion and proceeds by opposite pairs of snails, he may recall: (1) that the two left snails remained inside the loops and the two right snails outside; (2) that the two upper snails had their backs turned to each other, while the two lower ones faced each other. Hence, all he needs is to remember the four relations left/right; up/down; inside/outside and back/face, which does not seem unduly complicated.[3] In fact, however, we found that children have great difficulty in remembering this model; similarly, in our earlier study of anticipation by representative images, we found that children found it much harder to determine the positions and orientations of

---

[1] In collaboration with M. Levret-Chollet and A. Bauer.
[2] See J. Piaget and B. Inhelder, *Mental Imagery in the Child*, Routledge & Kegan Paul, 1971, Table 36.
[3] Because the snails themselves are paired; see Figure 59.

an object moving across a recumbent figure 8 than one moving along an oval or circle.

The probable explanation is that children can only fix images by reference to the positional order which, in both cases under discussion, involves two successive cyclic inversions: snail 2 has an orientation opposite to that of snail 1, and snail 3 has a position opposite to that of snail 2 (inside or outside); snail 4 points in a direction opposite to that of snail 3, and snail 1 has a position opposite to that of snail 4. That being the case, we were anxious to discover whether or not the memory and the anticipatory image were governed by the same laws,

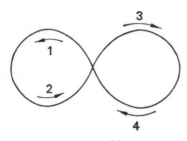

FIGURE 56

and whether they were impeded by the same obstacles (two reversible relations).

To settle this question, we first devised several preliminary tests and control experiments. In one of these, we substituted a circle for the recumbent figure 8, and found that the memory test produced the same results as the test of the anticipations. In another probe, we substituted three cars on a road-crossing for the snails, and in a third, we allowed the snail to describe somersaults so that it changed its position (inside/outside) on the ribbon, but not its direction, thus introducing the remembrance of chance as a fluctuation or singular class.

§1. *The main method*

During the first session, the material was brought out and the experimenter made sure that the child could clearly distinguish the snail's head from its back (the horns were conspicuously marked on the cardboard model). Once he had examined the snail at his leisure, the child was shown the figure 8-shaped metal ribbon, 8 mm wide and painted white on one side and red on the other. The loops had a diameter of 8 and 10 cm respectively. The child was told to look at the model carefully, because by next week the snails would have strayed, and he would have to put them back in their old places.

321

The second session was held a week later, and the child was asked, first of all, to specify the number and colour of the snails, and then to make a drawing of all he had seen (if he found it difficult to draw a large enough ∞, the examiner did it for him). The drawing was then hidden, and the child was handed the snails one at a time with the request that he place them back in their original position on the ribbon.

The responses of thirty 4- to 7-year-olds (including thirteen 4- to 5-year-olds) showed first of all that the remembrance of the contingent characteristics (number and colour) does not depend on age: ten of the thirteen 4- to 5-year-olds remembered one or the other, and so did seven out of ten 6- to 8-year-olds and six out of seven 9- to 11-year-olds.

The remembrance of the positions, on the other hand, clearly develops with age. Thus, only one of our thirteen 4- to 5-year-olds, a boy aged 5;11 years, produced the correct positions both in his drawing and in his construction, while another 5;11-year-old failed to do so in his drawing but offered the correct reconstruction. By contrast, five of our ten 6- to 8-year-olds produced the correct drawings (only one correct reconstruction), and so did four of our six 9- to 11-year-olds.

The positional errors of four- to seven-year-olds consist almost exclusively in placing all the snails inside or outside the loops, whereas the errors of older children consist mainly in mistaken alternations: thus snail 1 (Figure 56) may be drawn on the outside of the ribbon and snail 2 on the inside, when the correct opposition is between 1 and 3, etc.

However, in addition to the general position of the snail, we must also consider its 'local position' on the particular sector of the strip it occupies: instead of attaching it to the bottom of the ribbon by the foot (positions 1 and 4), the child may attach it by the shell: this type of error occurs in 25-30 per cent of all subjects between the ages of four and seven years. More generally, the local position was remembered by only fifteen out of twenty-three 4- to 7-year-olds (and of these, five did so exclusively in their reconstructions and one exclusively in his drawing), and by most eight- to eleven-year-olds.

On the other hand, the orientation of the snails was remembered with complete accuracy by only two out of four 10- to 11-year-olds and by one 7;9-year-old; the remembrance of the orientations is thus clearly much harder than that of the positions. Now, our previous study had shown that children found it easier to anticipate the orientation of the snail in 1 than its position (67 per cent as against 33 per cent seven-year-olds): this was because the demonstrator had gestured the direction of the motion and had simply asked the child to anticipate a few successive positions. In the present test, on the contrary, the positions are fixed and the child is simply asked to recall them, and it is left to him whether he tries to fix and retain his memory by relying on (1) the reconstruction of the motion responsible for the successive positions, on (2) partial schemata, or merely on (3) the opposition of single or combined pairs.

An examination of the errors and partial or complete successes of our subjects is highly instructive in this respect. All successful responses were manifestly due to the application of an ordination schema: once a starting position had been chosen, the other three were added step by step by an operational reconstruction of the motion. However, in addition to these completely schematized memories, there were some that were schematized in respect of only three of the four orientations: this reaction was produced by one 6;5 year-old, by two 7- to 8-year-olds and by two older subjects. Moreover, several subjects transformed the ∞ into two circles, with separate and unrelated pairs of coherent orientations: this was done by one 5-year-old and by three 7-year-olds, though only in their reconstructions and not in their memory-drawings. Others again treated the ∞ as an oval, and chose the orientations accordingly: this was the response of two 4- to 5-year-olds. Other subjects relied on paired oppositions based on the figure as a whole, inverting the orientations from right to left or from top to bottom: this tendency was found to decrease with age (in contrast to what happens with partial anticipations): it accounted for 50 per cent of the responses of our four- to five-year-olds (i.e. for thirteen out of twenty-six drawings and reconstructions); for 46 per cent of the responses by six- to eight-year-olds; and for 20 per cent of the responses of the older subjects. Finally, some subjects produced orientations partly chosen at random.

It should also be noted that a combination of orientations with positions gives the same results as do the orientations alone, which means that success with orientations implies success with position, but not vice versa.

The relation between memory-drawings and reconstructions based on responses to the three distinguishing features of the model—general position, local position, and orientation (plus number of elements added in brackets) are set out in Table 49.

TABLE 49   *Comparison of drawings and reconstructions*

	N of characteristics	$D > R$	$D = R$	$D < R$	*Subjects*
4– 5 years	27 (36)	2 (2)	19 (27)	6 (7)	9
6– 8 years	33 (44)	4 (4)	19 (29)	10 (11)	11
9–11 years	18 (24)	2 (2)	15 (21)	1 (1)	6

We see that the reconstructions of young subjects are slightly better than their drawings, because reconstructions force them to engage in a partial re-elaboration; nine- to eleven-year-olds, on the other hand, produce equivalent responses, thanks to the better schematization of their memories.

In other words, mnemonic progress with age is due to the replacement of the static schema with one based on the order and direction of the motion. The result is similar to the one we obtained in the case of rotations (Chapter 7) except that, with the latter, the static schema led to the pseudo-conservation of the positions and orientations prior to the retention of the correct inversions, while, in the present case, the pseudo-conservation bears exclusively on the positions.

§2. *The control experiments*

I. The model was shown to six subjects aged from 5;0 to 5;9 years.

(1) During the presentation, the demonstrator draws attention to the path of the snail and to its four characteristic positions;

(2) A week later, the subjects are asked to draw the path (inside and outside the loops) and the orientation of the snail at various specified points chosen at random from the four positions marked on Figure 56, plus two at the extreme right and left of the figure, and two close to the centre;

(3) After another week, the subject's operational level is determined by means of the plane-and-pilot test,[1] which also involves a displacement along a recumbent figure 8.

Now, the results of (1) and (2) were found to differ markedly from those described in §1. Of our six subjects, two (5;7 and 5;9) provided the correct drawings (one of them later proved successful with the plane-and-pilot test, while the other one proved half-successful); three had perfect recall of the positions and orientations of four out of the eight points, and one failed completely. Moreover, of the twenty-one errors, fifteen were in respect of the positions and only six in respect of the orientations, which suggests that the latter are easier to remember as soon as the memory is brought to bear on the path as well. A comparison between these reactions and the responses to the operational test (3) showed that the two were equivalent in two cases, that the former were in advance of the latter in one case, and the latter in advance of the former in another case.

However, though this test produced interesting results, we decided to abandon it, because we found it exceedingly hard to distinguish the rôle of mnemonic conservation from that of deductive reconstruction or actual reanticipation.

[1] See J. Piaget and B. Inhelder, *Mental Imagery in the Child*, Routledge & Kegan Paul, 1971, pp. 94–7.

II. In another control experiment, eight subjects aged from 4;10 to 5;10 years were presented with a snail moving along a circular path instead of the recumbent figure 8. The presentation was similar, except that four cardinal points now served as the positions.

We found that seven of our eight subjects had perfect recall of the general positions, six of the local positions and six of the orientations. Now, these proportions are highly reminiscent of those we obtained when testing the anticipation by representative images of five-year-olds (twenty subjects);[1] the corresponding figures were 88 per cent as compared with 80 per cent in respect of the positions, and 75 per cent as compared with 66 per cent of the orientations.

It should be noted, moreover, that the results of our main test (§1) too, were in close agreement with those of the anticipation test: correct anticipations of the position and orientation combined accounted for 0–12 per cent of the responses of four- to five-year-olds, for 20 per cent of the responses of six-year-olds and for 28 per cent of the responses of seven-year-olds.

III. In the most crucial of our control experiments, twenty-eight of the four- to eleven-year-olds who had taken the main test (twelve 5-year-olds; ten 6- to 8-year-olds and six 9- to 11-year-olds) were given a 'pure' memory test, i.e. one that involved neither reasoning

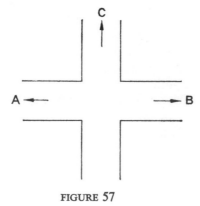

FIGURE 57

nor anticipation. Three model cars, differing only in colour and pointing in various directions (inwards or outwards), were placed near an intersection (Figure 57). In other words, all the elements—the number and colour of the cars, their positions and orientations—were quite arbitrary, so that sensori-motor anticipation could not help the child to arrive at a successful solution.

[1] J. Piaget and B. Inhelder, *Mental Imagery in the Child*, Routledge & Kegan Paul, 1971, Table 36.

Our problem here was to discover whether or not the memory developed with age in a manner comparable to that established by the main test: no evolution at all of the non-schematizable characteristics (number and colour) and a more or less regular development of the remembrance of the positions and orientations.

Now, the results were quite unequivocal. The number of cars which is contingent (three instead of four possibilities) is remembered best at the age of four to five years (twenty out of twenty-four cases), slightly less well at the age of nine to eleven years (nine out of twelve cases) and worst of all at the age of six to eight years (fourteen out of twenty cases)—hence this development follows no law. The colours which are equally contingent, on the other hand, are partly associated with the positions, and these are more readily schematized: whence there is some progress of the memory with age, both in respect of the number and of the order of the colours.

As for the positions themselves, they were remembered by 37 per cent of our five- to six-year-olds (nine cases in twenty-four), by 50 per cent of our six- to eight-year-olds (ten cases out of twenty) and by 85 per cent of our nine- to eleven-year-olds; while correct recall of the orientations increased from 25 per cent at the age of five to six years to 60 per cent at the age of six to eight years, and to 66 per cent at the age of nine to eleven years.

Remarkably enough, therefore, the drawings, no less than the reconstructions of these children (though not always both at once), show that the memory of the positions and directions develops very regularly with age, whereas the memory of the number 3, which would seem much easier to retain, does not. This shows once more that the characteristics of a model, even if they are completely contingent, are remembered to the extent that they fit into the child's construction of schemata which, in turn, evolves in the course of his operational development, and proves, *inter alia*, that our main experiment (§1) is a valid memory test. It could, in fact, have been argued that success or failure in that test was not due to success or failure in restructuring the model by deduction alone, had not the results of the present test suggested another interpretation; recall no less than reconstruction admittedly involves inferential constructions, but the underlying schemata are precisely the same as those governing the organization of the memory from its very fixation.

We must still make our customary comparison of memory-drawing with reconstructions. Here, it may also prove of interest to make a separate comparison of the remembrance of the number of elements N, a completely contingent characteristic, with the remembrance of the colours C and their order OC (characteristics that depend partly on the positions) and with the positions and orientations PO (which are more easily schematized inasmuch as they evolve with age). In that case we have a comparison as in Table 50 (T = total).

This shows that, with nine- to eleven-year-old subjects, there is no appreciable difference between drawings and reconstructions, that, in general, there is no difference between the remembrance of the contingent (and not readily schematizable) characteristics N and OC, and that as far as the orientation and position PO are concerned, the

TABLE 50 *Comparison of recall with reconstruction*

	$D > R$				$D = R$				$D < R$			
	N	COC	PO	(T)	N	COC	PO	(T)	N	COC	PO	(T)
4– 5 years	1	1	7	(9)	10	19	13	(42)	0	2	2	(4)
6– 7 years	0	2	2	(4)	10	16	14	(40)	0	2	4	(6)
9–11 years	0	0	0	(0)	6	10	12	(28)	0	2	0	(2)

drawings of four- to five-year-olds are slightly in advance of the reconstructions. There can only be one explanation of this apparent exception to the general rule that young children invariably produce better reconstructions than memory-drawings, namely that, as a precaution, we had provided our subjects with more material than was strictly necessary and that, in this particular case, arranging three pairs of cars instead of the original three units encouraged them to vary the positions and orientations, partly for playful reasons.

IV. In two final control experiments we introduced an element of chance. In the first (Figure 58), the snails moved across two separate ribbons A and B (meandering past a house or through a garden). As

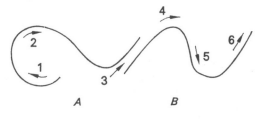

FIGURE 58

they came to the end of path A and switched over to path B, they had perforce to change from the upside down to the 'normal' position, i.e. to undergo a rotation of 180°.

327

The presentation was the same as that described in §1. A week later, the child was asked: (1) for a memory-drawing of the ribbons and the positions and orientations of the snails; and (2) to take a recognition test based on the selection of the correct model from a total of six, two of which included a single, continuous ribbon, and the other three continuous ribbons as well, but with the snails in the wrong positions or orientations.

The only results worth noting in this and the second, similar test (in which the snail had to be rotated through 180° as well, but followed a more complex path that led it to a flower), were in respect of the orientation of the snail and of the rotation imposed by the chance discontinuity of the ribbons. As for the direction of the snail, we found that, in the absence of the flower, the recall of four- to five-year-olds follows no discernible law, whereas in the presence of the flower, ten subjects aged from 4;5 to 5;9 years all produced adequate memories: the schema of an object-directed action obviously polarizes the memory much more strongly than even the geometrical form of the circular motion.

The recall of the chance discontinuity of the ribbons and of the 180° rotation had far more important implications. In the presence of the flower, only four out of our ten 4- to 5-year-olds remembered what to them must have been an unimportant detail, and, with the model shown in Figure 58, the five-year-olds forgot the discontinuity as well, while eleven out of the thirteen 6- to 10-year-olds remembered it correctly. This provides us with yet another illustration of the double significance of chance: while some subjects dismiss it as an unnecessary obstacle to their schematizations, others treat it as a singular class and remember it for that very reason. The youngest of our subjects had no problem in that respect: to them, the snail advanced smoothly from A to B (Figure 58) as from any other point to the next, and this the more readily as they themselves had moved it forward in action or in thought while trying to reconstruct the original path. In this they behaved very like young children who tend to submerge a piece of wood which they have previously declared would not float, as if natural laws depended on their own actions. If, on the other hand, their thought is sufficiently decentred from their own action to allow them to retrace the actual path of the snail, the discontinuity of the path and the rotation assume an importance quite distinct from that of the other changes in position or the other conservations of orientations: chance assumes the status of a remarkable and singular class and, for that very reason, is remembered much better than more regular events, in which the general schema alone is of importance.

§3. Conclusions

A comparison of the results of our control experiments with those of the main test (§1) may help to highlight the mnemonic problems

328

posed by the latter, and hence throw fresh light on the mechanism of the memory.

The most striking feature of our main model, and of the way in which the four snails are positioned in it, is that they can be remembered in two distinct ways. The first of these is figurative, and can be schematized by a matrix operation: one of the dimensions (left/right) is occupied by the dichotomy 'inside or outside the curve', and the other dimension (upper/lower) by the dichotomy 'back to back/face to face'. The second way is kinetic and involves the schematization of the displacement along the ribbon (but without change of side or direction of path): this somewhat more complex approach is quite simple to use in the case of a circle (§2, II), but, in, the case of our ∞, it involves an alternation of reversibilities: 2

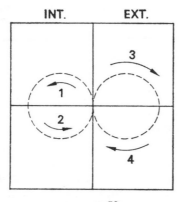

FIGURE 59

represents the inverse orientation of 1, and 3 the inverse position of 2 (inner or outer); 4 represents the inverse orientation of 3, and 1 the inverse position of 4.

If we dissociate these two approaches, the picture becomes much clearer. Thus, the road intersection test (Figure 57) brings out the matrix aspect of the model: here the positions and orientations are easy to remember, which accounts for the many successful responses. With the kinetic approach, on the other hand, the child need merely pay attention to the path traversed by the snail (§2, I), which explains why the memory of five-year-olds proved so good that we felt no need to continue the investigation with older children.

The reason why our subjects had such difficulties with the main method was therefore that their memories failed to come down squarely in favour of one or the other of the possible schematizations, and this because memorization is not an act of the reflexive intelligence or of conscious choice, but oscillates between the two methods, thanks to a set of mixed schematizations as inefficient as they are profuse: this explains why the child will sometimes produce kinetic but partial anticipations and at other times incomplete pairs of oppositions.

But though remembrance is not a complete act of the intelligence, it nevertheless is an active process; mnemonic retention cannot be reduced to the mere conservation of the perceived data. It is precisely the profusion of unco-ordinated schemata which impairs the memory of our main model (Figure 56), each of whose elements has special implications, but implications that vary with the particular schema the subject employs.

If the rôle of these implications is limited by the reduction of all the elements to arbitrary characteristics, as in the crossroads experiment (Figure 57), the schematism nevertheless persists, as we can tell from the fact that the memory of the positions and orientations continues to improve with age. But what entitles us to speak of a schematism in the case of contingent elements, or to identify a schema by its evolution with age? It is the fact that a schema must necessarily be involved just as soon as the subject begins to look for regular features in the data, and tries to assimilate the latter to a system or frame of reference (classification, or correlation of motions with anticipations), and thus transcends the data. And the reason why his schematizing assimilation can be identified by its evolution with age is precisely that it transcends the data, which do not, of course, evolve with time. If there were such a thing as a 'raw memory', it would remain identical throughout the child's life or, indeed, be the better the younger the subject and the less encumbered with memories; or perhaps improve with age but in purely quantitative terms (as in the well-known fifteen-word remembrance test). The explanation, then, of the progressive structuring of the memory is the existence of a mnemonic schematism, which becomes organized with age, or else that the memory comes to rely increasingly on the schemata of the intelligence, or a combination of both factors.

CHAPTER NINETEEN

Remembrance of Contingent Figural Combinations with or without Classification[1]

The resemblance between the remembrance of an operational presentation and that of the simple figurative models to which we have drawn the reader's attention can only be verified in part, since the figures presented to the child might be considered (and from a certain level onwards, rightly so) as representing states resulting from operational transformations. Hence, we shall now go on to examine the remembrance of a model to which the above qualification does not apply. Admittedly, all configurations whatsoever constitute so many states involving prior transformations, but these do not generally correspond to simple operations.

In the present experiment, our subjects were shown eight good or 'pregnant' forms: two circles, two squares, two triangles and two ovals, and a number of black bars affixed to these figures in what,

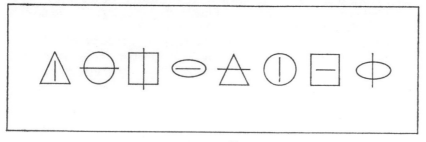

FIGURE 60

from an operational point of view, was a purely contingent way, though it involved certain figural regularities (Figure 60): each pair of identical figures had one bar on the inside and another crossing its periphery; the bars were placed vertically (in two pairs) or horizontally (in the remaining two pairs) and there was no correspondence between their orientation and length.

[1] In collaboration with P. Mounoud and P. Petrogalli.

331

Our problem here was to establish the manner and methods of perceptive recording or schematization by which the subject remembered these figures. In order to assess the degree of schematization used, we decided to divide our subjects into two groups, one of which was encouraged to engage in schematizing activities, and the other one not. More precisely, the first group was asked to classify the figures during the first session: a week later they were examined for their remembrance of the figures and not of their classification. The second group, by contrast, was not invited to engage in any form of classification, so that only their visual inspection of the figures could affect their subsequent recall.

§1. *Methods*

Method I (with classification) was applied during four sessions. The material (Figure 60) consisted of two triangles of side 4·5 cm; two circles of diameter 4 cm; two squares of side 4 cm; and two ovals with axes 5, 5 × 2, 8 cm. The bars measured 2 × 0·5 cm and 6 × 0·5 cm respectively. The eight figures were pasted to a sheet of white cardboard measuring 48 × 12 cm.

During the first session, the subjects were asked, first, to describe the material, and their attention was drawn to the bars if these had been omitted from their descriptions. Second, they were invited to cover the figures with a set of identical but loose elements (to encourage perceptive analysis). Third, they were asked to classify the eight loose figures in any way they chose, and then (if necessary) to proceed to a classification by pairs. Next, they were asked for another correlation of the loose figures and those pasted to the cardboard. Finally, they were invited to remember as many of the figures as they possibly could.

The second session was held a week later. The children were told to describe what they had done and seen during the previous week and then to draw everything they could remember. Next, they were handed the eight figures together with ten short and ten long bars, and asked to reconstruct the model. Finally, the demonstrator removed one element from a pair of figures and asked the subjects whether or not they could tell from the remaining element what the other one had looked like (this was done in order to determine their mnemonic strategies).

The third session was held six months later and was identical to the second. After recall and reconstruction, the material was brought out again for the purpose of memory 'retraining' (we should have liked to defer this part of the experiment until a day later, but had to fit in with the school routine). The retraining consisted of:

(1) Correlation of the loose and pasted-up figures;
(2) Classification of the loose figures; and
(3) Fixation for the purpose of memorization.

The fourth session was held a week later and was identical to the second.
Method II. Here, there was a deliberate attempt to eschew all forms of

classification and manipulative correlation. The first session, accordingly, involved nothing more than a visual inspection of the model, and whenever a subject found it difficult to keep his attention riveted on the latter, the examiner would say to him: 'Do look carefully at what is stuck to that card. In a moment, I shall be showing you another card and you will have to tell me if the same things are stuck to it.' After at least thirty seconds (if necessary repeating his admonition) the examiner brought out a second, identical, piece of cardboard and asked the child if it was the same as the first. If the child said it was not, he was shown the original card once again, and so on, until he changed his mind. Finally, he was asked to look carefully at everything once more so that he might recall it as soon as the material was removed.

The second session was similar to the second session of Method I, and the third session (six to sixteen months later) was identical to the second.

§2. *Recognition of the model*[1]

Before we look at recall and reconstruction, let us first try to determine to what extent recognition varies with age.

To that end, a separate group of subjects was shown the model for thirty seconds, and told by the demonstrator to look carefully at everything pasted to the card. 'I'd like you to remember it all. In a moment, I shall bring out a pile of other cards, and you'll have to pick out the right one.' Younger subjects did not know how to 'look' and fixed their attention on any point on the card (or even on the opposite wall!): we accordingly asked them to trace the eight figures with their finger, as if following a text in a book, or we did it for them, pointing deliberately to each element. Next, we told them to close their eyes for two to three seconds, and then showed them the old card and asked them whether or not it was the same. If they said no, we asked them to close their eyes once more and brought out the card for a further fifteen to thirty seconds, saying: 'This one is the card you looked at earlier. Look at it a bit longer.'

Next, the child was sent back to his classroom. He was called back an hour later, and shown the original model (M) in a pile of nine cards; $A = 8$ figures without bars; $B = 8$ figures with horizontal bars only (4 large and 4 small); $C = 5$ correct figures out of 8; $D = 8$ figures with vertical bars only (4 large and 4 small); $E = 8$ figures arranged in different order with two double oppositions (size and direction of bars), two pairs of identical figures among them; $F = 4$ isolated figures; $G = 8$ figures with bars running in the right directions but all of the same size (large); $H = idem$, but with small bars.

Choice 1. The cards were arranged in two columns, with M placed second from the top left and the rest at random. The child was told: 'Please find the card you looked at before.'

Choice 2. The cards were presented in a pile, and drawn out at random,

[1] In collaboration with A. Papert-Christophides.

and the child was asked: 'And what about this one?'; 'How do you know?; Why?', etc.

Most of our subjects chose several cards, and the examiner then asked them to make a final choice, having first arranged all the cards as in choice 1.

The responses of three 4-year-olds, eleven 5-year-olds, nine 6-year-olds, ten 7-year-olds, eleven 8-year-olds and two 9-year-olds are set out in Table 51. Let A represent the subjects who choose M exclusively; B the subjects who choose other cards; and C the subjects who choose several cards including M. Let $A2$ be the category A plus all those subjects who chose other cards before finally selecting M; and $A3$ the category A plus all those subjects who originally chose M and then changed their minds:

TABLE 51 *Types of recognition (expressed in %; absolute numbers in brackets)*

	N	Choice 1				Choice 2			
		A	$A2$	$A3$	B	A	$A2$	C	B
4 years	(3)	0	0	0	100 (3)	0	0	100 (3)	0
5 years	(11)	27 (3)	45 (5)	45 (5)	35 (4)	0	0	72 (8)	18 (2)
6 years	(9)	22 (2)	33 (3)	22 (2)	66 (6)	24 (2)	24 (2)	33 (3)	45 (4)
7 years	(10)	50 (5)	50 (5)	60 (6)	45 (4)	33 (3)	50 (5)	30 (3)	20 (2)
8 years	(11)	63 (7)	63 (7)	90 (10)	9 (1)	27 (3)	36 (4)	27 (3)	9 (1)
9 years	(2)	(2)					(1)		(1)

One 5-year-old and three 8-year-olds rejected all the cards when asked to make choice 2.

For the rest, Table 51 shows (as we hoped it would) that model M is difficult to memorize and recognize in the absence of analytical thought. More precisely, if we treat categories $A2$ and $A3$ as recognitions (because subjects belonging to category $A3$ and not to A, namely, two 5-year-olds, one 7-year-old and three 8-year-olds, began with 'global' recognitions and were then confused by the analysis associated with recall), we find that children below the age of five years do not recognize the model, and that correct recognitions do not account for more than 75 per cent of all cases below the age of eight years (choice 1).

Now, this difficulty in picking out the model shows that recognition is far from immediate, and that it calls for the kind of elaboration to which we commonly refer as 'analysis'. What precisely does the latter involve? The second essential lesson to be drawn from the Table is that it depends on the age level and, more precisely, that it does not become effective before the child reaches the operational level at about the age of seven to eight years: 'analysis', in fact, constitutes a structuring process based on classificatory schemata (in the present case, figures and bars) and on correlative schemata (size, positions and orientations of the bars). Moreover, if we compare the evolution with age of categories A and B (choice 1) with that of types III and IV on the one hand (IV, like A corresponding to M) and that of type I and II on the other (cf. §3, Method I, below) we find that the schemata supporting recognition are largely the same as those involved in reconstruction and recall.

The rôle of these schemata becomes particularly clear when we compare columns C and A (or $A2$) of choice 2. Column C, in fact, represents what we might call a choice bearing not only on the singular class M, but also on the equivalent class of cards the child has failed to distinguish from one another. We find that this non-differentiated choice declines with age (from 78 per cent in four- and five-year-olds combined, to 27 per cent in eight-year-olds), which can only mean that the pre-operational schemata of the younger subjects are much too blurred and vague to allow of exact recognition, and that the operational schemata of eight-year-olds prove more adequate. In fact, four- to five-year-olds generally choose all the cards except C and F, whereas eight-year-olds only choose M, D and H (choice 2) and M, D, E, G and H (choice 1).

The total number of choices per figure was as follows:

Choice 1

M	A	B	C	D	E	F	G	H
28	1	6	0	7	6	2	3	7

Choice 2

M	A	B	C	D	E	F	G	H
32	2	7	0	21	7	0	9	11

On analysing the reasons on which these choices are based, we find that they involve schemata of correlation (correlation of size of bars with their positions or those of the figures) and of classification (especially in the frequent joint choice of both M and D), which latter are essential for distinguishing the new class represented by the card M. However, these subjects also pay heed to a number of special signs: thus, one of them believed that the last oval was vertical, another that it was horizontal, etc. Moreover, card D, like the model itself, begins with a triangle and ends with an oval (and card E begins with a triangle and ends with a circle). Now, the search for special signs in no way runs counter to the search for a classificatory or relational schema: on the contrary, at the perceptivo-motor level, the 'understanding' of a class or of a schema is nothing other than the grasp of the set of common signs characterizing the objects constituting the 'extension' of that schema.

§3. *Results with Method I one hour after presentation*

Let us begin by describing the mnemonic levels in terms of their qualitative organization, and then go on to compare them with the classifications offered during the first session.

I. It is possible to distinguish four main levels:

Level I. No clear pairs (figures or bars). This level can be sub-divided as follows:

IA. One, more often two (and sometimes three), distinct figures; absence of bars from one or from several figures[1] (the total omission of bars was never observed until six months later);

IB. Two or three distinct forms; figures with bars, generally seven of the same size and direction (the somewhat more advanced case of alternation between figures with and without bars has been treated as an elementary form of pair formation, and hence consigned to Level II);

IC. Three or four distinct figures, one of which may be repeated, and two (or sometimes several) types of bar. Attempts at classification are primitive; for instance, there may be an irregular series of large and small bars, all of them horizontal.

Level II. Emergence of schematizing co-ordination, as reflected in (still rudimentary) pair formation. The figures are distinguished, and there is at least one pair of them. The pairs themselves are still constructed by simple opposition, either in respect of the bars (large and small, or horizontal and vertical but never both) or else in respect of the figures (two different figures bracketed together because they have identical bars or sometimes because the first has a bar and the second has none).

Level III. Beginning of co-ordination based on opposition by pairs. At least two pairs with simple opposition or at least one pair with double opposition.

Level IV. Generalization of pairs based on double opposition. (There are, of course, many intermediate levels between IV and III, and, for that matter, between any two successive levels.)

It must be stressed that this classification is rather arbitrary, the only certain fact being the general progress from one level to the next. Thus, the data were processed by at least four of our collaborators, and their joint conclusions bear out, not so much the detailed results set out in the Tables, as the relations they express; for example, an improvement in the drawings and reconstructions with age, the

---

[1] We have treated as IA one drawing of a single figure with bar, because of the omission of the other seven figures and bars.

fact that the reconstructions are in advance of the drawings, or that the initial results of Method I are better than those obtained by Method II, etc.

II. If we now apply the same classification to: (1) simple recall (descriptions and drawings); and (2) reconstructions with the help of mobile figures, we find the usual advance of the latter over the former: of our twenty-seven subjects, seventeen produced better reconstructions (including three cases of slight progress), six produced equivalent responses, and four produced inferior responses (including three that were almost equivalent). Here are some cases of progress:

GIL (4;0) produced a Level IA–B drawing (Figure 61 *a*) one week after the presentation; a week later he produced the same type of drawing but with three circles and three triangles, two of which were closed. In his reconstruction, on the other hand, he used eight figures, to all of which he attached horizontal bars (five long ones and three short ones), having first thought that two of the original figures had been without bars. His progress was therefore slight (IA).

YVE (4;0) drew Figure 61 *b* (IB) one week after the presentation. His reconstruction consisted of: two triangles and two squares with long horizontal bars, and two circles and two ovals with short horizontal bars (IC).

MAR (4;9), by contrast, had made spectacular progress. One week after the presentation she produced Figure 61 *c* (Level IB) but her reconstruction was of type IV: she had remembered everything except that the bars in the two squares and the two ovals ran in opposite directions.[1]

ANI (7;0) produced a Level II drawing, but a Level III reconstruction (Figure 61 *d*).

From these responses we can learn two things. On the one hand, they show that, as always, reconstructions, which involve both recognition and recall, enable the child to proceed to more highly developed co-ordinations and schematizations, while pure recall, which lacks the support of a sufficient number of mnemonic data, does not. On the other hand, the organization of the memory becomes a function of the intelligence, which explains why the memory-drawings of children from four to seven years of age do not show signs of clear improvement, except for the almost total disappearance of type I after the age of five years. The reactions of forty-seven subjects were, in fact, as shown in Table 52.

---

[1] Among children suffering from dyslexia (word-blindness), we also found one 6;10-year-old whose drawing consisted of figures without bars and whose reconstruction was of type III/IV (generally correct except that one square had a small vertical bar instead of a horizontal bar).

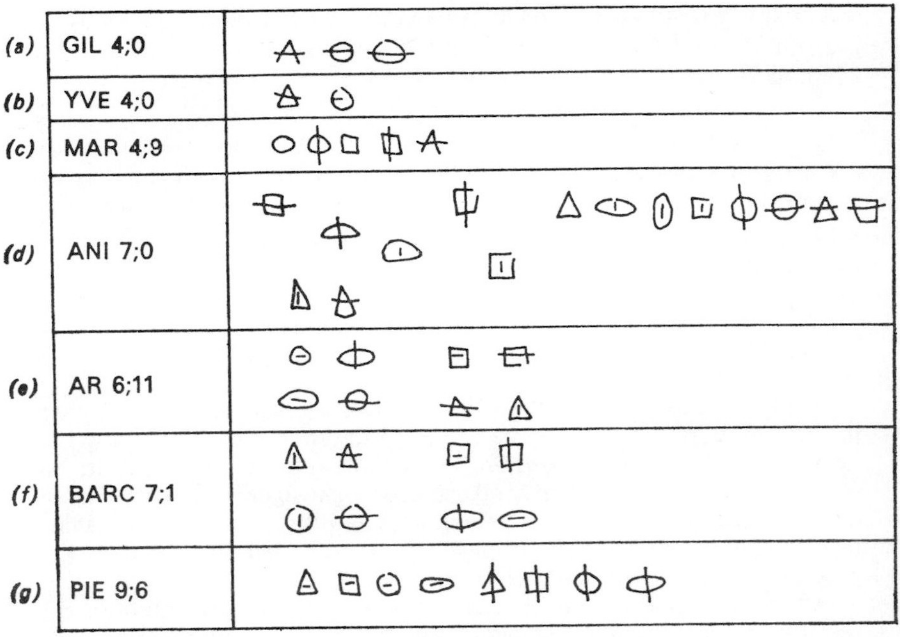

FIGURE 61

In addition we examined 20 dyslexic children[1] aged from 6;9 to 10;7 years, who, though suffering from word-blindness, were otherwise of normal or even of superior intelligence. All of them had just joined a logopedic re-education class (in the French language).

The main results obtained with these children were as follows:

(1) In respect of recall, they were all considerably behind the normal children. However, their mnemonic levels followed one another in precisely the same order as they do in normal children—only the average ages associated with the different levels proved to be greater;[2]

(2) In respect of the reconstructions, too, we found an important shift in favour of the normal children, though one that was less pronounced than in the case of recall. It follows that dyslexic, like normal children, find it easier to reconstruct than to recall the model (cf. Table 53);

(3) Dyslexic children suffer from a number of mnemonic deformations, such as the opposition of figures and bars, or of figures without any bars. Now, these two types of mnemonic degradation, which occurred in the recall of five dyslexic children out of twenty one week after presentation, also occur in normal children, but only after six months (or after twelve to sixteen months with Method II);

[1] In collaboration with Dr Luka.
[2] It should be mentioned that Dr Luka used slightly different criteria from ours to define the different levels; for all that, the hierarchical succession proved to be the same in both systems.

TABLE 52   *Distribution of types*

Levels	N	Memory-drawings				Reconstructions			
		I	II	III	IV	I	II	III	IV
4–5 years	(17)	11	3	3	—	7	6	3	1
6–7·5 years	(13)	4	3	3	3	0	5	4	4
7·5–9 years	(17)	2	1	8	6	1	1	8	7

(4) The classificatory levels of dyslexic and normal children are similar as well, and we find once again (see IV below) that classification influences recall.

A comparison of the reconstructions and memory-drawings of the forty-seven subjects listed in Table 52 with those of twenty dyslexic children reveals the picture shown in Table 53 ($R > D$ means that the reconstructions were of a higher level than recall, etc.):

TABLE 53   *Comparison of recall and reconstructions*

	$R > D$	$R \geqslant D$	$R = D$	$R \leqslant D$	$R < D$
47 normal subjects (4;9–9;10)	19	6	16	4	2
20 dyslexic subjects (6;9–10;7)	6	6	4	2	2

It should be noted, *inter alia*, that the reconstructions were rarely identical with the drawings made immediately beforehand (during the third session), except, of course, in the case of correct responses. In other words, the child is more concerned with structuring his memory than with perfecting its 'raw' state. As the reader knows, factor-analysts distinguish between what we may call the 'raw' or coarse memory (Thurstone's *M*-factor) and the remembrance of meanings (cf. the work of H. B. Carlson). However, we are entitled to ask whether the spontaneous memory is not always a memory of meanings whose different expressions reflect the subject's ability to assimilate the data to his schemata, and whether the 'raw' memory is not a limiting case in which the subject is forced by social constraints (scholastic demands or laboratory conditions) or by other external factors to accommodate his schemata momentarily to the task in hand, only to forget everything soon afterwards or merely to retain what has been assimilated.

Now, the material we presented to our subjects was an intextricable and deliberate mixture of schematizable and contingent elements:

(a) There were first of all two series of figures repeated in the same order (triangle, circle, square, oval), but the order itself was purely contingent;

(b) There were thus four pairs of figures, each involving a double opposition (length and orientation of the bars): if one term of a pair had a short vertical bar, the other had a large horizontal bar, etc. However, of the four multiplicative possibilities (large or small × vertical or horizontal) only two are realized in any one pair, irrespective of the nature of the figure (another contingency);

(c) The model comprised two long and two short vertical bars, and two long and two short horizontal bars. This is a schematizable relation, but the order of the vertical (v) and horizontal (h) or long (l) and short (s) bars was doubly contingent (vhvh–hvhv and slls–lssl), even though it presented internal regularities in each half of the series (vhvh or slls) and even though each half was a symmetrical reversal of the other.

The subject could therefore offer two possible solutions: he could either 'memorize' the model, i.e. have recourse to his 'raw' memory, or else make use of schematizations, i.e. fall back on the meanings inasmuch as it was in his powers to rediscover part of the system of classification (pairs and contrasts) or seriations. Method I, which called for a classification during the first session, might have favoured the second of these possibilities, but the presence of irreducible, contingent elements ought nevertheless to have led to passive memorization in a purely accommodative sense.

III. Now, the striking result of our tests of recall and reconstruction one week after the presentation (only a few children attended the second session, but this did not affect the results in any way) was that only one subject remembered the original configuration in all its details, and he had been tested by Method II (classification). True, a few subjects (cf. Mar at the age of 4;9) managed to reconstruct the four pairs of figures and an equal number (4 + 4) of vertical and horizontal, and of long and short, bars, but they failed to conserve the correct order of the figures or the bars, and even the best of them inverted the internal characteristics of at least one pair.

Thus, of ninety-five subjects, only four 8-year-olds and nine 11- to 12-year-olds succeeded in reproducing the correct order of the figures in their drawings, and one 13-year-old did likewise but added two rectangles which he placed between the squares and the ovals with perfect assurance. Of the forty-seven subjects tested by Method I, eleven produced an identical number of vertical and horizontal bars, and ten an identical number of long and short bars. However, only eight of these subjects observed both of these equalities at once.

By contrast, none of the forty-seven subjects tested by Method I (except for the reconstruction of one 8-year-old) reproduced the order *vhvh–hvhv* or *slls–lssl*, though one 5-year-old and one 7-year-old did offer *vhvhvhvh* and a 6;11-year-old came up with a similar alternation of *s* and *l*. Another common response was 4 *v*s followed by 4 *h*s or vice versa, often with all the *v*s as *s*s and all the *h*s as *l*s or vice versa. Many subjects also produced alternations of pairs of figures (two successive squares, two triangles, etc.),[1] but varied the order of the oppositions *sl* and *vh*.

As for the pairs themselves, which were contingent because each represented one combination in four, or one possible arrangement (combination and order) in eight, we found that the correct series (*C*) and the erroneous series (*F*) depicted in Figure 62 produced a choice of 49 *C* and 25 *F* in

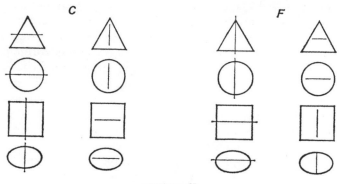

FIGURE 62

respect of the triangles, of 36 *C* and 36 *F* in respect of the circles, of 39 *C* and 27 *F* in respect of the squares, and of 24 *C* and 30 *F* in respect of the ovals. This distribution is not fortuitous; it depends on the schematization of the double oppositions, on the relative 'pregnancy' of the forms of the figures and on their position in the series.

All in all, it seems clear that the 'raw' memory plays no more than a limited rôle in these responses, while schematizations are of considerable importance. But it is equally clear that the use of schemata cuts both ways: it leads to errors no less than to the adequate organization and consolidation of the memory. When the original model is logico-mathematical, as in seriations or transitive relations, the subject assimilates it to his particular schemata, which leads to memory distortions at the lower levels and to increasingly correct

[1] By way of a control experiment, we presented the series in successive pairs (two triangles, two circles, two squares and two lozenges) to several subjects from 5;11 to 7;5 years. To our surprise, we discovered that the responses (after a week) were in no way improved: one 6;0-year-old drew nothing but horizontal bars and one 6;1-year-old omitted the bars altogether (Level I). Quite possibly the greater simplicity of this model served to diminish these subjects' analytical efforts.

recall at the higher level. On the other hand, if the model consists of a mixture of rationalizable and contingent elements, schematization produces useful results in respect of the former, but mistaken simplifications or total forgetfulness in respect of the latter. It is a very long time since Claparède first pointed to mistakes of eye-witnesses resulting from a tendency to reconstruct past events in the most probable way, when reality is so often the result of low-probability combinations. The same remarks apply to our present model, in which the memory often tends towards rationalizations based on the rejection of the contingent elements.

IV. Let us now look at the classifications produced during the first session. The problems these reactions threw up were not fore-seen by us when we devised the present series of tests. It was on the assumption that the 'raw' memory would play a considerable part in the remembrance, particularly by younger subjects, of the model, and because we were anxious to remedy the lack of attention frequently shown by young children when they are simply asked to memorize a model, that we decided to call for a classification of the figures. In this way we hoped to draw our subject's attention to the details of the model, or more precisely to encourage the most com-plete recording or encoding of the data to be retained. But then we discovered that schematization played a much greater rôle than we had expected, and that classifications became both an obstacle to our analysis (whence the use of Method II as a control) and an additional source of information.

In fact, if we assume that our subjects merely recall or reproduce the classificatory schemata they used during the first session, then we must also take it that classification must act as a supplementary impediment to the study of the memory as such. However, if we should find that recall and reconstruction are independent of the original classification and that they constitute the schematizations proper to mnemonic conservation and mnemonic reconstruction, then we can use the prior classifications to establish the level of the sub-ject's classificatory schemata and hence learn a great deal about their levels of mnemonic schematization.

In other words, our problem is to determine whether the classifica-tions supplied by the subject and his levels of recall or reconstruction are directly related, whether they merely converge, in detail or in general, or whether they are completely independent of one another. This is admittedly a delicate problem to resolve, but the comparison of Methods I and II provide an adequate check of our conclusions.

Here, then, are the classificatory levels we observed, having been careful not to press our subjects for exhaustive dichotomies, and bearing in mind that young children are more inclined to focus their attention on the differences and constant factors than on general similarities.[1]

Level I: a series of responses, which can be graded in part (IA with respect to IB and IC) or may represent the same stage of development (IB and IC).

IA: figural sets (generally rows) sometimes leading to alternations (large–small) and to differentiation based on one criterion (generally the shape of the basic figure).

IB: emergence of structuring with, for example, one-to-one correspondence based on a single criterion (such as the shape of the figure) or on two undifferentiated and unco-ordinated criteria, or on oppositions involving mixed criteria: though not generally exhaustive, this mode of classification culminates in the construction of random sets.

IC: small successive sets and a few complementary classes.

Level II: a whole range of reactions, with differentiation of the first and second criterion but not of the third (for example, long and short bars but no distinction between verticals and horizontals).

IIA: juxtaposition of sub-sets into sets (or division of one set into sub-sets) but no double multiplication.

IIB: beginning of double multiplication.

Level III: use of three successive classifications, but with suppression of one of the oppositions (for example, all the figures are placed in such a way that all the bars are horizontal).

Level IV: three criteria, applied successively or simultaneously.

The reader will see at once that though this hierarchy of levels is neither identical with, nor yet completely different from, that associated with recall or reconstruction, there is a clear functional correspondence between the two. If we merely consider Levels I–IV, and ignore the sub-levels (which, of course, makes our determination less precise and reliable), we find that our forty-seven 4;9- to 9-year-olds tested by Method I produced the following responses:[2]

$$Cl > D \quad Cl = D \quad Cl < D \quad Cl > R \quad Cl = R \quad Cl < R$$

$Cl > D$	$Cl = D$	$Cl < D$	$Cl > R$	$Cl = R$	$Cl < R$
11	26	10	4	26	17

These figures show that the classificatory level of these subjects corresponds very closely to that of recall, while that of the reconstructions is in advance of either. This becomes particularly clear from an examination of individual cases. For comparison, let us also

---

[1] The figures offered for classification were detached and mobile, but the bars had been glued to the cards, so that the children could fit the figures in such a way as to make the bars run horizontally or vertically across them.

[2] Explanation of symbols: $Cl > D$ means that the classification is of a higher level than the memory-drawing, etc; and $Cl < R$ that the classification is of a lower level than the reconstruction.

look at the corresponding responses of twenty dyslexic subjects aged from 6;9 to 10 years:

$$Cl > D \quad Cl = D \quad Cl < D \quad Cl > R \quad Cl = R \quad Cl < R$$
$$5 \qquad 9 \qquad 6 \qquad 2 \qquad 4 \qquad 14$$

Here again, the advance of the reconstructions on the classifications seems to persist with age, and this despite the fact that the classifications involved were quite simple.[1]

Level I classifications no less than Level I memory-drawings thus reflect a lack of structuring activities expressed differently in the two cases but springing from the same schematic difficulties.

GIG (4;11) began his classification with pairs of opposites: a triangle with a vertical bar and a square with a horizontal bar; a triangle and an oval, etc. Next, he constructed a row of figures which, except for the extremities, consisted of horizontal bars, followed by a row of alternating long and short bars, etc., but ignored the directions (IA). On recall, he produced three circles, one square and one triangle, all of them with long bars and running in different directions. In his reconstruction, the eight figures were aligned at random (no pairs) and all, except for the penultimate one, had horizontal bars (IC). The structure was therefore the same, but the contents had been changed.

SYL (5;0) based her classification on pairs; one triangle and one square with vertical bars; two circles with opposite bars (*sv* and *lh*); two ovals (*sh* and *lv*); two triangles (*sv* and *lh*) and two squares (*sh* and *lv*). As a result, she arrived at two sets, one with four distinct figures bearing large horizontal bars, and the other with the same four figures (not in correspondence with the first) bearing four small vertical bars (Level I-II). Her memory-drawing (IB) showed four different figures with all the bars horizontal (3 *l* and 1 *s*), and her reconstruction eight mixed figures all with horizontal bars but alternation of *s* and *l* (Levels I and II).

Clearly, at this level, remembrance one week after the presentation does not constitute a simple reproduction of the classification offered during the first session, but quite naturally represents the same structuring level. Nevertheless, the memory has become reorganized so as to comprise

---

[1] In this connection, it should be noted that the classifications of dyslexic children bear a remarkable resemblance to their memory-drawings: two subjects aged 6;9 and 5;10 years, respectively, who based their classifications exclusively on the shapes of the figures, also omitted the bars from their drawings (which did not prevent them from differentiating between *sv*, *sh*, *lv* and *lh* in their reconstructions!). Two subjects, aged 6;9 and 7;7 years respectively, based their classifications on the shapes of the figures, and the length of the bars, but neglected the directions of the latter: their drawings, on the other hand, consisted of horizontal bars only. A 7;5-year-old subject based his classification on shapes and directions, but, in his drawing, introduced horizontal and vertical bars all of the same (large) size (small bars, however, appeared in his reconstruction), etc. These cases illustrate the relationship between *Cl* and *D*, but also reflect the advance of the reconstructions on the classifications.

certain elements of the classification: this reorganization is, however, based on general convergence rather than on pure repetition. In this connection we must also mention the case of Mar, who straddled several levels:

MAR (4;9), whose remarkable progress from a memory-drawing of type IB to a reconstruction of Type IV we have already mentioned, produced a series of classifications that explained her exceptional advance: she began with four small sets based on pairs of figures, and hence with a double opposition of the bars (the reader will recall that the bars were glued on during the classification but not during the reconstruction). When asked to make another arrangement, she began with two circles (*sh* and *lv*) and placed two triangles underneath them (*lh* and *sv*), thus constructing a square matrix with *h* and *v* as the columns, and the figures as the rows. Next, she placed two ovals to the right of the original matrix, but one on top of the other, and then arranged two squares in the same way, thus constructing a new matrix, this time with the figures as the columns and the bars *hl* and *vs* as the rows. The two matrices did not correspond or constitue a unique system, but their use bore witness to a capacity for co-ordination that was absent from her memory-drawing (IB).

Level II sees the emergence of intermediate classifications with differentiation of the criteria and the appearance of sub-sets and matrices. In respect of the memory, too, this level is associated with the emergence of pairs and dichotomies:

JOS (6;0) began her classification with a combination of figures (two circles and two triangles), followed by a combination of long vertical bars (square and oval) and horizontal bars (triangle and circle). She thus arrived at two sets of rectilinear and curved figures, sub-dividing each into elements with vertical and horizontal bars respectively, but failed to construct a complete matrix (Level II). Her memory-drawing showed two pairs of figures (squares and triangles) each with *sh* and *sv*, and a circle with *sh*, i.e. an early attempt at (non-exhaustive) pair formation with all the bars of uniform size (Level II). Her reconstruction was complete and based on successive pairs, but again there was similarity in structure and a difference in content between the memory-drawing and the reconstruction and classification.

Classificatory Levels III and IV involve co-ordinations based on three criteria, first incomplete and then complete, which agrees precisely with the organization of the memory at the corresponding stages:

AR (6;11) began her classification with two pairs of figures with short and long bars respectively, but with inversion of the position in the case of the triangles. Next, she clustered all the curved figures on the left side and all the rectilinear figures on the right side (Figure 61 *e*), i.e. she constructed two square matrices, with corresponding figures paired diagonally in the left matrix, and horizontally in the right matrix, and the length of the bars in diagonal correspondence in the latter (Level III). Her memory-drawing and reconstruction consisted of almost correct pairs (III–IV).

BARC (7;1) produced two rows of pairs, with the rectilinear figures at the top, and the curved figures at the bottom. The bars were in correspondence, except for one switch as between the third and fourth columns. Her drawing (Figure 61 *f*) and reconstruction were of the same type (complete pairs and double opposition).

There is thus an undeniable correlation between the classification and the organization of the memory, but no direct interaction inasmuch as the contents are not generally identical in detail, except of course at the higher levels.

This poses two distinct problems; namely that of the convergence of the classification with the structure of the memory, and that of their possible, or even probable (indirect) interactions.

Convergence follows quite naturally from the preceding remarks: the mnemonic responses obtained by Method I are due in only small part to the 'raw' memory and rest chiefly on the schematization of resemblances and oppositions, which means that they are closely related to the classificatory schemata. As we shall see, the same schematism also enters into the responses obtained by Method II, so that it cannot possibly be due to the classifications demanded by Method I. However, we must still establish whether or not this schematism is of the same level as the operative schemata of children of comparative mental age.

As for the indirect effects of the classifications on the memory, they can be of two kinds, and it is important to define them before we go on to a discussion of Method II. They may, first of all, affect the correctness and general scope of the memory. As we have shown in our study of mental imagery,[1] the memory-image of an experimental model is generally better when the experiment involves some action or manipulation on the child's part than when the child confines himself to a simple perceptive examination (except at the higher levels, where perception affords an immediate glimpse of the possible actions). It is therefore only to be expected that, once the child has classified the figures he has been asked to remember, his memory should be more complete than when he merely looks at the model.

But there can also be a second type of effect. Let us suppose that a subject makes use of Level III schemata (classification by several criteria though not always systematically). This in no way prevents him from also employing Level II schemata (two criteria only) or even Level IIA and Level I schemata in other situations. Now, a prior classification would have brought out all his potentialities, thus

[1] See J. Piaget and B. Inhelder, *Mental Imagery in the Child*, Routledge & Kegan Paul, 1971, Chapter IX.

activating his Level III schemata: in that case, the prior classification would have been a cause of mnemonic progress, not directly and by simple transfer of its own contents or even of its own form, but by the stimulation of schemata that might otherwise have remained dormant.

§4. *The results of Method II one week after presentation*

The responses elicited by Method II (no prior classification of the figures) had the following, highly instructive, characteristics: (a) they proved to be of the same type of organization and the same succession of levels as the responses to Method I, thus demonstrating that neither the types of organization nor the levels were the result of the prior work of classification; and (b) successive levels proved to appear relatively late in the child's life, which corroborates our hypothesis that the preliminary classification stimulates the memory, not necessarily in a formative way (since the schemata are constructed even in its absence) but at least by activating the schematism inherent in the spontaneous development of our subjects (by 'spontaneous' we simply refer to the fact that the construction of schemata is the result of a host of activities and experiences, and not merely of laboratory tests).

I. The first thing we had to establish, therefore, was the qualitative identity of the responses. Now, the latter could once again be fitted into the levels we have established—from IA, through IB and IC to II, III and IV, so much so that there is no need to quote further examples. Moreover, we found once again that the reconstructions were well in advance of simple recall (drawings and descriptions): see Table 54.

As for the forms of the schematization, they proved to be so similar to those we have described that, for the sake of brevity, we felt entitled to combine the results of the two methods (see §2, III). Thus, the only two subjects who remembered the order of the figures were examined by Method II, and some of the drawings and reconstructions elicited by that method had the appearance of classifications. Pie (9;6), for example, produced a reconstruction (and his drawing was of the same type except for one inversion) containing several mistakes (Figure 61 *g*) but the correspondence schema of which was identical with that of many of the classifications.

When our subjects were questioned about the method of memorization they employed, which could easily be done with the older ones, their replies showed quite clearly that they relied on schemata of serial alternation or of classification: '*I saw that it was a series of standing and lying bars* . . . (12;6) '. . . *ovals, triangles, circles divided horizontally and vertically*' (12;8); '*It was*

347

the same thing twice over, but not with the black lines. You see, when one of the circles had a vertical line, the other was horizontal. And some of the lines stuck out, while others did not. It was all a bit of a gamble' (12;11). In other words whatever can be classified is remembered and the rest is forgotten. *'It was all done twice, because there were two kinds of lines'* (13;9), etc.

II. But though, qualitatively speaking, we find the same processes at work in the organization of the memory, no matter whether or not the child is asked for a prior classification, it is undeniable that successive levels of organization appear more slowly with Method II than they do with Method I.

Table 54 lists the distributions of Levels I–IV in comparable age groups (five to 7;8 years) (forty-seven subjects tested by Method I,

TABLE 54   *Drawings and reconstructions with Methods I and II*

	I	II	III	IV	I–II	III–IV
Drawings:						
Method I	17	7	14	9	24	23
Method II	18 (21)	7 (8)	6 (9)	4 (10)	25 (29)	10 (19)
Reconstructions:						
Method I	8	12	15	12	20	27
Method II	11 (13)	10 (12)	12 (17)	2 (6)	21 (25)	14 (23)

and thirty-five 5- to 9-year-olds tested by Method II; with the responses of forty-eight 5- to 14-year-olds in brackets).

The reader will see that the advantage, at all ages, is plainly with those subjects who began with a classification: 24 drawings of Levels I and II as against 23 of Levels III and IV, and 20 reconstructions of Levels I and II as against 27 of Levels III and IV; the corresponding figures for subjects who did not take the classification test were 25 to 10, and 21 to 14. This reflects a clear retardation in the organization of the memory, even though the levels, let us repeat, are qualitatively the same. If, on the other hand, we compare the reconstructions of these subjects with their drawings, we find that the two are almost identical (see Table 55).

In other words, when they are handed the experimental material, even those subjects who did not engage in a prior classification make immediate progress in co-ordination and schematization, and hence improve their memories. The reader will recall (§3, IV—comparison of *Cl* with *R*) that though the recall by subjects tested by Method I was roughly of the same level as their classifications, the reconstructions were well in advance (17 *Cl* < *R* as against 4

$Cl > R$) of the latter. It is this relative independence of the reconstructions that we find again in the present case; it would seem to support our view that subjects tested by Method II utilize the same schemata as those tested by Method I. True, they are less strongly stimulated by a task involving no more than simple memorization but during the reconstruction they show a clear tendency to improve their schematizations, though they are, of course, quite unable to recover what information they have lost when recording the data.

All in all, the similarities and dissimilarities of the responses of our two groups of subjects (Methods I and II) show how small is the difference between the 'raw' memory and the 'memory of meanings'. One of the boys (12;6) we questioned about his approach, said at first: 'It's my memory! I kept thinking of my subject and tried to get it straight in my head.' Thurstone would have been delighted by this remark, but the commentary that followed immediately afterwards

TABLE 55 *Comparison of Methods I and II ($R > D$ means that the reconstructions are in advance of the drawings)*

	$R > D$	$R \geqslant D$	$R = D$	$R \leqslant D$	$R < D$
Method I	19	6	16	4	2
Method II	18	7	18	3	2

would have warmed the heart of Carlson, because, as we saw earlier, this boy added: 'I saw that it was a series of standing and lying bars . . .'[1] And, in fact, no matter how empirical the set of objects or figures presented, and no matter how elementary the spatial, causal, ordinal, and other relations or the similarities and differences they introduce, these relations are nevertheless meaningful, and their systematization, however rudimentary, calls for schematization— without it the set of objects or figures would neither have been grasped nor retained by the memory.

§5. *The memory after several months*

Because our model did not readily lend itself to logical schematization (classification and ordination), and because its contingent aspects were considerable, there was no reason to expect that the memory after six months would show the least progress, or that there would even be a great deal of mnemonic conservation. We

---

[1] An 8;8-year-old (Method I) said similarly: 'When it was evening (horizontal bars) on one side, it was morning (vertical bars) on the other.'

349

nevertheless thought it worth while to make sure, and above all to examine the effects of a second presentation ('re-learning').

I. *Results with Method I after six months.* By and large, our assumption was proved correct except for one remarkable reconstruction. As far as graphic recall was concerned, sixteen of the original nineteen subjects tested by Method I produced responses greatly inferior to their original ones, three had remained at the same level, and there was not a single case of progress.

The regressions took the following form. One subject had completely forgotten the model. Another thought the model had comprised the letters SAMO. Eight subjects remembered the figures but not the bars; some of them only recalled two figures (triangle and circle) or three figures (square, circle, triangle plus a rectangle and a lozenge) or even 6–16 figures, including the square. One subject drew a triangle, a rectangle and two circles, one of which had a very thin bar, another subject drew two white squares and two black lozenges. Two subjects recalled the principle underlying the arrangement of the figures and bars, but carried their schematizations to absurd lengths: one of them merely produced a circle with a horizontal bar, and the other a triangle with *sv* and a recumbent oval with *lv*. The remaining drawings resembled those produced during the second session: only four of the eight figures were provided with bars (one case) or else all the figures (generally 4–6) had two bars each. These subjects are all at Levels 0 (no figures at all) IA–IC or II, the optimum case being one subject at Level II–III.

II. The material reconstructions several months after the presentation presented quite a different picture and a perfect justification of our distinction between the reconstructive memory and simple recognition and recall. Of seventeen subjects, only eleven had reverted to a lower level, five had remained stationary (including two cases of very slight regress) and there was even one case of clear progress!

The eleven regressive cases included two subjects who used the figures but omitted the bars, six subjects who placed the bars between the figures (the extreme case is illustrated in Figure 63), and three subjects who produced incomplete series with 1, 4 or 5 figures only (the single figure was offered by the same subject whose memory drawing had consisted of a single circle with a horizontal bar). The five stationary cases were at Level II–III.

As for the one subject who had made clear progress (Ris, 7;0), his responses are worth closer scrutiny. A week after the presentation he had produced a drawing of four figures all with vertical bars (Figure 64, I) and seven months later he made a drawing of five figures without bars (Figure 64, III). His mnemonic recall was therefore plainly inadequate (Level II followed by Level I). His reconstruction a week after presentation (Figure

64, II) showed that he had remembered the double opposition (*sl* and *hv*), though he produced seven horizontal bars and only one vertical one. His distribution of long and short bars, by contrast, was symmetrical: 4 and 4.

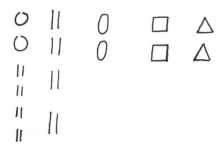

FIGURE 63

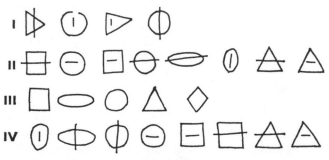

FIGURE 64

I. Drawing after one week; III. Drawing after six or more months; II. Reconstruction after one week; IV Reconstruction after seven months

Now, seven months later, his reconstruction took account of two symmetrical oppositions: two long vertical bars and two long horizontal bars, one small vertical bar and three small horizontal bars. Most significantly, Ris started with an oval bearing a large vertical bar, for which he himself substituted a small vertical bar to re-establish the opposition by pairs.

This advance allows of three interpretations: (1) pure chance, which must be ruled out in view of the correction he made quite spontaneously; (2) the effect of the new schemata that had emerged during the interval of seven months (Ris was 7;7 years old during the final test) and caused the subject to take a greater interest in questions of symmetry; and (3) the effects of a more or less schematized memory of the contrasts and symmetries based on the schemata of ordination and classification that were already at work 6½ months earlier, and merely became more active during the last reconstruction.

Now, without wishing to deny the rôle of mnemonic reconstruction (or the fact that the memory is always reconstructive in part and

351

not merely reproductive; see Chapter 16, §3, II), we think that the second interpretation does not meet the present case. Ris, in fact, had a schematized memory of the contrasts and symmetries even during his first reconstruction; moreover, in his original classification, he had divided the figures into two categories: four with long horizontal bars and four with small horizontal bars. No doubt, therefore, he must have retained part of his earlier schemata when he reconstructed the model six months later; he simply used them to better effect than he had originally done, and now linked part of the figurative material more closely to the conservation of his schemata. We shall meet the same problem in Section IV, where we shall be analysing five similar responses elicited by Method II.

This response, though exceptional in the present case, would therefore seem to fit into the same pattern as did mnemonic progress in the case of seriation, of transitive relations and of the sole advance in the domain of associative relations. But, as a general rule, mnemonic regress prevails over mnemonic progress, and this is particularly true of situations in which the rôle of the schemata is greatly reduced and in which the contingent data become lost for lack of a suitable framework.

III. We must now examine the effects of re-learning on subjects tested by Method I. Six months after the presentation, and immediately after the memory-drawings and reconstructions, twelve subjects were again presented with Figure 60, and invited to make a new classification and analysis. A week later, i.e. during a fourth session, they were asked for another memory-drawing and reconstruction. On comparing their responses with those we obtained six months earlier, we found:

(1) The memory-drawings of six subjects out of twelve proved to be at a higher level than they had been six months earlier; three had remained at the same level, and three had reverted to a lower level.

(2) In their reconstructions, nine of our twelve subjects had made progress (including one slight advance); three had remained at the same level; and not a single subject had regressed.

(3) A comparison of the memory-drawings and the reconstructions offered after the re-learning session showed that nine of the reconstructions were superior to the drawings and that three were of an equivalent standard.

Two facts are worth special mention. The first is that what progress in memory-drawings resulted from the re-learning session proved to be slight (50 per cent) when compared with what happened in the case of associative relations (Chapter 6, §3): with the latter, ten of the eleven subjects below Level V advanced to higher levels; whereas, in the present case, not a single subject remembered the model completely. This is because associative relations force the subject to solve a problem, while the present model is more akin to that used in classical re-learning experiments, in which the improvements are cumulative.

The second striking fact is the advance of the reconstruction on recall, which is in line with our observations in Sections I and II of this chapter on the relationship between recall and reconstruction six months after the presentation.

IV. *The results of Method II (no classification) after twelve to sixteen months.* Since every one of our tests necessarily extends over several sessions, it is often difficult to retrace the same subjects after a fixed interval, or, for that matter, to find collaborators with enough spare time to continue the research at a given date. Thus, in the case of Method II, we were unable to resume the tests six months after the presentation, as originally planned, but had to defer them until the following year. Ought we therefore to have abandoned the whole investigation? In genetic psychology, nothing ventured means nothing gained, because the unclaimed territory is so vast that every road is more or less uncharted.

We had a number of surprises. The first was that of the twenty-six 5;3 to 10;9-year-olds we were able to bring back (and who, like ourselves, were now one year older), only a single one (6;1) remembered nothing at all of the model. Our second surprise was that the remaining twenty-five subjects remembered either two figures (one 8;3-year-old: circle and triangle); three figures (four subjects: circle, triangle and square sometimes transformed into a rectangle); four, five and up to six figures (eight subjects). Twelve subjects also recalled the bars (which three of them admittedly placed outside the figures). Another subject drew a small black square inside a bigger one and a small black triangle inside a square, while one drew a square containing a series of letters.

Our third surprise was that, of the twenty-six memory-drawings, three had improved slightly during the interval (cf. the case of Ris), while one was comparable to the original drawing.

PAR (6;1), who, a week after the presentation, had drawn three figures only, drew six 15 months later, including three pairs with simple opposition of bars[1] (orientation). He began by furnishing each figure with two bars (one vertical, the other horizontal), but then corrected himself. All his bars were long, as in his first drawing.

MAN (7;0) also produced three pairs with simple opposition of bars, while his drawing six months earlier had been of three isolated figures.

[1] Admittedly one of his pairs consisted of a circle and an oval, but the other two were squares and triangles.

GEN (7;8) also drew three pairs with simple opposition of bars, while his drawing twelve months earlier had been of four figures and one singly opposed pair.

AN (6;3) produced a drawing that bore a striking resemblance to her first attempt: an empty triangle and two pairs of figures (circles and triangles) with two simple oppositions.

Of those subjects who offered inferior drawings, three nevertheless remembered the presence of at least one pair with a simple opposition of bars; the others drew empty figures (generally correct in shape, but with the frequent addition of rectangles) or figures filled with bars at random. A single subject transformed his figures into semi-empirical forms: circular and triangular traffic signs.

As for the reconstructions (demanded after the drawings but during the same session), they were, as expected, generally in advance of the drawings. Thus, fourteen of our twenty-six subjects produced a second reconstruction that was better than their second drawing, while the other twelve had remained at the same level. Of the fourteen superior reconstructions, ten divided the eight figures into four pairs; seven of these subjects introduced simply opposed bars, and the other three even offered doubly opposed bars (orientation and size), thus showing that they had made remarkable progress since their reconstructions twelve to fifteen months earlier:

PAR (6;1–7;4), offered a second reconstruction (fifteen months after the first) of four pairs of figures with all the bars correctly placed, while his first reconstruction had shown two simply and two doubly opposed bars.

MAN (8;11), who, in his memory-drawing, had transformed the four figures into traffic signs, was able to reconstruct one double and three single oppositions; whereas, twelve months earlier, he had merely aligned six figures, including one pair with doubly opposed bars, one pair with singly opposed bars and two isolated figures.

LIL (9;1), who, during her first reconstruction, had offered seven figures (one of them isolated), two simple oppositions and one double, offered four pairs, three simple oppositions and one double, twelve months later.

Such, then, were the responses a year or more after the presentation, of subjects originally examined by Method II, i.e. without a prior classification. We see, first of all, that these responses are clearly superior to those elicited six months after the presentation from subjects tested by Method I—the drawings of the latter never went beyond Levels I and II (except for one case at Level II–III), while, in the present case, there were at least three Level II–III responses. Similarly the best reconstructions obtained six months after the presentation with Method I were six Level II–III responses, plus the case of Ris (III–IV), while Method II produced one clear

Level IV and two Level III–IV responses. But, above all, Method I produced just one case of progress after six months, and that in respect of the reconstructions, while Method II, as we have just seen, gave rise to three advances over the earlier drawings (offered after twelve to sixteen months) and to three advances over the earlier reconstructions (after twelve to fifteen months)!

In other words, if it is true to say that the classifications and analyses called for by Method I serve to improve the memory (but, as we saw, in a chronological rather than a qualitative sense), then it follows that at least some subjects tested by Method II must employ similar procedures or schemata, since they ended up by surpassing the first group. Admittedly this advance was not the general rule, for there were marked memory deteriorations as well, and that with both methods. But it nevertheless occurs in five subjects out of twenty-six, and we must now try to explain the reason for this unexpected result.

Now, Man, before making his drawing, gave the following answers to our questions: 'Do you remember the little game we played?—*Yes, there were circles and bars.*—Anything else?—*Yes, there were rectangles, triangles with bars, and squares.*—And what can you tell me about the bars?—*They were straight* (vertical) *or flat.* Par, having finished his reconstruction, explained that he remembered *a circle with a big straight bar.*—And that one (the second circle)?—*I knew that one ran in the other direction.* And Lil had this to say of the triangles: '*Yes, they were* (crossed by bars) *in opposite directions.*' In other words, these subjects made use of *at least* two schemata: classification (of the simplest geometrical figures) and opposition of directions. None of them remembered the complete model, but they all recalled some of the figures and part of the compositional schema. The fact that the latter should give rise to greater improvements in composition after a lapse of a year or more can only be explained in one way: because the subject has grown older (from 6;1 to 6;4 years in the case of Par; from 7;0 to 8;4 years in the case of Man, etc.) he has also become more capable of performing mobile compositions and hence of restructuring the original mnemonic material. After all, we adults, too, behave in much the same way in a great number of cases.

§6. *Conclusion: the nature of the reconstructive memory*

The main lesson to be drawn from this chapter, quite apart from the fact that it brought out the remarkable resemblance of the responses elicited by Methods I and II, relates to the nature of the reconstructive memory.

One might have expected that a configuration with as many contingent elements as our present model would only give rise to mediocre memories, so mediocre, in fact, that the reconstructions could not be expected to be greatly superior to the drawings. However, we found that twenty-five of our forty-seven 4- to 7-year-olds (53 per cent) tested by Method I offered superior reconstructions a week after the presentation; that thirteen out of twenty 6- to 10-year-old dyslexic subjects (65 per cent) produced similar responses, and that twenty-five out of the forty-eight subjects (52 per cent) tested by Method II did likewise. Again, six months after the presentation, subjects tested by Method I produced six superior reconstructions out of seventeen (35 per cent), and this proportion went up to 75 per cent (nine subjects out of twelve) after the re-learning session. Finally, twelve to sixteen months after the presentation, 53 per cent of the subjects tested by Method II offered superior reconstructions (fourteen subjects out of twenty-six without the re-learning test).

This poses an interesting problem: in a situation that so closely resembles those normally studied in connection with the 'raw' memory (remembrance of objects, words, numbers, etc.) how is it possible that reconstructions should be so much superior to mnemonic recall, and how is it that the reconstructive memory should, in so many respects, resemble the recognitory memory, when reconstruction calls for the additional recall of relations and combinations that are not given in the material itself (if a child is simply handed eight figures, in four pairs, and twenty bars of two different lengths, he does not necessarily know what to do with them)? Now, we saw that, though Mar (4;9) and one dyslexic subject aged 6;10 years had very poor recall of the model one week after the presentation (Levels IB and IA), they nevertheless produced near-correct (Level IV) reconstructions. We also saw that, six months after the presentation, Ris (7;0) drew five figures without bars (including an additional lozenge), but immediately afterwards came up with an almost perfect reconstruction, and one, moreover, that was greatly superior to the reconstruction he himself had offered one week after the presentation. Finally, there was the case of Par, who at the age of 7;4 years, produced a reconstruction based on four double oppositions, while at the age of 6;1 years he had merely offered two double and two single oppositions.

The first explanation to spring to mind is that reconstructions are actions and that actions presuppose the use of schemata. Now, schemata are more readily conserved than figurative memories, simply because they conserve themselves, much as habits do. However, the particular reconstructions we are considering here, though admittedly so many actions, cannot possibly be of the re-petitive kind normally associated with habits: the subject has never copied the actual configuration but has merely produced correla-tions and classifications, and even this, only with Method I.

In the case of habits, the underlying schema is elaborated as a function of its very formation and involves the construction of meaningful signs, whose recognition is thus dependent on the schema; in that case, the memory (or rather the recognitive memory) is essenti-ally based on the conservation of the schema, and mnemonic reten-tion does not raise a distinct problem.

In the case of reconstructions, on the other hand, the only schemata involved are those activated during the presentation, i.e. by the perceptive examination of the model or by the correlations and classifications demanded in Method I, none of which calls for a manipulative reproduction of the model. The real problem, therefore, is to explain why it is that these schemata—if schemata are indeed involved!—are more easily reactivated and reorganized in the course of manual reconstructions than they are in the course of verbal or graphic recall.

Now, the main importance of the fact that the reconstructions are superior to recall is precisely that it proves the intervention of schemata. If 'remembrance' were based exclusively on memory-images, that superiority would be quite inexplicable. True, associa-tionists would contend that the very presence of the figures and bars sets up associations tending to awaken old memories. But in that case, the same associations and memories would also be produced by the child's drawings. It might, of course, be argued that the pro-vision of cardboard figures and bars identical to those included in the original model creates more vivid associations than do the child's imperfect drawings. True enough, but why does it? Pre-cisely because the child manipulates such figures and bars much more actively than he does his drawings and thoughts, so that his so-called associations turn out to be assimilations to his action schemata. Hence, the advance of the reconstruction over pure recall.

Let us now return to our central problem: why it is that schemata activated momentarily during the presentation should become re-activated so much more easily, and above all why they should be-come co-ordinated so much better during the reconstruction than they do during recall. In the case of transitive or associative relations, the answer is much simpler, because, in that case, we are dealing with operative sequences, and the reconstruction is, in fact, an action. In the case of the present model, on the other hand, which is pre-dominantly figurative, it seems most strange that the memory-image

357

constituting pure recall should lend itself less readily to the conservation and reproduction of the model than does an active reconstruction.

Now, this paradoxical situation proves simply that the memory-image cannot be conserved without a support. When it was first formed, it involved the assimilation of the perceived data to a number of schemata: succession (actions to be ordinated); similarity and contrasts (actions to be classified); size (coincidence or non-coincidence of the end points); direction (active orientation), etc. The same schemata are admittedly at work in simple recall as well, but they are not activated, because the memory-image symbolizing them does not suffice to reconvert them into actions—it has been forgotten to a large extent, and before it can reappear or be reconstructed, it needs the support of the relevant schemata. In the case of active reconstructions, on the other hand, manipulation activates the schemata directly, and the latter, in turn, determine the quality of the memory-image. In other words, recall is inferior to reconstruction simply because it reverses the order of events: actions $\rightarrow$ schemata $\rightarrow$ memory-images; whereas the reconstructive memory, based on actions, constitutes an 'active genesis', i.e. it repeats the genetic order.[1]

This fundamental fact explains why schemata combine into a more adequate whole during reconstructions than they do during recall; because recall reverses the genetic order and starts from the results, it cannot be complete in the absence of an over-all representation, in which all the elements are already co-ordinated; a reconstruction, on the other hand, repeating as it does the actual order of events, proceeds in such a way that every partial co-ordination involves the next, as in the original process.

It is therefore in the fullest sense, and not just for the sake of symmetry, that we are entitled to speak of the reconstructive memory as a distinct stage situated between mnemonic recognition and recall by images. At the sensori-motor levels, recognition is bound up with repetitive actions (suction reflexes, habits, etc.) which, in turn, are quite obviously bound up with schemata. Recall in its superior forms relies on memory-images which have a far greater mobility and independence and whose links with the schemata of the intelligence continue to pose a problem: we believe that these links are quite general, but this is only one hypothesis among many and, if we are right, it follows that the schemata of which the memory-image is the symbolic representation must be highly differentiated and particularized. Situated between recognition and recall, mnemonic recon-

[1] More precisely, reconstructions involve the order actions $\rightleftharpoons$ schemata $\rightarrow$ memory-images, because every action reactivates a schema.

structions represent a form of recall by actions, and, as such, promote recall by images, while remaining quite distinct from them.

Now, if there are indeed three distinct mnemonic spheres, we must expect the existence of a host of sub-levels, and these we shall be examining in greater detail in the final chapter (§3, III).

CHAPTER TWENTY

The Reconstruction of a Geometrical Configuration with Partly Regular and Partly Contingent Elements[1]

The mnemonic reconstruction of spatial configurations deserves further consideration, not so much in order to demonstrate that it is easier to effect than pure recall (which, we think, has been established) but for the purpose of analysing its components more closely. To that end we deployed a model more difficult to remember than the last, and one in which the rôle of the organizing schematization was not only more pronounced, but also increased with age.

The model is shown in Figure 65, and the reader will see at once that it comprises a number of regular, as well as a number of contingent, features. It may be asked why we did not simply choose a

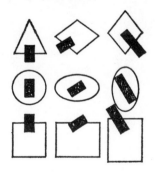

FIGURE 65

model with purely contingent features, so that the attribution of meanings, which may vary from one individual to the next, is neutralized as much as possible. However, this suggestion reflects a double bias, namely: that it is possible to effect a maximum dissociation between the memory and the intelligence, and that meanings can be eliminated.

[1] In collaboration with J. and M.-J. Delcourt and G. Voyat.

360

The first objection to all such attempts to isolate the 'raw' memory is that they blur the distinction between reconstruction and recall: thus, to evaluate the remembrance of nonsense syllables, we must ask the subject to repeat them, which amounts to a reconstruction. But there is a second and even graver objection: no matter what material we present to our subjects, we are invariably inviting them to engage in mental co-ordinations based on a regard for order, resemblances and contrasts, spatial structures, etc. Now, inhibitory, prospective and retrospective actions abound in relations of this type, for instance when resemblances to a newly learned name suppress the memory of an earlier name, albeit momentarily. These complex relations, which intervene continuously in all presentations, are in fact meanings, for we are not entitled to reserve this term for purely abstract and highly conceptualized notions. In fact, perception itself is a system of meanings that are partly isomorphous with conceptual and even with operational meanings—the same criteria apply to both perceptive and conceptual 'good forms'. Intellectual operations involve spatio-temporal or causal factors as well as systems of formal concepts, and hence apply to all models whether the subject realizes this fact or not; genetically speaking, they all start out as concrete forms that help to structure the perceptive and figural data. It follows that the logical memory is of necessity involved in all forms of remembrance, be they 'raw' or 'meaningful'.

That is precisely why we decided not to use a purely contingent model (i.e. one in which the logical and operative relations intervene no less than they do in other models, but in a highly complicated way and, moreover, in a way that differs from one individual to the next), but to employ a mixed configuration, the mnemonic structuring of which we can observe more easily and relate more closely to the subject's intellectual development. It is, in fact, essential to bear in mind that, no matter what material we present, the subject's intelligence necessarily intervenes during the three essential phases of mnemonic activity: during fixation, by determining the general structuring of the data to be retained; during retention, by presiding over the organization of the 'memory traces'; and during recall and reconstruction, by determining the re-elaboration of what has been retained. It was therefore in order to come to closer grips with the organizing, and possibly operational, schematism at work in each phase of the mnemonic process, that we thought it best to employ a model reflecting a large variety of relations: number and orientation of the figures; size and orientation of the bars; order of succession of the figures and bars; general presentation of the model in the form of a matrix involving the bars and partly the size of the figures, but not the vertical succession of the latter. In this way we hoped to discover the extent and the rôle of the schemata involved in the reconstruction. In particular, we were anxious to determine whether, in a model so much more complex than the one we described in the last chapter, a prior classification of the figures would facilitate and accelerate the structuring of the memory with age or whether, on the contrary, it would add nothing from a certain level of development onwards, i.e. from the moment when the attentive inspection of the figures suffices to impose the necessary classifications.

§1. *Methods used*

We began by dividing our five- to thirteen-year-old subjects into two groups. The first, consisting of thirty children, began with a classification of the material (Method I) and then went on to copy the model (by manipulating the figures and mobile bars). The second group (thirty-eight subjects) was asked neither for a classification nor for a copy, but proceeded directly to a reconstruction one hour, one week and several months after the presentation (Method II). The responses showed that five- to six-year-olds, as well as twelve- to thirteen-year-olds, are not greatly influenced by the classifications and copies they have been asked to provide, the former because they fail to appreciate their significance for lack of sufficient powers of assimilation, and the latter because they have no need of them to take stock of the situation during perceptive inspection. By contrast, seven- to eight-year-olds produce clearly superior responses when tested by Method I. We accordingly added two special groups each of ten 7- to 8-year-olds, demanding a classification but no copy from the first (Method IA) and a copy but no classification from the second (Method IIA). This brought the total number of subjects to eighty-eight.

Method I. The following material was used:

(a) a model board measuring 25 × 20 cm, to which were glued the nine figures: the circle having a diameter of 25 mm, the rectangle measuring 25 × 40 mm, and the bars measuring 10 × 5, 20 × 5 and 30 × 5 mm. The figures were pink and the bars black;

(b) nine cardboard rectangles, each measuring 5 × 5·5 cm (with a black line underneath) and each depicting one of the nine figures and the appropriate bars;

(c) a blank sheet of cardboard measuring 25 × 20 cm, on which the model could be copied;

(d) a ruled sheet of cardboard measuring 25 × 20 cm and divided into nine empty compartments each measuring 5 × 5·5 cm;

(e) a reference board with the nine shapes glued on (each inside a circle of diameter 17 cm) and an assortment of black bars;

(f) four sets of nine figures each (Figure 65), three of which were placed in a pile on the fourth which was glued to the board (without bars).

The first session began with a classification: the figures were jumbled up and placed on the cardboard (b) and the subjects were asked to make 'small piles of those that are alike'. Their justifications were noted, and the examiner tried (but without too much insistence) to get the subjects to classify the whole material. Next, he asked for a second classification: 'Can you arrange them differently and find other things that go together?

There followed a classification on the ruled sheet (d): the figures were again jumbled up and the child was told: 'Place all the figures into these compartments so that everything fits together.' Next came the copy: the examiner produced the model board (a) and the blank sheet (c) and said: 'Look carefully at this board. You can see that these are the same shapes you saw earlier. Copy them all on the blank sheet, taking all the figures you need from here (f) and all the bars from there (e).'

The examiner then concluded with: 'In a moment, you will have to do the same thing again but without the model. So look carefully and try to get everything properly into your head.' The inspection took thirty seconds.

During the second session (at most an hour after the presentation), the subjects were asked for a reconstruction $R1$ (without any prior drawing), for which purpose they were handed the experimental material (plus a number of additional elements) in disarray.

The third session (reconstruction $R2$) was held a week later and was identical with the second.

The fourth session was held six to nine months later, and consisted of a reconstruction ($R3$) followed by a recognition test, in which the child had to pick out the correct set of figures (no bars) from a total of six models.

Method IA. Same procedure, but no copy during the first session.

Method II (no classification or copy). During the first session the subject was shown the model sheet (a) and told: 'You see this sheet with the small pink figures, don't you? Can you tell me their names? (...) And then there are some bars running like this ... (gestures). I should like you to keep it all in your head, because, after your break, I shall ask you to do the same thing by yourself.' The demonstrator then uncovered the reference board containing three sets of each of the figures together with an assortment of loose bars and said: 'You will have to repeat it all (sheet (a)) on this bit of cardboard (sheet (c)). I shall hand you whatever figures you point out on this board (the reference sheet). As for the black bars, you will have to pick them out for yourself and arrange them in the right order. Meanwhile look carefully at the sheet and try to remember it all, so that you will be able to do the same thing by yourself.'

The second session was held an hour later and it was only now that the child actually proceeded to the reconstruction $R1$.

Third and fourth sessions: as with Method I.

Method IIA. This method involved manipulative copying during the first session, but no classification.

§2. *The hierarchy of characteristics*

I. We set out to establish a hierarchical order, based on a number of characteristic features of the model, which we intended to use as potential criteria of evaluation, and we selected nine of these in the assumed order of increasing difficulty. There is no need to mention

that order, though the reader might like to know that only characteristics VII, VIII and IX proved on further analysis to fit it quite
unequivocally, which shows that the hierarchy we were trying to
establish proved resistant to all prior interpretations. We were all the
more pleasantly surprised to discover that all thirty-three subjects we
were able to bring back several months after the interpretation
(seventeen of whom had been tested by Method I, and sixteen by
Method II) fitted almost perfectly into a hierarchical series based on
the work of Guttmann, and in such a way that the successful use
of any one criterion K meant success with all the preceding criteria
A, B, etc., but not with the subsequent criteria L, M, etc. Moreover,
we discovered that this hierarchy, which applied quite generally
during the first reconstruction $R1$ (one hour after the presentation),
also applied, except for a few exceptions (for example, two out of
twenty-nine cases in respect of characteristic I, two out of twenty-
seven in respect of characteristic II, etc.) with the same regularity to
the second reconstruction ($R2$; one week after the presentation) and,
again, with some exceptions, to the third reconstruction (several
months later). In other words, though our findings were, of course,
partly relative to our method of evaluation, which was based on the
all-or-nothing principle that approximate successes count as fully
correct responses, the conventions themselves did not change with
time, and hence, lent themselves to ordination. Here, then, are the
characteristics we discovered, in order of increasing difficulty, and
with an indication of their use as criteria of evaluation.

The first group of characteristics (I–III) relates to the number of
distinct orientations of the figures and bars, and to the number of
distinct sizes of the bars:

(I) *Number of distinct orientations of the figures.* The responses to this
characteristic are of four types: remembrance of random orientations;
remembrance of one orientation only (recumbent or vertical); remembrance
of two distinct orientations; and remembrance of three distinct orientations (only the fourth response has been treated as successful).

(II) *Number of distinct sizes (bars).* There are three possibilities: remembrance of a single size; of two distinct sizes; and of three distinct sizes
(only the last response has been treated as successful).

(III) *Number of distinct orientations (bars).* There are four reactions: one
or several orientations not found in the model; a single orientation; two
distinct orientations, and, finally, three distinct orientations (success).

The second group of characteristics (IV–VI) relates to the absolute
number of figures and bars, and also to the general form of the
nine-figure model:

(IV) *Absolute number of figures.* The number given varied from 0 to 20,
especially in the case of five- to six-year-olds, but four 7- to 8-year-olds out

of the twenty-three tested by Method II came up with more than nine figures, no doubt because they confused the model with the figures provided during the selection test. The only response treated as successful was nine figures.

(V) *Total number of bars*. Here, again, the number ranged from nine to twenty and we only accepted the number nine.

(VI) *General form of the model*. The responses included random alignments of vaguely rectangular or square forms but not in rows or columns, or correct forms without classification of the figures. If we may take it that the remembrance of this characteristic presupposes the prior retention of characteristics IV and V, then we may treat as successful responses, not only completely correct solutions, but also arrangements that are correct except in respect of one position; arrangements with a correct first column but an irregular arrangement of the six remaining and otherwise correctly classified figures; and, finally, the correct matrix (rows, columns, shape and number of figures) with some of the elements in the wrong positions.

The third group of characteristics (VII–IX) is the most difficult to remember because it relates to the position and order of the bars:

(VII) *Position of bars relative to the horizontal median of the figures*. There were four responses: random positions; correct position of one of the bars; correct position of two of the bars; and correct positions of three of the bars (success).

(VIII) *Number of different positions of the bars with respect to the figures*. The most common response was to start from one correct relation (for example, the triangle with the small vertical bar on its base) and then either to extend it to all the other figures, which is erroneous, or else to deduce all sorts of oppositions, most of them quite arbitrary. When we asked five adults to reconstruct the model soon after the presentation, only one of them was able to reproduce the nine positions (but he, too, reversed the position of the circle and one of the ovals and of the square and one of the rectangles). Not a single child was able to reconstruct all nine positions; hence, we treated as successful responses all reconstructions with three to seven correct positions.

(IX) *Order of succession of bars and figures*. This characteristic differs from the last in that, instead of bearing on the number of positions, it bears on the relational or classificatory criteria employed by the subjects: no classification at all; distribution by pairs; distribution based on two criteria (rows and columns) but with the figures themselves misplaced; etc. Of five adults, not a single one proved successful; the best of them reproduced the correct size, orientation and position of the bars but, as we saw, misplaced the circle and the square. With children, we accordingly treated as successful all responses involving the correct use of at least two criteria: correlation of bars and figures, of rows and figures, or of columns and figures.

Applying the same conventions we used to assess success with characteristics VII–IX, we found that the whole set constituted a more or less clear-cut hierarchical order. Here, then, in Table 56, are the details of the three reconstructions offered by the thirty-three subjects we were able to bring back six to nine months after the presentation (in absolute number of successful reactions).

The rare inversions (i.e. the fact that 17 follows 16 in the top row, that 18 follows 17 in the second row, and that 11 follows 10 in the third row) were all due to the exceptions we have mentioned, namely, that one subject who remembered VIII successfully, did not remember VI, etc. However, though these exceptions leave some doubt as to the sequential order of our nine characteristics taken individually, the hierarchy of the three major categories I–II, IV–VI and VII–IX seems to be established beyond reasonable doubt, especially if we compare the results of the three successive reconstructions—an hour, a week and several months after the initial presentation.

II. The significance of the three major categories is not as obvious as it would seem at first sight. Thus, it is tempting to rely mainly on a comparison of the first group of characteristics (I–III) with the last (VII–IX), and to consider those characteristics which are easiest to remember (I–III) as expressions of the most figural or contingent aspects, and those hardest to remember (VII–IX) as involving a schematizable relational structure. But why, for example, should the number of distinct orientations (I) be the easiest property of all to retain? Clearly, because the general configuration is regular in this respect (Figure 65); had the same nine forms been presented as in Figure 66, the remembrance of the orientations would have proved

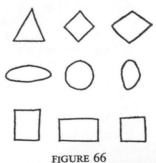

FIGURE 66

considerably more difficult. It could accordingly be argued that the order is inherent in the over-all figure and that it has not been constructed by the subject. But the most obvious result of the Table is that this over-all figure did not impress itself on the memory (see point VI); if, therefore, the remembrance of the distinct orientations of the figures is due to the regularity of the general arrangement, it is because that regularity served as an instrument of classification or

TABLE 56 *Successful use of the nine characteristics during three reconstructions*

Characteristics	I	II	III	IV	V	VI	VII	VIII	IX	I-III	IV-VI	VII-IX
R1 (1 hour)	29	28	26	23	23	16	17	16	7	83	62	40
R2 (1 week)	29	24	23	23	23	17	18	14	6	76	62	38
R3 (6–9 months)	15	10	11	8	6	8	4	3	3	36	22	10

ordination and not as a purely perceptive stimulus. The same remark applies *a fortiori* to the three distinct lengths of the bars and to their three distinct orientations. One might therefore consider category I–III as a rudimentary form of schematization of the figural data, but of data whose regular features are treated in what is already a classificatory or ordinative way, based on resemblances and contrasts that have been noted and combined as such. The result is a primitive organization of the memory, which explains why characteristics I–III are remembered better than the rest; whereas, if all that was involved was the remembrance of the fortuitous or figural elements, our subjects would have remembered characteristics IV–IX just as often, seeing that these characteristics include as many contingent and figurative aspects.

Characteristics IV–VI, which might have been thought even easier to remember, in view of the so-called 'global' aspect of perception and of infantile thought, in fact represent progress in schematization: reconstructing the model with the exact number of figures and bars, does not mean relying on a global effect, but calls precisely for a restructuring effort. To do so, the subject can no longer content himself with isolating the fairly regular sequences of orientations and lengths by their similarities and contrasts, as he can with characteristics I–III; the elements must be classified in accordance with these relations, no less than in accordance with their position in a figural system (VI) corresponding to that classification, which presupposes the correct evaluation of their number (IV and V). Here, we have a new schematization, and, as it were, of a logical 'type' directly superior to the preceding one.

With characteristics VII–IX, we reach a third stage in this process of schematizing the so-called 'global' factors involved in the reorganization of characteristics IV–VI. When applied to the present case, no less than to most others, this word, which many authorities use as a blanket term, simply refers to a lack of structuring activity, which comes back to posing, and not to resolving, the problem of why there should be such a lack. Now the over-all forms schematized in VI are 'global' precisely because they still lack the relational analysis of characteristics VII–IX.

Characteristic VII provides us with a striking illustration of this point. As Table 56 shows, it is remembered almost as frequently as characteristic VI: 17 against 16 in respect of $R1$; 18 against 17 in respect of $R2$, but 4 against 8 in respect of $R3$.[1] Now, the reader will

---

[1] Most subjects succeed with VI and fail with VII in $R3$ (5 against 1), whereas success with VII and failure with VI in $R1$ and $R2$ was chiefly confined to four young subjects who succeeded with I–II or I–III and VII, and none of the other characteristics.

see at once that, in order to position the bars correctly (characteristic VII), the subject must be concerned with the over-all form of the model (characteristic VI), so much so that remembrance of characteristic VII is simply the result of a relational analysis within the framework of characteristic VI, and vice versa. Similarly, the analysis of the different positions of the bars (characteristic VIII) and, above all, of the order of succession of the figures and bars (characteristic IX), constitutes a more extensive schematization than that of characteristic VI, in such a way that we are again faced with a transition to a higher logical 'type'.

III. In short, the hierarchy of the characteristics I–II, IV–VI and VII–IX reflects schematic progress in the organization of the memory. Now, as we have already noted in connection with a similar model (Chapter 19) and as we are about to establish more precisely in this chapter, mnemonic schematization can have two distinct results, as, indeed, can all methods based on trial and error: success and adequate organization, or failure and distorting simplification, the former naturally increasing with age.

In respect of the successful schematizations, we found that of the thirty-three 5- to 13-year-olds we re-examined after an interval of six to ten months and more, twelve remembered nothing at all, fourteen remembered no more than one to three characteristics (of these, twelve in the category I–IV, the remaining two retaining characteristics VI or I–II and VII); and seven remembered four to eight characteristics, and, of these, five in the category VII–IX. Now, of the fourteen subjects who remembered one to three characteristics, only seven had recalled characteristics I–III during R1 and R2, while the other seven and the seven who remembered four to eight characteristics had all recalled characteristics I–VIII or I–IX. There was thus a clear correlation between the schematizations produced during R1 and R2 and retention during R3; in particular, the three subjects who produced the most successful responses in R3 (characteristic IX) had all engaged in schematization during R1 and R2. In other words, we discovered once again that the more organized the data the better is their conservation, though it should be added that the organization we have in mind cannot be loosely defined in the way that perceptive *Gestalts* can, but that it is more or less isomorphous with the process of operational schematization, even though the data are figural (classification, order, correspondences, matrices, etc.). It was thus that a 6;6-year-old told us: 'I *see* it all in my mind, not in words', and that a twelve-year-old declared: 'I remember it all by logic.'

As for the mistaken or completely unsuccessful schematizations, which decrease with age, they are due chiefly to the fact that elements originally forgotten are subsequently misconstructed and substituted for others: this, too, is a form of schematization, and as such obeys the same laws, but nevertheless leads to errors because the model is partly fortuitous and contingent. And this distorting schematization can intervene during mnemonic conservation no less than at the point of recall or reconstruction.

IV. This brings us to the more difficult, though closely related, question of the remembrance of the fortuitous or contingent aspects of each of the characteristics I–IX. To begin with, it is quite impossible to divide these characteristics into two distinct groups: one contingent and the other more or less logically organized. Each characteristic contains both aspects: the orientations, numbers, sizes, etc. are all partly ordered and partly contingent, since they could all have been otherwise than they are.

What, then, are the reactions of our subjects to the contingent elements (for example, to the fact that the bars protruding from the bottom of the figures are all in the upper row, that those protruding from the top are all in the lower row, or that columns two and three of the first row are occupied by lozenges and not by triangles, etc.)? Our collaborators advanced all sorts of hypotheses: that young subjects have better retention of the fortuitous elements than do older subjects, because these elements are figural (characteristics I–III); or that older subjects are more successful in that respect, as witness their superior retention of the positions and succession of the bars (characteristics VII to IX); that both these interpretations are correct (as reflected in the percentages) but for quite different reasons; that remembrance of the fortuitous elements is the better the poorer the schematization, or that, on the contrary, the more highly structured the reorganization of the memory, the better is the conservation of the arbitrary elements, etc.

Now, these apparent contradictions revolve round three fundamental facts, which must all be taken into account:

(1) We have seen that schematizations have two poles—depending on whether the organization of the schemata is differentiated and adapted or whether it is simplifying and distortive—and the same is true of the contingent or arbitrary elements. On the one hand, they can impede the schematizations or tend to eliminate them. Thus, it would have been reasonable to expect that the first row of triangles and lozenges would have been followed by a second row of rectilinear figures (square–rectangles) and a third row of curved figures (circle–ovals): since the order was arbitrarily reversed, two adults out of five restored what they wrongly thought was the correct order, and

370

so did several seven- to eight-year-olds. On the other hand, the fortuitous or arbitrary elements can also be treated as 'singular classes', distinct from all others. For example, if we had placed a bright green cross next to the pink oval in the centre of the model, it seems almost certain that all our subjects would have remembered it as a singular class.

(2) Remembrance of the fortuitous or contingent elements cannot therefore be divorced from the schematizations: it is largely as a function of the schemata he employs that the child treats the arbitrary elements as so many obstacles to be eliminated or, on the contrary, as so many elements to be retained because of the contrasts or special classifications they introduce.

(3) Since it depends on schematizations, the remembrance of contingent elements must also depend on the child's level of development. It follows that the conservation of arbitrary elements should be the better, the more highly structured the organization of the schemata. But this in no way prevents younger subjects from having better recall of certain, apparently insignificant, details; applying rudimentary classifications and series based on pairs or triplets, they remember a pair or triplet where older subjects would have recalled subtler and more complex structures.

§3. *The evolution of the memory*

The remembrance of characteristics I–IX thus provides us with the most telling argument in support of the influence of schematizations, and the very fact that we did not have to distinguish between the two groups of subjects examined by Methods I and II to establish the hierarchical order of these characteristics shows clearly that the schematizations involved were of a spontaneous no less than of an habitual type. We saw in the last chapter that subjects who were not asked for a prior classification, nevertheless attained the same levels of mnemonic organization as those who were, though with some delay, and that these levels corresponded closely to the classificatory levels of successive age groups. Hence, we thought it important to test our subjects' responses to the present, more complex model.

I. The results of our analysis provided us with a striking corroboration and amplification of the findings we presented in the last chapter, and this precisely because of the greater complexity of the new model:

(*a*) Once again, we found that the mnemonic organization and reconstructions of seven- to eight-year-olds who had been asked for a classification and a copy (Method I) were well in advance of those tested by Method II, but that twelve- to thirteen-year-olds do not benefit from the prior classification in any way.

(b) We again discovered a close correspondence between the spontaneous classifications of subjects tested by Method I and the organization of their memories. Now, since the mnemonic organization must be the same in both groups of subjects (§2), it follows that the spontaneous schematization of subjects tested by Method II is indeed of a classificatory kind, i.e. that it is quasi-operational.

In respect of point (a), we can draw up Table 57, based on the average successes as defined in §2 (number of subjects in brackets).

TABLE 57   *Comparison of the two methods*

	Method I (with classification)			Method II (without classification)		
	R1	R2	R3	R1	R2	R3
5– 6 years	36 (7)	22 (8)	19 (7)	36 (7)	22 (8)	19 (7)
7– 8 years	80 (12)	90 (23)	7 (6)	34 (12)	43 (23)	5 (9)
12–13 years	85 (10)	76 (10)	34 (6)	85 (10)	87 (10)	55 (5)

(The reader will recall that R1 took place an hour, R2 a week, and R3 6 to 10 months, after the presentation.)

Table 57 therefore throws a good deal of fresh light on the problem under consideration:

(1) Five- to six-year-olds produced the same responses with Methods I and II: thirty-six and thirty-six successes, etc. This shows that they were not influenced by the prior classification (or copy), and this because the classification was rudimentary (a six-year-old, for instance, suggested that the bars were 'all the same', though they plainly protruded in different directions).

(2) Seven- to eight-year-olds produced R1 and R2 responses that were roughly twice as good with prior classifications and copies than they were without: 80 per cent and 90 per cent as against 34 per cent and 43 per cent. This was either because the additional effort led these subjects to a closer examination and fixation of the model during the first session, or else because, as with the five- to seven-year-olds described in the last chapter (§4 and Tables 54–5), the classification facilitated and accelerated their schematizations by leading to a superior mnemonic organization. However, in the present case, the second interpretation seems doubtful, since, if the

372

newly acquired schematizations did, in fact, influence the memory, they could only have done so in a negative way: the mnemonic degradation shown by subjects tested by Method I was considerably greater after several months (a drop from 90 per cent to 7 per cent) than that of subjects tested by Method II (a drop from 43 per cent to 5 per cent).

(3) Twelve- to thirteen-year-olds, on the other hand, effect reconstructions without prior classification which are superior or equal to those obtained with Method I: 85 per cent and 87 per cent as against 85 per cent and 76 per cent for $R1$ and $R2$ and, remarkably enough, 55 per cent against 34 per cent for $R3$. In other words, the prior classification in no way improves their schematizations and simply encumbers their memory.

II. This development is also borne out by the following observations. Our analysis of successful responses shows that five- to six-year-olds find it easy to retain characteristics I–III, not too easy to retain characteristics IV–V, and hard to retain VI–IX. Seven- to eight-year-olds, on the other hand, find it easier to remember characteristics IV–V (numbers of figures and bars) with Method I than they do with Method II (curiously enough, they have greater difficulties with characteristics II–III than do five- to six-year-olds). Moreover, they remember characteristic VII (position of bars) before they can remember characteristic VI (general form) when tested by Method I, but react in precisely the opposite way when tested by Method II (whence the fluctuations in their respective positions). Twelve- to thirteen-year-olds, finally, tested by either method, find characteristics I–VI easy, characteristic VII not too easy, and characteristics VII–IX difficult to remember.

In other words, it is possible to express the hierarchy of characteristics I–IX in terms of mnemonic levels and thus to return to the language we used in Chapter 19: if we do so, we find that while seven- to eight-year-olds progress more quickly to the higher levels with the help of classifications, five- to six-year-olds, no less than twelve- to thirteen-year-olds, produce the same responses, no matter by what method they have been tested.

III. With regard to the copy which we demanded in addition to the classifications, in an attempt to encourage schematization even further, we decided to distinguish its effects from those of the classifications by means of a control experiment. To that end, we tested ten 7- to 8-year-olds by Method I but without a copy (Method IA) and ten other 7- to 8-year-olds by adding the copy to Method II (Method IIA).

The results had an interesting bearing on the problem of spontaneous schematization. The elimination of the copy from Method I (Method IA) did not have the least effect on our subjects' responses; in other words, the copy added nothing to the classifications. On the other hand, the addition of the copy to Method II produced effects similar to those due to the classification. Thus, while no more than 43 per cent of the subjects tested by Method II reproduced the general form of the model (characteristic VI) during their second reconstruction (R2), eight subjects in ten tested by Method IIA produced the correct response.

The reactions of these younger subjects teach us two things. In the first place, we see that a copy is not a schematization: if it has the effect as a classification, it is simply because the attentive examination of the figures stimulates the formation, or helps the development, of classificatory schemata. In the second place, the work of copying the model produces the same results in seven- to eight-year-olds as Method II (no classification or copy) produces in twelve- to thirteen-year-olds: the rôle of spontaneous schematizations is therefore quite evident, though it can, of course, be accelerated or retarded by the supplementary activities.

IV. We must therefore look again at the convergence of spontaneous with induced classificatory schemata (see Chapter 19). Let us recall that our subjects were asked (Method I) to classify the material on a square matrix with nine empty compartments, which, needless to say, is not enough to enable the younger ones amongst them to construct a multiplicative classification, i.e. to bear two or three criteria in mind at once.

In fact, their spontaneous classifications generally take the form of rows of more or less regular figures (figural collections), which, lacking qualitative identity, are simply combined into unco-ordinated pairs. Now, the same pattern is generally repeated in the classifications produced on the empty matrix, and quite particularly in the reconstructions R1 to R3:

INC (8;3), despite her age, still produced a spontaneous classification of three pairs of identical figures. During her second classification, she connected a circle to an ellipse, and then joined up two rectangles with one bar. On the matrix, she placed four pairs, all unco-ordinated except for the third, whose second element served as the first element of the fourth pair. During R1 she constructed two rows (no correspondence) consisting of three pairs and an isolated figure; during R2 she used three pairs.

VIO (5;0) produced a spontaneous classification of three superposed pairs: two ovals, two lozenges (saying 'these two are squares') and two rectangles. Her second classification yielded four superposed pairs: square and rectangle, circle and oval, etc. During R1 she produced three pairs in alignment and another pair beneath; $R2$ represented clear progress: a single pair (two ovals), a triplet (two rectangles and a square) and a second triplet containing all the remaining elements: circle, triangle and lozenge.

It goes without saying that such classifications by pairs based on a single criterion (shape of figures) also appear in the reconstructions of subjects examined by Method II:

PAT (5;0) produced two separate pairs during $R1$, one consisting of rectilinear figures (triangle and rectangle), the other of curved figures (circle and oval) with identical bars (slightly inclined to the upper right in the first pair and almost horizontal in the second).

IS (5;0) contented himself with a single pair (triangle and lozenge) during $R1$, and simply added an oval during $R2$.

MIC (5;11), by contrast, offered eleven figures during $R1$, again combined into pairs, and placed them in two rows: triangle with rectangle, circle with oval, lozenge with rectangle, lozenge with recumbent oval, circle with oval, plus an isolated lozenge.

At more advanced stages, we have classification by sets of three figures, selected in accordance with a single criterion, followed by combinations of two and finally of all three criteria. There is no need to go into details, since we have already done so in Chapter 19 (except that classification by pairs sufficed in that case). The important thing to note is that each of the successive stages appears not only in the reconstructions associated with Method I, but also in those associated with Method II. Suffice it to say, therefore, that the final stage, i.e. the multiplicative classification based on three criteria, is also reached by subjects who have not been asked for a spontaneous classification or for a classification with the aid of the empty matrix.

In this connection it is interesting to note in what way the descriptions preceding the reconstruction $R3$ (several months after the presentation) of twelve- to thirteen-year-olds tested by Method II often differ from those of subjects in the same age group tested by Method I. The latter generally content themselves with saying: 'Everything had to be put on a piece of cardboard like the model', or 'You showed them to me and then they had to be put back as they were', while those subjects whom we merely asked to take a good look at the model paid greater attention to the order: 'We had to put the triangles and rectangles in a certain order', or 'We were shown all sorts of things which we had to put back in the same way.' Here, then, are a few responses of subjects tested by Method II:

MAD (twelve years) produced a first reconstruction ($R1$) that was correct in all details except that the recumbent oval had a horizontal bar and the other a vertical one. During $R2$ (one week later) she repeated the same arrangement, but first placed all the bars '*right at the bottom*' (first row), '*right inside*' (second row) and '*right at the top*' (third row). Next, she added the figures, saying: '*Here* (last column) *they all stood up and there* (centre column) *they all lay down.*' In other words, she not only had a figurative memory of the model, but also proceeded to a co-ordination of the schemata. Eight months later, she repeated the multiplicative classification but altered it in a way that left no doubt as to the predominance of the schemata: the first row now consisted of a circle and two ellipses, the second of a triangle and two lozenges, and the third of a square and two rectangles, but in the first column (circle, triangle and square) all the bars were vertical and protruded from the top; in the second column (oval, lozenge and upright rectangle) all the bars were vertical but did not protrude, and in the third column (recumbent figures) the bars were vertical and protruded from the bottom.

MUL (12;5) produced a matrix (R1) in which all the figures were correct as well as all the bars in the first column and in the first row. However, in the second row the recumbent oval bore a horizontal bar, and in the third row the bar of the recumbent rectangle protruded from the top and pointed to the left, and the bar in the erect rectangle protruded to the lower right. During R2 (a week later) the inclination of the bar in the recumbent rectangle was corrected, but not that of the upright rectangle; for the rest nothing was changed. Several months later (R3), Mul placed a triangle above a square, by the side of which he placed an upright rectangle followed by a recumbent one, but, not knowing how to continue, he placed a circle beneath the recumbent rectangle. At this point, he abandoned the whole attempt, and substituted a matrix with a triangle, a square and a parallelogram in the first column; a lozenge, a recumbent oval and a rectangle in the second column; and a circle, a square standing on one of its corners and a rectangle in the third column. All the bars were vertical and protruded from the lower left in the second column, and from the lower right in the third column. His reconstructions, too, were therefore based on a mixture of correct and distorting schemata in multiplicative co-ordination.

To sum up: at all levels there is convergence between the classificatory levels and the levels of mnemonic schematization, and this regardless of whether or not the subjects had been asked to supply prior classifications.

V. Before we conclude this chapter we must still examine the results of a recognition test based on a choice from six distinct models. Table 58, showing successful responses, is expressed in percentages.

TABLE 58 *Recognition with Methods I and II*

	Method I			Method II		
Ages (years)	5–6	7–8	12–13	5–6	7–8	12–13
Successes (%)	14	25	86	14	20	100

We see once again that seven- to eight-year-olds tested by Method I were, if anything, superior to those tested by Method II, while twelve- to thirteen-year-olds tested by Method II were superior to those tested by Method I.

More remarkable still is the fact that, while five- to eight-year-olds have greater difficulty in selecting the right model than in reconstructing it, the opposite is true of twelve- to thirteen-year-olds. This bears out our assumption that, considered from the hierarchical, no less than from the genetic, point of view, mnemonic reconstruction fits between mnemonic recognition and pure recall. But since, in the present case, the child was expected to recognize, not an isolated sign, object or process, but a complex configuration involving the multiplication of three variable criteria, we can easily understand why young subjects should find it much easier to reconstruct the model with the help of material provided by the examiner than to recognize it—after all recognition calls, at the very least, for the co-ordination of signs.

It follows that the reconstructive memory is a natural entity obeying the laws of general development and of mnemonic structuring. In respect of the first of these laws, we find that the reconstructive memory evolves with age, just as do recall and recognition, and hence that it cannot be considered a provisional or vicarious form of conduct bridging the gap between the time when the child relies exclusively on his recognitive memory and the time when he comes to rely on the more highly organized recollective memory. As regards mnemonic structuring, we hope that we have shown to the reader's satisfaction that reconstructions presuppose schematizations, the levels of which can be determined by means of the hierarchical order of the characteristics I–IX (see §2) and also by an examination of the stages of the child's development. The schematizations, moreover, turned out to be of a logico-mathematical, pre-operational or quasi-operational kind, and, as we saw, they were isomorphous with the classifications elicited by Method I. In short, the reconstructive memory, compounded as it is of manipulation and representation, provides a link between the conservation of schemata, which sets in with the formation of the recognitive memory, and the retention of memory-images, which seems to predominate (if we go purely by the subject's awareness and do not enter into the underlying structures) in the recollective memory.

General Conclusion

At the end of these studies of the memory of children, which followed our earlier studies of mental imagery, our main impression is that though the two pose many similar problems—after all the memory makes use of images—there is a fundamental functional difference between them. An image is only a symbol and, as such, it can be employed in operational representations (i.e. in the solution of a problem and above all in the anticipation of that solution); in the reconstruction of past events; in recall of all sorts of objects; or in fantasies, dreams, play or artistic activities. The memory in the wider sense, on the other hand, is not symbolic in the same way, even though it does make use of symbolic images: it is a mode of knowledge like any other (or a kind of know-how)—unlike perception, it is not bound up with the immediate data and, unlike intelligence, is not involved in the solution of new problems—its special province is the reconstruction of the past. However, this reconstruction poses a special problem which the subject cannot solve without reflection, and this is precisely why the memory cannot be divorced from the intelligence.

Now, the specific functions of knowledge of the past are as innumerable as those of knowledge of the present or anticipations of the future. However, because one of the most important of these functions helps to ensure the identity of the ego (which is what Pythagoras meant when he based his proof of metempsychosis on the remembrance of mathematical figures), the memory appears as a special faculty tending to preserve the continuity of mental life. Moreover, because it helps to conserve acquired knowledge, while the intelligence bears on new problems, the memory seems to be an instrument of pure retention, and it is as such that it has been treated by experimental psychologists.

There are, in fact, two distinct interpretations of the functions of the memory in the wider sense: while some authorities treat it as a basic mental faculty, or even as the central mental mechanism, whose rôle it is to conserve the entire past (Freud and Bergson), others treat it as that part of the intelligence which is concerned with knowledge of the past, the difference being that in the second case the memory involves active and selective structuring, or rather a perma-

378

nent reorganization, while in the first case it is organized direct\
and determined down to the last detail by the very passage of time\
Again, if we consider the memory in the strict sense, i.e. mnemonic\
recognition, reconstruction and recollection, we discover two similar
contrasts (but, as it were, in reverse): for some the memory is nothing
but retention or reactivation, and hence an instrument of pure conservation quite distinct from the intelligence in its various modes of
adaption to novel processes; for others it is a form of organization
which, though mainly figurative, rests on the general schematism of
the intelligence.

It is the second of these interpretations which we have tried to
submit to the searchlight of the facts, and the time has now come to
list some of our conclusions.

§1. *The development of the memory with age*

I. The problem of memory changes in the course of the child's
intellectual development can be solved in two ways, reflecting the
difference between those who consider the memory as a mere instrument of conservation and those who treat it as a transformative
organization. This explains why, though most students in the field
agree that mnemonic performance varies with age, they nevertheless
offer two distinct interpretations of this phenomenon:

(1) According to the first of these interpretations, the reason why
the qualitative content of the memory is transformed with age is
that the subject's interests in, and general understanding of, the
world changes with time. Now, though this change involves the
emotions and the intelligence and not the memory, once a content
has been registered by the emotions and the intelligence, it is retained
by the memory with the help of mechanisms that remain identical at
all levels of development, though the quantity of information retained may be greater or smaller at different levels, and the mnemonic
acquisition and extinction curves may have a steeper or gentler slope.
In short, this interpretation is tantamount to saying that if the
memory does indeed show signs of becoming more efficient at encoding and decoding data as the child matures, the code itself remains
unchanged.[1]

(2) According to the second interpretation, attention must be
paid, not only to these quantitative changes in the acquisition,
retention and loss of data or the capacity for immediate or deferred
recognition and recall (with considerable variations due to the
experimental variables), but also to a fundamental qualitative factor,

---

[1] See, *inter alia*, Chapter 14, §5.

379

namely, the organization of the memory (and hence of the code itself), which may emerge suddenly during the process of mnemonic fixation, but may equally well develop gradually or even manifest itself in the form of successive re-organizations. In that case, it is no longer possible to distinguish between the intelligence as the faculty of understanding and invention and the memory as the faculty of conservation and retention. In fact, the memory, as the organization of the past, would then make use of the pre-operational or operational schemata of the intelligence, though in quite a specific way, namely, in the construction, conservation and reconstruction of the concrete images of particular events, judged to have occurred in reality (which is a judgment resembling the existential judgments proper to the intelligence, but referring to the past and in singular form, while the intelligence in its normal activity is concerned with general, foreseeable and more or less abstract structures).

Seen in this light, the development of the memory with age is the history of gradual organizations closely dependent on the structuring activities of the intelligence, though regulated by a special mechanism, namely, the structuring of the past or of past experiences. This is precisely what this entire book has been trying to show, and we have now reached the point where we must assess the validity of this demonstration.

II. A first and well-known argument in favour of the second interpretation lies in the very logic of those facts on which we have based all our experiments. Everyone admits, in fact, that the recognitory memory emerges before the recollective memory, and that the latter does not appear before the formation of the semiotic function and of conceptual representation or representative images. Nor would anyone deny[1] that the organization of the memory of a subject incapable of recalling the past, and hence restricted to sensorimotor recognitions, is quite different from that of a subject who can conjure up the past by means of representative images or conceptualized language. Now, if this difference in structuring ability does indeed exist, then we must also grant the possibility that once the intelligence has become representative, its successive pre-operational and operational structures may continue to transform the organization of the memory and provide the schematizations which modify its adequacy and conservation. The main objection to this interpretation is that, as soon as self-preservation becomes the main subjective function of the memory, enabling the self to delve into the

---

[1] Except for some psychoanalysts who have stuck rigidly to Freud's somewhat imprudent views of the early memory: among them Melanie Klein and her disciples.

past at will, the conservation and accuracy of the memory are affirmed by strong emotional forces.

Thus when people engage in psychoanalytical investigations, they are often delighted to discover how much further the memory can probe into the past, resuscitating a large number of forgotten scenes, and this in a concrete and visual manner by even the most abstract of minds. But precisely because these memories do not flood back at random but appear in the context of 'complexes' or conflicts, we are bound to conclude, on the one hand, that the past provides a partial explanation of the present, and this was Freud's great discovery (except that, for him, the present was less strongly influenced by the memory as a form of representation as by the over-all schemata of interpersonal behaviour—which, for short, we may call affective schemata—acquired in contact with one's closest relatives), and, on the other hand, that the individual continuously reorganizes the past in his schemata—which have quite obviously become modified and adapted to the present—and above all in his ideas and representations,[1] and hence in his memory. This means that, throughout our life, we reorganize our memories and ideas of the past, conserving more or less the same material, but adding other elements capable of changing its significance and, above all, of changing our viewpoint. As for self-identity, it goes without saying that this term has no other meaning than continuity within a constant restructuring process, and that this so-called 'identity' cannot possibly serve as proof that the mechanisms of the memory remain identical while the intelligence continues to develop.

III. Now, the most general result of our investigations has been to reveal the importance of mnemonic schematizations in all age groups, and to show that they develop as the intelligence does. True, the idea of applying schemata to the memory is quite old, and F. Bartlett, basing his work on that of Head, has defended it brilliantly,[2]

---

[1] This applies to both conscious or 'sub-conscious' representation. Seen in this light, the subconscious does not, moreover, differ from the conscious, except in respect of a, possible or real, lack of accommodation on the part of the cognitive or affective schemata. See J. Piaget: *Play, Dreams and Imitation in Childhood*, Routledge & Kegan Paul, 1951, pp. 212–27.

[2] See F. Bartlett: *Remembering*, Cambridge University Press, 1932. Bartlett used a model consisting of two squares, and found that his subjects could reproduce this model correctly if they saw it as two distinct figures, but that they would draw in the shapes shown on Figure 67, II and III if they treated it as a picture frame. Bousfield, for his part, has drawn attention to the rôle of word combinations in mnemonic retention (thus introducing some of the schematizations to which we have referred). By contrast, we shall see (§4, III) that the *Gestaltist* hypothesis, according to which the memory is the more stable and durable the closer its correspondence to 'good forms', has not been confirmed: mnemonic schemata

but the study of the development of mnemonic processes with age does provide a number of new and valuable pointers:

(1) Let us first of all recall our distinction between schemes and schemata, which we have discussed at some length in our previous writings. A mnemonic scheme is a simplification of a memory or of a memory-drawing; for example, the reduction of the number of peaks on a mountain range; or the reduction of the element A' (Chapter 4, Figure 13) to a more symmetrical form ($\lfloor\rfloor$ or $\lfloor\rfloor$). A scheme is a law governing the behaviour (mental or graphic) of the image as such, and develops very slightly with age, its main advantage at all levels being that it leads to mnemonic economies, and hence to useful or distorting mnemonic procedures. A schema, by contrast, is an instrument of generalization, and while it, too, can be adequate or distortive, it depends on the intellectual level of the subject. In the case of the element A' we have just mentioned, the subject transforms his memory of Figure 12, II into Figure 13, III, not in accordance with a scheme which would have been a purely figurative transformation, but under the influence of an equalization schema based on the fact that the elements A and A' of Figure 12 are in one-to-one correspondence: this explains why children will reproduce this particular model correctly when it is presented to them in the form of continuous strokes.

(2) The schemata used by the memory are borrowed from the intelligence, and this explains why they follow one another in stages corresponding to the subjects' operational levels. In the case of serial configurations (Chapter 1) in which the model had a good perceptive form, which even five-year-olds could copy (55 per cent successes at this age), the memory and the operation advanced by remarkably similar stages. In all the other experiments described in this book, the fundamental rôle of the schemata and their correlation with the operational levels has been equally obvious, even in the case of essentially figurative models (Chapters 19 and 20) or of the purely operational tests in which many of the elements (vessels, geometric figures, etc.) might have been remembered in a passive or figural way. The most striking illustrations were provided in Chapters 16 and 4

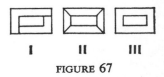

I   II   III

FIGURE 67

are not governed by *Gestalt* laws, which means that the memory-image is not identical with elementary perceptive structures, and that mnemonic schemata are genuine assimilatory schemata, not mere 'schemes'.

(recumbent or inclined vessels, and equal but unaligned lengths); here, the models were purely static or figural, and yet the child's remembrance of them was clearly based on assimilation to pre-operational or operational schemata.

(3) The memory thus borrows its schemata from the intelligence, and not merely during the perceptive recording of the data, since, in that case, the memory would be confined to the conservation of what has been recorded, and we should be back with interpretation No. 1. Rather do the schemata serve as instruments of mnemonic organization and, as such, they are active during retention and recall no less than during the fixation of memories. This becomes perfectly clear in recall immediately or an hour after presentation of the model (Chapters 4, 14 and 16). Here, the data are subject to such profound mnemonic transformations that the changes could not possibly be attributed to perception.

(4) This brings us to the relationship between schemata as cognitive instruments of generalization and memory-images as concrete and singular images; in other words, to the relationship between the operational and figurative aspects of the memory: this is a complex problem because it touches not only on the respective modes of conservation of schemata and images, but also, and necessarily so, on their interactions. It is, however, impossible to treat the conservation of schemata as a mnemonic problem, because the characteristic feature of the memory, except in the case of ideas or arguments that are reconstructed rather than recalled, is precisely that they are concrete, individualized and bound up with existential judgments about the past. That is why, in the Introduction to this work, we have distinguished between the memory in the strict sense and the memory in the wider sense. But how, precisely, does the self-conservation of schemata affect the conservation of memories?

§2. *Memory transformations during retention and mnemonic inferences*

The most convincing proof that the schemata of the intelligence intervene in the very organization of the memory considered as a form of retention is provided by an examination of memory transformations during successive recollections or reconstructions. In the classical view, according to which the memory is nothing but conservation, memory transformations must necessarily result in mnemonic distortions or memory losses; indeed, ultra-conservationist theories (we deliberately refrain from calling them ultra-conservative theories) such as those put forward by Freud and Bergson go so far as to assume that no memories can ever be lost or modified, though social pressures (Freud's repressions and Bergson's expedients) can lead to their exclusion from consciousness or to their distortion until they are summoned back from the subconscious by catharsis or by intuitive knowledge of the 'pure self'.

I. As against this view, our observations have shown that besides these distortions or omissions, there can also be qualitative mnemonic improvements with time. It is quite conceivable that the memory of a lecture or a long passage should be better once progress in reflection has enabled the subject to reconstruct certain connections, not merely forgotten but unnoticed in the first place; or, again, that practical experiences gained in the meantime (for instance in horticulture or mountaineering) should lead to the improvement, by reorganization, of defective memories. In the emotional sphere, it is no less conceivable that the memory of past feelings should improve with the grasp of certain elements previously ignored.

In any case, we were able to establish a number of mnemonic improvements in the course of time.

These improvements were most spectacular in the case of simple seriations, in which 74 per cent of our subjects showed an advance between the second session (one week after the presentation) and the third session (several months after the presentation). Again, with the M-shaped seriation described in Chapter 2, 38 per cent of our subjects made mnemonic progress in the course of ten weeks. In the case of double classifications (Chapter 8), graphic recall showed a decline of 61 per cent after six months, but 48 per cent of our six- to eight-year-old subjects offered improved reconstructions. Graphic recall of the horizontal level in an inclined bottle improved in 30 per cent of our subjects during the course of several months. We also observed several cases of clear mnemonic progress in the case of transitive relations (Chapter 5) of the causal sequences involved in transitive motions (Chapter 12), etc.,[1] and even in the case of the semi-contingent and semi-schematized configurations described in Chapter 19.

True, whenever mnemonic progress is plainly bound up with the subject's operational level, the advances might arguably have been due purely to a better grasp of the mnemonic contents: a subject,

[1] The unusually large number of advances in the case of seriations was possibly due to the fact that, with a series of ten elements, we were able to distinguish a host of sub-stages, and consequently to detect more subtle changes. If the remembrance of transitive relations had also been studied by means of a model consisting of ten elements ($A = B = C \ldots = J$ or $A < B; B < C; C < D \ldots$ hence $A < J$) it is quite possible that we might have been able to distinguish as many sub-stages as we did in the case of seriations, so that the number of partial advances would have been increased.

recalling the presence of unequal rods, and having meanwhile reached the stage of operational seriation or of spatial co-ordination, may remember them as constituting a serial configuration. It nevertheless remains a fact that he did not remember them as such during (a) the fixation of his memory and (b) on immediate recall. In other words, the code itself must have changed in the interval— and it seems obvious that this change involves the memory and not merely the intelligence.

As far as the memory is concerned, the improvement quite often appears during immediate recall: the subject feels dissatisfied with the fact that his memory-drawing does not fully correspond to the model he has been shown. In other words, mnemonic progress is based on a conflict between recall and recognition. Now, if knowledge of the model were based purely on the memory-image, it seems difficult to explain how that image could be judged unsatisfactory, or, for that matter, how it could make subsequent progress—after all, it was responsible for the deformation of the model and lacks a dynamism of its own. Hence, if the memory does make progress, it can only be because the model was not registered with the help of the memory-image alone, but also with the help of the schema to which it has been assimilated, and it is precisely the action of this schema which alone accounts for the fact that the subject fails to recognize the model in his memory-drawing (recognition involves a confrontation of the perception of this drawing with a prior schema, and this confrontation appears as an assimilation that the subject may or may not find satisfactory). The schema then develops and finds its own equilibrium, based purely on the subject's actions; during the next recall, the memory-image is improved, thanks to advances of the schema, but—and let us bear this essential fact in mind—this improvement generally occurs by stages, and not by a sudden leap from a lower level to correct recall.

All these facts tend to show (a point to which we shall be returning) that the memory-image is bound up with the conservation of schemata, which greatly simplifies the problem of mnemonic conservation: a schema, in fact, conserves itself by virtue of its own functioning.[1] In this way, we can explain mnemonic reorganization without the help of deductive or reflexive efforts on the subject's part, and this is as true of the remembrance of his own past and of his own ideas as it is of the facts we have just mentioned.

II. But these facts show, above all, that schemata do not merely intervene during the apprehension of the model, at the point of memory fixation, but that they continue to act, as organizational

[1] See Introduction, §3, I and IV.

factors, throughout the retention of that memory. Admittedly it is equally possible to argue that schemata act exclusively during the two extreme phases of memorization, viz. during apprehension and final recall, so that there is no need to postulate their continuous action throughout retention.

Here, we come up against the major problem of whether the memory is conserved in the 'subconscious' or whether it is a reconstruction at the moment of recall, and whether the essential rôle we have attached to operational schemata in the organization of the memory ought not to be attributed instead to mnemonic reconstructions. If that were the case, it would follow:

(1) That mnemonic fixation is the result of simple perceptions, etc., assimilated to a system of schemata;

(2) That these schemata subsequently conserve themselves—they were, after all, in existence before the fixation of the memory and continue to function independently of the memory (no matter whether they are habitual or operational);

(3) That the subject reconstructs the initial situation at the point of recall and hence 'fabricates' a memory-image based on (a) external material signs (he recognizes the demonstrator, the laboratory, the situation, etc.); and (b) on the schemata he applied during the 'fixation'.

However, though this type of mnemonic reconstruction played an obvious part in all our experiments, and though, in some cases, it perhaps suffices to explain mnemonic progress for lack of further information, a number of supplementary facts entitle us to add that the schemata are at work even during the retentive phase, and therefore play a more continuous rôle in the organization of the memory, the final reconstruction being no more than one phase in a long and convergent process.

These are the facts to which we have referred as mnemonic inference, and of which we have quoted striking examples in connection with the remembrance of inclined or recumbent bottles (Chapter 16) and of lines divided into segments of equal length but not in perfect alignment (Chapter 4). In either case, the inference involved both the schemata and the memory, whereas in the case of simple seriation (Chapter 1), the rôle of the memory could not be proved, so that we might easily have concluded that the reconstruction was based exclusively on the schemata (this was no longer the case with the M-shaped series discussed in Chapter 2). In the case of the bottle standing on its head (Chapter 16, §1), memory served to turn it back on its base (in the case of five-year-olds), which involved recourse to habitual schemata, but these children also remembered that the liquid covered the side of the bottle, which involved recourse to the memory-image. Again, our subjects assumed that the extremities of lines in one-to-one correspondence must necessarily coincide, thus relying on a pre-operational schema of ordinal evaluation. On the other hand, they did have an authentic memory-image of the actual correspondence. We are therefore dealing with inferences (in the sense of implications *sensu lato* or 'signifiers' of the kind we employ when we say that a face implies a nose), but inferences whose premises are derived simultaneously from schemata and authentic memories: they could not have been drawn at the moment of mnemonic fixation, when they would have been refuted by perception, and they cannot be considered as pure reconstructions because one of the two premises could not have been reconstructed either with the help of material signs (there was no further presentation) or by means of schemata alone, but presupposes the existence of an authentic memory. In other words, the schemata must have intervened during retention, to become co-ordinated with that memory. Can it be argued that this inferential co-ordination was nevertheless produced at the moment of recall and not during the interval? We can, if necessary, admit it in one sense, i.e. in the sense that dreams are said to occur at the moment of waking and not during deep sleep (a fact on which electrical recording devices have recently cast grave doubt). However, the fact that dreams are produced at the moment of waking in no way proves that they constitute so many products of the awakened consciousness. In fact, the choice between the hypothesis of reconstruction during recall and that of mnemonic inference during retention depends on the integral or partial character we attribute to that reconstruction: if, as everything tends to suggest, recall always involves a mixture of reconstruction and conservation, mnemonic inference must begin with retention.

The great importance of these mnemonic inferences is therefore that they offer us a means of synthesizing interpretations of the memory based respectively on conservation and reconstruction: both factors undoubtedly intervene simultaneously and at all times, but with this essential rider that mnemonic conservation can comprise transformations and reconstructions, and that the reconstructions involved in mnemonic retention converge with those involved in recall, because they are based on the same schemata and the same organizing dynamism.

§3. The relations between the memory and the intelligence and successive levels of schematization

The 'memory in the wider sense', as we have defined it in the Introduction (§1), is the conservation of everything that has been acquired in the past, including the various systems of schemata (from habits to operations) but excluding hereditary schemata, reflexes, etc., not due to learning. By contrast, the 'memory in the strict sense' (also defined in §1 of the Introduction) merely includes those forms of conduct that reflect the past in terms of the subject's consciousness: recognitions, reconstructions, recollections and their respective fixations. One might say that the memory in the strict sense is simply the observable (and, from the observer's point of view, the operational) side of the memory in the wider sense, and hence that their genetic or actual interconnections pose no further problems. In fact, however, they do, and this because a memory is always the remembrance of a particular object or event, while the schema involved in the memory in the wider sense always tends towards generalization (from habits to the higher operations). Thus, when we remember the Mediterranean, we remember a particular landscape previously perceived and not simply a series of schemata, and if we remember the Mediterranean as it appears in an atlas, we are still remembering a particular configuration and not a series of geodesic operations, etc. The remembrance of an idea either coincides with that idea, and hence falls within the province of the memory in the wider sense, or else it is the particular memory of a given discussion, a given lecture by a living person or at a given moment in time. In short, the problem of the relationship between the 'memory in the strict sense' and the 'memory in the wider sense' is the complex and difficult problem of the relationship between (particular) memories and the intelligence in all its varied forms.

I. There are four possible solutions to the central problem of the conservation or retention of memories:

(1) First of all, one could postulate that the only effective conservation is that found in schemata of all levels, and that memory-images do not so much conserve as reconstruct themselves by means of symbols, and that they do so in the course of mental reconstructions of a particular situation in the past; this is the hypothesis of the integral reconstruction of the memory, and we have seen why the facts of mnemonic inference entitle us to discard it.

(2) Alternatively, one might postulate the existence of mnemonic conservation in the strict sense (memory-images, remembrance of ideas, etc.) quite independent of the self-conservation of schemata: in that case, the conservation of the latter must be attributed to the memory in the strict sense; much as a pupil needs his memory to recall that $7 + 5$ makes 12 and not 11 or 13, so the memory also enables him to construct the correct syllogisms, to conclude that $A = C$ if $A = B$ and $B = C$, to apply the principle of identity during

an argument, etc. But then we would also have to assume that it is thanks to well-conserved memories and not thanks to the conservation of habitual schemata that we keep our balance on a bicycle, that we go down an escalator without falling off, and that we write from left to right, and not in the manner of the Arabs.

However, two types of fact stand in the way of this interpretation, the first relating to the memory and the second to the intelligence. In respect of the former, we have seen, throughout this book, that memories are invariably supported by existing schemata; we have never come across the case of independent memories on which schemata were gradually constructed. In respect of the intelligence, the hypothesis is clearly untenable, because the conservation of a schema differs from that of a memory. The conservation of a schema is, in fact, the direct consequence of an act of generalization,[1] while the conservation of a memory consists in its rediscovery. Now, rediscovering a memory or its object (by images, descriptions, etc.) is the opposite of generalization, because it involves a search for the particular, the unique and, above all, for what, by its very nature, no longer exists (in time) or only exists elsewhere (in space), while generalizing means applying an action to a new situation and seeking its continuation, i.e. it is future-directed. True, in addition to the acts of rediscovery characteristic of the memory and the continual generalizations characteristic of the operational schema, we also have actions that are repeated or reproduced directly, for instance, elementary habits. But, on the one hand, reproductive assimilation leads to generalizing assimilation and, on the other hand, the repetition or reproduction of an action leads towards multiplicity, while mnemonic rediscovery tends towards unicity and means restoring to the past object or event the individualized and irreversible property of having existed on one occasion only. It is, of course, true that we can remember repetitive events bound up with the action itself or external to it; but in that case we have memories attached to schemata, and that is a point to which we shall be returning.

(3) Third, we could postulate the existence of two independent types of conservation: the conservation of schemata at all levels, from sensori-motor habits to operations, all resulting from their generalizing function and all independent of any mnemonic support, and the conservation of memories (memory-images, memory of ideas, etc.) resulting from special retentive powers that enable the past to be 'rediscovered'. This, in fact, is the most widespread view, and according to it there is a clear distinction between the 'memory in the strict sense' and the intelligence, so much so that the former becomes a function sufficient unto itself.

[1] See Introduction §3, I and IV.

Now, the findings set out in this book contradict the second part of that interpretation, and this for a very obvious reason. Not a single model used in our experiments was anything but 'infantile' in its simplicity, and this precisely because all our models were intended to enable even the youngest subjects to perceive and fix in their memories what they were specially shown for this purpose, regardless of whether or not they could grasp the reasons for the experiment. Now, very few of our subjects fixed in their memories what they had actually seen; instead they fixed their own ideas of the model.

(4) The last hypothesis, and the foregoing remarks persuade us that it is the correct one, is that there are indeed two forms of conservation, but that they are interdependent. There is, first of all, the conservation of schemata resulting from their generalizing function, and then there is the conservation of memories, i.e. the constant restoration of particular and past existences, each needing the support of the other, but with the first playing the leading rôle. That the conservation of memories rests on the conservation of schemata has, we hope, been proved exhaustively by everything we have said about mnemonic schematizations and their transformations (the resulting distortions being due to the excessive application of schemata). The converse of this proposition, namely, that the schemata of the intelligence have need of the memory in general and of individualized memories in particular is equally obvious, not because the conservation of schemata rests on the memory (cf. hypothesis 2), but because the memory and the image supply the intelligence with useful 'representations', in the mathematical sense of the term, i.e. with the particular and concrete models it needs in order to engage in constructive activities. But, above all, every schema of the intelligence tends to accommodate itself either to the present (accommodation to the objects themselves) or the past (accommodation extended as inner imitation or in the form of memory-images). Hence, the connection between schema and the memory in the strict sense (see §4, IV, below).

II. It follows that the memory in the strict sense is part of a general set of cognitive functions, of which the intelligence represents a higher and balanced form, and that the conservation of memories rests on special but related schematizations in certain cases, but participates directly in that of the intelligence in others. Before we go on to examine how all this affects the relations between the figurative and operative aspects of the memory, we must first justify our thesis by a more detailed summary of our results.

The main evidence in support of the links between the memory and actions, and hence between mnemonic accuracy and action schemata, is our general finding that mnemonic reconstructions (with the help of material provided by the demonstrator) come so much more easily to the child than does pure recall.

In an earlier work (*Mental Imagery in the Child;* Chapter IX) we were able to demonstrate experimentally that memories based on the simple perception of a model are less complete and less accurate than memories based on actions (copying, etc.). Moreover, and this is essential, on comparing two groups of subjects who began with either perception or active copying, we found that whereas actions enhance perceptions, the opposite is not the case. In other words, a prior perception does not add very much to the organization and final retention of the memory, while a prior action leads to better perception of the model and, above all, to its perception in terms of actions, i.e. to its assimilation to virtual action schemata.

In the present series of experiments, we arrived at very similar conclusions, but by a comparison of recall (memory-drawings) with material reconstructions, the latter corresponding to the copy drawings to which we have just referred as actions, and the former to the memory-image obtained by perception. Now, in almost all the cases we investigated, the reconstructions were clearly in advance of recall up to about the age of seven to eight years,[1] while eight- to nine-year-olds and older subjects often produce drawings and reconstructions of the same level (for example, in the case of rotations (Chapter 15, §2, III, Levels III and IV)), which can only mean that both have come to rest on similar procedures.

The fact that reconstructions should so often be superior to pure recall is highly instructive. Reconstruction, too, is a form of recall (since the model is no longer in sight) but by actions instead of images. Now, as we explained in Chapter 19, §6, whereas reconstructions restore the supposed genetic order of the formation of memories (actions → schemata → memory-images), simple recall reverses that order by starting from the images. This is precisely why the superiority of reconstructions as mnemonic instruments confirms our hypothesis that the conservation of memories rests on the conservation of schemata.

III. However, active reconstructions represent a mnemonic form half-way between recognition and recall, and a form whose originality and importance have been largely ignored[2]—a gap which, we hope,

---

[1] A single but slight exception among our younger subjects appeared during the crossroads experiment (Chapter 18, §2, II), but here the reconstructions may well have been deformed for partly playful reasons.

[2] The subject was first broached by H. Münsterberg and J. Bigham in 1894.

the present work may have helped to bridge. Now, the very fact that reconstruction fits between recognition and recall constitutes its genetic importance, for it demonstrates that the close links between the conservation of memories and the conservation of schemata apply to all forms of the memory, from the lowest—recognition (whose connection with the habitual schemata is indisputable and generally admitted)—to the highest.

The hypothesis we have adopted is almost diametrically opposed to the philosophy of Bergson, who contended that memories were the life of the spirit, and tried to free both from their attachments to the body and the nervous system. The reader may know how anxious Bergson was to introduce a radical antithesis between memories in the form of acquired habits or motor mechanisms, and memory-images uncontaminated by actions whose sole purpose it was to record and conserve the entire past. Now, the reconstructive memory, in its many varieties, already constitutes a refutation of that thesis, because it proceeds from actions and leads to recall. Moreover, habits involve both motor schemata whose conservation does not concern the memory in the strict sense, and the recognition of signs which is a form of memory but one closely dependent on these schemata. Finally, between recognition and recall by images, we find a host of transitions (see below) by which we can demonstrate that all mnemonic forms share a fundamental mechanism: they all fit into schemata ranging from the lowest (motor schemata associated with habits) to the highest (intelligence and operations).

We can, in fact, establish three major hierarchic types of memory, each with several sub-levels: the recognitory memory (1–3); the reconstructive memory (4–7) and the recollective memory (8–10). We shall not treat mnemonic improvements due to re-learning as a special category (see Introduction, §1), for, though they certainly bear witness to the conservation of memory traces, we have to establish in each case whether they involve the consolidation of motor schemata or of memories as such, and at what mnemonic levels (see Chapters 6 and 19).

Type I: the recognitive memory. Recognition at all the levels is an assimilation of the data to schemata of various kinds, ranging from reflex and elementary habits to the motor schemata of sensory exploration:[1]

(1) Elementary recognition is bound up with the continuation or repetition of a reflex action or a potential habit extending that reflex: a baby recognizes the feel of the nipple he has let slip, or the moving

[1] Cf. R. Frances: 'La perception des sons' in Fraisse and Piaget: *Traité de psychologie expérimentale*, Vol. VI.

object that he followed with his eyes and that he has momentarily lost from sight.

(2) Next, there is recognition by assimilation to an existing schema (in the repetition of the schematized action): this is the recognition of signs as signifiers and is bound up with habits and acts of the sensori-motor intelligence—the fact that the signs are treated as signifiers is due precisely to their links with the schemata.

(3) Recognition at the higher levels is bound up with mobile and differentiated schemata (classifications, etc.). In our various recognition tests, the subjects were asked to select the correct model from a whole batch: we found that the younger ones found it difficult to make a choice (absence of correlation and of implicit classification) and that successful subjects invariably had recourse to the underlying schemata (cf. the experiment described in Chapter 20, §3, V). Now, in everyday life, recognition also involves the spontaneous and continuous classification of known objects, with new 'pigeonholes' for whatever unknown elements may appear: a known road is recognized by details missing from other roads, and the latter are thought to be unknown precisely because they lack the expected features, etc.

However, in the case of these differentiated recognitions we have to determine where exactly the memory ends and where the intellectual schemata begin: the recognition of a melody is an act of the memory, but the recognition of Vivaldi's style in an unpublished score calls for judgment and for highly schematized comparisons; similarly, the recognition of a Scotch pine is an act of memorization, but the identification of that tree as a member of the species *Pinus sylvestris* is an act of classification. Moreover, there are all sorts of intermediate stages between the two, and this is precisely what makes our hypothesis so useful: classification, in fact, reaches down to the individual object or event as a singular class and, even during perception, there is every possible gradation between J. Bruner's schematizing identification ('This is an orange') and individualized identification ('This is the orange I put to one side an hour ago').

Type II: mnemonic reconstruction. In contrast to elementary habits, which involve the reproduction, intentionally or otherwise, of schematized actions or of sensori-motor schemata tending towards generalization, a reconstruction is the intentional reproduction of a particular action and of its results. Hence, it involves the recognition of signs, etc. but goes beyond recognition proper in that it constitutes a form of recall by action: it tends to reconstruct a model no longer available for perception, while recognition occurs in the presence of the model.

(4) We may seek the elementary form of the reconstructive memory

393

in sensori-motor imitation, considered as the intentional reproduction of an action performed by oneself, or by somebody else, and often of the motion of an object. Now, this interpretation of the reconstructive memory bears out the genetic point of view, because sensori-motor imitation heralds recall and already constitutes a kind of recall by actions. Moreover, in its deferred and above all in its internalized forms, it becomes representative recall and constitutes the source of the mental image which plays so important a rôle in the recollective memory.

(5) Next comes the reproduction of an isolated and not fully schematized action and reconstruction of its result: this is the situation examined in Chapter 20, where the model was copied before it was reconstructed.

(6) Then there is the reconstruction of an object or a configuration (without prior constructions of an imitative or spontaneous kind): this is the situation examined in Chapter 19, where the model was recalled by memory-drawings and reconstructions, with the latter producing considerably better responses than the former.

(7) Finally, we have reconstruction of a schematized action: for example, the reconstruction of the transitive sequences examined in Chapter 6. In the experiments described in Chapter 1, the subjects were not asked for a reconstruction of the seriation, because with rods measuring from 9 to 16·2 cm, a reconstruction would have been equivalent to an operational seriation: the subject would have been forced to compare the rods two at a time before he could put them in order. But by using only five or six rods from 10 to 20 cm in length, we were able to reduce the number of operational factors encumbering the reconstructive memory.[1]

Type III: mnemonic recall. There is no need to stress the fact that even the recollective memory depends on actions and action schemata, thus ensuring the complete continuity as between reconstructions by actions (type II) and internalized reconstructions represented by the memory-image as the instrument of recall:

(8) The memory-image of a schematized action: a good example was provided by the rotation of a triangle (Chapter 15); here, we found precisely that from the age of seven years, and from mnemonic levels III and IV, simple recall produces the same results as reconstruction (Chapter 15, §2, III), which proves the complete internalization of reconstructive procedures.

(9) Recall by images of any non-schematized action: this is the direct result of the internalization of imitation by images.

[1] However, since our aim was to compare the levels of recall with the operational levels, we were forced to re-examine the material from an operational point of view.

(10) Recall by images of objects or events extraneous to the action: this is the 'pure' memory of classical psychologists, but as we saw in Chapters 19 and 20, these 'ill-assorted' configurations are nevertheless subject to active schematizations, the *sine qua non* of their retention.

From the foregoing remarks, the reader will have gathered by what slight transitions children advance from elementary recognitions, closely bound up with actions, to the higher forms of recall,[1] which, thanks to their links with the operational schemata, cannot be entirely divorced from actions because, as we saw, operations spring directly from the latter.

§4. *The figurative and operative aspects of the memory and its functional unity*

Though the conservation of memories is based on that of schemata, it nevertheless remains a fact that memories are not schemata but consist of images whose importance varies from case to case. We shall therefore return to this twofold nature of the memory and examine the problem of the unity of the memory as it evolves through its different stages.

I. If mnemonic reconstruction, which ensures the transition from recognition to recall, is indeed rooted in imitation, as we have supposed, it must have the same origins as the mental image. And, in fact, every type of mnemonic recall involves an image, and every mental image is, to some extent, a memory (the anticipatory image must needs base itself on reproductive images which it recombines in a novel way). The image nevertheless remains distinct from recall: the image is a symbol and recall a mental act which includes (attributive, relational and existential) judgments precisely because it is not exclusively an image but also comprises a schematism.

It is perfectly legitimate to postulate, as we have done in the Introduction, that the memory in the strict sense constitutes the figurative aspect of the conservation of schemata. This postulate has two implications. The first of these we have stressed in §2: the conservation of memories must rest on the conservation of schemata. The second is that there is nevertheless a conservation of memories as such. A schema, no matter of what kind, is by its very nature an instrument of generalization, and hence appears as a signification,

---

[1] In his *Les Maladies de la mémoire*, Presses Universitaires de France, 1965, Delay distinguishes three forms of memory: sensori-motor, autistic and social. We must confess that we have experienced some difficulty in trying to fit most of our intermediate levels into these categories.

and just as soon as the semiotic function is constructed, that signification becomes a significate demanding a signifier. The signifier may consist of words or images, and the images best suited to a mental schema are those representing situations to which the schema has been applied in the past and to which, so to speak, it gives concrete expression. This is the case with the memory-image (visual image, verbal memory, etc.); and shows why the conservation of schemata should be accompanied by a form of conservation (mnemonic retention) dependent on the conservation of schemata, while yet having a relatively consistent signifying function and continuity of its own. And the more differentiated the schemata, the greater that consistency.

This explains the existence of memory gaps no less than of mnemonic successes. In respect of the former, it should be obvious that, if the conservation of memories rests on the conservation of schemata, two fundamental circumstances are bound to impair remembrance: the first is that schemata conserve themselves by their very functioning but that all of them do not function permanently, and the less so as they become differentiated or particularized; the second is that the differentiation of schemata cannot be continued indefinitely and that an indefinite number of them is needed to embrace every detail of past events.

According to William James, the main function of the memory is to forget useless information, lest we become completely encumbered by our past. This is undoubtedly true, and moreover in full agreement with the assumption that the memory collaborates with the schemata of the intelligence. But it nevertheless happens in everyday life that the addition of a few exact memories more would greatly facilitate the functioning of conceptual, and quite particularly of practical, schemata of all kinds. However, the conservation of memories is dependent upon the constant use of highly differentiated schemata, and not of the more general schemata we ordinarily employ, and the sad experience that each one has had of forgetting a great deal of what he learned at school shows clearly what happens to the memory once it has become divorced from the exercise of the corresponding schemata (and this is a polite way of putting it, since the absurdity of a number of school practices is precisely that they divorce the memory of spontaneous activities from the intelligence and its operational schemata).

Nevertheless, gaps in the memory are compensated by specific mnemonic achievements. By that we do not mean simply that the memory is capable of conserving as well as shedding its contents, but that its exercise (when it is functional and not merely based on learning by rote) is useful to the development of schemata, be they pre-operational or operational. Schemata are general by their very nature, while memories are particularized and differentiated down to the singular and fortuitous, and this opposition renders a double service to the schematism.

In the first place, it leads to the retention of a series of concrete situations in which the schemata worked well or badly, and this serves to infuse life into a set of forms and transformations that would have remained purely abstract, but which, thanks to the memory, are incorporated into the web of living experience.

In the second place, and above all, by its very use of the schemata of the intelligence, the memory leads to their indefinite differentiation. A classificatory schema may remain general, but the greater the number of objects and details retained by the memory, the more the schema must be differentiated into sub-systems down to singular classes. Relational schemata, too, may remain very general, but if chance gives way to regularities and introduces fluctuations that capture the attention and become fixed in the memory, these relations become differentiated as well. In short, the conservation of schemata and of memories can only co-exist by virtue of their mutual dependence, and their interactions are generally to the advantage of both systems, however different they may be, or precisely because they are so different. Hence, though the 'memory in the strict sense' is mainly bound up with the feedback *FR* (Introduction, §2), it also reacts on the feedback *FA*, to the extent that it is bound up with 'memory in the wider sense'.

II. However, the closer the co-operation between the operative elements (action and intellectual schemata) and the figurative elements of the memory (from the perception of the *déjà vu* in recognition to the memory-image associated with recall) the more blurred becomes the memory in the strict sense, whose two chief characteristics are and remain the individualization of memories and the localization of the past in time. While the schematism of the intelligence tends towards the extra-temporal, for instance in the mathematico-logical sphere, the function of the memory in the strict sense is not only the conservation of the contents of the past, regardless of the time of their occurrence, but also, and in many cases predominantly so, the comprehension of the past by the representation and temporal localization of events or objects belonging to that past as such.

As we have been chiefly concerned with the relations between the memory and the operational schemata, we have paid little attention to that localization in time. We shall now look at it more closely, the more so as several of our experiments have shown that subjects who

397

had apparently exhausted their mnemonic resources in answering our questions, suddenly recalled (or behaved as if they had suddenly recalled) certain aspects of the model they had previously ignored: whence, the disturbing impression that, in addition to the schematized or 'logical' memory, they also and despite all, relied on something like a 'raw memory', and that the latter was, in fact, their true memory!

The problem can be posed in the following way: how do perceptions accompanied by recognitions differ from a new or 'pure' perception; how do reconstructions treated as such by the subject differ from reconstructions guided by attempts to find a solution to the problem that has been posed, and how does a memory-image differ from a representative or any other form of image? Claparède was right when he stressed the constant links between recognition and self-identification and pointed out that an unrecognized perception is not accompanied by the impression of 'I-ness'. The same can be said of mnemonic reconstructions and of the memory-image, but this merely shelves the problem, for we must still establish whether it is the subject's self-identity which confers their individual identities upon the memories and localizes them in the past, or whether the opposite is the case, and also whether that self-identity is ready-made or constructed by the subject.

Now, all the data we have been able to gather, and moreover all we know about the memory (particularly of children) tends to show that there is no intrinsic, qualitative difference between the contents of a false memory and those of a true one: a false recognition gives the same *déjà vu* impression (and the same impression of I-ness) as a correct recognition, and the same is true of reconstructions. There is nothing, moreover, that entitles us to distinguish 'reconstructed' from pure, or false from correct, recall. And when our subjects have apparently searched their memories, and suddenly remember certain supplementary features, or show by their behaviour that these have not been forgotten, the addition of these features to the initial memories in no way justifies the distinction between a 'raw' and hence automatically correct, memory and mnemonic illusions during recognition.

Clearly, therefore, the attachment of a memory to the past involves some element of decision or judgment on the subject's part. Actions no less than the exercise of the intelligence (whether in the service of the emotions or of social demands or simply of a cognitive kind) call for the representation or practical knowledge of all sectors of reality, past, present and foreseeable. However, the difference between representations of the past and representations of the present is so great that we rarely think of comparing the details of their cognitive mechanisms. In particular, the present is open to the future and can therefore be transformed: whence the subordination of all modes of knowledge (from perception to concrete or abstract representation) to the means of that potential transformation, i.e. to actions and operations. The past, by contrast, is just what it was and cannot be altered in any way: what knowledge of the past we try to obtain or to conserve is essentially centred, not on the general instruments of transformation, i.e. on the operational structures that enable us to grasp a maximum number of changeable situations, but, on the contrary, on the individualization and localization of events, persons or objects encountered in the past, and of their various actions. However, to recover them as 'things past', to define their existing relations, and above all to fit them into existing causal series and hence into the flow of lapsed time, we are forced to have recourse to a number of schemata of the practical intelligence or to operations similar to those enabling us to structure present experience, namely classifications leading to the combination of memories by their similarities and differences; multiple correlations (and especially the spatial or 'infra-logical' operations involved in the organization of figures) leading to the co-ordination of memories; causal inferences permitting the comprehension of filiations; and above all temporal seriations permitting the (more or less approximate) re-discovery of the order of succession of the contents recalled. It is these infinitely differentiated schemata that alone enable us, generally for better but sometimes for worse, to reach back into the past, and to distinguish true memories from false.

Seen in this light, the 'memory in the wider sense' becomes an integral part of the intelligence, except that it is orientated, not towards present reality with its possible transformations, but towards the comprehension of the past, with its limited and frozen characteristics.

Now, it is these characteristics which most clearly distinguish our knowledge of the past from our knowledge of the present: while the past is individualized in respect of the events and objects constituting it, the present and future also abound in specific elements, but within a general framework that multiplies their possibilities *ad infinitum*. In particular, in present and future situations the aleatory elements can be mastered by probability judgments bearing on the situations as a whole and ensuring the effectiveness of these operations; while, in the case of past experience, chance bears on individual events, whose occurrence and order of succession were partly fortuitous as well, but which cannot be deduced and must be reconstructed by the co-ordination of signs. However, this is no reason at all for thinking that the same schemata do not intervene in both cases. Thus, a subject may remember that he owned at least three dogs in his childhood, first a St Bernard, then a Great Dane and, finally, a sheep-dog. How does he know that all this happened when he was a child? He does so by means of temporal seriations, which help him to localize in time what few signs he has retained in his memory (the presence of dogs in his parents' large garden; how small he himself was compared with the St Bernard, etc.) and which could only have occurred during that particular period of his life. How does he know that the Great Dane came after the St Bernard, and before the sheep-dog? Because he remembers that the St Bernard died and that his parents were forced to replace the Great Dane with a smaller dog—the large Great Dane had caused too much damage in the neighbourhood. How does he remember the size, shape and colour of these dogs? In respect of the first two dogs, the fact that they belonged to well-known breeds obviously facilitates recall, the more so as the subject believes that he has always known that his first dog was a St Bernard, and the second a Great Dane. If, on the other hand, our subject himself were trying to buy a dog, he might hesitate between a host of breeds; and perhaps be more interested in their intelligence or responsiveness. In short, whether his powers of representation are devoted to the recovery of fragments of the past or whether they are applied to his present situation, they are bound to involve a great many schemata and operations identical in both cases, but directed in one towards the particularization of the predicates, relations and spatio-temporal localizations, and in the other towards the over-all system and transformations.

III. Why are these obvious facts not clear to everyone? First of all because most psychologists believe, not only that all reality is organized (which is quite probable once chance has been eliminated) but also that it is organized in a form directly accessible to the subject, who has only to open his eyes or to copy reality to grasp that organization and to become moulded by it (this is what Bacon believed before he put the matter to the test, and before the whole history of science showed that the problem was much more complex than was formerly believed). Thus, while the organization of present reality is thought to result from perception and learning, the organization of the past is said to be handed down ready-made, even though it involves a succession of largely fortuitous states; moreover, it is assumed that this organization cannot be lost, because it is the special function of the memory to restore it as such. However, once we realize that, in order to discover an organization we must either construct it or at least reconstruct it, things begin to look quite different, and once we consider the memory adequate to this construction or reconstruction, we must also grant that it has an inner capacity for organization or reorganization, isomorphous with that of the intelligence. But, in that case, there is no reason for separating the two, rather must we consider the memory as part of the intelligence, though differentiated and specialized to perform a precise task, namely, the structuring of the past, and this the more so as the past can no longer be controlled directly, and since its organization involves the use of relations and of a schematism that are all the more important because that organization is subject to constant deterioration and because so many of its contents are aleatory.

We cannot set ourselves up as judges of the extent to which this approach resembles, or differs from other current views, since, in order to do so, we should have to be less committed than, in fact, we are. The reader will nevertheless permit us a few comments on recent trends in the USSR and in the English-speaking world.

In the USSR, the subject was discussed at some length at the XVIIIth International Congress of Psychology held in Moscow, and especially in the symposium on *Memory and activity* organized by P. I. Zinchenko with the collaboration of A. A. Smirnov, *et al.* The general thesis, which agrees with everything we have been saying, is that the memory depends on the structure and contents of actions much more so than it depends on external stimuli, and that it is a permanent component of all behaviour patterns, no matter whether remembrance be 'involuntary' or intentional. The memory depends, *inter alia*, on classifications in their genetic order, and the classifications on language, etc. Soviet psychologists also stress the importance of 'significations', which they compare to the 'operators' in a cybernetic model. But though we can only applaud these conclusions, they nevertheless strike us as being incomplete. What, in fact, are the actions on which, as these psychologists keep telling us, the memory depends? 'Mental activity', declared Zinchenko, 'is a reflection of reality in the brain.'[1] No doubt this is so, but one of the founders of dialectical materialism also said that acting means begetting, and hence transforming and enriching reality. Moreover, Zinchenko himself points out[2] that 'before the image of an object can fulfil its function of guiding and regulating actions, it must be moulded by a corresponding activity'. But in that case, what precisely is involved: the moulding of the object by the action (i.e. what we call assimilation) or the moulding of the action by the object (which we call 'accommodation' but to which Leonid refers as 'assimilation') or both together? Of course, it is both together, but the two are quite distinct activities, or distinct poles of one and the same activity: for while we can copy or manufacture images and language, we can also engage in structuring activities by which we subordinate the object to activities that enrich rather than copy reality. The advantage of the concept of 'reflection', but

---

[1] 'Memory and activity' (Symposium 22), *Proceedings of the XVIIIth International Congress of Psychology*, 1966, p. 6.
[2] *Ibid.*, p. 22.

also its possible ambiguity, lies in the implication that, in order to be effective, all mental activity must correspond with 'reality'; but copying reality is something quite other than fitting it as living organisms do, into structures and organizations that lend it a previously unrealized 'potential'.[1] Now, if these are the two poles of action, and consequently of knowledge, considered as the extension of action, the memory must have two similar poles: it must admittedly be based on images and the use of language, but it also involves constant organization or reorganization, and this is precisely what we have tried to establish in this book.

As for English and American views before 1961, they have been summed up extremely well by D. A. Riley.[2] Two things strike us in his summary. The first is, that, apart from introducing the *Gestalt* factor in the classical sense of that term, English-speaking psychologists have made no attempt to explain the adequation of the memory, which becomes the central problem the moment we cease to treat knowledge as a simple 'copy' of reality. Instead, these authors concentrate on the factors tending to deform the memory, and in this respect, the second circumstance to strike us is that they classify these factors as if they fitted into one of only two categories: those which one might call external or at least relative to the stimulus (verbal labels applied to the stimulus on presentation, exaggeration of conspicuous details and of forms that are more familiar than, or resemble, the stimulus, and that may be perceived at the same time as, or before or after, the latter), and those which we might call endogenous but which the *Gestalt* psychologist Wulf in 1922 has called 'autochthonous' (organization of the cortex so as to impress 'good forms' on the memory). Now, seen in the light of the interpretation we have put forward in this book, this type of dualism seems rather artificial and ought to be dropped, for the very good reason that exogenous factors cannot intervene without some inner, schematizing activity by the subject, and that endogenous factors, too, cannot operate without similar activities, but which in their case, serve to correlate the external data (the stimulus and the general context in which it appears).

As for the influence of 'good forms', it should be noted that their alleged rôle has not been corroborated in the numerous writings of J. J. Gibson, Brown, Zangwill, Hanawalt, Hebb and Fours, George, *et al.* Thus, when Irwin and Seidenfelt presented their subjects with six figures, they found a tendency to impress good forms on three of them (open circle and triangle, imperfect square) but not on the other three, etc. In other words, memory-images are not stamped by good forms to the same extent, or of the same kind, as perceptive structures, and wherever *Gestalts* intervene, they do not do so as innate or 'autochthonous' factors, or as mere patterns, but as

---

[1] In short, we, too, believe that human thought is a 'reflection' of reality, but a reflection of the unobservable as well as of the observable aspects; now the unobservable aspects have to be constructed, reconstructed or deduced, particularly in the case of an unrealized potential. . .

[2] D. A. Riley: 'Memory for form', Chapter XII in L. Postman (ed.); *Psychology in the Making: History of selected research problems*, Knopf, 1962. In what follows we shall also be quoting from sources not mentioned by Riley.

assimilatory schemata (see §1, III). Again, when Perkins in 1932 presented his subject with sets of two lines of unequal length forming acute angles, and found that they tended to equalize the lines in their memories, we need not agree with him that what was involved was an 'autochthonous' factor; it is far more reasonable to assume that the subject relied on the familiar schema of the equilateral triangle.

Conversely, the so-called external or empirical factors such as the verbal 'labels', the exaggeration of certain features, or the assimilation to familiar objects are never purely exogenous and, in their turn, call for the intervention of action schemata or operations. For instance, most of these authors treat the rôle of the verbal 'label' in quite different ways, and this simply because words or 'verbal' signs cannot be reduced to 'labels': they are signifiers, and as such the purveyors of concepts or of conceptual schemata as the significates, and, depending on the case, the stress can be laid either on the schema as the operative aspect of the memory, or else on the figurative or accommodative aspects of the schema (whence the extension of the latter by internal imitation or images). As for the exaggeration of certain conspicuous details (to which Wulf also refers as 'pointing'), the real problem is to discover why these details should be stressed; now, since 'good forms' cannot be involved in this case, it goes without saying that the exaggerations are rooted in the significations, and that, if a detail is found to be 'conspicuous' it does so by virtue of a schema introduced by the subject and to which he assimilates the model. As for the effects of 'similar' or familiar forms, it is even more obvious that they must be assimilations, and hence schemata, since every assimilation is precisely a schema-forming activity.

In brief, we oppose the artificial duality of the empirical and endogenous or 'autochthonous' variables, with the necessary interaction—the source of accurate no less than of distorted memories—of a schematizing activity or operative assimilation with its figurative accommodation to the data. Instead of dualism, we therefore prefer to speak of bipolarity, which is not the same thing because it implies an inseparable link instead of a plurality of factors, and it is this bipolarity of the schema and the figurative memory-image to which we must now return.

IV. Generally speaking, a schema is an instrument of assimilation, and hence of generalization, and one that intervenes in all problems of the intelligence or even of sensori-motor and practical adaptation. But every schema must accommodate itself to a given situation, and its application therefore involves balancing assimilation with accommodation. Now, the latter, when it predominates and becomes an end in itself, leads to imitation, i.e. to the more or less pure accommodation to an object or a process considered as the external model of an action, and imitation itself, once it has been internalized, becomes the source of the image.

It follows that, to the extent that the intelligence becomes attached to knowledge of the present and the future and that the problems to be resolved call for generalizing anticipations and operational transformations, the schemata act chiefly as instruments of assimilation and generalization, while knowledge of past experiences, which are particularized and not easily deduced because of their inextricable mixture of successions or elements of chance and causal sequences bound up with individualized objects or events, calls for a much greater accommodation to realities no longer subject to change. That is precisely why the memory in the wider sense needs a large number of differentiated types of accommodation in the form of perceptive schemata, as instruments of recognition; in the form of imitation as the source of reconstructions; and above all, though only from a certain level of development onwards, in the form of internalized images as instruments of recall. This is a general process found in all types of knowledge, because the comprehension of the present and of the future calls, in its turn, for the constant collaboration between the operative elements, as the mainspring of all structuring activities and transformations, and the figurative elements (from perception through imitation to the image) as the mainspring of representation in the strict sense of that term. By contrast, when it comes to knowledge of the past or remembrance, the figurative elements can no longer be deployed at will (or rather, if they are, they lead to errors and distortions) because past reality can only be what once it was: whence, the fundamental, and in this case the privileged, rôle of the figurative factors in what we have called the memory in the strict sense.

However, if recognitions can be distinguished from perceptions, mnemonic reconstructions from imitations, and memory-images from representative images in general, this, as we saw (in II) is so, not by virtue of their figural properties or the particular qualities of their contents, but by virtue of judgments that attach or fail to attach these properties or contents to the past. Their localization in time is therefore essentially due to the context, i.e. the problem to be resolved, and hence to the functions assumed by the perceptions, images and scheme in the subject's present-day activities. Seen in that light, the sharp dividing line between acts of the memory and general acts of the intelligence makes way for a series of mobile boundaries: without the memory in the wider sense there could be neither understanding of the present nor even invention. At the same time, the memory in the strict sense becomes the more differentiated the more specialized is the accommodation of the schemata to objects, momentary states and past events rediscovered as such. That is why 'I-ness' and references to the past seem, at first sight, to appertain to the figurative aspect of the conservation of schemata, but since this figurative aspect is rooted in the imitative accommodation of the

404

schemata, and hence in their differentiation by virtue of the singular and non-modifiable character of the data to be rediscovered, we are fully entitled to argue that it is the system as a whole which alone permits the localization and recovery of past events, and which also provides the necessary checks.

This brings us to our final problem, namely, the unity of the system: if all figurative memories are indeed based on more or less differentiated schemata, and if this is true even of 'raw' memories, which are most closely bound up with the original model (for even combinations of sounds or of visual shapes are subject to spatio-temporal correlations), we still want to know whether identical schemata intervene in the different types of recognition, reconstruction and recall, or whether they constitute an irreducible plurality, or perhaps a series of ordered variations within a hierarchy.

Now, the problem of the unity of the various forms of the memory resembles that of the unity of the intelligence, both in respect of the hierarchical levels of development and also in respect of the relationships between the figurative and the operative aspects. With regard to the levels, we know that the intelligence manifests itself in three successive forms which, once established, correspond to three co-existent divisions in the hierarchy of behavioural levels: a sensori-motor stage, a representative stage culminating in 'concrete' operations, and a stage of propositional or 'formal' operations. However, while each of these stages has characteristic structures of its own which help to make it much richer than the preceding one, there is nevertheless a remarkable functional continuity between them; the earlier stages pave the way for the next and are integrated in them; the later stages start with a reconstruction of the earlier, which they finally transcend and generalize by adding new combinations: this explains why even such partial structures as displacements (including the rotation of triangles discussed in Chapter 15 and the translations and rotation of the snails discussed in Chapter 18) are expressed in similar, but increasingly general, form at the sensori-motor, concrete and formal levels.

The memory, too, appears in successive forms which, though differing from those of the intelligence, can easily be fitted into the same framework. Thus, early recognitions correspond to the sensori-motor stage; reconstructions mark the transition from the sensori-motor to the representative stage, while recall corresponds to the stage of the representative, pre-operational or operational forms of the intelligence: in almost every chapter of this book we have come across mnemonic transformations in the course of the child's advance to 'concrete' operations; thus we saw in Chapter 10 that 'formal' combinatorial structures do not become fixed in the memory until

405

the subject has attained the corresponding level of intelligence (at about the age of eleven to twelve years). This raises the question of whether the different mnemonic forms (recognition, reconstruction and recall) are functionally united in the same way as the forms of the intelligence, i.e. by integration of the earlier forms into the later, or whether these forms are heterogeneous. And, when all is said and done, it is on the answer to this question that we must base the decision whether the figurative aspects (perceptions, imitations and images) and the operative aspects (schemata) of the memory are interrelated or completely independent.

In this connection, the reader will recall that all forms of the memory, including recognition, involve the use of schemata, and the succession of the same mnemonic levels with age; the only difference between them is that, in some, the stages succeed one another more quickly than in others. In particular, none of our observations suggest, as well they might have done, that it is possible to have immediate and massive recognitory successes (complete correspondence to the model) when the corresponding reconstructions and recollections advance by stages that vary distinctly with age. These two facts—the general presence of schemata and the identity of the order of succession of the mnemonic levels—already bear witness to the general functional unity of the memory. However, this is not enough, for a given figurative memory may be based on one of several schemata, and there is no doubt that the perceptive or sensori-motor schema underlying recognition is different from the representative schema underlying recall: we must therefore go on to examine the links between them.

The links between reconstructions and recollections pose few problems, for the underlying schemata are quite obviously identical. However, since reconstructions are made with the help of the material that went into the construction of the original model, the accommodation of these schemata is greatly facilitated, so that the influences of the figurative elements become reinforced. This explains the almost general advance of reconstructions over recall, particularly when the model contains arbitrary elements (Chapter 19) which the schemata cannot reconstruct during recall and which recur to the mind in the presence of the objects. By contrast, when the schemata needed for successful remembrance surpass the subject's level of development, as in the combinations discussed in Chapter 10, reconstruction and recall produce identical results (three advances and three regressions in a total of sixty subjects).

The problem of the links between the schemata involved in recognition and those involved in reconstruction and recall is a much more delicate one. It has been raised by many authors, including

Zangwill, who was not concerned with schemata, but with the respective rôle of external and 'autochthonous' factors, which latter might have been expected to produce identical errors during recall and recognition; when, according to Zangwill, they often do not. We think that the only satisfactory explanation is one based on the child's level of development, because different errors may well be due to differences in intellectual level.

Now, the results of our various experiments on recognition (Chapters 2, 4, 6, 10, 14, 15, 18, 19 and 20) show precisely that there is a similarity in the types of error committed at different levels: the succession *a*, *b*, *c*, etc. may, at a given age, cause *c* to predominate in recognition, while recall may not yet have gone beyond *a* or *b*. By and large, recognition quite naturally produces better results than recall or even reconstructions, but, instructively enough, its degree of superiority varies from one experiment to the next, and depends essentially on the subject's comprehension and not merely on his perception: this points very strongly to a functional process similar to that involved in recall although all that is involved in recognition is the co-ordination of perceptions and not of images.

Whenever the subject does not understand the model, or whenever its characteristics are, or appear to be, distributed at random, recognition after six months is no better than recall (cf. the U-tube experiments described in Chapter 14), and can even be inferior to the reconstructions, particularly of younger[1] subjects (cf. the recognition of the geometrical figures described in Chapter 20). This is because recognition involves selection. Now, whenever the subject comprehends the model (e.g. the rotating triangles described in Chapter 15) selective recognition produces much better results than recall, though the two are based on precisely the same schemata. By contrast, in the case of the associativity of triangles (Chapter 6, §5), we observed excellent recognitions (an hour, but not so six months, after the presentation) by four- to five-year-olds, a deterioration at the intermediate levels (II–IIIA) and a further improvement at the higher levels (IIIB–IV), which would seem to point to the existence of two types of recognition, the first figurative and passive and corresponding to the 'raw' memory, and eventually suppressed by the nascent schemata, and the second schematizing and corresponding to the 'logical' memory. But, as we have seen throughout this book (and quite particularly during the analysis of the characteristics I–IX described in Chapter 20, §2), the figurative memory of shapes is by no means independent of schemata. Not only are there infra-logical or spatial operations (partition and partitive addition based on proximity and not on resemblances or differences, as in the addition of classes, ordination, etc.) but these operations are prepared from the pre-operational level onwards, and the perceptive schemata involve an entire schematism, some of whose consequences have

[1] It becomes better than the recall at the age of about twelve to thirteen years.

been correctly analysed by *Gestalt* psychologists, though not the fundamental factors of the assimilatory activity leading up to it. In the case of
the broken triangles (Chapter 6, §§4 and 5), young subjects produce such
remarkably good recognitions because the movement of their eyes follows
the outline of the triangular model and not because they choose the 'good
forms' so beloved of *Gestalt* psychologists. Though the schemata they
applied were not identical with those used by children at higher levels (on
which infra-logic is incorporated into a more general type of associativity)
they were nevertheless of a similar type, and may therefore be considered a
first stage in a generalizing process culminating in the emergence of more
abstract schemata. In this case, too, we can therefore conclude that the
schemata underlying recognition are by nature analogous to those underlying recall.

In brief, the mnemonic process seems to be largely continuous
and integral, with the schemata proper to recognition preparing the
way for those proper to reconstruction and recall. The former nevertheless have a much greater accommodation potential, and hence a
much greater figurative power, because, in the case of recognition, the
model is present and perceptible, and all the memory has to do is to
distinguish it from other models. It is this union between imitative
(and later, figurative) accommodation and schematizing assimilation
which explains all the mnemonic successes or deformations we have
observed, so much so that all distinctions between the so-called 'raw'
memory and the logical memory, and hence the intelligence, appear
to be purely arbitrary.

V. If we were asked to express this conclusion in the language of
information theory, we should do it in the following way. Let 'data'
refer to information in the ordinary, and not the technical sense, of
that term, i.e. to the various characteristics of the model. The reader
may remember that, on the one hand, the quantity of information
per signal depends on the number of signals included in the code
(and is maximal if the different signals are independent of one another)
and, on the other hand, that the introduction of syntactic rules
determines the redundancies which reduce the amount of information per signal. It follows that, if the data 1, 2, 3 . . . N are encoded in
a code with independent signals $A, B, C . . . N$, the amount of information contained in A, B, C, etc. is maximal. The greater the number
of syntactic rules linking the signals to one another, the greater the
redundancy, and the less the quantity of information per signal. In
the case of the memory, the encoding of data at the point of perception, their storage during mnemonic retention, and their possible
decoding or recoding are therefore closely dependent on the particular code the subject employs. Now, we have seen that in the course
of operational development, the code itself becomes transformed;

while it is not highly structured, i.e. involves few rules (or schemata) in the case of four- to five-year-olds, and is mainly directed towards accommodation and the figurative extension of the latter, the code subsequently acquires an increasing schematization as the subject advances towards the age when he can perform and co-ordinate operations. This is the first important conclusion to be drawn from our investigations. The second is that mnemonic progress at all levels goes hand in hand with a tendency to retain the *maximum* number of data with the minimum amount of 'information'. Now, since the latter is relative to the code, and to its degree of schematization (which, in particular, determines the characteristics of the redundancies involved at the different levels), it follows that, depending on the model and its correspondence to the operational structures available to the subject, the evolution of the memory with age can tend towards simplifications or even distortions of the data no less than towards accuracy and progress. It nevertheless remains a fact that, at all ages, the code itself depends on the assimilative structures of the intelligence, and that the accommodation of these structures to the data offered for memorization is subject to the same law of thought economy as governs the equilibrium between assimilation and accommodation in general, and which, in the case of the memory, comes back to the retention of the *maximum* number of data with the *minimum* amount of information.

In sum, this final discussion points once again to the fundamental unity and even the common nature of the memory and the intelligence, not only because both pass through the same stages but also because the evolution of the mnemonic 'code' is a direct function of the construction of operational schemata. All this is, of course, quite self-evident, but we nevertheless felt the need to confirm it by a genetic analysis that, though fairly detailed on the whole, proved, if anything, too summary in respect of any one sector.

Index

accomodation, 22–3, 47, 137–9
Ammons, R. B. and Irion, A. L., 48
Ampère, A., 11
arrangement, remembrance of, 189–196; method, 189–92; results, 192–4; after six months, 194–6
assimilation, 1, 4, 21–3, 26, 46–7, 75, 94, 118, 139, 358, 389, 393, 403
associative operations, remembrance of, 115–39; method (II), 127–33; methods, 118–20; recognition of triangles, 133–9; result of method (I), 120–3; after six months, 123–6
associativity, 4, 115, 118, 123

Babich, 24
Ballard, P. B., 19, 47–9
Bally, Charles, 13
Baron and Cohen, 25
Bartlett, F., 17, 381
Bergson, H., 7, 17, 378, 383–4, 392
Bousfield, W. A., 381n
Bruner, J., 393
Bubash, 24

causal problem, remembrance and growing appreciation of, 238–64; conclusions, 262–4; method (I), 239–41; methods (II)–(IV), 252–262; recall, 241–8; recognition, 248–52
causal process, remembrance of incomprehensible, 224–37; conclusions, 234–7; level (I), 227–9; level (II), 229–32; level (III), 232–234; method, 224–7
causal process, represented by

levers, remembrance of, 199–211; conclusion, 210–11; method, 199–202; after six months, 208–10; stage (I), 202–5; stages (II) and (III), 205–8
causal structures, remembrance of, 197–264
Claparède, E., 398
classification(s), 355, 374–6
classifications, remembrance of double, 156–71; later responses, 160–5; methods, 157–9; poor figurative presentation, 165–71
cognitive functions, figurative, 9–14; place of memory in, 8–14; operational, 9–10; organization, 8–9, 131, 400–1
condensation, 105–8
conflict, 76–97
conservation, 2–8, 23–4, 26, 47, 388–9; of acquired schemata, 3; of action schemata, 17; of areas, 311, 317–19; of correspondences, 70; of habitual schemata, 3, 16; of lengths, 20, 24, 74; of memories, 13–21, 23, 25–6, 306–8, 387, 389–92, 396; of operational schemata, 14–19, 21, 24, 61; of perceptive schemata, 1; of a schema, 15–17, 383, 385, 389–92; subconscious, 21
contingent figural combinations, remembrance of, 331–59; conclusion, 355–9; memory, 349–55; methods, 332–3; recognition, 333–6; results (I), 336–47; results (II), 347–9
co-ordination of dimensions, 318

411

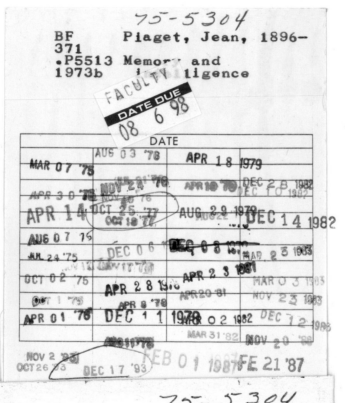